Contents

THE LEGAL RIGHTS MANUAL

The Legal Rights Manual

A guide for social workers and advice centres

Second Edition

Professor Jeremy Cooper

arena

First published 1990 by Gower Publishing Ltd

Second edition 1994 published by
Arena
Ashgate Publishing Limited
Gower House
Croft Road
Aldershot
Hants GU11 3HR
England

Ashgate Publishing Company
Old Post Road
Brookfield
Vermont 05036
USA

British Library Cataloguing in Publication Data

Cooper, Jeremy
Legal Rights Manual: Guide for
Social Workers and Advice Centres
– 2 Rev. ed
I. Title
344.2

ISBN 1 85742 136 1

Typeset in 11pt Times by Manton Typesetters, 5–7 Eastfield Road, Louth, Lincolnshire, LN11 7AJ, England.

Printed in Great Britain at the University Press, Cambridge

Abbreviations

AAC	Adjudication and Appeals Committee
ABWOR	Advice by Way of Representation
ACAS	Advisory Conciliation and Arbitration Service
ACE	Advisory Centre for Education
ADC	Ability Development Centre
AIMS	Association for Improvements in Maternity Services
ALAS	Accident Legal Advice Service
AMCTB	Alternative Maximum Council Tax Benefit
ASW	Approved Social Worker
BASW	British Association of Social Workers
BGS	British Geriatrics Society
BT	British Telecom
CA	Children Act 1989
CAB	Citizens' Advice Bureau
CBI	Confederation of British Industry
CCE	Counsel and Care for the Elderly
CCETSW	Central Council for Education and Training in Social Work
CCG	Community Care Grant
CEPD	Committee for the Employment of People with Disabilities
CHAR	Housing Campaign for Single People (formerly Campaign for the Homeless and Rootless)
CLH	Common Lodging House
CPAG	Child Poverty Action Group
CRC	Community Relations Councils
CRE	Commission for Racial Equality
CSA	Central Services Agency

CSDPA	Chronically Sick and Disabled Persons Act 1970
CSE	Centre for Studies on Integration in Education
CTB	Council Tax Benefit
DAS	Disability Advisory Service
DAT	Disability Appeal Tribunal
DB	Disablement Benefit
DC	District Council
DEA	Disability Employment Adviser
DFG	Disabled Facilities Grant
DHA	District Health Authority
DLA	Disability Living Allowance
DLF	Disabled Living Foundation
DOE	Department of the Environment
	Department of Employment
DOH	Department of Health
DPSCRA	The Disabled Persons (Services, Consultation and Representation) Act 1986
DSS	Department of Social Security
DWA	Disability Working Allowance
EAT	Employment Appeal Tribunal
EC	European Community
ECC	Electricity Consumers' Council
ECT	Electro-Convulsive Therapy
EHO	Environmental Health Officer
EOC	Equal Opportunities Commission
EPA	Equal Pay Act
ERS	Employment Rehabilitation Service
ESW	Exceptionally Severe Weather (payment)
FC	Family Credit
FHSA	Family Health Services Authority
FIAC	Federation of Independent Advice Centres
FRU	Free Representation Unit
GDC	General Dental Council
GIA	General Improvement Area
GLAD	Greater London Council for Disabled People
GMC	General Medical Council
GOQ	Genuine Occupation Qualification
GP	General Practitioner
HA	Housing Association

HAA	Housing Action Area
HASAW	Health and Safety at Work Act 1974
HAT	Housing Action Trust
HB	Housing Benefit
HMO	House in Multiple Occupation
HMSO	Her Majesty's Stationery Office
HRP	Home Responsibilities Protection
HSE	Health and Safety Executive
IB	Invalidity Benefit
ICA	Institute of Consumer Affairs
	Invalid Care Allowance
ILF	Independent Living Fund
IR	Inland Revenue
IS	Income Support
IYSH	International Year of Shelter for the Homeless
LEA	Local Education Authority
LSO	Legal Services Ombudsman
MAT	Medical Appeal Tribunal
MAVIS	Mobility Advice and Vehicle Information Service
MENCAP	Royal Society for Mentally Handicapped Children and Adults
MHAC	Mental Health Act Commission
MHRT	Mental Health Review Tribunal
MIND	The National Association for Mental Health
MODU	Major Organisations Development Unit
MSC	Medical Services Committee
NAA	National Assistance Act 1948
NACAB	National Association for Citizens' Advice Bureaux
NAFD	National Association of Funeral Directors
NAHA	National Association of Health Authorities
NCC	National Consumer Council
NCIP	Non-Contributory Invalidity Pension
NCVO	National Council for Voluntary Organisations
NFA	No Fixed Abode
NHS	National Health Service
NHSA	National Health Service Act 1977
NHSCCA	National Health Service and Community Care Act 1990
NI	National Insurance
NISP/NSP	Notice Seeking Possession

NSPCC	National Society for the Prevention of Cruelty to Children
OFFER	Office of Electricity Regulation
OFGAS	Office of Gas Supply
OFTEL	Office of Telecommunications
OFWAT	Office of Water Services
OPAS	Occupational Pensions Advisory Service
OUP	Oxford University Press
PACE	Police and Criminal Evidence Act 1984
PACT	Placing, Assessment and Counselling Team
PAYE	Pay As You Earn
PCA	Police Complaints Authority
PCC	Professional Conduct Committee of the Bar
PTRP	Private Tenants Rights Project
RAC	Rent Assessment Committee
RADAR	Royal Association of Disability and Rehabilitation
RHA	Regional Health Authority
RMO	Responsible Medical Officer
RRA	Race Relations Act
SB	Sickness Benefit
SDA	Sex Discrimination Act
	Severe Disablement Allowance
SDT	Solicitors' Disciplinary Tribunal
SEPACS	Sheltered Employment Procurement and Consultancy Services
SERPS	State Earnings Related Pension Scheme
SFC	Social Fund Commissioner
SFI	Social Fund Inspector
SFO	Social Fund Officer
SHA	Special Health Authority
SHAC	The London Housing Centre
SOSR	Some Other Substantial Reason (for dismissal)
SSAT	Social Security Appeal Tribunal
SSI	Social Services Inspectorate
SSP	Statutory Sick Pay
TAC	Telecommunications Advisory Committee
TPAS	Tenant Participation Advisory Service
TUC	Trades Union Congress
UB	Unemployment Benefit

UHH	Unfit for Human Habitation
UPIAS	Union of the Physically Impaired Against Segregation
YHG	Young Homelessness Group

Acknowledgements

The first edition of this book grew from my work as a teacher of law and legal rights to a generation of social work trainees at the Universities of Middlesex and East London. The second edition has been substantially rewritten and expanded to reflect the considerable speed of change and development in the various areas of law and practice covered by the book. I am particularly grateful to David Lewis, of Middlesex University Law School, who wrote Chapter 7 of this edition, and to Bill Bowring, of the University of East London Law School, with whom I jointly wrote Chapter 3. I am also grateful to Benjamin Andoh, Michael Mandelstam, Clare Picking, Stuart Vernon and Alan Wilson for taking the time to read various sections of the text and to offer a number of helpful comments.

I gratefully acknowledge permission from the Police Complaints Authority to reproduce Table 2.1 on page 35, MIND to reproduce Table 5.1 on page 161 and the Benefits Research Unit (Service) Ltd to reproduce Table 8.1 on page 284.

Chapter 1

Introduction

> 'Law!' said Bunce, with all the scorn he knew how to command. 'Law! Did ye ever know a poor man yet was the better for law, or a lawyer?'
>
> From *The Warden* by Anthony Trollope

This book is about legal rights in their widest sense. It is designed as a manual to assist anybody working with clients who wishes ready and clear access to information about these rights. Those who seek the assistance or advice of social work agencies rarely perceive of the law as a positive instrument for improving their position. All too frequently the law has been identified with the source of their greatest discomfort: a brush with the police, care proceedings against their children, a 'section' under the Mental Health Act, or an intransigent, rule-bound Benefits Agency officer refusing financial assistance. Confronted with the law, they feel at best powerless, at worst afraid. It is the purpose of this book to present the law in a different perspective and to encourage those engaged in such work to use it positively and creatively for the benefit of their clients. The task is not simple, as the prejudice against law runs deep among advisers and clients alike. For many engaged in social work, law is something that is 'done by lawyers', who in any event are not to be trusted. They fear that if they become themselves knowledgeable in the law's scope and uses they will somehow become surrogate lawyers, which will in turn restrict their freedom to exercise a wider range of social work and advice skills. This view I believe to be seriously misguided, and I offer this book as an opportunity for social workers and others in the caring and advice professions to embark upon a reappraisal of this common perception.

Although I write the book as a lawyer, it is written in the firm belief that some of the best and most imaginative use of the law is made by those who are not themselves lawyers. Lawyers all too frequently take the narrow view, the cautious interpretation, too influenced at times by their sense of the mathematical risk of failure which is bred in them by their training. The possibility of success must always be balanced against the risk of failure: the scales of justice on the roof of the Old Bailey are more than mere metaphor. Lawyers seem too often little concerned with justice, underlining Samuel Johnson's observation that 'a lawyer has no business with the justice or injustice of the cause which he undertakes. … The justice or injustice of the cause is to be decided by the judge.' In contrast, those who work at the social work coalface have no need to exercise such restraint in their endeavours to assist their clients and need specifically to help their clients in the active enforcement of their legal rights. If their client has legal rights it is surely the duty of the social worker to help the client obtain them. But to embark upon this task of encouraging client self-assertion the adviser must have an appropriate level of knowledge of the possibilities that the law presents either to consolidate or to improve their client's situation. *The CCETSW Law Report* published in 1988, which exposed the serious inadequacies in the teaching of law to trainee social workers throughout the country, serves as a clear indication that too many social workers are entering practice poorly prepared to assist in the assertion of clients' legal rights. The independent advice sector is equally concerned with such training issues. It is intended that this book may help to address this inadequacy.

In designing the structure and content of the book a number of choices had to be made as to what to leave out. A deliberate decision was taken at an early stage to leave out all the areas of strict 'statutory' work for which some specialised social workers have responsibility, e.g. child care work, child abuse, and participation in the process of the committal of people to detention in a mental institution. There are two reasons for this decision. The first is that to include such material would be to focus on professional specialisms within social work, and a number of specialised manuals on these areas already exist. The second is more complex but essential in order to expose the central philosophy of the book. It is premised upon the belief that there is a basic core of legal knowledge that should be available to all who are engaged in caring for people in trouble, whatever their particular specialism. It is essential for all those doing social work or advice work to be able to recognise the general circumstances in which the law can be of assistance to their client, to be able to provide their client with a basic outline of their legal rights and to be in a position to help them explore in more detail their legal position with the aid of appropriate specialised assistance. It is for this latter reason that the book provides at every stage details of where to go for further assistance, either in the form of specialised agency advice or in further written advice.

The selection has deliberately omitted one important area, that of family law, i.e. the laws on divorce, cohabitation, custody, access, maintenance, wardship, adoption and so forth. The principal reason for this omission is that by and large the solicitor's profession is very well placed to provide detailed legal advice and assistance under the legal aid scheme (see p.5) in this field, for largely historical reasons connected with the way in which legal aid was developed in this country. As this very extensive, skilled and heavily subsidised legal advice service exists for those with problems in this area, it seems unnecessary to include it in this book.

Inevitably a great deal of the focus of the book is upon the problems of those experiencing poverty. There is more than a grain of truth in Oliver Goldsmith's comment in *The Traveller* that 'Laws grind the poor, and rich men rule the law'. Social workers and advice workers know that most of their clients are poor. And poverty is not just about a shortage of money. It is also about relative deprivation compared with the other members of the society in which we live. As the Church of England report on inner city deprivation, *Faith in the City*, observed in 1985, 'poverty exists ... if people are denied access to what is generally regarded as a reasonable standard and quality of life in that society'. Elsewhere in the same report is another statement whose message provides the motivation for this book and the approach that it adopts: 'Poverty is not only about shortage of money. It is about rights and relationships; about how people are treated and how they regard themselves; about powerlessness, exclusion and loss of dignity. Yet the lack of an adequate income is at its heart.'

One of the key themes that runs through the book is the need to be aware of the precise pressure point at which to press a claim. Knowing where an adverse decision was made, knowing in which department, in which office, and by which individual, can all be key factors in the pursuit of a challenge on behalf of a client. A very large number of the decisions that affect the lives of social work clients are made in the offices of departments of central and local government. Two invaluable reference works that are annually updated and provide a mass of detailed addresses and other information about all such departments are *The Municipal Yearbook* (Municipal Publications Ltd) and *The Social Services Yearbook* (Longman).

Wherever appropriate throughout the book, details have been provided of where to go for further assistance. But how do advisers know when they have gone as far as their knowledge will safely allow them in giving assistance and it is therefore time to refer the client to a specialist? This is a difficult question to answer and will always be a matter of individual judgement. As the aim of the book is to encourage self-help, both on the part of the lay adviser and the client, the general answer is that you can normally go a lot further than you realised! Nevertheless, it should be stressed that there are in particular two large-scale networks of professional legal advice provision that are always available for referral at the appropriate moment: the Citizens' Advice Bureau network (CABs) and legal aid solicitors.

CABs. There are close on 1000 CABs in operation in England, Wales and Northern Ireland (Scotland has its own separate though similar system). CABs provide a wide range of general advice, much of it legal advice, free of charge to anybody who requests it. The quality and accuracy of the advice is maintained by the fact that every CAB has to register as a member of the National Association of CABs (NACAB) in order to operate and NACAB has an extensive programme of training, research, information retrieval and back-up that it makes available to all its local offices. NACAB itself operates from a central office in London and 22 area offices throughout the regions. It is essential that any person engaged in social work makes contact with their local CAB in order to familiarise themselves with the range of matters upon which the CAB is able to advise and also on any secondary specialist services they may operate such as the use of the services of local solicitors, accountants, surveyors and so forth on a volunteer basis. In some rural areas peripatetic CABs also operate. For further information on the operation of the service contact NACAB, 115 Pentonville Road, London N1 9LZ (tel: 071 833 2181).

In addition to CABs a number of independent advice centres exist throughout the country which, though not affiliated to NACAB, often provide a similar sort of service to a CAB. To discover if there is an independent advice centre in your area contact The Federation of Independent Advice Centres (FIAC), 4th Floor, Concourse House, Lime Street, Liverpool L1 1NY (tel: 051 709 7444) or 13 Stockwell Road, London SW9 9AU (tel: 071 274 1839/8), or consult the *FIAC Directory of Independent Advice Centres 1990*.

Legal aid solicitors. Since 1949 solicitors (and if necessary barristers) have been able to represent clients in the civil courts on a subsidised basis as a result of the legal aid scheme. They have been able to represent clients on this basis in the criminal courts for a much longer period. Although no solicitor is obliged to participate in the scheme, the majority do, particularly those working in small to medium-sized firms. Thus if a client has a problem that may involve an action in the civil court (county or High Court), either as the plaintiff or the defendant, it is always advisable to refer them to a local legal aid solicitor.

Legal aid is not automatically granted to a person involved in a civil court action. The client (or their solicitor) will have to apply for it to the local legal aid committee. They will also have to submit to a means test. The legal aid committee, which is composed of solicitors and barristers, will grant legal aid if they think there is a reasonable chance of success and that the case can be financially justified (i.e. a person would still engage in the litigation if they had to pay for it themselves!). It can, however, take a few weeks for the decision to be made and legal aid is not backdated. If the client satisfies the means test they will be granted legal aid, which means that all or some of their legal fees will be met by the state. The amount, if any, that they will be asked to contribute to the cost will depend upon their income. On current figures, approximately 50 per cent of the population of the country would be entitled to at least partial assistance. Legal aid is not, however, available to cover the cost of legal representation in most tribunals, although limited financial support known as ABWOR (Advice by Way of Representation) is available in Mental Health Review Tribunals (see Chapter 5, p.157), for the representation of parents or guardians in certain child care proceedings and in proceedings before boards of visitors of custodial institutions.

Legal aid in criminal cases (magistrates' and Crown Courts) is granted by the clerks or the magistrates at the first appearance of the defendant in those courts. It is also subject to a means test, albeit a more generous one. In addition a magistrate need only grant legal aid if s/he considers that the defendant is at risk of losing their liberty, or would be unable to follow the proceedings without a lawyer representing them, or if there is a point of law to argue. The great majority of magistrates' courts (and a few county courts) also operate a Duty Solicitor Scheme (see Chapter 6 at p.214) whereby a duty solicitor will represent any unrepresented defendant who turns up at the court and who requires their services.

Parallel to the legal aid scheme there has been in existence since 1973 the legal advice and assistance scheme, commonly referred to as the Green Form Scheme. Under this scheme a solicitor can give advice and assistance (e.g. write a letter, make a telephone call and so forth) to a client on any matter of English law, subject to a simple means test that the solicitor will carry out in the office. If the client satisfies the means test the solicitor can give a limited amount of advice and assistance to the client free of charge and recoup the cost from the state. It is possible that in the near future, by way of a franchising agreement with the Legal Aid Board, the Green Form Scheme may be extended to include other advice agencies, in particular the CABs. The Law Society has produced each year a detailed booklet for each region of England and Wales providing details of all the solicitors in that region who provide services under the legal aid scheme. The booklet is called the *Legal Aid Referral List*. A copy should be obtained by all those engaged in social work. The area legal aid committee can provide a copy (address in local telephone book). Alternatively, local CABs and libraries normally have their own copies. For further information on the legal aid scheme contact Legal Aid Board, 5th Floor, Newspaper House, 8–16 Great New Street, London, EC4A 3BN (tel: 071 353 3794). For a detailed practical guide on legal aid consult Hansen, O. (1993), *Legal Aid in Practice: the Guide to Civil and Criminal Proceedings* (Legal Action Group).

The two networks described above are by no means the only sources of specialist front-line legal advice and assistance. A number of specialist agencies cover specific subject areas and offer a limited back-up service to advisers who cannot solve the problem themselves. Where appropriate these have been referenced in the text of the book. In some parts of the country (particularly large cities) there may also be an independent law centre, which can offer some form of free legal service to clients in their catchment area. Law centres normally prioritise the matters on which they are able to help, to reflect the major concerns of their local area, but most law centres offer assistance in the areas of housing, social security, family, employment and immigration law. To find out whether there is a law centre in your area contact The Law Centres Federation, Duchess House, 18–19 Warren Street, London W1P 5EB (tel: 071 387 8570). Finally, mention should be made of three organisations which provide specialist advice in specific areas which are not covered in the chapters of this book. First, Community Relations Councils (CRCs) which exist in most regions of the country to help foster good race relations and which can therefore advise on ways of trying to resolve disputes in this field. If the address of the local CRC cannot be found in the local telephone directory contact the Commission for Racial Equality (CRE), Elliot House, 10–12 Allington Street, London SW1E 5EH (tel: 071 828 7022). Second, the Children's Legal Centre exists as a pressure group to provide legal advice, back-up and research on any issue that involves the legal rights of children. They can be contacted at 20 Compton Terrace, London N1 2UN (tel: 071 359 6251). Third, the Family Rights Group provides a limited telephone advice service, to families with children in care or the subject of other related proceedings. They can be contacted at The Printhouse, 18 Ashwin St, London E8 3DL (tel: 071 249 0008 for advice, 071 923 2628 for enquiries).

This book is devoted largely to the legal rights of social work clients in England and Wales and to a lesser degree in Scotland. For historical and political reasons the law-making process in Northern Ireland is a little different from that on the mainland, which accounts for the fact that while the law in that country is in general terms broadly similar to that in England and Wales there remain sufficient differences of detail for a different book to need to be written, were it to accommodate the law of that country. Scotland, with its own very different legal system, presents another set of problems to anyone writing a book of this nature. However, as many of the laws of England apply in more or less the same way to Scotland, the book is more accessible to the Scottish reader, and the text will indicate where appropriate if the law in Scotland differs in any way.

One final point should be made regarding this book and national boundaries. The only courts that will have any direct interest for the great majority of social work clients and their advisers are the domestic courts of the United Kingdom, and of course the large number of administrative tribunals. There are, however, two other courts outside the United Kingdom whose deliberations can have a considerable impact on the lives of those living in this country. These are the European Court in Luxembourg and the European Court of Human Rights in Strasbourg. The European Court is the final Court of Appeal, whose decisions will bind the courts of the United Kingdom on matters relating to the Treaty of the European Community (EC). This may not at first sight appear to have much to do with the daily life of those doing social work, but occasionally the European Court has been used by pressure groups working within the United Kingdom to challenge the legality of a government action, on the grounds that it is in breach of EC law. The most spectacular example of this in recent years has been the challenge by the Child Poverty Action Group (CPAG) to the provision in the Social Security Act 1975 preventing a married or cohabiting woman from receiving invalid care allowance (see Chapter 4, p.126), a weekly benefit paid to the carers of disabled people. The CPAG successfully argued that this provision was in breach of an EC Directive concerning the Equal Treatment of Women and in consequence the government was obliged to extend the benefit to married and cohabiting women at a cost in excess of £70m. The European Court of Human Rights is a very different institution which is based in the Council of Europe and is concerned with the upholding of human rights in European countries, in accordance with the Convention for the Protection of Human Rights and Fundamental Freedoms of 1950. Unlike EC law, this Convention does not form part of the law of the United Kingdom although the Court of Appeal has stated that United Kingdom courts should 'have regard' to it when applying national law. The Convention, which is essentially a human rights charter, covers a wide range of rights including the right to life, the right not to be subjected to torture or to inhuman or degrading treatment or punishment, the right to a fair hearing, the right to respect for private life and freedom of correspondence, and the right to freedom of thought and expression.

A person who believes that one of these rights has in their case been violated can apply to the European Commission on Human Rights, setting out the basis of their claim. They can only do this, however, if they have first exhausted all legal remedies in this country. If the Commission believes that the applicant has a strong case they may then refer the matter to the European Court of Human Rights which will decide whether the alleged conduct has violated the Convention. If the Court finds in favour of the applicant, it will become the duty of the member state concerned to enforce their decision, although the only sanction for failure to enforce is suspension of membership of the Council of Europe. More cases have been brought against the United Kingdom than any other member state and in many cases violations of the Convention have been found to have occurred. In three areas of particular concern to those engaged in social work the Court rulings have had a significant impact in the United Kingdom: the recognition and development of prisoners' rights;

the rights of mentally disordered patients (see Chapter 5), and in areas of legislation relating to immigration. Those who are interested in learning more about the operation and the potential use of this court should write to Interights, 5–15 Cromer St, London WC1H 8LS (tel: 071 278 3230). Finally, those with the confidence to 'go it alone' who simply need to know what to do, should obtain the following invaluable guide: *Taking Your Own Case to Court or Tribunal* (1985, The Consumers' Association). An excellent update to much of the material in this book (and more) is *The Adviser* magazine published jointly by NACAB and Shelter at regular intervals.

Chapter 2

How to help your client complain

The right to complain, if a service is inadequate, should be considered a fundamental human right. All too frequently, that right to complain remains unexercised because people are unaware of the procedures that are available for making a complaint. There are in fact a surprisingly large number of complaints procedures in this country that are little used. Not only do the major providers of professional services such as doctors, nurses, lawyers, psychiatrists, paramedicals, teachers, surveyors, architects, banks, local authorities, estate agents, travel agents and the police have their own internal complaints procedures, but increasing numbers of trades are also developing Codes of Practice within their own associations that include procedures for handling complaints from customers. This chapter will provide the social worker and general adviser with an outline of the complaints procedures that exist for dealing with some of the more common types of complaint their clients might wish to make. As in other chapters, the chapter will demonstrate how the law provides a much wider framework through which common frustrations can be expressed than is often supposed. Although it may often be the case that the most effective way of addressing a problem is by collective action, this chapter will concentrate upon the procedures available for individual complaints. Complaints about local authority employees, including social workers, are dealt with in Chapter 3.

The particular complaints procedures to be outlined in this chapter are as follows:

1. complaints about public utilities: gas (p.11), electricity (p. 14), water (p.18), telephone (p.18), postal service (p.21);
2. complaints about faulty goods and services (p.23);
3. complaints about police misconduct (p.31);

4. complaints about lawyers: solicitors (p.37) and barristers (p.42);
5. complaints about medical services and paramedical services: general practitioners (p.46), dentists (p.50), hospital staff and paramedical professions (p.51).

Whatever the subject, whether it be n unhelpful doctor, an aggressive police officer, a badly mended washing machine, a ruined holiday, or poor legal advice, dissatisfaction with a service invariably gives rise to a sense of injustice in the person on the receiving end. This sense of injustice normally manifests itself in the desire to complain. This chapter sets out to clarify the relevant procedures.

COMPLAINTS ABOUT PUBLIC UTILITIES

Although most of the utilities in this section have passed into private ownership as part of the policies of the Thatcher and Major governments, they can still be described as public utilities in the sense that the great majority of households in this country receive these services as a matter of course. This is of increasing importance, as more and more utilities are passed from a state monopoly to a 'private' monopoly. Furthermore, every one of the public utilities in this section has its own complaints procedures, details of which can be obtained free of charge by writing to the addresses provided.

Gas

Source of law: Gas Act 1986

There are 18 million gas users in the United Kingdom. Responsibility for gas provision rests with British Gas, which is divided into geographical regions. A number of the legal duties, both of the consumer and British Gas, are set out in the Gas Act 1986, which was the Act that privatised the industry. They can be summarised as follows:

General duties of British Gas. To supply gas to any occupier of premises within 25 yards of a live gas main who so requests; and not to disconnect that supply unless a bill is unpaid for at least 28 days, and 7 days' notice of disconnection has been given (see also p.16 on effects of Code of

Practice on Disconnection), or in an emergency. Although British Gas employees normally need a warrant to enter private premises, they may enter without a warrant in an emergency to take steps to avert danger to life or property.
General duties of consumer. To ensure that air is freely available to a gas appliance; to have gas appliances fitted by a competent installer; not to use a gas appliance that might be unsafe; if there is a gas leak, to shut off the supply and contact the local gas emergency service (number in telephone book under British Gas). Failure to do any of these things is an offence carrying a heavy fine.

Can a consumer be made to pay for gas, after they have vacated the premises?

If a consumer is vacating premises to which gas is supplied they must give British Gas 24 hours' notice of their departure, otherwise they may be obliged to pay for gas used up to whichever of the following first occurs:

- the 28th day after notice is eventually given;
- the date of the next meter reading;
- the date on which a subsequent occupier requires a supply of gas.

What can you complain about?

British Gas publishes a *Commitment to Customers* leaflet which sets out in broad terms what it aims to do for customers. Clearly, a customer is entitled to complain if British Gas fails to comply with any of its legal duties set out above, or any of the commitments set out in this leaflet. They may in addition wish to complain about faulty maintenance by British Gas contractors, faulty goods purchased from a British Gas showroom (on this see also 'complaints about faulty goods', p.23), or mistakes in a gas bill. Any failure on the part of British Gas to follow their Code of Practice regarding disconnection (see p.16) will automatically give rise to grounds for complaint. If the customer is a tenant, paying for gas through a meter, the law regulates exactly how much a landlord can charge for the gas. The up-to-date figures are contained in a leaflet which can be obtained from any gas showroom or Gas Consumers' Council. If the landlord is overcharging, the tenant is entitled by law to a refund when the meter is emptied. For further information see the Gas Consumers' Council leaflet *Gas: How Much Can your Landlord Charge?*, and the National Consumer Council paper (1987), *The Minimum Resale Price of Gas*. Finally, the Gas Act 1986 requires British Gas to send to any consumer on request a copy of a statement issued by the Secretary of State for Energy relating to the tests of the gas supplied to the consumer during the preceding quarter.

Who do you complain to?

Initially, all complaints should be made either to the local British Gas showroom, or if this is inconvenient, to the relevant British Gas Regional Office whose address will be on the customer's last gas bill. If the matter cannot be resolved over the telephone the complaint should be put in writing. If the matter is not resolved by this method, the next stage is to write either to OFGAS, the statutory body, at Stockley House, 130 Wilton Road, London SW1V 1LQ (tel: 071 828 0898), if the complaint relates to anything up to and including the meter (e.g. installation costs, meter defect, gas price), or to the regional Gas Consumers' Council, whose address should be on the customer's last gas bill, for any other type of consumer complaint. The central office is at Abford House, 15 Wilton Rd, London SW1V 1LT (tel: 071 931 0977). The Scottish office is at 86 George St, Edinburgh EH2 3BU (tel: 031 226 6523), and the Welsh Office is at Caradog House, St Andrew's Place, Cardiff CF1 3BE (tel: 0222 226547). These Gas Consumer Councils are independent consumer watchdog organisations that represent the interests of gas consumers in a whole range of ways, providing a free, advisory and mediation service to gas consumers about gas supply, appliances, installations and repairs, lobbying the government for safer supplies, ensuring that any price increases are scrutinised, and representing individuals with grievances against British Gas that have not been resolved at a local level. It also publishes a number of pamphlets, research studies, and a comprehensive annual report, which lists all the available publications.

Is there a time limit?

There is no time limit for complaints about British Gas services. If, however, the complaint is serious enough to lead to possible legal action, as for example when the customer has been injured by the negligence of

British Gas employees, any legal action must normally be commenced within three years of the incident.

How do you make the complaint?

If a complaint is not immediately satisfied, it should always be put in the form of a letter, copies being kept by the complainant.

Will you need help to make the complaint, and will it cost anything?

Gas Consumer Councils (regional and national) should normally handle the complaint once it has been made. There is no charge. Further help will be needed if the complaint might lead to legal action. A Citizens' Advice Bureau, or Consumer Advice Centre, will advise on the likelihood of this.

What remedies are available?

For further information see the leaflet *Help and Advice from the Gas Consumers' Councils* which can be obtained from any British Gas showroom.

Electricity

Source of law: Electricity Act 1989

The procedures governing complaints about electricity services are very similar to those governing complaints about gas services. Responsibility for the provision of electricity rests with the Regional Electricity Board. The general duties of both the Regional Electricity Board and the consumer are laid down by several statutes which can be summarised as follows:

General duties of Electricity Board. To provide a supply of electricity to any occupier of premises who so requests providing they live within 50 yards of a distributing main; to continue to supply the electricity unless the customer fails to pay for it. There is no statutory procedure for disconnection as for gas (but see p.16 on the Code of Practice on Disconnection). Electricity Board employees may only enter private premises without a warrant in an emergency to take steps to avert danger to life or property, e.g. to prevent an imminent fire.

General duties of consumer. There is no special requirement by law that electricity consumers ensure that their appliances are safe, although it is obviously in their own interests that they do so!

Can a consumer be made to pay for electricity after they have left the premises?

By law the consumer must inform the Electricity Board in writing at least 24 hours before they move so that the meter can be read. If they do not do this they will be liable to pay for any electricity up to the next meter reading or the time the next person moves in, whichever is the first to occur.

If a customer has a complaint about any aspect of their electricity service, they should follow exactly the same procedures as set out above for complaints about gas. The statutory body intended to serve as the main protector and enforcer of consumer's rights in the electricity industry is the Office of Electricity Regulation (OFFER), whose area address can be found in the local telephone directory or on the back of the last electricity bill. If the complaint is serious and has not been resolved by the local OFFER, the customer can contact the national office of OFFER in Birmingham (tel: 021 456 2100). The national trade and lobbying association for the distributors and generators of electricity is the Electricity Association (tel: 071 344 5700).

Completely independent of all the above bodies is the Electricity Consumers' Council (ECC), set up as a watchdog to 'represent the interests of electricity consumers in England and Wales at national level'. The ECC does not normally take up individual cases, but it is a very useful body to approach concerning any general or persistent difficulties or problems experienced by clients in connection with their electricity supply. The ECC has direct access to the policy-making level of the electricity industry and is willing and able to lobby hard and effectively on behalf of dissatisfied electricity consumers. Its particular areas of concern are the cost of domestic electricity, methods of helping consumers to meet their electricity bills, the circumstances in which area boards can disconnect customers, and consumer education on the wise use of electricity and energy conservation. The address of the ECC is: The Electricity Consumers' Council, Brook House, 2–16 Torrington Place, London WC1E 7LL (tel: 071 636 5703).

Special rules on disconnection of services (gas and electricity) for non-payment of bills

One of the most distressing problems facing clients of those engaged in social work is the threat of disconnection of gas or electricity services for non-payment of bills. Since 1982 the electricity and gas industries have operated a joint Code of Practice for domestic users of their services regarding disconnection for non-payment of bills. The Code of Practice is essential reading for anybody engaged in social work, and can be obtained from any gas or electricity showroom. Reference to the Code of Practice will be invaluable if a social worker is negotiating on behalf of a client threatened with disconnection. Failure to comply with the Code will give rise to automatic grounds for lodging a complaint.

The most important points contained in the Code of Practice are, in summary, as follows:

- Once either service has been informed that the DSS or Social Services are involved in trying to help the customer, no supply will be disconnected for at least 14 days. If necessary a longer period than 14 days can be negotiated, in which case written confirmation should be requested. Longer periods should always be sought where possible to enable the agency to try to find ways to alleviate the problem. It is particularly important that this right is observed where children are in the home. The statistics on the effects of cold weather on children make grim reading. For example, in the winter quarter of 1980, there were 51 per cent more deaths of male children and 21 per cent more deaths of female children than in the summer quarter of that year. Social services departments are empowered to make financial payments to families in emergencies if this is likely to reduce the risk of their children being taken into care.
- If the house is lived in by a person who is blind, severely sick or disabled, the Code states 'we will try to agree with you a payment arrangement to avoid disconnection'. The clear implication of this section is that only in quite exceptional circumstances (e.g. blatant

refusal to pay) can disconnection occur to people in these categories.

- If all the people living in the house who have incomes are old age pensioners (see Chapter 9) the supply will not be disconnected between 1 October and 31 March. This rule does not, however, apply if the people can pay but refuse to do so. In the latter case not only can disconnection take place but the supply may not be reconnected for the following winter. (For general advice to elderly people on ways of paying for fuel and insulation consult Age Concern's *Your Rights* which provides many useful ideas.)
- The actual disconnection should not take place if there is no adult at home at the time, unless warning has already been given that disconnection will take place after a certain date, that date has passed, and the employee who has come to disconnect the service has an entry warrant.
- Disconnection will not take place because of a debt in the name of a previous customer, nor if it is safe and practical to install a slot meter which can be set to incorporate payment of the debt in the future, nor if the debt is only for a hire purchase item, nor if the customer has made and kept to a proposal in writing to pay off the debt by instalments over a reasonable period.
- If the debt is in the name of a landlord to whom the tenant has paid money for the use of gas and electricity, disconnection will not take place for at least 14 days. This is to enable the customer to apply to their local council (if in England or Wales) to pay the landlord's debt, and reclaim the sums from him. It is very important, if these are the circumstances, that the council is informed promptly in writing by the consumer (or their adviser) of the request.

Further assistance. A very good handbook to assist in all problems connected with fuel bills and problems with the fuel supply utilities is Hoffland, A., and Nicol, N. (1992), *Fuel Rights Handbook, 1992–3* (CPAG). The book includes an account of the structures of both the gas and the electricity industries, the complaints procedures, the related consumer organisations, and how to deal with debt, and offers information on a range of related benefits.

Water

Source of law: Water Industry Act 1991

Water is another of the great public utilities to have undergone privatisation in recent years, although as with the others this has effectively meant no more than the replacement of one monopoly with another. As each area has its own regulations and by-laws, any customer wishing to complain about their water service should obtain details about the local situation before taking any action. This information can be obtained from the local water office, whose address can be found on the last Water Services Charges Bill. The overall responsibility for overseeing the water services rests with the Director-General of Water Services, who is independent of the local services and appointed by central government. The national body with overall statutory responsibility for protecting and enforcing consumer rights with respect to water is the Office of Water Services (OFWAT), Centre City Tower, 7 Hill Street, Birmingham B5 4UA (tel: 021 625 1300). OFWAT is independent of the water industry and is responsible for controlling price increases, monitoring standards of service and value for money, and protecting customers in such matters as billing errors, methods of payment, new connections, interruptions to supply, debt and disconnection, flooding, leakage and low water pressure. Each area has its own Code of Practice for Customers, which can be obtained from the area office, whose address will appear on the Water Services Charges Bill. The new customer charter will set out minimum standards for keeping appointments, answering complaints, dealing with bill queries, the installation of meters, interruption of water supplies and so forth, and will offer fixed levels of compensation of around £10 per 'failure' to customers in the region. To register a complaint contact the Customer Services Committee of the area office. In cases of hardship, the water company is not permitted to give rebates on charges but will be prepared to negotiate payment by instalments.

Telephone

A convenient starting-place to consider whether to make a complaint about the telephone service is to read the *British Telecom Code of Practice for Consumers*, which is printed in full in the back of the local Residential Telephone Directory. This explains in some detail the rights of the consumer of telephone services and the practice that should be followed by British Telecom, the public utility licensed by the government to run the telecommunications services throughout the United Kingdom.

What can you complain about?

The Code of Practice deals with the standards of service that can be expected in a number of areas as follows:

- installation (including connection charges and deposits);
- provision of telephone books, and entries of name and address of subscribers;
- explanation of content of bills, and procedures for payment;
- procedures for querying of bills;
- procedures when subscriber has difficulty paying bills;
- disconnection and reconnection of telephone;
- the fault repair service (repairs normally to be effected within 2 days of complaint; if not, financial compensation is paid to the customer under the Customer Service Guarantee);
- procedures for reimbursement of calls where difficulties are experienced after connection.

The Code of Practice should be consulted for further details of the above, together with the BT leaflet *What We're Doing to Improve our Service for You.*

Selling by telephone

Another telephone usage that often provokes a wish to complain is the use of the telephone for selling unsolicited services or goods. The Office of Fair Trading in a report published in October 1984 (*Selling By Telephone*) has set out guidelines for companies engaging in this type of selling, laying down what it considers to be fair and unfair practice. These guidelines are published in full at the back of the Telephone Directory. In summary, they state that there should be no telephone selling at the customer's place of work; no selling after 9 p.m.; no calls to ex-directory numbers; a 'cooling-off' of 7 days between the date of the call and the receipt of any papers relating to any agreement to purchase;

and a rule that all calls should begin with the caller explaining who they are, and the purpose of the call. If a customer feels that this particular practice code is not being followed by an unsolicited caller, they should obtain the name and address of the caller and complain to: The Office of Fair Trading, Field House, 15–25 Bream's Building, London EC4A 1PR (tel: 071 242 2858).

Who do you complain to?

The Code of Practice answers this question as follows:

> All problems should be taken up with the local British Telecom Office who will try to solve your difficulties. You may also obtain independent advice from a Citizens' Advice Bureau, Consumer Advice Centre or Trading Standards Department. British Telecom is very happy to work together with any of the independent advisory bodies if you decide you need their help to resolve your problem.

The telephone numbers of all local British Telecom Offices are listed in the Telephone Directory after the Code of Practice.

For more serious complaints, or complaints that are not satisfied by the above method, contact the local Telecommunications Advisory Committees (TACs), which are the independent bodies set up to monitor and regulate telecommunications in the United Kingdom. There are regional offices of TACs in Edinburgh (tel: 031 244 5576), Cardiff (tel: 0222 374028), and Belfast (tel: 0232 244113). The addresses are listed in the Telephone Directory after the Code of Practice. The central office for the United Kingdom is in London: OFTEL, Export House, 50 Ludgate Hill, London EC4M 7JJ (tel: 071 634 8764). OFTEL also publishes a range of literature intended as guidance for consumers, a list of which can be obtained from the OFTEL librarian.

If the complaint is serious enough to be likely to lead to legal action, and the customer does not wish to engage in court proceedings, British Telecom offers an alternative to court action in the form of legally binding arbitration through the Chartered Institute of Arbitrators, who can be contacted at the International Arbitration Centre, 24 Angel Gate, City Road, London EC1V 2RS (tel: 071 837 4483). The Centre covers the whole of the United Kingdom. Complaints to the Chartered Institute of Arbitrators should normally be made within 12 months of the cause of the complaint, and the Institute will only accept complaints after that period in exceptional circumstances. If the arbitration service is to be used, application is in writing for the relevant application forms, and explanatory leaflet, directly to the Chartered Institute of Arbitrators. The arbitration procedure is very simple, and based entirely on what is written by the complainant and British Telecom on the relevant forms. It is thus important to fill out the application form with great care, putting in all relevant details, dates, charges, costs and so forth, after consultation with any relevant documents, such as diaries. There will be a small registration fee of £15. Each party bears its own costs in the application. The arbitrator may refund the fee in the light of the outcome of the arbitration.

What remedies are available?

The arbitrator has the power to come to a decision that is legally binding on both parties, which includes the power to award compensation of up to £5000. Any claim in excess of this will probably have to go to the county court, which will involve the employment of a solicitor. For a detailed appraisal and criticism of the standard contract conditions for the provision of services by British Telecom, see the *National Consumer Council Response to the OFTEL Consultation Document* PD 41/87, which can be obtained from the NCC, 20 Grosvenor Gardens, London SW1W 0DH (tel: 071 730 3469).

Postal services

Unlike the other services outlined above, there is no contractual relationship between the Post Office and its customers. This means that the areas of legal complaint are rather limited. There is, however, a Code of Practice governing most areas of Post Office contact with the public, and a failure to follow the Code of Practice will give grounds for a complaint. A copy of this Code of Practice can be obtained from most large post offices.

What can you complain about?

The most common type of complaint relates to late delivery. Unfortunately, there is no legal redress for such a complaint, but redress (up to a point) is allowed for under the regulations for registered mail and special delivery. If the delay is flagrant or persistent, it is nevertheless worth registering dissatisfaction by writing to the local head postmaster who will at the very least acknowledge the complaint. If it can be shown that the Post Office was in some way negligent in its handling of the relevant delivery, and damage was suffered by the complainant, compensation may be paid.

The other common type of complaint relates to lost or damaged mail. Post Office leaflet P58 *Enquiry about a missing or damaged letter or parcel* explains the procedure for such a complaint, and can be obtained from any post office. The level of compensation payable will depend on whether the item was sent by ordinary mail, recorded delivery, registered mail, or special delivery. Evidence that the item was actually sent must be produced. This should be in the form of a certificate of posting, which can be obtained from the post office at the time the item is posted (it obviously will not be given retrospectively).

NB Complaints about standards of direct mail operations (including misleading information) should be addressed to the Direct Mail Services Standards Board, at 26 Eccleston Street, London SW1N 9PY (tel: 071 824 8651).This organisation seeks to monitor and promulgate the ASA good practice codes on advertising standards.

Who do you complain to?

In the first instance all complaints should be addressed to the local head postmaster, whose address can be obtained from the local post office. If still dissatisfied, the complainant can complain to the regional director, of which there are seven in England, and one each in Scotland, Wales and Northern Ireland. The national, independent advisory bodies dealing with complaints about the Post Office are as follows:

Post Office Users' National Council
England: Waterloo Bridge House, Waterloo Rd, London SE1 8UA (tel: 071 928 9458).
Wales: Caradog House, St Andrew's Place, Cardiff CF1 3BE (tel: 0222 374028)
Scotland: Alhambra House, 45 Waterloo St, Glasgow G2 6AT (tel: 041 248 2855).
Northern Ireland: Chamber of Commerce, 22 Great Victoria St, Belfast BT2 7BJ (tel: 0232 244113).

The Chartered Institute of Arbitrators is also available as an alternative method for resolving any dispute. For details of this procedure see p.20 under 'Telephone'.

Is there a time limit?

The usual advice applies about the desirability of making a complaint as soon as possible after the event. The head postmaster normally takes at least 6 weeks to reply to a complaint! If the complaint relates to a lost or damaged item, and court proceedings become necessary, they must be initiated within 12 months of the date the item was posted. If an application is to be made to the Chartered Institute of Arbitrators it must be filed within 18 months of the date the item was posted.

How do you make the complaint?

Complaints should be addressed to the head postmaster in a letter, or if still dissatisfied to the regional director, also in a letter. If arbitration is being used, follow the procedure set out on p.20 under 'Telephone'.

Will you need help to make the complaint and will it cost you anything?

See p.20 under 'Telephone' (same answer).

What remedies are available?

Both the Post Office and the arbitrators can make offers of money compensation if they feel the complaint is justified. In the latter case the offer is legally enforceable.

COMPLAINTS ABOUT FAULTY GOODS AND SERVICES

The law relating to faulty goods and services is quite complicated, and cannot be dealt with in any detail in this book. In addition, it should be made clear that for Scotland and Northern Ireland, while the general principles set out below apply, there are differences of detail that ought only to be referred to local experts. As a starting-point, advisers should obtain from the Office of Fair Trading (address at p.29) the relevant general pamphlet:

How to Put Things Right (England and Wales).
Dear Shopper in Scotland (Scotland).
Dear Shopper in Northern Ireland (Northern Ireland).

An excellent and readable summary of the various ways to complain about faulty goods and services can be found in a book by Brigid Avison (1986), *How to Complain* (Longman Self-Help Guide). A more detailed and comprehensive account of the main legal rights of consumers, together with procedures for redress and useful addresses, is the *Handbook of Consumer Law* (1989), produced by the National Federation of Consumer Groups and published jointly by Which? and Hodder and Stoughton. A Citizens' Advice Bureau (and, if one exists in the area, a Consumer Advice Centre) is normally a good place to go to seek more detailed advice on how to complain about faulty goods or services. Set out below, however, is a summary of the main factors of importance when considering complaints of this nature.

Trade associations

Some traders belong to trade associations, and the majority of these trade associations have Codes of Practice which members are supposed to follow in their dealings with customers. A typical Code of Practice would be likely to cover most of the common areas of customer complaint, such as shoddy work, overcharging, slowness, and incompetence. Most of these Codes of Practice provide for conciliation and arbitration procedures which a dissatisfied customer may use as an alternative to lengthy correspondence or legal proceedings. At the time of writing, official Codes of Practice (i.e. those drawn up in consultation with the Office of Fair Trading) exist for the purchase of all the following goods: mail-order catalogue goods, party-plan selling, cars and motor cycles (including parts and accessories), electrical goods, furniture, shoes, glass and glazing, and photographic equipment.

In addition official Codes of Practice exist in connection with all the following services: repair and servicing of cars and motor cycles and body repairs to cars and caravans; repair and servicing of electrical goods, furniture, shoes and other footwear; laundry, dry cleaning, double glazing, photographic services and package holidays. All these Codes of Practice can be obtained from the Office of Fair Trading (see below) which will also provide an updated list. (*NB* If the complaint is about selling by telephone, see p.19).

The addresses of all the trade associations concerned with all the above goods and services can be found in Avison (see above, p.24) and can also be obtained from the Office of Fair Trading. They are also conveniently listed at the back of the *Handbook of Consumer Law* (above at p.24). It must be stressed, however, that traders or retailers are under no obligation to belong to the relevant trade association, and will only be expected to follow the Code of Practice if they are members of that trade association or if they pretend that they are. Even then, they are not *legally* bound by the Code, although it is an offence under the Trade Descriptions Act 1968 to claim to belong to a trade association of which they are not members.

If a client is about to employ somebody to do work in their house, such as home improvements or repairs (e.g. builders, plumbers, electricians), they are well advised before employing any such person to obtain the pamphlet *Home Improvements* from the Office of Fair Trading, which sets out in simple language how to avoid legal pitfalls so often associated with such work. A common problem in such circumstances is a failure to agree the terms in advance. In particular, if a fixed price for the job is important to the client, they should make sure that it is expressed as a quotation, or a firm and definite price, rather than an estimate.

Goods bought from a trader (including shop, but excluding private sales)

All purchases of goods from a trader (i.e. person selling goods in the course of a business) have the following terms automatically implied into the sale, whatever the trader may or may not say to the contrary. If it subsequently transpires that one of these terms was not complied with by the seller, the purchaser has a legal remedy against the seller and should complain direct to them, either rejecting the goods in exchange for a refund or seeking financial compensation, which will normally amount to the cost of the repairs. The purchaser may need to seek legal advice on which of these various remedies is the most appropriate in the circumstances of their case as the law here can be complicated. In 'faulty goods' cases, the law operates harshly if the customer does not reject the goods quickly. In one recent case, for example, the purchaser of a new car lost the right to a refund after only three weeks. In the circumstances, therefore, if a client wants a refund it is important to advise them to reject the goods straightaway. If they do not obtain satisfaction, they should consult a Citizens' Advice Bureau or a Consumer Advice Centre. In addition, if the complainant's income is below a certain level, they can ask a solicitor to write a letter of complaint for them, under the Green Form Scheme (see Chapter 1). Ultimately, if they obtain no satisfaction they may have to take legal proceedings in the local county court. They will be most unlikely to receive legal aid for such a claim, whatever their income. If, however, the claim is for £1000 or less, the purchaser can use the *small claims procedure* in the local county court, which was set up to enable individuals to pursue the case themselves without legal representation. A claimant can be represented by a friend or adviser, who need not be a lawyer, and the forms are all written in plain English, which makes the experience relatively informal.

The terms that are *automatically* implied into a contract are as follows:

- That the trader has the *legal right to sell the goods* (i.e. they are not stolen). So if the goods do not belong to the seller, the purchaser has a right to a *refund.* This rule applies even if the purchaser has used the goods for some considerable time. Sometimes the purchaser can *keep the goods,* even if they did not belong to the seller at the time of sale. An example of when this will happen is where goods are bought in a 'market overt', i.e. a market held on days and at times prescribed as 'market days' by statute or charter. Another is where an individual purchaser buys a car which is subject to a hire purchase agreement. If any of the above circumstances arise, the client should always seek legal advice.
- That the goods *match their description* (e.g. in size, colour, quality, shape, smell and so forth). Description may be by label, advertisement, or by the word of the trader themselves (e.g. if the trader describes an item as a 'leather coat', it must be made of leather).
- If sold in the course of a business (i.e. not a private sale), that they are of *merchantable quality* and they are *fit for the purpose* for which they were bought. These terms need further explanation:

  a) *of merchantable quality.* Essentially this means that the goods supplied should be satisfactory, taking into account their age, the price and any other description applied to them. The case law here is extensive and the Law Commission has recommended that the term *merchantable quality* should be replaced by a clearer and more up-to-date phrase (see *Sale and Supply of Goods,* Law Commission No. 160, May 1987). A change in the law is expected in the next decade! However, it is now generally accepted that safety factors, durability, and minor defects in appearance and finish will all be taken into account in determining whether goods are 'merchantable' or not. The term also applies to second-hand goods but these are not required to be of the same high quality as brand-new goods. It is a question of what is reasonable in all the circumstances.

Purchasers should further note that the trader is not liable for any defects specifically drawn to the attention of the purchaser prior to the purchase. Also, if the purchaser examines the goods before buying, the trader will not be liable for any defects that examination ought to have revealed. But note that the purchaser is *not* bound to make an examination, and this rule only therefore applies if they did do so.

b) *fit for the purpose for which they are bought.* If a purchaser tells the trader that they want the goods for a particular purpose, e.g. boots suitable for hill-walking, or a coat that is fully waterproof, etc., and the item is *not* suitable for that purpose, the trader will be in breach of this implied term. But the trader can, however, get themselves off the hook if they can show that the purchaser did not rely upon the trader's skill or knowledge, or that it would have been unreasonable to have done so.

For more detailed information on all the above implied terms consult Lowe, R. and Woodruffe, G., *Consumer Law and Practice* (3rd edn) (Sweet and Maxwell).

Note that if any goods are bought on credit the whole transaction is subject to a set of special rules under the Consumer Credit Act 1974. Details on these rules, which are designed among other things to protect the consumer from being rushed into credit sales, are set out in the leaflet *Shop Around for Credit* (Office of Fair Trading). A short summary of the rights of consumers to know what credit reference agencies say about them is contained in *No Credit?* (Office of Fair Trading). Details of the risks involved in paying in advance for goods and services are contained in *Don't Wave Your Money Good-bye* (Office of Fair Trading). For details on the protection of consumers who make 'doorstep purchases' and then wish to withdraw, consult Consumer Protection SI 1987 No. 2117 (HMSO), or a simple leaflet *How to Cope with Doorstep Salesmen* (Office of Fair Trading).

There are also a number of criminal offences that may be committed under the Trade Descriptions Act 1968 in connection with false or misleading descriptions of goods that are offered for sale. Convictions can lead to heavy fines and compensation orders. Misleading price indications are covered by the Consumer Protection Act 1987 (see Lowe and Woodruffe, p.27).

The responsibility for enforcing these criminal laws on trade description and misleading prices rests with the Trading Standards Consumer Protection Department of the local authority (see Chapter 3), which should be consulted on any problem that may arise. You will find them in the telephone book under the local authority.

Services

There are further laws which protect the consumer of services. Any goods supplied as part of a service will be subject to what has been written above. That is to say, the seller must have the right to sell the goods, they must be as described, of merchantable quality, and fit for their purpose. But in addition the service has to reach certain basic standards. The law is set out in the Supply of Goods and Services Act 1982, which states that any supplier of a service to a consumer must provide that service:

1. With reasonable care and skill, to the standard expected of a reasonably competent practitioner of that trade. If a client is unsure about the required standard, they can get a reputable contractor in the same field to inspect the work and write a report;
2. Within a reasonable time. If a client wants a service provided by a particular date they must make this an essential term, before the contract is made. It is a good idea to get this in writing;
3. For a reasonable charge. If a client is unsure about what is reasonable, they can consult a trade association, or ask another reputable contractor to price the work.

If a customer feels that they have been given a service that falls short of the expected standard, they should first give the contractor a chance to put the matter right, unless the workmanship is so appalling that they have lost all confidence in the contractor. If the original contractor fails to put the work in order, for whatever reason, the customer will probably be entitled to claim some compensation, for the inconvenience, and the cost of putting things right. A Citizens' Advice Bureau, Consumer Advice Centre or solicitor can advise on such a claim. If not settled informally the claim will have to be settled in the small claims division of the local county court. Most county courts provide initial advice to claimants on how to make an application. Legal costs cannot be claimed if the amount of compensation is less than £1000, which substantially reduces the risk of incurring legal costs, if the claimant actually loses the case.

For further information on all the above aspects of consumer rights contact the Office of Fair Trading, Field House, 15–25 Bream's Building, London EC4A 1PR (tel: 081 242 2858; telephone orders, 081 398 3405). A further valuable source of up-to-date information is the quarterly journal of the National Consumer Council, *Consumer Voice*.

All the leaflets and booklets of the OFT described above can be obtained from this address or in Northern Ireland from the Department of Economic Development, Trading Standards Branch, 176 Newtownbreda Road, Belfast BT8 4QS (tel: 0232 647151). Stocks of these publications should also be available in CABs, Consumer Advice Centres and Trading Standards (or Consumer Protection) Departments.

General assistance with consumer complaints

Since 1974 there has been in existence the *Institute of Consumer Advisers* (ICA), 14 Delawyk Crescent, London SE24 9JB (tel: 081 403 5867). The membership comprises people who are professionally employed as consumer advisers within consumer advice centres. The ICA aims to encourage, maintain and seek to improve standards of consumer services. While it does not deal with individual complaints it can refer enquiries to advisers in the relevant area.

The *Institute of Trading Standards Administration* (ITSA), County Offices, Kendal, Cumbria L79 4RQ (tel: 0539 21000, extension 4327) is the professional body for trading standards officers, and is able to advise members of the public with regard to the problems encountered in the commercial transactions of everyday life. Finally, the *Consumer Con-*

gress Directory produced by the National Consumer Council, 20 Grosvenor Gardens, London SW1W 0DH (tel: 071 730 3469) provides details, including addresses and telephone numbers, of 295 organisations involved in the consumer movement in the United Kingdom. It is an invaluable reference source on a very wide range of consumer issues as a means to finding the best back-up assistance available for a particular problem.

COMPLAINTS ABOUT POLICE MISCONDUCT

This section deals only with the position in England and Wales and does not extend to Scotland or Northern Ireland, which operate under a different system. For details of the complaints systems in these countries consult:

Scotland: the Police (Discipline) (Scotland) Regulations 1967 available from any Scottish Police Station or from the Scottish Police Federation (041 332 5234).
Northern Ireland: the Independent Commission for Police Complaints (0232 244821) should be contacted for further information on the complaints system currently in operation in Northern Ireland.
England and Wales: Any person who is a victim or a witness of misconduct by a police officer has a right to lodge a complaint against that officer. If a person suffers actual physical harm, damage to their property or is wrongfully arrested or imprisoned by a police officer, they may also be able to sue that officer or the relevant police authority in the county or High Court. While the decision whether or not to sue the officer is best taken following legal advice, the lay adviser should be able to advise a client as to whether or not to make an official complaint about police misconduct.

An adviser whose work brings them into regular contact with clients who brush with the police should obtain a copy of the best existing guide on the subject, Harrison, J. and Cragg, S. (1991), *Police Misconduct: Legal Remedies* (2nd edn) (Legal Action Group). The book also includes PACE Codes of Practice (see Chapter 6) and the Police Discipline Code 1985. This book contains detailed information on the procedures available, draft complaints letters, explanations of how to present evidence and find witnesses, examples of successful outcomes, and a range of interesting statistics concerning the effectiveness of police complaints. For the adviser whose work only occasionally brings them into contact with alleged police misconduct, the following outline should suffice.

The police complaints procedure

Any person, whether victim or witness of alleged police misconduct, has the right to lodge a formal complaint about the misconduct. The complaint must relate to the action of an identifiable officer, or officers, and not just to 'police action in general'. 'Misconduct' means any breach by a police officer of the *Police Discipline Code* (Police Discipline Regulations 1985 SI No. 518 Sch 1). The Code should be consulted in detail if possible before deciding whether to lodge a complaint. Offences under the Code are in summary as follows:

- discreditable conduct (e.g. acting in a disorderly manner);
- misconduct towards another member of the police force (e.g. abusing or assaulting a colleague);
- disobedience to orders (e.g. any breach of the Code of Practice, see Chapter 6 on Civil Rights and the Police);
- neglect of duty (e.g. failing to react promptly to a request for assistance from a member of the public);
- falsehood or prevarication (e.g. making up or destroying evidence);
- improper disclosure of information (e.g. handing over confidential police records to a third party);
- corruption or other improper practice (e.g. accepting bribes);
- abuse of authority (e.g. being violent, oppressive or abusive to any member of the public);
- racially discriminatory behaviour;
- neglect of health (e.g. not carrying out doctor's instructions when off sick);
- improper dress or untidiness while on duty;
- damage to police property, wilfully or through lack of due care;
- drunkenness while on duty or preventing officer coming on duty;
- drinking on duty or soliciting drink;
- entering licensed premises without good cause, on duty, or off duty if still in uniform;
- criminal conduct;

- being an accessory to a disciplinary offence.

The Police Discipline Code is clearly extensive, even draconian, demanding from officers very high standards of behaviour. In 1990, for example, nearly 35,000 complaints were investigated. It should be noted, however, that only 2.4 per cent were substantiated and in only 0.42 per cent of cases were officers charged with disciplinary offences, with charges being proved in 0.3 per cent of the total number of complaints. Furthermore, in 42 per cent of the cases the complaint was subsequently withdrawn, and in 23 per cent of the cases the matter was resolved informally. It is clearly immensely difficult to succeed in attributing blame to any police officer under the existing complaints procedures. In the words of Sir Cecil Clothier, Chairman of the Police Complaints Authority, writing in the *Guardian* in response to criticism of this low 'success' rate (17 April 1987): 'It remains the fact that in the great majority of cases no disciplinary proceedings follow investigation, either because there is no cause for them or, more commonly, because there is insufficient evidence.'

Information on police computers

In 1988 the Association of Chief Police Officers published a detailed *Code of Practice for Police Computer Systems* which states that 'any failure to comply with the Code could amount to disciplinary offence'. The Code can be obtained from the Communications Department, Merseyside Police, PO Box 59, Liverpool L69 1JD (see also Chapter 6 at p.180).

Procedure for making a complaint

The procedure for making a complaint about a police officer who is alleged to have breached the Police Discipline Code is very straightforward. It costs nothing. The complainant, or somebody acting on their behalf, simply writes a letter addressed to the Chief Constable (or to the Commissioner of Police if in London) setting out the circumstances of the complaint. The letter should give the date, time and place of the incident. It should identify the officer or officers involved, either by name, by number, or, if that is not possible, by description. It should describe the incident fairly and concisely, including details of any damage or injuries sustained. It should also give details of any other witnesses to the incident. A copy should always be kept of this letter. Once the complaint has been received by the relevant police chief, there are two possible paths they may take, either an informal resolution or a formal investigation.

Informal resolution

This is only permissible if the conduct complained of, if proved, would not justify a criminal or disciplinary charge and the complainant agrees that the matter can be resolved informally. The Home Office has suggested the following as examples of misconduct that should be investigated informally: 'The use of obscene language or the disciplinary offence of incivility, or an assault in the nature of a mere push without aggravating features such as an endeavour to obtain an admission.'

If the officer appointed by the police chief to investigate the complaint feels that informal resolution is the best way of dealing with the complaint, an interview will be arranged between that investigating officer and the complainant to discuss this possibility. An adviser can be present at this interview to ensure that undue pressure is not placed upon the complainant. It is important to ask the investigating officer before the interview begins for an agreement that the complainant will be sent a photocopy of any statement they may make in the course of the interview. Any statement made by either party in the course of an interview for informal resolution will be inadmissible in any future criminal trial, so all parties can express themselves freely.

If, following the interview, the complainant is willing to drop the complaint, or is satisfied with the investigating officer's explanation or apology, the matter will have been informally resolved. If the complainant is not satisfied with the informal resolution, they must make this clear. In these circumstances the complaint will follow the formal complaints procedure.

Formal investigation

If a complaint cannot be resolved informally, or is not appropriate for informal resolution because of its serious nature, it will be investigated formally in one of two ways, either by an Internal Formal Investigation or by an Investigation Supervised by the Police Complaints Authority (PCA).

Internal formal investigation

This procedure runs along similar lines to the informal resolution procedure, but if there has already been an informal resolution attempt which has failed, a different investigating officer will be appointed. Investigating officers are always appointed by the police chief who received the initial complaint. They may be from another force, but this is not essential. The officer will always be a senior officer of at least the rank of chief inspector. The investigating officer will arrange an interview in the same way as for the informal resolution. The complainant can be accompanied at this interview by a person of their choice.

Investigation supervised by the Police Complaints Authority (PCA)

The most serious types of complaints are referred to the PCA, a special independent body set up in 1985 with wide powers to investigate serious complaints against the police. Broadly speaking, these will be where it is alleged that the conduct complained of:

- resulted in death;
- resulted in serious injury (a fracture, damage to an internal organ, a deep cut or laceration, or an impairment of bodily function);
- amounted to an assault occasioning actual bodily harm;
- amounted to corruption;
- constituted a *serious arrestable offence* (see Chapter 6 at p.197).

A police chief may refer any other complaint to the PCA but is under no obligation to do so. Controversial cases are often referred to the PCA in an attempt to allay public anxiety about the independence of the inquiry. In addition, the PCA may itself require a police chief to submit a particular complaint to its supervision. A complainant may themselves request the PCA to investigate their complaint. This is only likely to be allowed if there are special 'disadvantages' in the complainant's position, e.g. they are very elderly, mentally ill, or a juvenile.

The role of the PCA is supervisory, i.e. it does not carry out the investigation itself. It does, however, have wide powers to dictate the way in which the investigation is carried out, for example by requesting that certain witnesses be interviewed, by requiring specific forensic tests

Table 2.1 Analysis of disciplinary outcome of complaints Period 1 January–31 December 1992

Type of complaint	No disciplinary charges preferred	Disciplinary charges preferred by Chief Officer and admitted by officers S.91(2)	Disciplinary charges preferred by deputy chief officer not admitted by officer		Disciplinary charges recommended by Police Complaints Authority		Dispensations		TOTAL
			Complaints	Charges	Complaints	Charges[1]	Refused	Granted	
1 Incivility	1427	1	24	14	9	1	2	678	2141
2 Assault	3401	1	47	48	16	9	2	2627	6094
3 Irregularity in procedure	1379	0	19	26	22	13	1	393	1814
4 Traffic irregularity	117	0	1	0	0	0	0	31	149
5 Neglect of duty	1454	0	25	37	28	17	2	295	1804
6 Corruption	63	0	3	7	3	1	0	17	86
7 Mishandling of property	442	0	2	1	3	0	1	205	653
8 Irregularity in relation to evidence	1467	0	16	13	9	5	1	184	1677
9 Oppressive conduct	857	0	5	14	11	5	5	634	1512
10 Racially discriminatory behaviour	67	0	0	0	0	0	0	6	73
11 Irregular arrest	1130	0	15	8	8	1	4	497	1654
12 Irregular stop/search	152	0	0	0	0	0	0	79	231
13 Irregular search of premises	314	0	0	0	2	1	2	138	456
14 Other	663	2	15	24	14	3	0	251	945
Total	12,933	4	172	192	125	56	20	6035	19,289

[1]These figures are not included in the TOTAL column.

to be carried out, or by insisting on vetting the choice of investigating officer. When the investigating officer has completed the investigation they will send a report to the PCA. The PCA will then send a statement to the relevant police chief in which they will indicate whether they feel the investigation is satisfactory. A copy of this statement should normally be sent to the complainant (unless, for example, criminal charges are being advised).

What are the possible outcomes of any of the above investigations?

The purpose of the investigation is to decide whether the officer(s) in question breached the Police Discipline Code. There may be three possible findings:

- there has been no breach of the Police Discipline Code;
- there has been a breach but no action will be taken (because it was too minor, or the officer has left the force or cannot be identified);
- there has been a breach and disciplinary and/or criminal proceedings will be initiated against the officer(s).

The PCA can be contacted at 10 Great George St, London SW1P 3AE (tel: 071 273 6450).

Will the complainant receive any compensation?

It should be noted that the complainant will not receive any compensation under any of the above procedures even if their claim is substantiated and action is taken against the officer. If the complainant wishes compensation (because, for example, they have suffered some injury, damage to their property, or have suffered the indignity of false imprisonment) they will have to initiate court proceedings against the police (see Chapter 6, p.214). This should only be done after careful consultation with a solicitor. In really serious cases of police misconduct involving wider questions of civil liberties contact Liberty (formerly the National Council for Civil Liberties), 21 Tabard St, London SE1 4LA (tel: 071 403 3888), who may be able to help.

COMPLAINTS ABOUT LAWYERS

Legal services are provided by lawyers who are either solicitors or barristers. They may be in private practice, or they may be working for a law centre, a Citizens' Advice Bureau or an independent advice agency, in which case they are paid a salary from public funds. Although in private practice, the solicitor or barrister may receive payment for the case from the government, through the legal aid scheme (see Chapter 1). Regardless of the nature or the place of the lawyer's practice, or form of remuneration, every solicitor or barrister is expected to provide a service of high professional skill. Any client who feels that in their particular case they have not received such a service has the right to make a formal complaint. The complaint will always be against the individual lawyer, and not against the practice, the chambers or the organisation for which they work, for every lawyer is personally responsible for their own standards of work. This section deals first with lawyers practising in England and Wales and second with lawyers practising in Northern Ireland and Scotland.

England and Wales

Solicitors

What can you complain about?

A complaint about a solicitor is likely to be one of three types:

- a complaint about the solicitor's bill;
- a complaint that the solicitor has proved incompetent, as a result of which the client has suffered some loss;
- a complaint about the way a solicitor has handled a case but no financial loss has been suffered by the client.

A complaint about the solicitor's bill

For further information, obtain the free leaflet *Complaints About Solicitors' Charges* from the Solicitors Complaints Bureau (see below at p.41).

Solicitors run a business and therefore have to make a profit in order to pay their salaries and meet their overheads. It is perfectly proper, therefore, that anybody visiting a solicitor for the first time should enquire as to how much the solicitor's service is going to cost. If the client is eligible for legal aid, a special procedure will be followed (see Chapter 1). If, however, the client is not eligible for legal aid, or the matter is not one for which legal aid is available (e.g. conveyancing, and making of wills), the client will have to pay. It is essential that a client is aware from the outset that solicitors charge for all the time they spend on the case, including time spent perusing letters and making telephone calls at an hourly rate. This means that even the friendly, reassuring chat on the telephone may end up as an item on the bill! Solicitors' bills are thus often higher than the client expected at the outset. Nevertheless, if a client feels that they have been overcharged there are two procedures they may follow to challenge their bill:

1. *Apply for a remuneration certificate.* This procedure is only available for work that has not involved court proceedings. The client who, having received a bill, feels they have been overcharged, should ask their solicitor within one month of receiving the bill (or of being informed of their right to apply for a remuneration certificate, whichever is the later) for a remuneration certificate from the Law Society. They can make this request in writing to their solicitor to avoid embarrassment, and in the meantime should not pay the bill. The solicitor must then write to the Law Society enclosing their file and justifying the bill. The client will be given the opportunity to comment on the solicitor's justification. If the solicitor gave the client an estimate of the bill prior to the work, that estimate will normally be the maximum amount chargeable. Eventually the Law Society will reply to the client enclosing a certificate stating the amount they feel should be paid. The client cannot challenge this certificate and will have to pay whatever amount is shown. The solicitor can charge interest on the amount to cover the delay. It should be noted that where the bill concerns any conveyancing charges the solicitor should have followed the procedure laid down by the Law Society in their *Fact Sheet on Solicitors' Conveyancing Charges* which is available free of charge from the Law Society, 113 Chancery Lane, London WC2A 1PL (tel: 071 242 1222).
2. *Apply for taxation of the bill.* This procedure is available whether or not the work has involved court proceedings. It could involve the client in expense, however, and is a procedure that is not advisable for relatively minor matters. It is probably best to seek advice from a Citizens' Advice Bureau, or another independent solicitor, before embarking upon the procedure. Under the procedure, which involves an application to the court by the client (which court will depend on the size of the bill), the court may reduce the bill, having listened to representations from both sides. The procedure is complicated because the court cannot reduce every aspect of the bill, and in addition

if they only reduce the bill by 20 per cent or less, they can order the complainant to pay the solicitor's costs of defending the application. There is thus a very real danger that the client will end up paying more than the original bill, even if the bill is reduced! In addition, the procedure is slow and cumbersome.

A complaint that the solicitor has proved incompetent as a result of which the client has suffered loss

Under this procedure, the client is in fact suing their solicitor for negligence. One can therefore imagine the reluctance of a client who has already suffered loss as a result of their solicitor's alleged incompetence, to embark upon yet more legal proceedings. In recent years, however, the Law Society has tried to make the system more accessible to such complaints, in an attempt to improve the image of the profession, and allay public criticism.

What can you complain about?

A client can complain about any action (or inaction) by their solicitor that has caused them loss for which compensation should reasonably be paid. The missing of deadlines for the issue of court proceedings, failure to seek expert advice that might have increased the client's claim, the giving of negligent advice leading to the client losing money, are all common grounds for negligence claims against solicitors. But the issues here are complex and certainly need legal advice. If in any doubt, seek the advice of the Negligence Panel (and see below). The services of the Negligence Panel are not available to limited companies or businesses.

What is the procedure?

As the complaint is one whereby the client is seeking compensation directly from the solicitor, the complaint has to be directed to the solicitor in question. The solicitor is unlikely to accept the complaint without a fight and it is thus advisable to seek legal assistance in the drafting of such a complaint before it is formally made. But where can you seek that advice? Since 1986 a scheme has been in operation whereby a client who is considering making such a complaint can receive a one-hour diagnostic interview with an experienced solicitor free of charge, to decide whether grounds for such a claim exist. The diagnostic interview will be with a member of the Negligence Panel. For access to this panel the complainant must write directly to the Solicitors' Complaints Bureau. The Bureau will not normally refer an applicant to this panel, however, unless they can show clear evidence that they have made efforts to contact local solicitors to advise them and have not been successful. The local CAB can provide a list of solicitors to contact in the first instance.

The solicitor on the Negligence Panel may recommend a number of alternative options:

- no action if, having heard the story, they believe there is no case in law;
- the use of the independent Arbitration Scheme which might be proposed as a simple way of resolving small disputes where the alleged loss is minimal;
- legal action against the solicitor in question. If this is the conclusion of the Negligence Panel member, they will advise the client to obtain legal representation, for which legal aid will be available (see Chapter 1). Otherwise the client will have to pay. The Negligence Panel solicitor is personally allowed to offer to take the case for the client;
- no legal action should be taken but the matter should be referred to the Solicitors' Complaints Bureau as 'shoddy work' (see below).

A COMPLAINT ABOUT THE WAY A SOLICITOR HAS HANDLED A CASE BUT WHERE NO LOSS HAS BEEN SUFFERED

What can you complain about?

A. Poor Service

It sometimes happens that the client does not actually suffer direct financial loss as a result of the way their solicitor has handled their case, but they feel that their solicitor has generally given them a poor service that is below the standard they are entitled to expect. The Law Society gives the following as examples of the type of situation where the circumstances may give rise to a right to lodge a complaint under this heading. The list is not exhaustive:

- failure or delay in answering letters;
- delay in dealing with the case;
- failure to deal properly with the client's money;
- acting for both sides in a case, where there is a conflict of interest;
- overcharging (see also p.38);
- dishonesty or deception;
- failure to hand back papers when the client has asked for them, having paid the bill;
- 'shoddy work', generally defined as work which is substandard, causing distress and inconvenience though no entitlement to compensation.

Who do you complain to? The procedure for making one of the above complaints was introduced in 1986 and is relatively straightforward. The complaint must be made by the complainant in writing, direct to the Solicitors' Complaints Bureau, Victoria Court, 8 Dormer Place, Leamington Spa, Warwickshire CV32 5AE (tel: 0926 820082). The Bureau is a body of lawyers and lay representatives. Its complaints work is itself monitored by an internal Investigation Committee, and by the external Legal Services Ombudsman (see p.42). Once the Bureau has received the complaint, it will send a copy of it to the solicitor involved, inviting comment. It may also ask the complainant for more information. For initial enquiries ring the help line on 0926 822007/822008. The help line is a service provided free of charge and is staffed by solicitors. The help line cannot give legal advice, but it will give practical help and advice on how to proceed with a complaint.

If the Bureau agrees that the complaint is justified, it has various ways of dealing with the complaint. The solicitor can be ordered to reduce the fees charged for the poor work, refund all or part of the fees, or waive the right to recover any more fees. In addition, compensation up to a limit of £1000 can be awarded to the complainant.

B. Misconduct

Having considered all sides of the argument the Bureau may then choose to take no further action, it may deal with the matter itself, it may refer the matter to the Adjudication and Appeals Committee (AAC), and in very serious cases to the Solicitors' Disciplinary Tribunal (SDT). The AAC has 11 lay members and 11 solicitor members, and the SDT, which is completely independent of the Solicitors' Complaints Bureau, sits with two solicitor members and one lay member. The SDT in particular has wide powers, including the power to fine a solicitor, to suspend the solicitor from further practice, and the ultimate sanction of preventing the solicitor from continuing in practice at all.

Can anybody help you to lodge your complaint?

The Interview Panel. Another innovation in the complaints system is the Interview Panel. This service is available to clients of solicitors who wish to make a complaint, but who have difficulty explaining their case. In these circumstances an appointment can be made with a solicitor who will help to write out the complaint. It is potentially an innovation of great assistance to those engaged in social work, many of whose clients might not be conversant with legal jargon and procedures. Most parts of the country have now established their Interview Panels. All appointments with a member of the Interview Panel are made by the Solicitors' Complaints Bureau, and are free. Bureau staff will not themselves give interviews for this purpose.

The Legal Services Ombudsman (LSO). The LSO, appointed by the Lord Chancellor, exists as a further tier in the complaints system. The LSO cannot be a barrister or a solicitor. The first two LSOs (described then as Lay Observers) were in fact retired senior officers of the armed forces. The LSO exists to investigate complaints about the complaints procedure itself. If, once a client's complaint has been investigated, they are still dissatisfied either with the way in which it has been investigated or with the outcome of the investigation, they may complain to the LSO. They should write a letter to the LSO, within three months of being informed of the final decision of the Solicitors' Complaints Bureau, setting out the reason for their dissatisfaction, at the following address: The Legal Services Ombudsman, 22 Oxford Court, Oxford Street, Manchester M2 3WQ (tel: 061 236 9532). If the LSO, having investigated, is not satisfied with the way the case was handled, he or she can order a further investigation.

Barristers

A consumer of legal services will rarely have direct contact with a barrister. This is because under an ancient tradition of the legal profession it is to a solicitor that a client goes for the first line of legal advice and assistance. A barrister will only be engaged if the case requires certain specialist services, such as representation in the higher courts or a legal opinion on a complicated area of law. Even then it is the solicitor and not the client who engages the barrister, and the client may still have no direct contact with the barrister involved in their case. Nevertheless, if the client is in some way dissatisfied with the service provided by their barrister, there are procedures available for them to register a formal complaint which will be investigated. Social workers engaged in court work frequently tell of the frustration felt by themselves or their client when the barrister who has been working with the client on the case is replaced at the last minute by another barrister. This is the type of matter for which complaints procedures exist. These procedures are available regardless of whether the client is paying for the service or receiving legal aid.

What can you complain about?

As with the service of solicitors, a client who has suffered some financial loss as a result of a barrister's negligent work may wish to sue the barrister for damages. This right is, however, limited to the work that a barrister does outside the courtroom, e.g. giving written opinions that are inaccurate on points of law, or preparing faulty documents. A barrister cannot be sued for losses suffered by their court performance, however inadequate it may have been. If a client is considering suing their barrister they should consult a solicitor following the procedures for suing solicitors set out on p.39. The more likely circumstances in which a client may wish to register dissatisfaction are where the client feels that their barrister has acted unprofessionally, been guilty of inadequate preparation, sloppy conduct and so forth. All barristers are subject to a Code of Professional Conduct which they are obliged to follow. Failure to attend court in good time, refusal to take a brief for inadequate reason, unseemly behaviour in court, inadequate preparation, demanding of fees direct from the client, are all examples of behaviour that might give rise to a complaint. The *Code of Conduct for the Bar of England and Wales* can be obtained from the General Council of the Bar, as can a copy of the Professional Conduct Committee Rules.

Who do you complain to?

Complaints against barristers are investigated by the Professional Conduct Committee of the Bar (PCC). The PCC consists of members of the Bar and lay representatives who are drawn from a panel appointed by the Lord Chancellor. The Bar Council Notes for Guidance to complainants advise as follows:

- The complaint should be made in writing, preferably on the form provided for this purpose. As there is no equivalent of the solicitors' Interview Panel for barristers, it is likely that the complainant will need assistance from another source such as a CAB or a social worker in order to complete this form.
- The complaint should identify the barrister and set out in detail the respects in which it is alleged he was guilty of professional misconduct or a breach of professional standards.
- Any witness who can support the complaint should either provide a statement or be identified.

Once this information has been received by the PCC it will then obtain any further information that it feels might be appropriate, e.g. it might seek more evidence from the complainant or witness, and it will write to the barrister against whom the complaint is made.

Having obtained all the necessary information, the PCC will review the evidence. There are a number of options available to it:

- It may dismiss the complaint (but only if the lay representatives on the PCC agree).
- It may accept the complaint but determine that no action should be taken on it (because, for example, of its trivial nature).
- It may decide to deal with the complaint informally, and direct the barrister to arrange a meeting with the Chairman of the PCC.
- It may refer the matter to be dealt with by the Leader of the Court Circuit to which the barrister belongs, or the Treasurer of the Inn of Court to which they belong.
- In an appropriate case, it may require the barrister concerned to take a test in oral English and consider the result of that test.
- In serious cases, it may order a formal hearing of the complaint either before a Summary Tribunal (minor matters), or before a

Disciplinary Tribunal. The Tribunal will consist of a judge, a lay representative and three barristers. The complainant will normally be called as a witness to the hearing, which will normally be in private. The Tribunal has wide powers to discipline the barrister if it finds the allegation to be proved, including advice and reprimand, suspension for a period, a fine of up to £5000, an order to repay or forego fees, and in the most extreme cases, disbarment. A sentence of disbarment or suspension is made public. Other sentences are not normally published. A dissatisfied complainant can request the Legal Services Ombudsman to review the decision in writing, within three months of receiving the PCC written decision (see above at p.42).

The address to write to for further information and a complaint form is: The Secretary of the PCC, The General Council of the Bar, 3 Bedford Row, London WC1R 4DB (tel: 071 242 0082).

Scotland and Northern Ireland

Both the Scottish and the Northern Irish legal professions operate their own complaints procedures, which are similar to those operating in England and Wales but differ in certain aspects of detail. For further information on these procedures contact:

Scotland: For complaints against solicitors, contact The Scottish Law Society, 26 Drumsheugh Gardens, Edinburgh EH3 7YR (tel: 031 226 7411). For complaints against barristers (advocates), contact The Faculty of Advocates, Office of Clerks, Parliament House, Edinburgh EH1 1RF (tel: 031 226 2881).
Northern Ireland: For complaints against solicitors, contact The Law Society of Northern Ireland, Law Society House, 90/106 Victoria Street, Belfast BT1 3JZ (tel: 0232 231614). For complaints against barristers, contact The Secretary to the General Council of the Bar of Northern Ireland, Bar Library, Royal Courts of Justice, Chichester Street, Belfast BT1 3JX (tel: 0232 241523).

COMPLAINTS ABOUT MEDICAL AND PARAMEDICAL SERVICES

The Patient's Charter makes the following provisions:

> All regional and district health authorities must publish information about the services they provide and their performance in relation to local and national charter standards; about waiting times for outpatient, day care and inpatient treatment; about common diseases, conditions and treatments; and about procedures for complaining about NHS services, which include publishing details about the number of complaints received and the time taken to deal with them.

For more information on the above consult *The Patient's Charter*, HPC1 4/92, HMSO.

General practitioners (GPs)

GPs generally provide an excellent service to their patients. It sometimes happens, however, that a patient is not satisfied with the way their GP is treating them, or they may even claim to have suffered injury as a result of their GP's incompetence. In these circumstances it is important that the patient is aware that there are procedures that allow them to make formal complaints. The procedures should be explained to a patient when they first register with a GP. In practice this is rarely the case. The various procedures are therefore set out below. Before dealing with complaints, it would be helpful to set out the basic procedure by which a patient comes to be registered with a particular GP in the first place. Every resident of the United Kingdom is entitled to be registered with a GP. Family Health Service Authorities (FHSAs) (England and Wales), Health Boards (Scotland), and the Central Services Agency (CSA) (Northern Ireland), are the bodies with statutory responsibility to ensure that every person resident in the United Kingdom, who so requests, is registered with a GP. Every practising GP in the United Kingdom has a contract with one of these bodies to look after a given number of patients, normally between 2000 and 3000. GPs' names and addresses are published by the above bodies. Every patient has a right to change their GP without giving any reason. In these circumstances the local body has a duty to find them an alternative GP. GPs also have the right to remove a particular patient from their list without giving any reason. The addresses of the local FHSA (or equivalent) can be found in the local telephone directory or on the back of a client's NHS medical card. Despite the existence of this legal right to change GPs, there is evidence that in practice the procedure is not as straightforward as it seems. In May 1987 the Consumers' Association published the results of a survey of 2600 patients and 1300 GPs in which they claimed that:

> Nearly 4 out of 10 doctors in our survey told us they had refused to accept new patients in the last 12 months. The most common reason for such refusal was that the GP already had a full list of patients. A minority of refusals were, however, on the grounds that the GP thought the patient was likely to be 'difficult'; 'difficult' was all too often defined as a patient who was transferring from a neighbouring practice, or was known to have fallen out with their last GP. (*Which?*, May 1987)

What can you complain about?

A dissatisfied client is entitled to complain about any aspect of their treatment, about the way in which a practice is run, and about any professional or ethical misconduct by their GP.

Who do you complain to?

The nature of the complaint will determine the way in which the complaint should be made:

- An allegation that the GP has not shown proper skill or care, as a result of which the patient has suffered injury. This complaint should be made directly to the GP, or their solicitor, and should normally only be made after seeking careful legal advice, as the allegation is one of professional negligence, and is thus extremely serious for the GP in question.
- An allegation that the GP has breached their contract with the FHSA (or the Health Board or the CSA) in their dealings with their patient. This complaint should be made in writing, to the relevant body (see above), within 13 weeks of the alleged incident. If a patient wishes to check whether their GP has breached the con-

tract, they will obviously wish to know what the contract actually says, and the FHSA should provide a copy. The matters in the contract that most directly affect the patient are the duty to provide 'proper and sufficient accommodation' at the practice; the duty to render to patients 'all necessary and appropriate medical services of the type usually provided by general medical practitioners'; the duty to provide this care at a surgery or at the patient's residence 'if their condition so requires'; and the restrictions on the types of service for which a GP may charge.

- A minor complaint falling short of an allegation of breach of contract. This complaint should be made in writing, to the same body as for complaints of breach of contract.
- Allegations of serious professional or ethical misconduct. Any allegation of this nature must be made in writing directly to the General Medical Council (GMC), the statutory body set up to ensure standards of medical training and practice. The Council's address is 44 Hallam St, London W1N 6AE (tel: 071 580 7642).

If the complaint amounts to an allegation of 'serious professional misconduct', the complainant will be asked to make a sworn statement (called a 'statutory declaration') before a Commissioner for Oaths or Notary Public that their allegation is true. The following examples illustrate conduct that could give rise to complaints under this procedure. The list is not exhaustive:

- Improperly disclosing information about a patient.
- Abuse of drugs or alcohol.
- Indecent behaviour with a patient.
- Prescribing addictive drugs when not necessary.
- Failing to visit or treat a patient when necessary.
- Asking fees for services that should be provided free of charge.
- Entering into an emotional or sexual relationship with a patient that disrupts the patient's family life, or that damages or distresses the patient.

Procedures

Allegations of breach of contract

If the allegation is of a minor nature, the FHSA will normally try to deal with it on an informal, conciliatory basis, sometimes making use of its own lay conciliation service, which employs lay persons 'of tact and sympathy' specially trained to resolve disputes of this nature. If the matter is serious it will be treated more formally. Once the relevant body has received the letter of complaint (see p.47), a formal procedure has to be carried out by their Medical Services Committee (MSC). The Committee is composed of doctors and lay persons, the latter group having the majority. The GP will be sent a copy of the complaint and given the chance to respond.

If there appear to be any grounds for the complaint, a date will be fixed for a formal hearing of the complaint before the MSC, with at least 21 days' notice (14 days in Scotland or Northern Ireland). Both patient and doctor may attend the hearing, which will be in private. Either side may be assisted by another person, such as a social worker or a lawyer. Having heard the complaint, the MSC will compile a report to the relevant body, which has a number of courses of action available to it, ranging from dismissing the complaint to recommending that part of the GP's pay be withheld or even that the GP appear before the National Health Service Tribunal with a view to being stopped from practising.

Allegations of serious professional or ethical misconduct

Allegations of this nature can be dealt with in a variety of ways depending on the nature of the allegation. If the GMC decides to hold a formal inquiry, evidence will have to be given on oath, and will be subjected to cross-examination as in a court of law. The most serious allegations may lead to the GP being struck off the register of practitioners.

Access to medical reports

Since 1989 all patients have a right of access to reports written about themselves by medical practitioners for employment or insurance purposes, on payment of a small fee. Doctors can refuse patients access only if they believe access would cause them, or others, physical or mental harm, reveal the identity of a third party, or indicate the doctor's intentions.

ACCESS TO MEDICAL RECORDS

The Access to Health Records Act 1990 gives patients the right to see their medical records, on application to their doctor. The Act is not retrospective, and thus only allows access to records written after its operative date, which was 1 November 1991. The doctor has the right to refuse access, if s/he considers that this is not in the patient's interest, on the same general grounds as for denying access to personal housing or social service files (see Chapter 3 at p.68). They in turn can appeal against such refusal to the FHSA.

Dentists

The procedures for complaining about dentists are rather more straightforward than those for complaints about doctors. There is no formal procedure for registration with a particular dentist, and subsequently changing to another for whatever reason, so long as the particular course of treatment has been completed, is perfectly simple.

How do you complain?

Complaints about the standard of service should be addressed to the local Family Health Service Authority (FHSA) (Area Health Board or Central Services Agency) within 13 weeks of the incident coming to the complainant's notice, or 6 months after the end of the course of treatment, whichever is the sooner. The subsequent procedures will be exactly the same as those for complaints alleging that a GP has breached their contract of employment (see p.47). Complaints of serious professional misconduct (broadly similar to those relating to GPs) should be addressed to the Registrar of the General Dental Council (GDC), 37 Wimpole St, London W1M 8DQ (tel: 071 486 2171). A recent court ruling has decided that in such cases the GDC must establish 'conduct connected with the dentist's profession in which they have seriously fallen short of the standards of conduct expected among dentists'. Complaints of professional negligence that have caused injury or loss should only be made having sought the advice of a solicitor. For further information, consult

National Consumer Council (1987), *You and Your Dentist* (HMSO), a paperback guide to patients' rights.

Hospital staff and paramedical professions

Overall responsibility for the hospital and community health services in each area of the country rests with the District Health Authority (DHA). The Regional Health Authority (RHA) is concerned with planning the wider health provision, ambulance, and some other services provided direct to the public. Special Health Authorities (SHAs) manage certain special hospitals, the Health Education Authority and the London post-graduate teaching hospitals, and NHS Trusts manage themselves. If a person has a complaint about a hospital service they must first find out which of the above authorities has overall responsibility for the service in question. Complaints will normally be in one of two categories, each category having its own procedures for complaint:

1. Complaints about the quality of service;
2. Complaints about the clinical judgement of hospital staff.

Complaints about the quality of service (including conduct or behaviour of a member of hospital staff)

Complaints should always be made in the first instance to the person involved. If this proves impossible or too embarrassing, or the complaint is sufficiently serious, the patient should complain to a senior member of staff, preferably the member of staff responsible for the work of that particular individual. If the matter still remains unresolved, the patient, or somebody on their behalf, should write a formal letter of complaint to the Hospital Administrator, who will then be bound to investigate the complaint. Such complaints should normally be lodged within a year of the incident complained about.

Complaints about the clinical judgement of hospital staff

A three-stage procedure exists for the patient who wishes to complain about the clinical judgement of any member of the medical staff responsible for their treatment:

Stage 1. The patient should formally complain, verbally or in writing, to the consultant responsible for their treatment, or alternatively to the responsible authority (see above at p.51). The consultant in charge must then look into the complaint, and seek the opinion of the members of staff involved in the complaint. The consultant should try to resolve the matter by informal discussion with the patient.
Stage 2. If the patient is still dissatisfied, they must renew their complaint, at which stage the Regional Medical Officer will be informed (in Wales the Medical Officer for Complaints, in Scotland the Chief Administrative Medical Officer, and in Northern Ireland the Chief Administrative Officer). The consultant will be asked to try once more to resolve the matter informally, having received the views of this officer.
Stage 3. If the matter remains unresolved, and the patient is not considering any other proceedings (e.g. an action for negligence), the Regional Medical Officer (or equivalent: see Stage 2) can set up an independent professional review of the case. This will only happen if the complaint is of a serious nature. The review will be carried out by the independent consultants at a time fixed in advance. The patient can invite their GP, or a relative or friend (including, if appropriate, a social worker) to this review. The consultants will try to resolve the problem at the review, and will also submit a written report of the review and their findings to their district administrator, who will then write formally to the patient setting out their opinions.

Serious professional misconduct or unethical behaviour by a hospital doctor of whatever rank should be reported to the General Medical Council following the procedures set out on p.48.

The Health Service Commissioner (Ombudsman)

This is an independent body set up by the government to investigate complaints of maladministration concerning the health services. Separate offices exist for England, Wales, Scotland and Northern Ireland (known as the Commissioner for Complaints). The Ombudsman is a place of last resort for the complainant as the office will not investigate matters until all other complaints procedures have been exhausted, and they have an undertaking that no legal proceedings are pending. Normally complaints should reach the Ombudsman within a year of the incident, though this can be extended. The Ombudsman has wide powers of investigation, but will not investigate any matter directly involving the clinical judgement of a doctor; complaints about services provided by GPs, dentists, opticians or pharmacists; action taken by the FHSA under their formal procedure (see above at p.49); complaints about a personnel matter; complaints about a NHS authority's commercial or contractual dealings; or a complaint outside the time limit of one year. In broad terms, the sort of complaints the Ombudsman will investigate concern alleged failures of health authorities to provide services they have a duty to provide, and any maladministration. Each national office produces leaflets setting out their procedures and the scope of their activities in more detail. The addresses are as follows:

England: Church House, Great Smith St, London SW1P 3BW (tel: 071 276 2035).
Wales: 4th Floor, Pearl Assurance House, Greyfriars Rd, Cardiff CF1 3AG (tel: 0222 394621).
Scotland: 11 Melville Crescent, Edinburgh EH3 7LU (tel: 031 225 7465).
Northern Ireland: 33 Wellington Place, Belfast BT1 6HN (tel: 0232 233821).

Further assistance (including complaints about paramedical professions)

A detailed handbook to be consulted on most of the above is *Patients' Guide to the NHS*, Consumers' Association (1983), although some of its content is now out of date. The best short booklet setting out the main procedures and addresses for making complaints of this nature is *Patients' Rights* (1983) by the National Consumer Council. It covers the position in the whole of the United Kingdom. As well as dealing with complaints it also sets out patients' rights concerning such matters as home visits, urgent treatment, refusal to consent to treatment, maternity and contraceptive services, abortions, hospital treatment, sterilisation, second opinions and alternative medicine.

The Patients Association, 18 Victoria Park Square, London E2 9PE (tel: 081 981 5676) is a registered charity providing an advice service and collective voice for patients. It also publishes a quarterly news-sheet, *Patient's Voice.*

On the procedures for handling complaints by staff about patient care see *Protecting Patients: Guidelines for Handling Staff Complaints about*

Patient Care (1985) which is available from the National Association of Health Authorities and Trusts, Birmingham Research Park, Vincent Drive, Edgbaston, Birmingham B15 2SQ (tel: 021 471 4444). Available from the same address is an excellent book providing a detailed stage-by-stage account of the procedures for complaints about medical services in general: Capstick, B. (1985), *Patient Complaints and Litigation.*

The procedures for complaints about pharmacists and opticians are the same as those for GPs and dentists (see above at pp.47–50).

Complaints involving the nursing, midwifery or health visiting professions, where there is an allegation of professional misconduct, should be addressed to:

England: The English National Board for Nursing, Midwifery and Health Visiting, Victory House, 170 Tottenham Court Rd, London W1P 0HA (tel: 071 388 3131).
Wales: The Welsh National Board for Nursing, Midwifery and Health Visiting, 13th Floor, Pearl Assurance House, Greyfriars Road, Cardiff CF1 3AG (tel: 0222 395535).
Scotland: The National Board for Nursing, Midwifery and Health Visiting for Scotland, 22 Queen St, Edinburgh EH2 1JX (tel: 031 226 7371).
Northern Ireland: The National Board for Nursing, Midwifery and Health Visiting for Northern Ireland, RAC House, 79 Chichester St, Belfast BT1 4JE (tel: 0232 238152).

Instances where it appears that a nurse is practising unsafely due to physical or mental illness should be reported directly to: United Kingdom Central Council for Nursing, Midwifery and Health Visiting, 23 Portland Place, London W1N 3AF (tel: 071 637 7181).

Complaints involving speech therapists should be addressed to: The College of Speech and Language Therapists, 7 Bath Place, Rivington St, London EC2A 3DR (tel: 071 613 3855). A voluntary organisation offering advice to parents of speech-impaired children is AFASIC, 347 Central Markets, Smithfield, London, EC1A 9NH (tel: 071 236 3632).

Complaints involving other registered health professionals (e.g. physiotherapists, radiographers, chiropodists, occupational therapists) should be addressed to: The Council for the Professions Supplementary to Medicine, Park House, 184 Kensington Park Rd, London SE11 4BU (tel: 071 582 0866).

For a general specialist work covering many aspects of the use of the law to cover disputes in medicine and nursing, advisers should consult Cole, A., Tingle, J., et al. (1988), *Medicine, Nursing and the Law* (Blackstone Press).

Community Health Councils

These Councils were set up in 1981 (one per health district) to represent the interests of the public in the running of the health services of their district. In Scotland the equivalent is the Local Health Council, and in Northern Ireland the (limited) equivalent is the District Committee. The Councils normally have between 18 and 24 members, drawn from local authority nominees, regional and district health authority nominees, and voluntary organisations. Councils should be consulted by district health authorities on any 'substantial development' or 'substantial variation' of existing health services. Councils can also pass on to their district health authorities all general complaints about services, and will often provide representation to individual complainants involved in any of the above procedures. For the address of the local Community Health Council see the local telephone directory.

National Association for Patient Participation

This voluntary organisation encourages patients to form or develop patient participation groups. There are currently over 100 such groups in the United Kingdom. Groups are normally formed by the patients of one particular practice or health centre, with the co-operation of the doctors involved. Their work might include health education, preventive care, and representation of patients' views to the doctors in the practice. For further information on how to set up such a group contact: Mrs Joan Mant, 6 Landsdowne, 1 Sydney Road, Guildford, Surrey GU1 3LJ (tel: 0483 65882).

The Association produces a useful booklet, which explains the work of patient participation groups and gives practical advice on how to start one, called *Patient Participation in General Practice*, which can be obtained from the above address.

Association for Improvements in Maternity Services (AIMS)

This is a pressure group working from London, with 12 UK branches, which offers publications, information, support and advice to parents about all aspects of maternity care including parents' rights, technological interventions, natural childbirth and complaints procedures. For further information contact: AIMS, 40 Kingswood Avenue, London NW6 6LS.

The Maternity Alliance

This is a voluntary, campaigning organisation concerned to improve health care and legal rights of parents-to-be, mothers, fathers and babies. It provides an information resource to organisations, groups and individuals with an interest in maternity rights and services. Contact: Maternity Alliance, 15 Britannia Street, London WC1X 9JP (tel: 071 837 1265).

Chapter 3

Dealing with council services: rights and responsibilities

written with Bill Bowring*

Many local services are delivered by local authorities, which are public bodies headed by elected representatives, and are therefore usually known as councils. This chapter is designed to assist those advising people who wish to complain about council decisions, by explaining local authority structure and examining the various ways in which people can:

- exercise their legal right to information about the decision-making processes in their local council;
- exercise their legal right to information concerning themselves;
- make a complaint about council services or decisions, and if appropriate seek some form of redress.

Where advisers are themselves council officers, for example social workers, housing officers or environmental health officers, they may themselves be the subject of complaint. Indeed, elected councillors, who are ultimately responsible for council decisions, are often called upon to give advice. In such cases it is of particular importance that the adviser should have a clear understanding of the structure and duties of the council as a whole.

Where appropriate, the chapter will deal with collective action as well as individual action.

*Senior Lecturer in Law, University of East London.

WHAT IS A COUNCIL?

Councils are created by Act of Parliament (the basic statute which provides for the constitution, powers and duties of councils is the Local Government Act 1972; but beware, there have been many further Acts) and for that reason, even though councillors have been democratically elected on the basis of their own policy manifestos, the services they may provide and the way in which they provide them are limited to what Parliament has decided, as interpreted by the courts.

A good general introduction to the structure and working of a council is Hutt, J. (1988), *Opening the Town Hall Door: an Introduction to Local Government* (Bedford Square Press). For those who wish to acquire a deeper knowledge of the precise distribution of power between various types of council, and details of their structure and operation, Tony Byrne's non-technical and comprehensive (5th edn, 1990) *Local Government in Britain* (Penguin) is highly recommended reading. R. J. B. Morris's (1990) *Local Government Ground Rules* (Longman) is a compact and very useful and readable account, written for council officers, to help them stay out of trouble!

For those requiring detailed and specialist knowledge the best single book, looseleaf and regularly updated, is Stephen Bailey's (1991) *Cross on Local Government Law* (Sweet and Maxwell). There is a shortened paperback version of the most important chapters of this work, Stephen Bailey's (1992) *Cross on Principles of Local Government Law* (Sweet and Maxwell), while for the most comprehensive and frequently updated information, including the full annotated text of statutes, statutory instruments and circulars, consult the *Encyclopedia of Local Government Law* (3 volumes looseleaf, Sweet and Maxwell).

Each council is responsible for the provision of services in its own geographical area. The present local government system in England and Wales is basically three-tier. In Scotland there are just two tiers. The current system of local government in Northern Ireland is based largely upon district and borough councils. Most of the material in this chapter relates to the prevailing situation in England and Wales. Where the material also has specific application to Scotland or Northern Ireland the text indicates accordingly.

Which council does what?

England and Wales

At least 44 per cent of the population is now (since the abolition of the Greater London Council and the metropolitan county councils in 1986) locally governed in what are essentially one-tier metropolitan areas: the 36 metropolitan district councils (some boroughs, some cities) and 32 London boroughs.

The rest of England and Wales is divided into counties, each with a county council. There are 39 county councils in England and 8 in Wales. Each county is subdivided into districts, each of which has a council: 296 district councils in England and 37 in Wales.

County councils are responsible for education, personal social services, libraries, museums and art galleries, structure plans, highways and parking, national parks, refuse disposal, police, fire and rescue services, civil defence, weights and measures and consumer protection services, and residual housing powers.

District councils are responsible for housing, environmental health services, refuse collection, local plans and development control, some licensing and registration functions, markets, land charges, parks, recreation and leisure facilities, museums and art galleries (with county councils), car parks, allotments, crematoria and cemeteries.

The *metropolitan districts and London boroughs* are virtually unitary (that is, one-tier) authorities, having responsibility for all the combined functions of counties and shire districts, with joint committees to deal with police (except in London, where the Home Secretary is in charge), fire and civil defence, passenger transport, airports, and waste disposal.

Advisers must therefore be aware that, outside London and the metropolitan districts, one council will be responsible, for example, for housing, while another is responsible for social services. Where a disabled person, cared for by one council, is housed in accommodation provided by another, complex questions of responsibility can arise.

Parish or town councils (known in Wales as community councils) have minor local responsibilities in such matters as footpath protection, public lavatories, recreation and parking.

Scotland

In Scotland the equivalents of the county councils are called regional councils, and district councils are the same. There are no parish councils.

Proposals for reform

It has long been argued that local government would best be provided by a single-tier system, with just one council responsible for each geographical area, and the government is presently considering proposals for reform in England and Wales. A single-tier system is to be introduced in Scotland.

Council structure

A council is composed of elected councillors (also known as council members), who are elected by the local electors for a period of four years, and non-elected officers, who are the employed staff who carry out the decisions of the councillors and administer the council services.

Parliament has decided that there should be a number of features common to all councils:

- Most of the legal powers and duties of councils (for example, those concerning mental health, child care, disability, homelessness) are the legal responsibility of the elected councillors, and not of the officers.
- A number of these powers and duties may (and in some cases, such as education and social services, must) be delegated by the full council to its committees and subcommittees, also made up of councillors. Some powers may also be further delegated to officers. Some duties, such as the fixing of the amount of the annual council tax, and consideration of reports from the Monitoring Officer (p.64) or the Local Ombudsman (p.75), cannot be delegated, and remain the responsibility of the full council. An adviser should always check whether a power or duty has been properly delegated.
- All council committees and subcommittees will operate according to standing orders which are drawn up by the council and which must be available to the public for inspection. Some of these standing orders are obligatory, by virtue of Act of Parliament.
- All council meetings and committee and subcommittee meetings are open to the public, subject to the limited exceptions set out below.

- Questions coming before any council meeting must be decided by a majority of those present and voting.
- The names of those present at and taking part in all council meetings must be recorded and minutes taken which must be available for public inspection (see p.66).
- Every council has the power to appoint staff, of which some appointments are mandatory (e.g. Director of Social Services, Chief Education Officer, Monitoring Officer (see p.64 below)).

What services does a council have responsibility to provide?

The range of services that a council provides is vast and there is insufficient space to list them all here. As indicated above, these services are also often distributed between different types of council. Housing, social services, education, environmental health, public health, public libraries and recreation facilities are examples of some of the most important council services.

It is always important to distinguish between the service that a council provides through *political preference*, although always within the limits laid down by Parliament, and the service that a council provides through *legal obligation.* Failure to provide the latter type of service always leaves open the possibility of legal action against the council for a breach of statutory duty (see p.78), whereas failure to provide the former does not, although there may be other possibilities of legal redress.

It is seldom a simple matter to determine whether a service is a council's legal obligation or political preference. Only a thorough knowledge of the subject area will ultimately answer this question. There are, however, some clear areas of councils' legal obligation that are examined in this book:

- obligations to mentally disabled people (see Chapter 5);
- obligations to physically disabled people (see Chapter 4);
- obligations to homeless people (see Chapter 10);
- obligations relating to disrepair and public health (see Chapter 11);
- obligations to elderly people (see Chapter 9).

Since 1980, Parliament has implemented plans to subject a wide range of council services to 'compulsory competitive tendering': first construction services, then cleaning and catering, and now even legal and architectural services. These services may therefore be performed by private contractors, though the council will nevertheless remain legally responsible for provision of the service.

How are decisions regarding council services made?

Committees

Because it would be impossible for a full council meeting to make all the decisions regarding the provision of services, councils operate through a committee system, as mentioned above. Committees will be set up to cover all the main areas of council activity, e.g. housing, planning, social services, education, staff employment, recreation, public health and finance. With the exception of an Education Committee and a Social Services Committee, which each council must by law establish, it is a matter of choice for each council which committees to set up, and what they will be called. Some councils have set up decentralised, neighbourhood structures, in which many functions are carried out by neighbourhood committees.

A number of the council's decision-making powers will be delegated to committees: for example, decisions about council house allocation, planning permission, care proceedings, and the acquisition of property. Each committee will be made up of a number of councillors, who are advised by the relevant council officers. There are rules, contained in the Local Government and Housing Act 1989, which seek to ensure that the various political parties have fair representation on each committee. The chairperson of the committee will be the vital link between the officers and the committee in the periods between meetings.

COUNCILLORS

A councillor is somebody who has been elected by the local electors to serve as a member of the council for a period of four years (less if elected in a by-election). Councillors have collective and personal responsibility for making all the policy decisions of their council, and for ensuring that the council officers carry out these decisions. Councillors may claim expenses for attending council meetings, but they are not employees of the council.

Nowadays councils frequently operate on party political lines that follow national party politics fairly closely. This means that once all the votes have been counted, the majority group within the council will automatically have an in-built political majority in the council, and on all its committees, subject to the rules on proportionality of representation. Like a member of parliament, however, a councillor is elected to serve all the constituents whatever their politics. There is no doubt that, within any council, a councillor is a powerful figure.

Anybody fitting the following description may stand for election as a councillor: a British subject or Irish citizen who is 21 or over on the day of the election and who has a local connection with the authority in which they are standing for election. If a candidate is not registered as a voter in the area of the council they must demonstrate substantial living or working connections with the area for at least the previous 12 months.

Even if a person fits the above description, they may be disqualified from standing for election for a number of other reasons, for example bankruptcy, a recent prison sentence, or disqualification for a period of five years as a result of a finding of wilful misconduct resulting in a loss to the council. For more information on the powers and responsibilities of councillors see Turner, B., *Law For Councillors* (1986, Sweet and Maxwell), which contains a wealth of information on such questions as privilege and protection, corrupt practices, and the legal limits to councillors' powers. The adviser should be aware, however, that there have been many changes in the law since 1986; the *Encyclopedia of Local Government Law* is the safest source of detailed information.

A councillor who has a pecuniary (financial) interest in any proposed council contract must disclose that fact at any meeting where it will be considered, and then must not take part in discussion or voting. In addition, since 1992, every councillor must supply information on all direct and indirect pecuniary interests for publication in a 'register of members' interests', open to inspection at reasonable hours by the public free of charge (Local Authorities (Members Interests) Regulations 1992 SI 1992 618).

Every councillor must also be guided by the National Code of Local Government Conduct which expands and clarifies a number of the rules by which councillors operate. The full text of the Code can be found in the *Encyclopedia of Local Government Law*. The Code stresses that a councillor's overriding duty as a councillor is to the whole local community. It requires disclosure by councillors of all private or personal nonpecuniary (financial) interests, unless they are insignificant; and regulates the circumstances in which a councillor who has such an interest may take part in a discussion or vote.

Each council has, since 1989, a 'Monitoring Officer' (often the Chief Executive), who must warn the full council formally if there is or may be any contravention of a rule of law, or any code of practice, or any maladministration within the scope of the Local Ombudsman (see p.75 below).

What happens if a councillor does not attend any council meetings?

Failure of a councillor to attend any meetings of the council and its committees for a period of at least six months without good cause (such as illness) renders that councillor liable to be disqualified from office.

What powers do councillors have to investigate the work of their officers?

Because councillors must employ staff to carry out their policies it follows that they must have powers to check that their policies are actually being carried out. This employer's right is, however, subject to all the general laws of the workplace (see Chapter 7). The existence of these powers does not mean that councillors have the right of random access to officers' files. Any request for access to an officer's files must be justified by the councillor as reasonably necessary in order for that councillor to carry out their duties.

If a member of the public complains to a councillor about the actions of a particular officer, however, the position becomes clearer. Because councillors have a legal responsibility to keep themselves informed of all matters necessary for them to perform their duties, they have a basic right to inspect any files relevant to the matter they have been asked to investigate. This gives councillors who are investigating complaints very wide powers to inspect files. But are there any limits to these powers? According to the courts, a councillor is entitled by virtue of his or her office as an elected member of the council to have access to all documents relating to the business of the full council, as well as a committee or subcommittee of which he or she is a member; and to other documents if there is a good reason. Probably, the councillor must show that it is in the public interest that they should have access to the particular piece of information.

Parliament has enacted provisions for access to council information (these are complex, and are to be found in sections 100A–K of the Local Government Act 1972). These cover England, Wales and Scotland (but not Northern Ireland). There are a number of categories of 'exempt information' to which the public can be denied access (see p.67 below). A councillor without a 'good reason' for access to such information may be denied access to it. The councillor does not have the automatic right to show the information to which access has been given to the person whom it concerns (see below).

If an officer refuses to show a councillor a file, the line or senior manager should be consulted. If this manager upholds the refusal, the councillor has the right to take the matter to the full council for a decision, and ultimately to challenge any refusal in court.

To whom may councillors divulge any confidential information that they have obtained?

Having obtained information, a councillor has then to decide whether to divulge its contents. The Data Protection Act 1984 and the Access to Personal Files Act 1987 (which covers only housing and social services information) may in any event entitle the client to automatic access (see pp. 68–71). Otherwise, it will be a matter for the councillor to decide whether or not to divulge the contents of the file. If the document is contentious or is marked 'confidential' it is advisable for the councillor to seek legal advice, in the first instance from the council's own lawyers, before divulging its contents, as the document may be the subject of legal privilege, its contents may be defamatory, or it may contain confidential information about other people. In any of these cases, revealing the contents of the document may render the councillor liable to legal action.

FINDING OUT ABOUT COUNCIL SERVICES AND ACTIVITIES

Local government which is carried out in a spirit of openness will almost certainly be more accountable and more efficient. There will be less opportunity for corruption and unfairness. Parliament has for those reasons enacted legislation with a view to giving greater access to local government information.

Obtaining general information

Most councils have information departments usually based in their town hall, which employ officers skilled in guiding enquirers in the right direction. These departments will usually be able to indicate which particular section of the council is responsible for any service. In addition to providing general information councils have a statutory duty to provide certain specific information if requested, as follows:

- details of forthcoming meetings of council committees and subcommittees (including the agenda, copies of any reports that will be publicly discussed, together with copies of any relevant background papers – a reasonable fee may be charged for copies provided);
- similar details of similar meetings that have taken place together with the minutes of any such meeting;
- details about councillors, including each councillor's address, and the ward or division they represent;
- the register of councillors' interests (see p.63 above);
- the name and address of every member of each committee and subcommittee of the council;
- details of any powers that have been delegated for more than six months to a council officer, together with a description of the rank of that officer;
- details of the council's housing allocation policy.

Rights of a member of the public to attend council meetings

A member of the public has the right to attend any council meeting, committee or subcommittee meeting, unless the council has exercised its power to exclude the public from all or part of that meeting. This power to exclude can only be exercised in the following circumstances:

- *either* the presence of the public would result in a breach of confidence by the disclosure of confidential information supplied to the council on confidential terms by a government department or whose disclosure is prohibited by court order or statute;

- *or* the item(s) of business to be discussed may involve the disclosure of 'exempt information' (see below).

The power to exclude is exercised by a simple resolution proposed at the time that the need to exclude arises.

It follows from the right to attend meetings that, by law, proper notice must be given. In general, three clear days' notice must be given; this period excludes the day of the meeting but not the day of the giving of notice. Failure by the council to give the correct period of notice will be a ground upon which a court might set aside a decision taken at the meeting. Moreover, the agenda for the meeting and the copies of the reports prepared by the officers (except those containing 'exempt information' (see below)) must be open to inspection by members of the public for the same period.

Exempt information

There are a number of categories of 'exempt information', including information about any of the following: council employees and councillors past, present and future; council tenants or licensees; recipients of council services or financial assistance from the council; the adoption, care, fostering or education of any child. The full list can be found in the *Encyclopedia of Local Government Law*.

Disorderly behaviour

The chairperson of any council meeting has the power to ask any member of the public to refrain from 'disorderly behaviour' and, if necessary, arrange for them to be removed from the meeting with such reasonable force as is necessary to eject them. The police have no power to enter council premises in these circumstances, unless invited by the council to do so. They may, however, enter without permission if they have reasonable grounds to suspect that a breach of the peace is imminent. If the 'disorderly behaviour' is by a councillor, the councillor should be asked to withdraw voluntarily, and if they refuse to do so, the meeting can be adjourned or suspended. For further information on the running of council meetings, and the procedures that can be adopted within meetings, see Ward, S. (1985), *A–Z of Meetings* (Pluto Handbooks). For a more formal account see Moore, M. (1979), *The Law and Procedure of Meetings* (Sweet and Maxwell).

Obtaining information about council expenditure: public rights of access to council accounts

Every council's financial year ends on 31 March each year. A council is obliged by law to have its accounts audited by an external auditor appointed by the Audit Commission and to publish thereafter a summary of the accounts. Every council elector has the right to purchase from their council a copy of this summary, together with any explanatory tables, diagrams and statistical information that may accompany it.

If an elector wishes to make a more detailed examination of the council's accounts (including related books, deeds, contracts, bills and vouchers) they have the right to do so, and to make copies, provided they do so in a period of seven clear days before a date fixed and published annually by the district auditor. A period then follows during which an elector may question the auditor on the accounts and express any objections. In the event of objections being made, the auditor may call an informal meeting at which the objector(s) can pursue their objections further.

Auditors have extensive powers in the case of unlawful expenditure or loss caused by the wilful misconduct of councillors or officers, and formal procedures are also available to the public to challenge an auditor's action, or failure to act. These procedures are complex and time-consuming and advice should be sought before invoking them. For further information see Turner, B. (1986), *Law for Councillors* (Sweet and Maxwell). R. J. B. Morris's (1990) *Local Government Ground Rules* has a very clear and succinct (and more up-to-date) account of the auditor's powers and duties, Chapter 13, pp. 109–20.

It should be noted that, in all the above circumstances, the rights of access of councillors are even more extensive than those of members of the public (see Turner, above).

Obtaining information on personal council files: client rights of access

The desirability of open access of clients to the files held on them by council officers has been the subject of debate. On the one hand it has been argued that the willingness of officers to record their true impressions will be restrained by open access; on the other hand it has been argued that open access will encourage greater openness between officer and client and help reduce the possibility of inaccuracy or misunderstanding, particularly in the personal social services. Three years after the introduction of open files in the United States in 1974, a study of those files to which access had been sought revealed that inaccuracies had been discovered by clients in 90 per cent of files. More recently, the general trend in British social services has been towards an acceptance of the principle of open access.

A move to compulsory access was initiated by two important pieces of legislation, the Data Protection Act 1984 and the Access to Personal Files Act 1987. The position is now as follows.

Files and records held on a computer (England, Scotland, Wales and Northern Ireland)

Any person who is the subject of files or records held by a council authority on a computer has the right of access to those files or records. There are a number of exemptions to this right, for example as to information related to social work – see the Data Protection (Subject Access Modification) (Social Work) Order 1987 SI 1987/1903, to be found in the *Data Protection Encyclopedia* (Sweet and Maxwell, looseleaf). Every local authority holding information on clients on a computer has to be registered with the Data Protection Registrar and will appoint a Data Protection Officer whose duty it is to ensure that the authority complies with the Data Protection Act.

If a client wishes to have access to information held on them on a computer by any council department they should apply in writing for access to the council's Data Protection Officer. A small fee will be charged for the service. Having requested the information, the client must be given access to it unless it is claimed that the information falls within one of the following exemptions:

1. It is held by a local authority social services department, health authority, education welfare service, probation committee or the NSPCC, and revealing it would either prejudice the carrying out of social work by seriously harming the health or emotional condition of that client or some other person, or would lead to the identification of other individuals not employed in social work (e.g. informants).

2. It is held by a health professional (see below), and supply of the information would be likely to cause serious harm to the physical or mental health of the client or to lead to the identification of another person.

Health professionals include doctors, dentists, nurses, health visitors, midwives, various forms of therapists, and paramedical professionals such as speech and occupational therapists and physiotherapists. These provisions have been extended to data held by local authorities exercising education welfare officer functions, to council meals and recreation functions for old people, to guardians *ad litem*, to the NSPCC, and to probation committees.

For further advice and information on this subject contact: Data Protection Registrar, Wycliffe House, Water Lane, Wilmslow, Cheshire SK9 5AX (tel: 0625 535777).

For a comprehensive guide to the Data Protection Act, consult the *Data Protection Encyclopedia* (Sweet and Maxwell, looseleaf).

Personal files which are not held on a computer (England, Wales and Scotland)

Partly in response to a lengthy campaign by the Freedom of Information Campaign Parliament enacted a private member's bill, the Access to Personal Files Act 1987. This statute allows individuals the right to see their own housing or social services files, on payment of a small fee, in order to secure access to any personal information contained on their files, and the right to erasure or rectification of any inaccuracies contained in that information.

Personal information is defined as 'information which relates to a living individual who can be identified from that information (or from that and other information in the possession of the authority keeping the record) including any expression of opinion about the individual but not any indication of the intentions of the authority towards that individual'.

The local authority can still withhold access on grounds similar to those which apply to the Data Protection Act (p.69). Thus the course of action proposed for a particular client need not be disclosed, although there may be some difficulties where the course of action is based upon an expression of opinion. The identities of third parties will also be protected.

For full details see the Access to Personal Files (Social Services) Regulations 1989 SI 1989/206 and the Access to Personal Files (Housing) Regulations 1989 SI 1989/503.

In addition, a council must, on request, allow an applicant for housing details of any information it has been given by any party about themselves or their family, and which the council has recorded as being relevant to their application.

For further information on all of the above consult Harrison, T. (1988), *Access to Information in Local Government* (Sweet and Maxwell).

COMPLAINING ABOUT A COUNCIL SERVICE

How do you complain about a council service?

It is always helpful as an adviser to draw up your own formula concerning priorities of complaint on a sliding scale of seriousness. In the same way that an individual may not take a case to the European Court of Human Rights until they have 'exhausted their domestic remedies' by exercising all their rights of appeal, an individual with a complaint about a council decision, or inaction, should be encouraged to pitch the initial level of the complaint appropriately. The general rule should always be to make the initial complaint at the lowest appropriate level, and only if that does not achieve the desired result should higher-level complaints be considered.

First of all, a potential complainant should enquire from the council information officer whether the council has a formal complaints procedure, what matters it covers, and whether it is appropriate for the particular complaint. Some councils produce a booklet setting out their procedures, others adopt a much more informal approach.

How to use a council complaints procedure

The general rule should be that if there is a complaints procedure that is appropriate for the particular complaint, then it should be used. At the present time, however, only about half the social services departments in the country have formal procedures for the investigation of complaints by clients, although there are now special mechanisms for dealing with complaints in relation to child care and educational special needs. A whole new set of complaints procedures are also slowly coming into force to reflect the new local authority community care responsibilities (see Chapter 4 at p.90).

Alternative methods of complaint

Complain to the relevant officer

Although it is the elected councillors who have overall responsibility for the services that their council provides (which is why they are named as the defendants in any legal action against the council), it is the council officers who carry out all the day-to-day work of the council, and it is normally to them that any complaint should first be addressed. Because their work is carried out locally, council officers tend to have a much higher public profile than do government civil servants, although they also are required to act neutrally.

A complaint can either be addressed to a particular officer (for example, a social worker, housing official, or estate manager) or to that officer's line manager. As a general rule, complaints should always begin at the lowest level, to give the person most closely involved in the complaint the opportunity to resolve the problem or at least provide some explanation to the complainant. A complaint will always be more sympathetically received at a higher level if it has first been made at the level at which it originated. Complaints should always be made in writing, with a copy retained by the complainant. Complaints about policy are best directed to the relevant *council committee* (see below at p.73).

If the officer or their line manager fails to resolve the complaint satisfactorily the complainant then has two choices, either to go to a higher level of officer management, or to complain to a councillor.

Complain to higher level of officer management

The first problem will be to establish the officer hierarchy of the council in question. Most council information offices provide a booklet explaining the structure of each department. Every department will have a head, who has ultimate responsibility for the work of every member of their department (e.g. the Director of Social Services, Chief Education Officer, Director of Housing, or the Chief Environmental Health Officer). Each council has a 'head of the paid service' with overall authority, who is often called the Chief Executive; this officer should be reserved only for the most serious complaints. If the complainant is not sure to which department to address their complaint, however, they should address it to the Chief Executive who will ensure that it ends up in the right department.

Complain to a councillor

As it is councillors who have ultimate responsibility for the work of the council, it is to them that a complaint should be addressed, if it has not been resolved by one of the above two methods. As a general rule, it is better to complain to a councillor only when a complaint has been made to the officers and the complaint has not been resolved.

As has been shown above, councillors have wide powers to investigate a complaint, including the right of access to relevant files. An important consideration will be, which councillor to complain to? There are two main possibilities. The first is to approach a councillor representing the ward where the complainant lives. The second is to approach the chairperson of the appropriate council committee. This latter course would normally only be taken if the matter involved a major complaint about the department, which would include a complaint about departmental policy.

Presentation of petitions and deputations

If the subject matter of the complaint affects a number of people, e.g. the closing of a school or day centre, or a refusal to install a pedestrian crossing, the raising and presentation of a petition may sometimes be an effective way of airing the complaint. Most councils have strict rules regarding the presentation of a petition which can be found in the standing orders of the council (see p.60). Normally the following procedure should be adopted:

- The petition should have a clear and precise preamble which sets out the issue of concern and provides the names and addresses of the petition organisers.
- All those who sign the petition should give their name and address.
- The petition must be presented by a councillor, on behalf of the petitioners, to a full council meeting. The councillor will indicate

the nature of the petition, and hand it in. There may then be a debate on the petition, or if appropriate it may be remitted to the next meeting of the committee dealing with the subject matter of the petition. The petitioners may also, at the discretion of the meeting, be allowed to speak.

If the complainants are anxious to be given the opportunity to address the full council or one of its committees on the issue in question, an alternative course of action would be to organise a *deputation.* A deputation is when a group of complainants are given the opportunity to confront the council directly with their problem. It is particularly useful when a group of people are anxious that the full council should be aware of the particular issue, as for example when a very local campaign has failed to influence the council decision and insufficient publicity has been given to the issues involved.

Again the standing orders of the council should be consulted for details of the procedure. A typical procedure would be as follows:

- A written request must be addressed to the Chief Executive setting out the reasons for seeking a deputation, the names and addresses of those concerned in the deputation, and nominating a person to speak on their behalf. The subject-matter of the deputation must come within the general powers and duties of the council.
- The Chief Executive will convey the request to the mayor or chairperson of the council who has absolute discretion whether or not to allow the deputation. If the mayor or chairperson decides to allow the deputation, they can also decide whether it should be heard before the full council or before an appropriate council committee.
- If the deputation is allowed, limits can be placed upon the length of time the presenter will be allowed to speak, and the numbers that will be allowed on to the council floor. At the designated meeting (either the full council or committee) the presenter will be invited to address the members, and can then be questioned by any of them.

Complain to the Commissioner for Local Administration (the Local Ombudsman)

In 1974 Parliament established Commissioners for Local Administration, usually known as Local Ombudsmen, and gave them enhanced powers in 1989. The Local Ombudsman has wide powers to investigate complaints by members of the public that they have suffered injustice as a result of council maladministration. Maladministration is a very broad term that includes undue delay, bias, discrimination, failure to apply rules of procedure, and general misconduct or incompetence.

There are currently three Local Ombudsmen in England, and one each in Wales, Scotland and Northern Ireland. Each operates from a regional office with a full-time staff. Their addresses are as follows:

England
21 Queen Anne's Gate, London SW1H 9BU (tel: 071 222 5622) (covers Greater London, Kent, Surrey, Sussex and Southend);
The Oaks, Westwood Way, Westwood Business Park, Coventry CV4 8JB (tel: 0203 695999) (covers South-West, West, South, East Anglia, Central England);
Beverley House, 17 Shipton Road, York, YO3 6FZ (tel: 0904 630151) (covers East Midlands and North of England).

Wales
Derwen House, Court Road, Bridgend, Mid-Glamorgan, Wales CF31 1BN (tel: 0656 66325).

Scotland
23 Walker Street, Edinburgh EH3 7HX (tel: 031 225 5300).

Northern Ireland
33 Wellington Place, Belfast BT1 6HN (tel: 0232 233821).

The procedure for laying a complaint as set out below is the procedure for complaints in England and Wales, although the procedures in Scotland and Northern Ireland are broadly similar.

A complainant, or somebody on their behalf, can initiate a complaint by writing directly to the Local Ombudsman, setting out the nature of the alleged maladministration – a letter will suffice. Normally the complaint should be lodged within 12 months of the alleged maladministration, although exceptionally, if for good reason, this requirement can be waived. The complainant must have brought the complaint to the notice of the council, and given the council a reasonable opportunity to investigate and reply.

The following are matters that the Local Ombudsman is *not* empowered to investigate:

- matters where there is an existing right of appeal to a tribunal, minister or court which has not yet been used, for example, a decision to evict a council tenant where the tenant has grounds to defend the eviction, unless it would not have been reasonable for that right of appeal to be used;
- commercial transactions, other than those involving the purchase or sale of land, e.g. a council's decision to sell its office equipment;
- education matters affecting teaching in, or the internal organisation of, schools;
- personnel matters;
- matters affecting most or all of the inhabitants (e.g. the level of the rates or community charge);
- matters relating to the investigation or prevention of crime;
- the commencement or conduct by the council of civil or criminal proceedings.

How does the Local Ombudsman deal with the complaint?

The first stage of the procedure, assuming that the complaint is one that the Ombudsman has power to investigate, will be for the Ombudsman to invite the relevant council officers or councillors to give their side of the story. If the Ombudsman feels there is a case to answer, he or she will despatch an investigator to the council to interview the officers or councillors involved, and to look at all relevant files.

The council has a legal duty to allow the Ombudsman access to all relevant files unless they claim that the 'public interest' demands that the files remain confidential to them. This may raise complicated legal questions which the Ombudsman may wish to place before the court. The court will have to decide whether the 'public interest' that certain council documents remain confidential outweighs the 'public interest' that the Ombudsman can carry out a full and thorough investigation. This may well be relevant in cases involving the personal social services where sensitive questions have been raised prior to making a decision on, for example, the suitability of a foster parent. However, such applications to court are rare.

The investigator will also visit the complainant and any other relevant parties. All these visits and interviews are intended to be fairly informal. The Ombudsman has the power to reimburse any expenses incurred by those taking part in the investigation. All interviews are conducted in private. Having completed all these interviews and investigations the investigator will compile a 'statement of facts' which will be sent in draft form to both parties for their agreement.

The final stage of the investigation will be the preparation by the Ombudsman of a report which will decide whether maladministration has taken place. If the answer is affirmative, the Ombudsman may also suggest an appropriate remedy, e.g. some form of compensation. In addition, the report must be placed before a meeting of the full council for consideration. The Ombudsman has no power to enforce this remedy other than the pressure that comes from the status of the office, and public opinion; the Ombudsman now has power to publish a report in the press. The final report on the case will always be made available to the public. It will not, however, identify the parties unless the Ombudsman rules it to be in the public interest to do so.

The largest category of complaints to the Local Ombudsman relate to housing and planning, followed by highways, education and environmental health matters. Complaints range from allegations of excessive delay in the processing of council house applications to failure to take correct action or consult the right people, to racial and personal bias or simply gross incompetence.

Perhaps the biggest problem facing those who complain to the Local Ombudsman is the problem of the time that it takes to process the complaint: the average time is around 47 weeks from lodging the complaint to resolution. In England and Wales complaints to the Local Ombudsmen about social services are comparatively rare: in the first 2 years of the Local Ombudsmens' work only 20 of the 466 reports issued related to social services departments. In general local Ombudsmen receive between 2000 and 3000 complaints a year, on which only around 12 per cent on average do they find initial grounds to investigate. Once a formal investigation has occurred about 60 per cent lead to a finding of injustice.

The Ombudsmen offices in all four countries provide useful introductory leaflets, entitled *Your Local Ombudsman*, on how they operate.

Advisers should remember that the Ombudsman has far greater powers of investigation and inquiry than could be ordered by a court in a claim for damages or an application for judicial review. On the other hand, the remedies which may be obtained through the Ombudsman are limited.

Sue the council

Suing the council means issuing proceedings in the county court or the High Court against a council officer, or against the council itself, for damages to compensate injury or damage that has been suffered as a result of their negligence or breach of statutory duty. When the council officer has been carrying out council decisions or policies, it is usually the council which should be sued. This tactic should only be used as a last resort when all else has failed, and should never be adopted without first taking professional legal advice. In appropriate cases legal aid will be available (see Chapter 1). In addition, there are Law Centres in many areas which will provide advice and representation free of charge (contact the Law Centres Federation, Duchess House, 18–19 Warren Street, London W1D 5DB (tel: 071 387 8570) for details of your local Law Centre).

In what sorts of circumstances might somebody sue?

There are a great many possibilities, but in most cases a person suing a council will rely on the council's failure to provide a service which they have a statutory duty to provide, or their failure to discharge their statutory duty in accordance with the law. Such duties arise in the case, for example, of assistance to the disabled, the protection of children in care, or the care of people discharged from mental institutions. In addition, a council may be found to have acted negligently in cases where, according to the rules laid down by the courts, a 'duty of care' is owed. If councillors or officers have deliberately or recklessly acted unlawfully, because of malice towards the complainant, they may become liable to pay damages. But it should be borne in mind that, in general, the courts have no power to award damages for 'maladministration' as defined above.

Is the councillor or officer personally liable?

An officer or councillor enjoys considerable statutory protection (to be found in s.265 of the Public Health Act 1875 and s.39 of the Local Government (Miscellaneous Provisions) Act 1976) from legal action by aggrieved service users and others. No action will lie against councillors or officers by third parties (this would include all potential complainants) for an action done *bona fide* (in good faith) under the direction of their employing authority or by the authority itself. That means that a complainant must, in nearly every case, sue the council itself.

Independent social workers or independent paramedics (i.e. those who are 'brought in' by the council for a specific task, but are not normally employed by that council) remain personally liable for their negligent acts, and are strongly advised to take out private insurance against such an eventuality.

The council will not be liable for the actions or negligence of its employees if they have been acting in a manner which is not within the 'course of their employment' – for example, a social worker who carries out an unlawful assault, or steals. In such a case, the individual officer must be sued, or, where there is doubt, both the council and the officer.

Can officers sue the council for injuries suffered in the course of their employment?

All employees are covered by the general employment rights outlined in Chapter 7, including the provisions regarding health and safety at work, the provision of a safe system of work, handling and lifting regulations, and the provision of safe working conditions (pp. 233–8). This means, for example, that social work employees have a legal duty to ensure that their staff are given reasonable protection against violence from clients and the general public, and must not expose them to unreasonable risk of violence, e.g. by sending lone staff to visit clients who may become violent. A very useful short book on this topic, explaining the need for social work employers to carry out a detailed safety audit of the entire workforce, and how to do it, is More, W. (1993), *Ensuring Staff Safety* (Pepar Publications).

Specialised complaints: discrimination on grounds of race or sex

It is unlawful for any council to discriminate against a person or group in the provision of any council services or facilities, including housing. Discrimination means treating a person less favourably than others on grounds of their colour, race, nationality, sex, or ethnic or national origins. It also extends to 'indirect' discrimination, which is the policy of applying a similar requirement for obtaining a service or facility to all members of the population, knowing that certain groups are less able to meet that requirement because of their colour, race, nationality, sex or ethnic origins. (For further details on the concept of both direct and indirect discrimination as it relates to employment, see Chapter 7.)

Discrimination is notoriously hard to prove, as the evidence is rarely overt or written. The widening access to information described above will, however, make it easier to obtain evidence of discrimination, and the powers vested in the Local Ombudsman (see p.75) to obtain information and read files are another potential source of proof. Complaints about discrimination have to be brought in the local county court, within six months of the alleged act of discrimination. Anybody who believes they are the subject of discrimination in any of the above forms should seek further advice and assistance from one of the following organisations:

Equal Opportunities Commission (EOC) [sex], Overseas House, Quay Street, Manchester M3 3HM (tel: 061 833 9244);
Commission for Racial Equality (CRE) [race, colour, nationality, etc.], Elliot House, Allington St, London SW1 5EH (tel: 071 828 7022).

For a clear, comprehensive and accurate book on the key provision of the 'equality legislation', see Gregory, J. (1987), *Sex, Race and the Law* (Sage).

High Court review of the legality of council action

Since reforms were implemented in 1977 there has been a considerable increase in the number of people using the High Court to seek an order

- to force a council to do something they are legally obliged to do (this is called an order of *mandamus*),

- to cancel a decision already taken by a council (this is called an order of *certiorari*),
- to prevent them from a particular course of action (this is called an order of *prohibition*).

These unusual names date from the Middle Ages, but are still in use. Complainants may also seek a *declaration* as to what the law is, where there is doubt; an *injunction*, which is an order that the council does something or refrains from doing it; and, in a limited number of cases, *damages*.

The procedure involved in such action is called 'an application for judicial review', a procedure whereby the High Court literally reviews the legality of a council's decision or failure to act. A series of complicated rules have been developed over the years to govern the circumstances in which judicial review can be requested. Nobody should contemplate an action for judicial review without first seeking expert legal advice. Legal aid is available for judicial review as long as the applicant is within the legal aid limits, the local legal aid committee considers that there is a reasonable chance of success, and that the action is justifiable in cost terms (see generally Chapter 1).

The adviser should, however, be aware of the following general principles governing judicial review before advising a client to seek further legal assistance:

1. An applicant for judicial review must have 'sufficient interest in the matter to which the application relates' before the courts will entertain the application, i.e. a direct interest in the subject-matter of the application. Thus a homeless person or a disabled person would be entitled to initiate an action for judicial review of a council's decision, or failure to act, if it concerned them personally. If the action to be reviewed involves significant expenditure, then a local council tax payer will also probably be able to argue that they have 'sufficient interest' to justify an application. But an applicant with no interest, other than a moral or political interest, is unlikely to be able to persuade the court to allow them to initiate judicial review proceedings.
2. A judicial review case can only be initiated if the applicant is first given *leave to apply* for judicial review by the High Court. The application for leave must be made 'promptly and in any event

within three months from the date when grounds for the application arose'.

3. The court will not, generally, grant judicial review unless all internal appeal and review procedures available to the complainant have been completed. Thus, a disabled applicant seeking judicial review of their council's alleged failure to carry out their legal responsibilities under the Chronically Sick and Disabled Persons Act 1970 was refused permission as they had not gone through the existing appeal procedure to the Secretary of State, prior to making the application (for more detail on this case, see Chapter 4, p.92).
4. The applicant must show good grounds for applying for judicial review. The rules are made by the judges in individual cases, and therefore continually grow in number and complexity. It is, however, possible to group such grounds under the following technical headings:

   Illegality. This means that the council had no power to make the decision that it made (for example, because the committee making the decision was inquorate, or insufficient notice was given), or the council's decision was based on an error in law (for example, the council misinterpreted the meaning of a statute). A council will also act illegally if it unlawfully delegates its decision to another person or body; acts under the dictation of another person or body; or acts according to a self-made policy so rigid that individual cases cannot be considered on their merits.

   Procedural impropriety. This means, basically, that the council's decision was unfair, either because the complainant was denied consultation to which they were entitled, or the decision was taken in breach of the 'rules of natural justice'. These rules are that both sides should be heard before a decision is made and that a decision should not be based on bias. Breach of these rules might arise where the council only listened to one side of the argument before reaching a major decision, or a councillor who was involved in the decision had a personal financial interest in the outcome.

   Irrationality. This means that a council has taken a decision (or failed to act) of a kind or in a way that no rational council could have done, which one Law Lord has interpreted as meaning the council must have 'taken leave of its senses'. This is a highly complex provision, as it involves a number of subtle interpretations of the words 'reasonable' and 'rational'. For example, it is quite reasonable for a council to follow its political philosophy, according to the case law, so long as the decision based upon that philosophy is not 'irrational'. Many people engaged in social work, with experience of the courts, will be slow to suggest this particular course of action, given their experiences of the views of some judges on what constitutes reasonable action!

5. The courts are, to an increasing extent, requiring councils to give reasons for their decisions (in some cases – for example, decisions on homelessness – the council has a statutory duty to give reasons). A failure to give reasons may itself provide grounds for challenge.
6. Even if leave is granted to apply to the High Court for judicial review of a council decision, it may take between six months and a year before the application is finally heard, and a further lengthy period if the case goes to appeal. This is partly because judicial review has become such a popular means of securing the redress of grievances against councils.
7. If the applicant wins the case against the council, and the court finds that the council acted in some way unlawfully, it is by no means certain that the council will then make the decision that the applicant wishes them to make. This is because of the form taken by the remedies, outlined above, that are available to the High Court in a judicial review case. Judges have a complete discretion whether to grant a remedy in a particular case. If the court grants an order of *certiorari* cancelling a council decision, it will often be open to the council simply to reconsider, and then to take the same decision again! If this happens, the unhappy applicant will have won a battle but lost the war, and will be likely to feel extremely disillusioned by the whole process.

It probably goes without saying that some of the most controversial and important cases in recent years have been those using the judicial review procedure. On many occasions applicants have won, and significant improvements have been obtained. In others, where applicants have failed, it has been suggested that the judges have been motivated by conscious or unconscious political considerations. Because of judicial discretion, it is often hard to advise which way a case will go. This is a very creative and potentially useful use of the law for those engaged in social work, but clients must be warned, before they decide to embark upon this journey, that a lost case may be much more painful than one that has never been fought.

For those who are interested in looking in more detail at the issues surrounding this particular use of the law, the following book is particularly useful: Aldous, G., and Alder, J., (2nd edn, 1993), *Applications for Judicial Review* (Butterworths). See also, for a full and up-to-date treatment of all aspects of judicial review, Supperstone, M., and Goudie, J. (1992), *Judicial Review* (Butterworths).

The Public Law Project (Charles Clore House, 17 Russell Square, London WC1B 5DR (tel: 071 436 0964) operates as a national 'law centre' and resource, and can give advice and assistance on all aspects of the use of law, particularly judicial review, in challenging public authorities.

Changing the law

Finally, for those with their sights on influencing Parliament to bring about changes in the law for their particular cause, a useful guide has been produced: Dubs, A. (1988), *Lobbying: an Insider Guide to the Parliamentary Process* (Pluto).

Chapter 4

Legal rights of physically disabled people

GENERAL INTRODUCTION

Government statistics suggest that over 6 million citizens of the United Kingdom suffer from appreciable physical and mental disability. In these circumstances a great responsibility lies with social workers, doctors, occupational and speech therapists, physiotherapists and other professionals to ensure that those with physical disabilities are aware of the special legal rights the law has created for their benefit. The dedication and perseverance of a number of individuals and groups working with disabled people has borne them considerable fruit in the legislative field. Since the end of the Second World War, over 50 Acts of Parliament have contained specific reference to the particular rights of physically disabled people, and as a result of this legislation the legal rights of physically disabled people are now substantial. Enforcing these rights is a different matter.

This chapter will outline the special rights given by law to physically disabled people. It will begin by setting out the general statutory duties of local authorities towards disabled people. It will go on to describe in detail the specific legal rights of disabled people in the fields of employment, housing, financial benefits and education. As with the other chapters, addresses of useful organisations and details of helpful publications will be provided where appropriate.

STATUTORY DUTIES OWED BY LOCAL AUTHORITIES TOWARDS DISABLED PEOPLE

There are a number of statutes which lay down legal duties owed by local authorities towards disabled people. The key provisions, setting out these duties, are to be found in the following statutes:

1. National Assistance Act 1948 (NAA).
2. Chronically Sick and Disabled Persons Act 1970 (CSDPA).
3 National Health Service Act 1977 (NHSA).
4. Disabled Persons (Services, Consultation and Representation) Act 1986 (DPSCRA).
5. Children Act 1989 (CA).
6. National Health Service and Community Care Act 1990 (NHSCCA).

Central to all legal duties owed by local authorities are the duties laid down in the first two of these Acts, the NAA and the CSDPA (supplemented by the NHSA). As a result of these two Acts, a local authority has the following statutory duties:

1. A local authority must inform itself of the number of disabled persons in their area. For the purposes of this Act 'disabled' means 'suffering with a permanent and substantial handicap'. The definition clearly extends beyond physical disability to include those with learning disability so long as it is 'permanent and substantial'. A local authority will satisfy this duty by keeping a register of disabled people in their area. Any person who thinks they qualify as 'disabled' under the Act should contact their local social services department and ask to be registered. Councils employ occupational therapists, occupational therapy assistants and, sometimes, social work assistants specially trained for this task. Although registration is not a precondition to receive special services it is clearly administratively useful in organising and prioritising limited resources.
2. A local authority must assess the needs of each disabled person within their area for any one of a list of services below. In December 1992, the Social Services Inspectorate issued guidance on what is meant by *assessment* (CI(92)34), including guidance on the appropriate level of assessment, the procedures to be followed in each case, and publicity about such procedures. According to the guidance the overriding con-

sideration is 'to keep the process as simple and efficient as possible'. If the local authority is satisfied that any disabled person in its area has a need for any of the services listed below, and that that need is not being met, the local authority must inform that person of any welfare services it provides that could satisfy that need, and, if necessary, must make arrangements for the service to be provided to that person through any appropriate agency. The local authority can employ a voluntary agency, or an appropriately skilled individual, to provide all or any of these services. Its legal duty is to ensure that the needs are met. The local authority cannot use budgeting difficulties as a basis for refusing to provide the service. The local authority may charge for the services that it provides, but the charges must be reasonable. If an individual satisfies the local authority that their means are insufficient, the local authority cannot require the individual to pay more than they are practically able to pay. The relevant services are as follows:

- practical help in the home, which might include the support of a home help to do cleaning and shopping;
- the provision of a television or radio, and help in using the local library;
- assistance towards attending educational facilities, games or outings, and, if available, council day centres, where a variety of activities might take place;
- adaptations to the home such as ramps for wheelchair access, extensions, and the provision of other specialist equipment (grants may be available for this work: see below at p.101);
- help towards a holiday;
- meals at home, or in a day centre;
- provision of a telephone, and any special equipment needed to operate it.

The NHSA added a further list of discretionary powers (i.e. not legal duties, as for the above list) enabling local authorities to provide laundry facilities to people who need them because of illness, handicap or age, and to provide other services for those suffering from physical or mental illness, or in after-care from such illness, including day centres, meals, social work support, and residential accommodation. These latter services can also be provided 'for the prevention of illness'. Many of these discretionary powers relating to residential accommodation have now been subsumed within the contracts that local authorities will have to draw up with a home that is caring for somebody placed there by them (for further detail on these contracts see DOH Circular HSG(92)50).

All the services outlined above must now be included in the local authority's community care plans, by virtue of the NHSCCA (see below at p.89).

The 1986 DPSCRA further developed the responsibilities of local authorities, and strengthened the rights of disabled people as follows:

- If a local authority fails to assess the needs of a disabled person for any of the services listed above, it can be ordered to do so by a court.
- Where a disabled person is living at home and receiving a substantial degree of care from a carer (who is not a person employed to care for them by a statutory body), the views of this carer, and the extent of the carer's willingness and ability to continue giving such care, *must* now be taken into account when assessing the disabled person's future needs. The principal aim of this change appears to be to promote the concept of genuine shared care between informal carers and social services, where feasible.
- The local authority must inform a disabled person, whose needs it has assessed, of all relevant welfare services of which it has knowledge, from which that person might benefit. This duty extends beyond those services provided by the local authority to include all the relevant services from the voluntary sector of which the local authority has knowledge. Many councils produce comprehensive booklets setting out details of such services. The onus is clearly on those who provide a specialist service for the disabled to ensure that their local authority is aware of it.
- All disabled school leavers must receive statutory assessment by their local authorities prior to leaving school.
- There is a provision in the DPSCRA which states that any disabled person, who is not able to make representations on their own behalf, can appoint their own 'authorised representative' concerning any claim they may have under the CSDPA. This provision has never been implemented, but it can be argued that the wide consultation requirements associated with the provision of community care services under the NHSCCA can effectively be used to insist that, in appropriate cases, representatives of disabled people should

be appointed, be consulted at every stage of an assessment and be allowed to make representations to the local authority on the disabled person's behalf. For a useful summary and commentary on the DPSCAA see the *Handbook for Voluntary Organisations on the Disabled Persons (Services, Consultation and Representation) Act 1986*.

The NHSCCA has added further duties on the local authority towards adult disabled people in their area (for the new duties towards those under 18, see below, under 'Children'). The underlying principle of the NHSCCA is that every local authority must now produce and publish a plan for the provision of 'community care services' in their area. 'Community care services' includes services provided by the local authority, and those which they arrange to be provided by any other appropriate body. If it then appears to the local authority that any person for whom they provide or arrange such services may be in need of such services, they have a statutory duty:

- to carry out an assessment of that person's needs for those services *and*
- to decide whether any needs discovered by the assessment call for the provision by the local authority of any of their 'community care services'.

The Social Services Inspectorate of the Department of Health published in 1991 a *Practitioner's Guide*, and a *Manager's Guide* in respect of care management and assessment under the NHSCCA. The guidance covers publishing of information, determining levels of assessment, assessing need, implementing the care plan, and monitoring and reviewing of decisions. There are also a series of detailed inspection procedures relating to any premises in which 'community care services' are to be provided, and there is a new complaints procedure, allowing any person entitled to or receiving community care services to issue a complaint concerning any aspect of the local authority's discharge of this function.

Children

The CA has added a further raft of duties that are specifically related to 'disabled children'. For these purposes a 'disabled child' is one who is:

'blind, deaf or suffers from mental disorder of any kind or is substantially and permanently handicapped by illness, injury or congenital deformity or such other disability as may be prescribed'. These duties also extend to a child whose physical or mental health is unlikely to reach a reasonable standard, or is likely to be significantly impaired, or further impaired, without the provision of special services (for those with developmental or behavioural difficulties, see below at p.130).

The duty to this group of children is to provide services designed to minimise the effect on them of their disabilities, and to give them the opportunity to lead as normal a life as possible. In addition, they must consider whether it is also appropriate to provide disabled children who are living with their families with any of a list of services, including advice, counselling, home helps, laundry facilities, assistance with a holiday, and assistance with travel to special day facilities. It should, however, be noted that the local authority will in most cases already have a duty to provide these services under the operation of the CSDPA.

The complaints procedure

The government has laid down a series of new procedures for dealing with complaints about a local authority's discharge of (or failure to discharge) its 'social services functions'. Whenever a local authority receives such a complaint it should first try to resolve the matter informally. If this either fails, or is inappropriate, the complainant will be asked to submit a written statement of the complaint, which will be registered by the local authority and responded to within 28 days. If the complainant remains unsatisfied, a review panel of three people, chaired by an 'independent person', will be set up, which will be attended by the complainant and their representative who cannot be a practising lawyer. The panel will make its own recommendations to the local authority after the hearing, within 24 hours of the end of the hearing. The local authority is not, however, bound to follow this recommendation. For more information on the assessment and complaints procedures, see *The Right to Complain: Practice Guidance on Complaints Procedures in Social Services Departments*, HMSO 1991, and Gordon, R. (1993), *Community Care Assessments: a Practical Legal Framework* (Longman).

Miscellaneous duties

In addition to the above specific duties, a local authority must generally consider the needs of the disabled people in its area when designing new housing schemes. Furthermore, under a series of statutes and associated regulations, new 'non-domestic buildings', e.g. new public buildings, offices, shops, and ground-floor extensions to such buildings, must include a number of features designed to assist the access and mobility of those with disabilities, including impaired hearing and/or sight. These features include the construction of staircases with standardised hand-rail height; the use of marked glazed panels on entrance doors; the use of platform lifts as an alternative to a ramp where there is a change of level within a building; regulations on the scale and design of special toilet provison, and so forth. For the full details of these changes consult The Building Regulations 1991: Access for Disabled People, Approved Document M (amended 1992) DOE/HMSO. Although the changes are to be welcomed, these new powers and duties are, however, by no means comprehensive; they generally apply only to new buildings, and no significant grant aid is available for installation. The circulars do, however, encourage each local authority to appoint an 'access officer' to provide a clearly identified point of contact on questions of access for the disabled from members of the public, and it is important that local authorities should be pressed to make such an appointment.

How can a local authority be forced to carry out its statutory duties?

Since the 1986 Act it seems likely that any failure by a local authority to assess the needs of a disabled person could be enforced through the courts. Ensuring that those needs, once discovered, are provided for is, however, a different matter. If the failure relates to 'community care services' the new complaints procedures will be available for dissatisfied clients (see above at p.90). It should nevertheless be noted that the strict definition of 'community care services' under the NHSCCA does not extend to services provided to the disabled by way of statutory duty under the CSDPA or the DPSCAA. The only procedure available to disabled people who believe that they are not receiving the services to which they are legally entitled under the latter legislation is to write to the Secretary of State, requesting direct intervention on their behalf (for a summary of the Secretary of State's powers, see below). The Court of Appeal decided, in the case of *Wyatt* v. *Hillingdon LBC* in 1978 (see 78 Local Government Reports 727), that it is not open to a complainant to take the local authority to court for failure to carry out their statutory duties under the Act, unless the complainant has first gone through this written appeal procedure. This is unfortunate, as research by RADAR (see p.135), suggests that not only is the procedure extremely slow, taking up to one year from complaint to resolution, it is also extremely rare for a complainant to persuade the Secretary of State that a local authority is in default.

Another factor to take into consideration before mounting a complaint to the Secretary of State is that only individual complaints can be considered, even if a large number of people in one area have an identical complaint. This leaves the way open for large-scale non-compliance by hard-pressed, or negligent, local authorities, who can refuse to carry out some of their duties in the knowledge that it is most unlikely that they will be brought to task.

What can the Secretary of State do, if a complaint is justified?

The actual powers given to the Secretary of State, in the event of a finding that the local authority is in breach of their statutory duty to provide a particular service, are vague. They appear to be limited to making a declaration that the local authority is 'in default', which is clearly a serious defect in the whole system, as it effectively means that a local authority can be found in default, but the complainant may receive no relief unless they are prepared to take subsequent legal action through the courts. Throughout the early 1980s RADAR (see p.135) conducted an extensive research project into the level of dissatisfaction with local authority provision under the 1970 Act. Its conclusions, published in an interim report entitled *Putting Teeth Into the Act*, make depressing reading (RADAR is in the process of preparing an updated version of this study which should be available in 1994). Commenting on the complaints procedure to the Secretary of State, the report states:

> Referral to the Secretary of State has not led to the resolution of any problem if a general issue has been involved. Even when there is a cut-and-dried individual case the procedure may mean that provision is

made several months, or even years, after the need originally arose, when the time taken by the Secretary of State is added to the delay on the part of the local authority.

Perhaps more serious is the potential conflict of interest highlighted by the report for a Secretary of State who may be a member of a government which is forcing local authorities to cut back generally on their expenditure. When in practical terms the provisions a local authority can make are largely dependent upon central government decisions, the Secretary of State may be required to pass judgement on a local authority for actions for which he, as a member of the Cabinet, is largely responsible.

The new community care legislation has added a further line of attack for an individual or group dissatisfied with the inaction of social services in connection with their social services responsibilities towards disabled inhabitants, through the introduction of what are known as 'default powers'. Although these 'default powers' are only likely to be used in instances of extreme inaction, they do allow the Secretary of State to order a local authority to take a particular course of action. The way in which these powers are likely to be used was explained in the House of Lords as follows:

> We expect the default procedures to work in the following way. The first stage will be when it comes to the Secretary of State's attention that an authority is failing to discharge its functions. This may come from a number of directions – the work of the Social Services Inspectorate, information received from organisations representing disabled people or by direct representations to the Secretary of State by users of services. The first thing the Secretary of State needs to do is to satisfy himself that the authority has failed without reasonable cause to exercise its functions. This will entail some form of further investigation or inquiry and may include using the general powers of direction to direct the authority to exercise its functions in a particular way. ... When these powers are used the Secretary of State first has to issue an order then, if it is not complied with, he can seek an order from the court to enforce it.

Is there any alternative complaints procedure?

If the complainant considers that their failure to receive a proper service from their local authority is a result of maladministration by the relevant officers it is always open to them to complain to the Local Ombudsman, although the Ombudsman does not have any powers of enforcement (for further details see Chapter 3, p.75). It would appear that complaints about social services authorities' performance on home adaptations represent a large part of the caseload of a typical Local Ombudsman. In 1993, for example, Wirral Council on Merseyside was censured for extreme delay in no fewer than four separate cases, ranging from one in which a thalidomide victim in his early thirties had to wait five years, and in great pain, for essential adaptations to his home, to another in which a woman suffering from a heart condition, arthritis and cancer had to wait two years for the installation of a shower. In all these cases compensation, ranging from £300 to £2000, was recommended by the Ombudsman.

RIGHTS OF PHYSICALLY DISABLED PEOPLE IN THE FIELD OF EMPLOYMENT

Although 70 per cent of people with disabilities develop their disability after reaching working age, the rights of disabled people to special employment consideration are poor and remain largely unenforced. Both the National Audit Office and the Public Accounts Committee of the House of Commons have regularly voiced criticism of the system and called for strong action to reform the system. In recent years, largely in response to this criticism, the government Employment Service has reorganised its disability employment programme. While legislation in this area remains outmoded and inadequate, much can be done to assist disabled people to acquire or keep employment with adequate advice and information. A good starting-point for all advisers is to acquire and read the 1992 Employment Service booklet, *Employing People With Disabilities*, obtainable from the Employment Service Disability Services Branch (see below at p.95).

Legal rights to employment

According to the Disabled Persons (Employment) Acts of 1944 and 1958, certain categories of employer are obliged to operate a quota system whereby a minimum of 3 per cent of their workforce must be drawn from the Register of Disabled Persons. This register is the general responsibility of the Department of Employment, working through the Employment Service. It is a different register from the register kept by the social services department under the CSDPA 1970 (see p.86). At the local level the register is the responsibility of a service called PACT (Placing, Assessment and Counselling Teams) which is based in the local Job Centre, and run by specially trained officers called Disability Employment Advisers (DEAs). PACT is essentially a team of people skilled and experienced in helping people with disabilities in, and into, work. It brings together the former work of Disablement Resettlement Officers (DROs), the Disability Advisory Service (DAS) and parts of the Employment Rehabilitation Service (ERS) (see below at p.98). Local PACTs are supported by nine regional Ability Development Centres (ADCs), who work on developing new techniques in providing employment advice 'for disabled people entering work, or for employees who have become disabled and need to adjust to new circumstances'.

For further information on ADCs contact the Employment Service Disability Services Branch, DS1, Level 3, Steel City House, c/o Rockingham House, 123 West Street, Sheffield S1 4ER (tel: 0742 596151). Of particular benefit is the booklet, *Employing People with Disabilities: Sources of Help*.

For large employers, there is an additional good practice advisory service called Major Organisations Development Unit (MODU), based in London but available nationwide.

What is a 'disabled person' for employment purposes?

The definition of a disabled person for the purposes of this register is extremely long-winded. It reads as follows:

> a person who on account of injury, disease (including a physical or mental condition arising from imperfect development of any organ) or congenital deformity, is substantially handicapped in obtaining or keeping employment, or in undertaking work on his own account, of a kind

which apart from that injury, disease or deformity would be suited to his age, experience and qualifications.

In addition to falling within this definition the disabled person must be likely to remain disabled for at least 12 months and be actively looking for work, with some prospect of finding work. It is presumed that the prospect of finding work refers to the degree of impairment suffered by the disabled person and not to the general employment conditions in the area.

How does a disabled person get on the register?

The applicant has to fill out a form provided by the DEA at their local Job Centre, describing the nature of their disability. If the conditions described above are clearly satisfied, the DEA will immediately register the applicant and grant them a Green Card (certificate of registration). The certificate may be granted for a period of from 1 to 10 years, or until retirement. It can be renewed on further application. The registered person can apply to remove their name from the register at any time they wish by writing to the local Job Centre or to the Employment Service.

What happens if the DEA refuses to place them on the register?

If there is any doubt as to the applicant's eligibility, the application will go before a panel of the Committee for the Employment of People with Disabilities (CEPD). This committee includes representatives of employers and workers, doctors and people interested in the problems of disablement. The panel will include a representative of each of the categories listed above. The applicant will be invited to attend before the panel, and can be accompanied by a representative of their choice, e.g. a social worker, trade union representative or advice worker. The panel will require medical evidence, normally a letter from the applicant's GP. Alternatively the Job Centre can arrange a special medical examination. Any loss of earnings or travelling expenses incurred by this medical examination can be met by the Job Centre. The hearing is in private. After the hearing, the panel will make a recommendation to the DEA. If accepted, registration will take place as above. For further information on this procedure see MSC pamphlet DPL 1 (Employment Division) or *Employing People with Disabilities* (DRO) (Employment Service).

Which employers are covered by the Act?

Any employer with a workforce of 20 or more is subject to the Act, with the exception of the Crown and government departments. It is possible for an employer to apply to the local DEA for a temporary permit exempting them from compliance with the quota, normally for a period of six months. Such a permit should only be granted if the employer has produced convincing evidence why no job suitable for a disabled employee is likely to become available within the following six months. Official government figures published in 1988 stated that in 1986 only 27 per cent of employers met the 3 per cent quota, while 56 per cent had obtained exemption permits.

What happens if an employer does not comply with the Act?

Being below the quota is not an offence in itself. Being below quota when a suitable disabled person is available to do a job is, however, an offence, punishable on conviction in a magistrates' court by a fine not exceeding £400. If the employer is a corporate body, the maximum fine is £2000. But since 1944 there have only been 10 prosecutions under the Act. Not surprisingly, the Public Accounts Committee recently concluded that the quota system was 'ineffective, unenforceable and out of date'. For further information on this procedure see *MSC Employers' Obligations: Notes for Guidance* DPL(2), and *Code of Practice*.

Are any categories of work reserved specifically for disabled people?

Vacancies for electric lift operators and car park attendants must be offered by law in the first instance to registered disabled people. Only if no such person is available for the job should it be offered to non-disabled people. The failure to add any more substantial jobs to this list is a serious inadequacy of the system.

How can employers be encouraged to comply with the spirit of the Act?

PACTs are a good step forward in providing local centres that focus upon good practice in the employment of people with disabilities. PACTs can provide written guidance to employers in the form of the *Code of Good Practice on the Employment of Disabled People.* The 'disability symbol' (logo) can be awarded by PACTs to employers who wish to advertise the fact that they have taken positive steps to make employment of disabled people easier, and who encourage disabled employees to work for them.

The low prosecution rate for offenders is a clear indication that disabled people are not generally getting a fair deal under the terms and spirit of the Act. There are a number of factors that discourage employers from seeking out disabled employees, many based on ignorance or prejudice. Unfortunately, attempts to extend the anti-discrimination laws to include disabled people have so far failed. It is ultimately a job for government nationally, and DEAs locally, to encourage greater compliance with the Act. There are, however, practical sources of help for employers that may act as an incentive to employ more disabled people.

Under the Job Introduction Scheme the Employment Service will make a contribution of £45 per week for six weeks to an employer who agrees to engage a selected disabled employee. Employers can gain assistance in improving their premises in such a way that compliance with the Act need not cost them much money. For example, they can apply for grants of up to £6000 from the Employment Service to adapt their premises to accommodate the particular needs of disabled employees, such as installing access ramps, special toilets, rails or other adaptations. The Employment Service can loan employers special tools, or other 'high-tech' equipment such as Braille typewriters, talking calculators, hoists and hearing aids in appropriate cases. A special scheme exists to help self-employed people with the start-up costs of installing appropriate technology in the home.

Can a disabled person claim assistance with fares to work?

Registered disabled people (see p.95), unable to use public transport for all or part of their journey to and from work because of their disability, can apply to the local PACT for assistance towards their fares to work, up to 75 per cent of the cost of taxis to and from work five days per week (maximum ceiling in 1993–4 of £94.20 per week).

What are sheltered placements?

Finally, there is an alternative scheme offered by many local authorities in conjunction with their local DEA known as the Sheltered Placement Scheme. Under this scheme, certain disabled people (normally those who are able to do a particular job but at a very slow pace) are employed by a sponsor (normally the local authority or a charity) then 'leased out' to an employer offering suitable work. The employer will simply pay the employee for the work done, and their salary will then be 'topped up' by the sponsor, who should have this sum refunded. For further information on these schemes contact Remploy Ltd, 415 Edgware Road, London NW2 6LR (tel: 081 452 8020) or SEPACS, c/o Employment Service.

For further information on all the above schemes consult the Employment Service, Disability Services Branch, Steel City House, c/o Rockingham House, 123 West Street, Sheffield S1 4ER (tel: 0742 596151), or the local PACT (see p.95). The Employment Service is part of the Department of Employment.

Duty of companies to state their policy concerning disabled employees

Any company employing more than 250 people is obliged under the 1985 Companies Act to include in the Directors' Report a statement of the company's policy for that year concerning disabled employees. If the company has no policy, it should say so. Only the civil service, nationalised industries, health authorities and local authorities are exempted from this legal duty. Directors' reports are available for public inspection at: Companies Registration Office, 55–71 City Road, London EC1Y 1BB (tel: 071 253 9393, England; 0222 380801, Wales; 031 225 5774, Scotland).

Further information

The principal government agency responsible for co-ordinating and improving efforts to assist disabled people in finding employment is the Employment Service (see above at p.94). From this service can be obtained a host of leaflets and booklets providing further information on all of the above as follows. There are also a number of leaflets dealing with the specialist difficulties associated with the employment of those with mental illness or learning disability, with epilepsy, with multiple sclerosis and those who are visually or hearing impaired. Further publications of particular interest to advisers in this field are:

Getting on with Disabilities: an Employer's Guide (Institute of Personnel Management).
Employers' Guide to Disabilities (RADAR).
Employing Disabled People (CBI).
Guide on the Employment of Disabled People (TUC).
Monitoring People with Disabilities in the Workforce (Employers' Forum on Disability).
Disability Etiquette: Meeting, Interviewing and Working with Disabled People (Employers' Forum on Disability).

The Employers' Forum on Disability, 5 Cleveland Place, London SW1Y 6JJ (tel: 071 321 6591) is a national employers' organisation which aims to provide job prospects for people with disabilities and to help employers to recruit, retain and develop disabled employees. It provides practical support and advice to members wishing to improve employment practice, and works with government and voluntary agencies to improve policies on job and training prospects. It publishes a quarterly newsletter, a leaflet *Disability Etiquette*, an *Employer's Agenda on Disability*, and a variety of other booklets and information packs.

There is a further independent organisation that specialises in helping disabled graduates to find employment as follows: The Disabled Graduates Careers Information Service, Bulmershe Court, University of Reading, Woodlands Avenue, Earley, Reading RG6 1HY (tel: 0734 318659) offers careers advice and job vacancy information to graduates with disabilities. It also maintains a database with over 700 case studies covering many disabilities and professions.

HOUSING FOR DISABLED PEOPLE

For a disabled person a home can be a prison. While some disabilities do not affect the mobility of a person, the majority do, and consequently the internal arrangements for comfort and mobility within a home take on a special significance. If the home of a disabled person is unsuitable in some way for their particular needs, there are two possible ways of coping with the problem. The first is to carry out adaptations to their home to render it more suitable and comfortable for them. The second is to enable them to move to more suitable accommodation. What part do legal rights play in both these two alternative courses of action?

Adapting the existing accommodation

If a local authority is satisfied that the home of a disabled person is in some way failing to meet the special needs arising from their disability (e.g. no access for a wheelchair, inaccessibility of toilet and bathing facilities), it is under a statutory duty by virtue of the CSDPA 1970 (see pp. 86–7) to ensure that those needs are met by arranging for any necessary adaptations to be made. Any person on the local authority Register of Disabled People can apply for assistance of this nature. Although it is not strictly necessary to be on the register to receive help with housing adaptations it is advisable, as it is possible to obtain other benefits as a result of registration, e.g. travel passes. Applications to go on the register are usually processed by social services departments and occasionally by the area health authority.

What sort of adaptations are available?

DOE Circular 59/78 (now obsolete) set out in detail the sorts of housing adaptations that could be possible under the above legislation. In particular, Appendix I to the circular listed a large number of structural changes to property that might be made for the benefit of a disabled occupant, which would also now be eligible for inclusion in an application for a Disabled Facilities Grant when proposed for a disabled person in private sector housing (see p.102). The list includes building extensions, widening access areas and doors, constructing handrails, installing stair lifts, refixing water and electricity sources, acoustic insulation, kitchen conversion, and the installation of special baths and toilets.

Detailed technical advice on such adaptations may be obtained from the occupational therapist who works through the social services department and is also usually appointed to assess need and make recommendations as to the work to be carried out. Further ideas, particularly on up-to-date equipment, can be sought from: the Disabled Living Foundation, 380–4 Harrow Rd, London W9 2HU (tel: 071 289 6111).

Who will pay for these adaptations?

A new system for the renovation, repair and improvement of houses in England and Wales was introduced in 1990. Scotland retains a separate grant system, the details of which can be found in a pamphlet entitled *Improve your Home with a Grant*, available from the Scottish Development Department, St Andrew's House, Edinburgh EH1 3DD.

The most important grant concerning adaptations to a home to make it suitable for a disabled occupant is the Disabled Facilities Grant (DFG). The DFG is administered by the local authority, although the money comes ultimately from central government. The DFG is means tested, and the maximum DFG payable (1994 figures) is £20,000. Local authorities are under a statutory obligation to determine all DFG applications within six months of the date on which they are received.

Who is eligible for a DFG?

An application for a DFG is made by, or on behalf of, the disabled occupant of a dwelling. The disabled occupant is defined as 'the disabled person for whose benefit it is proposed to carry out any of the relevant works'. The word 'disabled' here means a person who is on the social services disability register (see above at p.86), or would qualify to be on the register if they chose to apply. The disabled occupant must normally live in the dwelling in question, but does not have to have a legal interest in the dwelling, i.e. as a tenant or an owner. The dwelling does not have to be privately owned, e.g. it can be a council dwelling, or belong to a housing association. If the applicant is a private tenant they must get the landlord's consent to the adaptation before the local authority can approve the application. The applicant must provide a Certificate of Future Occupancy, stating as follows:

Owner: that they or a member of their family intend to live in the dwelling as their only or main residence for at least a year after the works are completed. If the property is disposed of within a three-year period after the completion of the works, the owner may be ordered to repay all

or some of the grant. Advice should be sought from the local authority on the details of this provision before an application is submitted.
Tenant: that they intend to live in the dwelling as their only or main residence.
Landlord: that they intend to let the dwelling as a residence (not for a long lease, nor a holiday home, nor to a member of their family) for at least five years after completion of the works.

What adaptations does a DFG cover?

There are two types of DFG: the first is *mandatory,*[1] the second is *discretionary.*

The Mandatory DFG

Mandatory DFGs are available under the scheme, if the proposed work is 'necessary and appropriate to meet the needs of the disabled occupant' and if it is 'reasonable and practical to carry out the works taking into account the age and condition of the dwelling'. These phrases have been explained in government circulars in the following ways:

> The assessment of whether the works are 'necessary and appropriate' must involve consideration of whether the proposed adaptation or improvement is needed in order to enable any care plan to be implemented [see above at p.101], and to enable the disabled occupant to remain in his or her home, retaining or regaining as great a degree of independence as can reasonably be achieved. It is neither appropriate nor practical to impose strict boundaries on what works may be regarded as 'necessary and appropriate' to meet the assessed needs: much will depend on the circumstances of each individual case and on the judgement of the professional advisers concerned.

Subject to the above paragraph, Mandatory DFGs will be available for adaptation work that assists the disabled occupant in any of the following purposes:

[1]In June 1993 the DOE published a consultation document, *The Future of Private Housing Renewal Programmes*, canvassing, *inter alia*, the abolition of mandatory grants, the introduction of a queuing system, and the lowering of the maximum limit from £50,000 to *c.*£15–20,000.

- facilitates access to and from the dwelling or the building in which the dwelling or flat is situated;
- facilitates access to a room used as the principal family room, or to a room used or usable for sleeping, or providing such a sleeping room;
- facilitates access to a room in which there is a lavatory, bath, shower, or wash-hand basin, or helps them to use such facilities, or provides the facilities if they are not already there;
- preparing and cooking food;
- improves any heating system, or providing a new system to meet their particular needs;
- helps them use existing sources of power, light or heat, e.g. moving switches, adding levers, etc.;
- facilitates access around the dwelling to help them care for another resident of the dwelling in need of such care.

The Discretionary DFG

Discretionary DFGs are hard to get, but they are available for any other type of work that makes the dwelling or building 'suitable for the accommodation, welfare or employment of the disabled person'. This vague, catch-all phrase presumably covers changes to the home that would improve the quality of life of the occupant, but for which there is no statutory responsibility to provide under the CSDPA or the community care legislation.

Is a DFG means tested?

All DFGs are means tested. The test is applied not only to the disabled occupant, but to each other relevant person, which means any other person living or intending to live in the dwelling who has an interest in the dwelling (as an owner or a tenant). The means test is fairly complex, but is broadly similar to the means test for *housing benefit* (see Chapter 11 at pp. 404–7). There is no set capital or income point above which no grant is payable. For a detailed account of the working of the means test, see *Disability Rights Handbook* (18th edn), at 38(4).

Discretionary Minor Work Grants

In addition to the above grants an owner-occupier or a private-sector tenant can apply to their local authority for a Minor Works Grant, up to a 1993 maximum of £1080. Repeat applications are also possible, with a ceiling of £3240 over a three-year period. The grant is discretionary and means tested. To be eligible, the applicant must be in receipt of at least one of the following:

- family credit (see p.272);
- disability working allowance (see p.113);
- council tax benefit;
- housing benefit;
- income support.

Application is on a simple application form to the local authority. The grants cover, very broadly, the following types of work:

Thermal Insulation Grants

These would include the insulation of lofts, tanks and pipes and draught-proofing, but do not extend to improving heating or fixing a dampness problem (see below at 'patch and mend').

'Patch and Mend' Grants

These are to ensure that dwellings in areas scheduled for clearance are wind- and weatherproof.

'Staying Put' Grants

These are for householders aged 60 or over whose dwelling is reasonably sound but in need of some repair work, adaptation, improvement or basic security installation, and where carrying out major work would be too disruptive to the occupant(s).

'Elderly Residents Adaptation' Grants

These grants finance small adaptations like an extra toilet, more cooking facilities, a new shower unit and so forth, to enable a person of 60 or over who is not an owner-occupier or a tenant to live in the dwelling.

For more information on Minor Works Grants see DOE Circular 4/90, *Assistance with Minor Works in Dwellings*.

Where can an applicant go to top up any of the above grants?

It should be noted that in cases of grave hardship or other exceptional circumstances, local authority social services departments, and a range of charities, *may* be willing to cover all or part of the difference between the grant and the total cost of the work, so that the applicant pays nothing at all. For a list of relevant charities consult the *Charities Digest* available from the Family Welfare Association, 501–5 Kingsland Road, Dalston, London E8 4AU (tel: 081 254 6251).

Is a disabled person entitled to special council tax relief?

An outline of the workings of the council tax is contained in Chapter 11 at p.409. Disability reductions are available against council tax if anybody resident in the dwelling is 'substantially and permanently disabled' (see above at p.86), and because of that disability the dwelling contains *either* a second bathroom or kitchen or some other room which is predominantly used to meet that person's special needs *or* sufficient floorspace to enable a wheelchair to be used within the dwelling *and* the local authority is satisfied that the above are necessary because of the disability.

What is the procedure for applying for council tax relief?

Application is by letter to the local authority setting out the case for reduction. If a reduction is not allowed the applicant can appeal to a local valuation tribunal.

Moving to other accommodation

There are few legal obligations on local authorities to provide accommodation to disabled people. If a disabled person is actually homeless, their homelessness is not 'intentional', and they are considered to be 'vulnerable', the local authority will have a duty to house them (for details on these rights and duties see, Chapter 10, p.320). Once such accommodation has been provided, the disabled person will be able to apply to the council for any necessary adaptations to the new home, following the procedures set out above. The only other circumstances in which a local authority will be legally obliged to provide accommodation to a disabled person will be if that person's existing accommodation is unfit for human habitation, and the council have placed a demolition order or a closing order on it (see Chapter 11, pp. 386–8). Otherwise, the provision of alternative accommodation to a disabled person who already has accommodation, however unsatisfactory, is entirely a matter for the council's discretion.

Every local authority must by law publish the details of the allocations procedure that it follows concerning its vacant housing stock (for details, see Chapter 10, p.332). The most common procedure is the points system. A disabled person will almost certainly acquire extra points by virtue of their disability. The exact number of points awarded for a particular disability will normally be set out in a leaflet published by the local authority housing department. If no such leaflet is available, the local authority is under a duty to provide any enquirer with details of their allocations policy.

In addition to the points system or other allocations procedures, a council must by law consider the needs of disabled people in any new housing scheme it designs, and also in any new public building (see above at p.91). Although now obsolete, the DOE Circular 59/78 still provides useful guidelines on ways in which the former duty may be satisfied. The commonest way in which this duty is satisfied is in the form of Wheelchair Housing Projects or Mobility Housing Projects. Wheelchair Housing Projects are designed principally for those confined to a wheelchair in order to give them the maximum mobility within their home. Mobility Housing Projects are principally for those who are ambulant, but have mobility problems. While it lies entirely within the local authority's discretion how much housing of this nature they provide, it is clear that if they provide nothing at all they are failing to fulfil their statutory obligations. In these circumstances legal advice should be sought from a solicitor to investigate whether the local authority could be taken to court for failure to carry out its statutory obligations.

Finally, some housing associations specialise in providing accommodation adapted for disabled people, and direct application to these associations should always be encouraged. Local authorities frequently work closely with such associations in the allocation of this specialist accommodation.

Further sources of information

For specialised help in adaptation see the *Charities Digest* (p.106). All the DOE circulars mentioned above can be obtained direct from the Department of the Environment.

SPECIAL FINANCIAL BENEFITS

A number of the financial benefits referred to in Chapter 8 will also be available to a disabled person who satisfies the eligibility criteria. In particular, a disabled person who has to leave work because of their disability should check their eligibility for statutory sick pay, sickness benefit, or invalidity benefit. All claimants should pay careful attention to the additional benefits available to disabled people in receipt of income support (see Chapter 8).

It is unfortunately the case that very many disabled people are ineligible for the benefits referred to in the above paragraph for the simple reason that they have not paid any, or sufficient, national insurance contributions. This is normally through no fault of their own: they may have been unable to work, or unable to work long enough to acquire the appropriate number of contributions to become eligible. But even those disabled people who have not paid national insurance contributions are, however, entitled to claim a number of special financial benefits connected with their disability, subject only to satisfying the criteria laid down by law for the particular benefit. The benefits that fall into this category are as follows:

- benefits to compensate disability brought about by industrial injury or disease;

- war disablement pensions;
- disability working allowance;
- disability living allowance (care/mobility component);
- attendance allowance;
- severe disablement allowance (SDA);
- invalid care allowance (ICA);
- vaccine damage payments.

For detailed information on the effect of hospitalisation on claims consult the *Hospital Patients' Handbook* (Disability Alliance).

What are the payment rates of each of these benefits?

The actual amount of each benefit is not included in this chapter as it will change from year to year. For the current levels, advisers should consult the latest edition of the *CPAG Handbook* (see below at 'Further assistance', p.134) or *Disability Rights Handbook.*

Benefits to compensate disability brought about by industrial injury or disease

This section sets out the position in outline only. An excellent book to consult for a more detailed appraisal is Lewis, R. (1987), *Compensation for Industrial Injury* (Professional Books). Since 1948 there has been in existence in the UK a scheme to compensate any employee who suffers disability as a result of an accident at work or an industrial disease. This scheme does not depend upon national insurance contributions. All that needs to be proved is that the claimant was gainfully employed under a contract of service, i.e. it does not cover the self-employed (for clarification of this term see Chapter 7, p.218 and see also the *Rights Guide to Non-Means Tested Social Security Benefits*). In addition, a person who suffers injury or disability as a result of the negligence of another (including employers, car drivers and so forth) can sue that person, and often that person's employer, in the civil courts. Legal aid is available. Benefits paid as a result of the accident may, however, be deducted from the compensation (see Social Security (Recoupment) Regulations 1990).

Industrial Injury Disablement Benefit (DB)

MUST THE ACCIDENT THAT LEADS TO THE DISABILITY OCCUR AT THE WORKPLACE?

To qualify for compensation the accident must have arisen out of and in the course of employment. This will therefore include accidents which occur travelling to and from work, so long as it can be shown that this was 'employer's time', i.e. time when the employee was still being paid. If the employee was doing something outside the terms of their employment, or in contradiction of express instructions from their employer at the time of the accident, they may be denied the benefit.

HOW IS DB CLAIMED?

As soon as practicable after the accident the employee should report the details of the accident to their employer. By law, every employer of ten or more employees should have an accident book for this purpose. If not, a letter setting out the details will be a sufficient record. If the employer disputes the accident the employee should apply to the DSS for a declaration that they have had an industrial accident. This can be done on DSS Form BI 95. Once it becomes clear that the accident may have caused some disability to the employee (see below for definition of disability) the employee should apply for disablement benefit on DSS Form BI 100A. The benefit is not payable until 16 weeks after the date of the accident. The benefit should be claimed within three months of the day on which entitlement begins, though later claims will be considered. If the claim is late, arrears of only three months can be paid and only if there is 'continuous good cause' for the lateness.

WHAT DEGREE OF DISABILITY IS NECESSARY TO CLAIM DB?

This benefit is paid to those who have suffered disablement from a loss of physical or mental faculty. The amount of the benefit will vary according to the degree of disability. The degree of disability is determined according to a complicated scale of injuries drawn up by the DSS (for full details consult the *Disability Rights Handbook* or the *Rights Guide to Non-Means Tested Social Security Benefits*). The scale ranks severity of injuries from 0 to 100 per cent. In order to be eligible for the benefit, the claimant must be assessed as being at least 14 per cent disabled as a result of the accident.

HOW IS THE ASSESSMENT CARRIED OUT?

The assessment is carried out by a special medical board consisting of two or more doctors. The doctors will assess the extent and likely duration of the disablement by comparing the condition of the claimant with a normal healthy person of the same age and sex. They will make either a provisional or a permanent assessment, the former being subject to reassessment at a later date, the latter being for life. An appeal lies within three months to a Medical Appeal Tribunal. For further details see *DHSS Handbook for Industrial Injuries Medical Boards* (2nd edn) (HMSO). For details on social security appeal tribunals generally, see Chapter 8, p.260.

HOW IS THE BENEFIT PAID?

The benefit is paid weekly as a percentage of the DB for that year (e.g. if the DB is currently £90 a week, a person assessed as 50 per cent disabled will receive £45 per week). DB is not taxable, but it is treated as income for the purposes of claiming income support (see Chapter 8, p.263). It will continue regardless of whether the claimant is in work.

NB A person claiming DB may be entitled to additional benefits in certain situations. For example, if their disablement is assessed at 100 per cent, and they require constant attendance, they may be entitled to claim constant attendance allowance (paid at a higher rate than the normal attendance allowance), and exceptionally severe disablement allowance. In addition, if the disability is likely to lead to reduced earnings for the claimant in the future they may be entitled to claim a reduced earnings allowance. For details on these benefits see the *Disability Rights Handbook* or the *Rights Guide to Non-Means Tested Social Security Benefits*.

Industrial diseases

The alternative grounds for claiming disablement benefit are that the claimant has suffered disablement from a loss of physical or mental faculty caused by an industrial disease. The industrial disease must be one of the 63 diseases prescribed as industrial diseases by the DSS in

DSS leaflets NI 2 (general diseases), NI 3 (pneumoconiosis and byssinosis), HI 237 (occupational asthma) and NI 207 (occupational deafness). Prescribed application forms can be obtained from the DSS. The 'disease list' is quite extensive, and is worth consulting. For example, it includes secretaries who suffer from cramp of the hand or forearm.

IS THE PROCEDURE FOR APPLYING THE SAME AS FOR INDUSTRIAL INJURY?

The procedure is similar though not identical. The case is initially appraised by a combination of the DSS adjudication officer and a consultant. If they both believe there are grounds for a claim, they will refer the matter to a medical board which will operate in the same way as for an application based on industrial accident. Although the general time limits are similar as for industrial accident claims, there are complex details that vary according to the particular disease. For further details on disablement benefit, consult DSS leaflet NI 6 or the *Disability Rights Handbook* or the *Rights Guide to Non-Means Tested Social Security Benefits*. The application form is BI 95, available at all DSS offices.

There is also a free advice service on the possibility of claims, provided by volunteer solicitors, called ALAS (Accident Legal Advice Service); for details of this service consult your local CAB.

War disablement pensions

There is a special scheme of benefits for people whose disability has been caused or aggravated by military service, during the First World War, or at any time after 2 September 1939. Merchant seamen injured in either World War, and civilians whose disability was caused (though not aggravated) by the Second World War are also covered. The scheme is administered by the DSS and further details plus claim forms can be obtained from the Controller, Central Office (War Pensions), DSS, Norcross, Blackpool FY5 3TA. The basic payment takes the form of a tax-free weekly disablement pension. There are also a number of special related benefits. For further information see DSS leaflet NI 50, *National Insurance Guidance for War Pensioners*. There are also a number of leaflets available free of charge from War Pensioners' Welfare Offices as follows: *Rates of War Pensions and Allowances* (MPL 154); *Help for the War Disabled* (MPL 153); *War Widows* (MPL 152); *War Pensioners'*

Mobility Supplement (MPL 155); *War Pensioners: Help with Transport* (HI 211A); *War Pensioners and Widows Going Abroad* (MPL 120).

Disability Working Allowance (DWA)

This benefit is designed to top up low wages or self-employed earnings for people whose disability puts them at a disadvantage in getting a job (see also above at p.98).

Who can claim DWA?

Any person in Great Britain, aged 16 or over, who is normally working for 16 or more hours a week, who has a physical or mental disability which puts them at a disadvantage in getting a job, can claim DWA, as long as they 'qualify financially' as follows:

1. The claimant (plus partner, if relevant) does not have capital in excess of £16,000; *and*
2. *Either* the claimant is receiving at the date of the first claim at least one of a list of other benefits (known as the *qualifying benefits* (disability living allowance, attendance allowance, industrial/war pensions constant attendance allowance, war pensions mobility component, or DSS invalid trike), *or* the claimant has received during all or part of the previous eight weeks at least one of another list of benefits (invalidity benefit, severe disablement allowance, disability/higher pensioner premiums).

Is DWA taxable?

DWA is not taxable but it is taken fully into account for the purposes of calculating entitlement to other means tested benefits.

Can DWA be backdated?

DWA can only be backdated if the claimant can show 'good cause' for the delay in making the claim.

How is DWA claimed?

DWA is claimed on Form DWA1 obtainable from the local DSS office, or the Disability Working Allowance Unit, Freepost PR1211, Preston PR2 2TF. The claimant must satisfy all the DWA requirements on the day that the claim is submitted. All DSS offices are supposed to have available an officer who can advise the claimant on whether or not they will be 'better off' making a claim, rather than, for example, making a claim for family credit (see Chapter 8, p.272). The claim form must be sent to the DWA Unit in Preston, where it will be decided by an adjudicating officer. The DWA unit will send a written notification of their decision to the claimant.

Can the applicant appeal against an adverse decision?

A claimant who receives an adverse decision can ask for a review by another adjudication officer, within three months of receiving the notification. If the claimant remains dissatisfied with the reviewed decision they can appeal to the Disability Appeal Tribunal if the appeal relates to failing the 'disability test', and to a Social Security Appeal Tribunal, if it relates to any other reason. The appeal must be submitted within three months of receiving the final decision. The Disability Appeal Tribunal consists of a lawyer chairperson and two other members, of whom one is a medical practitioner and the other is a person either themselves disabled or experienced in dealing with the needs of disabled people. The address of the DAT central office is: Chaddesden House, PO Box 168, 77 Talbot Street, Nottingham NG1 5JX (tel: 0602 472942).

For how long does DWA continue?

Each award of DWA lasts for 26 weeks, regardless of any changes in the claimant's physical or financial situation during that period. There is no limit on the number of renewal claims that the claimant may make. On each renewal claim, the same criteria will be applied as for the first claim.

Disability Living Allowance (DLA)

This benefit, first introduced in April 1992, is a hybrid of the old attendance allowance and mobility allowance. In broad terms, it is available to people with disabilities who either need help looking after themselves or who have difficulty moving around unaided. DLA is divided into two components, the *care component*, and the *mobility component.* Each component has its own tests, and its own rates of payment. There is nothing to prevent a claimant from receiving both components as long as they satisfy the tests.

Is DLA taxable?

DLA is not taxable, is not means tested, and does not depend upon national insurance contributions. DLA does not count as income for the purposes of income support, except that for a person in a nursing home, or in residential care, the care component is taken into account by income support.

DLA: the care component

To claim the care component of DLA, a person must be under 66 on the day of first claim, must have been eligible to qualify before their 65th birthday (but see below under 'Attendance allowance') and must be so severely disabled, either mentally or physically, that they require from another person one or more of the following:

1. *Throughout the day.* Frequent attention in connection with their bodily functions.
2. *Throughout the day.* Continual supervision to avoid substantial danger to themselves or others.
3. *Throughout the night.* Prolonged or repeated attention in connection with their bodily functions.
4. *Throughout the night.* In order to avoid substantial danger to themselves or others, they require another person to be awake for a prolonged period or at frequent intervals for the purpose of watching over them.
5. *For part of the day.* Attention in connection with their bodily functions for a significant portion of the day.

There is also a sixth possible way of receiving the care component, called the *cooking test* (see below at p.116).

The start of 'night' is not defined by law but is generally assumed to be approximately between the hours of 11 p.m. and 7 a.m. The criterion is what a claimant reasonably needs, thus they are entitled to receive the DLA care component even if they are not actually *receiving* the care that they need. To be eligible a claimant must have been in this condition for at least three months, although they can submit their claim before the three months have expired.

What does 'frequent attention in connection with bodily functions' mean?

This means that the claimant needs regular assistance throughout the day to carry out any of a number of personal activities such as going to the toilet, washing all over, eating, drinking, washing hair, shaving, or dressing. It does not extend to assistance with shopping or cooking (but see below under *cooking test*). Profoundly deaf people qualify if they need frequent attention in connection with their deafness.

What does 'continual supervision to avoid substantial danger' mean?

This has been interpreted to mean 'frequent and regular' supervision, i.e. not non-stop supervision, 'in order to effect a real reduction in the risk', i.e. it is not necessary to demonstrate that the risk has been removed altogether. If the need for the attention is real but unpredictable, e.g. because the claimant may suffer an epileptic attack with grave risks attached, a claim is nevertheless permissible.

What is 'a prolonged period'?

A 'prolonged period' is at least 20 minutes.

What are 'frequent intervals'?

At 'frequent intervals' means at least three times.

What is the 'cooking test'?

The care component can also be satisfied through the 'cooking test'. To qualify, a claimant must be between 16 and 65 at the date of the application. They must also show that they are so severely disabled, either physically or mentally, that they cannot prepare a cooked main meal for themselves, if given the ingredients.

Is the DLA care component affected if the claimant moves into residential care or a nursing home?

If the claimant is moving permanently into either of the above types of accommodation their DLA care component will be withdrawn after four weeks if the accommodation is council owned or run (Part III accommodation, see Chapter 9 at p.297). The local social services department will, however, make an equivalent adjustment to the amount that the claimant is expected to pay towards their fees. If the accommodation is privately owned or run, and the claimant is meeting the full cost of the fees, there will be no changes made to their DLA care component.

How much is DLA care component?

There are three rates of payment, the *higher rate*, the *middle rate* and the *lower rate.*

The *higher rate* is payable if the claimant satisfies either (or both) of tests 1 and 2 above, *AND* either (or both) tests 3 and 4. In other words, the need for care is spread over both day and night.

The *middle rate* is payable if the claimant satisfies either (or both) of tests 1 and 2 above, *OR* either (or both) of tests 3 and 4. In other words, care is only required for either daytime, or night-time, but not both.

The *lower rate* is payable if the claimant satisfies test 5 or 6 above.

DLA: the mobility component

The mobility component of DLA is designed to help severely disabled people become more mobile. It is paid at two rates, according to two different tests.

Test one: higher rate

A person can claim the higher rate if they suffer from a physical disability such that *either*:

1. They are unable or virtually unable to walk; *or*
2. The exertion required to walk would constitute a danger to their life, or would be likely to lead to a serious deterioration in their health; *or*
3. They have no legs or feet, from birth or through amputation; *or*
4. They are both deaf and blind; *or*
5. They receive the higher rate care component (see p.117) and are severely mentally impaired with extremely disruptive and dangerous behavioural problems; *or*
6. They are switching from the pre-1976 invalid vehicle scheme.

TEST TWO: LOWER RATE

A person can claim the lower rate if they are 'so severely disabled physically or mentally that, disregarding any ability that they may have to use routes which are familiar to them on their own, they cannot take advantage of the facility to go out of doors without guidance or supervision from another person most of the time'.

This lower rate is particularly designed for people who do not have any obvious physical inability to walk in certain areas, but need assistance or company in doing so; for example, some learning disabled or agoraphobic people, some Down's syndrome or autistic people, some blind or deaf people, may fit this category, although they may alternatively be eligible for the higher rate. For a useful guide on the interpretation of the lower rate provision, see the *Disability Rights Handbook.*

A first-time claimant for the DLA mobility component must be between 5 and 65, and be likely to remain in the same condition for the next six months (*NB* there are special rules and procedures for those applicants who are terminally ill). It must also be clear that they will be in a position to benefit from the allowance, were it to be paid, i.e. they will be able to get outside of their home, albeit transported by another person.

How is DLA claimed?

DLA is administered from ten Regional Disability Benefit Centres and from the central Disability Living Allowance Unit, Warbreck House, Blackpool FY2 0UE. The Unit, Benefit Centres and local DSS offices can provide a DLA claim pack, Form DLA1. As long as the completed claim pack is returned to the appropriate address within six weeks, the date that the claimant requested the pack will count as the date of the claim for payment purposes. Payments cannot be backdated any earlier than this date. The application does not require a routine medical examination, although a claimant can ask for one. The decision whether or not to grant DLA, and at what level, is taken in the first instance by an adjudication officer, on the basis of the claimant's answers to the self-assessment questionnaire contained in the claim pack. The adjudication officer will be following the guidance laid down in the DSS/DLA Advisory Board Handbook.

Can an applicant appeal against an adverse decision?

A dissatisfied applicant can ask that the decision of the adjudication officer, which is made in the Regional Disability Benefit Centre, be reviewed by a second-tier adjudication officer, based in the Central Unit in Blackpool. If the claimant remains dissatisfied with the second-tier review they can appeal to the Disability Appeal Tribunal (see above at p.114).There is no longer any walking test applied to applicants appealing against a refusal to grant the mobility component.

For how long does DLA continue?

DLA is payable for the period that it is awarded, which may be for life or for a shorter fixed period. There is no limit on the number of renewal applications that can be made by the claimant.

Are there any residence requirements for DLA claimants?

All claimants must be ordinarily resident in Great Britain and have been so for 26 of the past 52 weeks at the time of the claim (unless they are less than one year old).

Does receipt of DLA act as a 'passport' to any other benefits?

Receipt of DLA gives claimants a passport to a number of further types of help as follows, of which the following are the most important:

CARE COMPONENT

(*Higher and middle rates only †All rates)

- * 80 per cent disablement for SDA (see below at p.124).
- * Disability test for DWA (see above at p.113).
- * ICA carer test (see below at p.126).
- * IS/HB severe disability premiums (see Chapter 8 at p.266 and Chapter 11 at p.405) and exemption from signing on (see Chapter 8 at p.267).
- † IS disability, higher pensioner, and disabled child premiums (see Chapter 8 at p.265).
- † DWA qualifying benefit (see above at p.113).

MOBILITY COMPONENT

(*Higher rate only †Both rates)

- * Exemption from road tax (see below).
- * Access to Orange Badge Scheme (see below at p.121).
- * Access to schemes to assist in acquiring special vehicles (see below at p.122).
- * British Rail concessionary railcard.
- * Help with fares to work (see above at p.98).
- * 80 per cent disablement for SDA (see below at p.124).
- * Disability test for DWA (see above at p.113).
- † DWA qualifying benefit (see above at p.113).
- † IS disability, higher pensioner, and disabled child premiums (see Chapter 8 at p.265).

EXEMPTION FROM ROAD TAX

A person in receipt of higher-rate mobility component of the DLA can claim exemption from road tax (Vehicle Excise Duty) if they are unable to leave their home without assistance from another person. When receiving higher-rate mobility component (or pensioner's mobility supplement) allowance a claimant should automatically receive a road tax exemption form from the DSS which they must produce at the post office in order to claim a tax exemption disc. Technically, the vehicle is only exempt while it is being used solely by or for the use of the disabled person. But if the vehicle is being used by another to do something for them, e.g. shopping, that would seem to be quite legal. A person in receipt of higher-rate mobility component may alternatively nominate another person's vehicle (e.g. their spouse) for exemption so long as that vehicle is used 'by or for the purposes of the claimant'. If exemption appears to have been wrongfully refused for any purpose the claimant should write a letter of complaint to Driver Vehicle and Licensing Centre, Vehicle Enquiry Unit Centre, Longview Rd, Swansea SA6 7JL, setting out the details of the complaint.

Finally, car tax (10 per cent on new cars) is not payable on cars supplied through the Motability Scheme (see below at p.122) and on vehicles built specifically for use by disabled people with seating or space for wheelchairs for more than 12 people. For further information see Customs and Excise Commissioners leaflet, *Car Tax Conversion of Vehicles*.

Access to the Orange Badge Scheme

A higher-rate mobility component claimant may also apply to their local authority for an 'Orange Badge' which gives them certain parking privileges, such as the right to park without charge or time limit on a parking meter. Details of this scheme can be obtained from local social services departments. It is at the discretion of the local social services department whether or not to grant an Orange Badge, and they can charge up to £2 for the privilege. Even if the applicant is not in receipt of higher-rate mobility component they are entitled to consideration for an Orange Badge:

- if they are registered blind, *or*
- if they drive regularly, and have a severe disability in both arms so they cannot turn a steering wheel by hand (even if the wheel is fitted with a turning knob), *or*
- if they have a permanent and substantial disability which causes inability to walk or very considerable difficulty in walking, *or*
- if they receive war pensioner's mobility supplement.

Orange Badges cannot be used in the Cities of London and Westminster (Central London) nor in parts of the London Borough of Camden. If the disabled person is not, or has not been, in the vehicle it is an offence to display the Orange Badge unless the driver is about to collect, or has just deposited, the disabled person.

Access to schemes to assist in acquiring special vehicles

Finally, there are also a number of schemes designed to assist people with mobility problems in obtaining specially adapted cars. The most prominent of these schemes is the Motability Scheme, whereby the claimant (or the parent of the claimant if the latter is too young to drive) can rent a car from a private trust at favourable rates by trading in their higher-rate mobility component, or their war pensioner's mobility supplement. (On tax exemptions for new Motability cars, see above at p.121.) The address of Motability is: Motability, Gate House, Westgate, The High, Harlow, Essex CM20 1HR (tel: 0279 635666). For further details on several other schemes, contact the Department of Transport Mobility Advice and Vehicle Information Service (MAVIS), TRRL, Old Wokingham Road, Crowthorne, Berkshire RG11 6AU.

For further information on assistance for those with mobility problems, there is a useful free guide called *Door to Door*, which can be obtained from the Department of Transport Disability Unit, 2 Marsham Street, London SW1P 3EB (tel: 071 276 5256/7).

Other organisations that can assist in this respect are:

Mobility Information Service, Unit 2A, Atcham Industrial Estate, Upton Magnor, Shrewsbury SY4 4UG (tel: 0743 761889). This is a voluntary organisation offering a wide range of information on cars, adaptations, and costs through a series of leaflets and direct assessment, if within a 100-mile radius of Shrewsbury.

Banstead Mobility Centre, Damson Way, Orchard Hill, Queen Mary's Avenue, Carshalton, Surrey (tel: 081 770 1151). This centre, which is part of the Queen Elizabeth's Foundation, is a combination of an advisory service on the different types of adapted vehicles available, and an assessment centre.

Attendance allowance

Attendance allowance is still available to people who become eligible for the first time for middle- or higher-rate DLA after their 65th birthday. Attendance allowance is paid to anybody satisfying any of the first four tests for the care component of the DLA (see above at p.115) who has been in that condition for at least six months at the date of the first payment. It will be paid at the higher rate only if both a daytime and a night-time need are demonstrated. For further information, see the *Disability Rights Handbook.* The position regarding continuing receipt of attendance allowance by those who have moved into residential accommodation or a nursing home is the same as for those in receipt of the DLA care component (see above at p.117).

The Independent Living Fund (ILF)

In 1988 the government, together with the Disablement Income Group (DIG), set up a special trust fund open to severely disabled people in receipt of attendance allowance and on low incomes (i.e. income support level) who have to pay for domestic care. The details of the fund were complex and payments discretionary. The initial aim of the fund was to keep people living in the community who would otherwise have to go into residential care. It was criticised as seeking to replace with a discretionary fund services which local authorities ought to be providing as a matter of right under the CSDPA 1970 (see p.86). The fund is still operating in respect of some 21,300 people who were receiving its assistance by 31 March 1993, under the new name of Independent Living (Extension) Fund.

The Independent Living Fund (for new claimants) has now been replaced by a new fund, known as the Independent Living (1993) Fund. According to the *Disability Rights Handbook*, the new fund:

> bears little resemblance to the old ILF. It is still aimed at enabling severely disabled people to live in the community, and can only provide cash as a top-up to services provided by the local authority to people in their own homes up to a specified ceiling. But compared to the old ILF, it provides less cash and less choice over personal care arrangements; its criteria are more restrictive and fewer people are expected to get help from the Fund.

In essence, the new fund is designed to help people between 16 and 66 with the most severe disabilities to live independently in the community. The fund is organised in partnership with local authorities, 'reflecting their primary role following the April 1993 community care changes'. The local authority will be expected to 'make a contribution by way of services equivalent to what it would have spent on residential or nursing care', and the fund then has the power to provide a top-up cash payment. For further details of the ILF, see the *Disability Rights Handbook* (18th edn, 1993–4), Chapter 34, or write to the Independent Living Fund, PO Box 183, Nottingham NG8 3RD (tel: 0602 290423 or 290427).

Severe Disablement Allowance (SDA)

This benefit was introduced in 1984 to replace non-contributory invalidity pensions (NCIP and HNCIP). Anybody receiving these pensions prior to the introduction of SDA is automatically entitled to receive SDA. The benefit is broadly designed as a weekly benefit for people with severe disabilities, who have not paid the necessary national insurance contributions, to claim the contributory benefits outlined at Chapter 8 (statutory sick pay, sickness benefit, and invalidity benefit). Inevitably, the level of SDA is lower than that of these three benefits. SDA is neither contributory, nor is it means tested. Although this benefit is often described as highly complex, the label arises more because of the number of different ways in which it can be claimed than because of any inherent complexity in the benefit itself. Nevertheless, it is normally advisable to consult a good manual before applying for the benefit, and in particular the *Disability Rights Handbook* is recommended in this respect (see 'Further assistance', p.134).

Who can claim SDA?

In addition to those already receiving NCIP/HNCIP when the benefit was introduced (November 1984), there are two other categories of claimant. To succeed, a claimant must fall into one of these categories:

Category 1: The claimant must have been incapable of work for at least 28 consecutive weeks prior to the date of the application, the relevant period commencing *before the claimant's 20th birthday*. The claimant must be aged 16 or over (and if in full-time education, aged 19 or over).

There are special – very complex – rules governing claimants in Category 1 who manage to find work for a brief period, then find, on reaching 20, they are being asked to reapply for SDA and establish 80 per cent disability. For a clear exposition of these rules, see the *Disability Rights Handbook*.

Category 2: The claimant must have been incapable of work for at least 28 weeks and disabled to the extent of 80 per cent (an assessment of 75 per cent is always rounded up to 80 per cent). The claimant must be below pensionable age, unless they were entitled to SDA (or NCIP/HNCIP) immediately prior to reaching pensionable age but for some reason failed to claim the benefit. If a claimant over pensionable age does receive SDA they will be entitled to receive it for the rest of their life. It should not be forgotten, however, that if a claimant is incapable of work (as above) but has previously worked and paid the appropriate number of national insurance contributions, they will be better off claiming statutory sick pay, sickness benefit and invalidity benefit.

What is meant by 'incapable of work'?

For an explanation of this term, see Chapter 8, p.256.

Are there any residence requirements for SDA?

At the time of claiming a claimant must be present in Great Britain, and have been present for at least 26 weeks of the year in which the claim is made. No continuing residence requirement applies once the claimant is in receipt of SDA. Certain categories of claimant are exempted from these resident requirements, e.g. members of the armed forces (for full list see either of the reference handbooks mentioned below at 'Further assistance'). There are special rules for those in full-time education.

How is the disablement percentage worked out?

The DSS has published a list of industrial injuries setting out prescribed percentages of disablement, which is essentially the same list that is used for assessing the degree of disability for a claim for *industrial disablement benefit* (see p.110). A summary of the list is produced by the DSS. The list sets out standard percentage degrees of disablement for particular disabilities ranging from 2 per cent to 100 per cent. If a claimant's disability does not fall into any clear existing category it will be up to the adjudicating medical practitioner (see below) and ultimately the Medical Appeal Tribunal to determine whether the disability amounts to 80 per cent. It seems that a 75 per cent assessment is always rounded up to 80 per cent.

Prescribed degrees of disablement

SDA is not taxable, nor is it means tested, but it counts as an income resource in full for the purposes of a claim for income support (see Chapter 8).

Can SDA be backdated?

A claim for SDA can be backdated if the claimant has 'good cause' for the lateness. Given the inevitable disability of the claimant (which may also include a mental disability) the 'good cause' clause is normally treated fairly liberally. SDA cannot, however, be backdated for more than one month.

How is SDA claimed?

A claim should be made on DSS Form NI 252.

Further information

In addition to the two handbooks detailed at the end of this chapter, there are two publications by the DSS that are particularly helpful in explaining how the 80 per cent test is carried out as follows: *The DSS Handbook on Non-Contributory Benefits for Disabled People*, and *The DSS Handbook for Adjudicating Medical Authorities*, both of which are available from the DSS Store, Primrose Hill, Clitheroe, Lancashire BB7 1BF.

Invalid Care Allowance (ICA)

This allowance is paid to certain carers, engaged full-time in caring for a severely disabled person. The level of remuneration is very low, for example it is approximately half the level paid in Sweden. (For a study of relative levels of this benefit in Europe, see *Paying for Care: Lessons From Europe*, HMSO 1993.)

Who can claim ICA?

Any person can claim this allowance if they are caring for a person who is receiving either DLA care component at middle or higher rate, attendance allowance at either rate or constant attendance allowance in respect of industrial or wartime disablement. The claimant must not be gainfully employed, nor in full-time education. They must be 16 or over, and under 65, unless in the latter case they were receiving or eligible to receive ICA at the time they reached 65. To be eligible a claimant must be both present and ordinarily resident in the United Kingdom.

What do the phrases 'caring for' and 'gainfully employed' mean?

As with all benefits the legal problems invariably centre on the interpretation of particular words. The words 'caring for' have been held to mean 'regular and substantial caring' which may be satisfied by being around and available for most of the day to help when necessary with the disabled person's personal needs, but will normally amount to 35 hours or more per week. Once a pattern of caring has been established, temporary breaks will not cause the carer to lose their benefit. In practice, a carer can have four weeks' holiday in any six months without losing their benefit. In addition, if the carer meets the requirements during part of the year (e.g. weekends, or school holidays) they may be entitled to claim ICA for those periods.

The words 'gainfully employed' have been held to mean 'earning £40 a week or more gross' (see Chapter 8 for explanation on how 'earnings' are calculated).

Is ICA taxable?

ICA is taxable, with the exclusion of any amount paid to the carer in respect of any dependent children. When receiving ICA the claimant is credited with Class 1 national insurance contributions (see Chapter 8, p.257, and Chapter 9, p.301, on relevance to pension rights). ICA counts as an income resource for the purposes of a claim for income support.

Can ICA be backdated?

ICA can be backdated for up to 12 months from the date of the application, if the applicant can show they met all the qualifying conditions during that period. Unlike for most other benefits, it is not necessary to show 'good cause' for the delay.

How is ICA claimed?

A claim for ICA should be made on DSS Form NI 212. The claim should be sent to the Invalid Care Allowance Unit, Palatine House, Lancashire Road, Preston, Lancashire PR1 1HB. A written decision regarding the claim will be sent directly to the claimant. Payment is by way of a book of orders cashable at a local post office.

Does an appeal lie against an adverse decision?

An appeal lies to the social security appeal tribunal in the normal way (see Chapter 8).

Does receipt by the carer of other benefits affect their entitlement to claim?

A person cannot claim ICA if they are receiving the same amount or more from the following benefits: unemployment benefit, maternity allowance, invalidity benefit, state training allowance, sickness benefit, retirement pension, widow's benefits, or SDA. In these circumstances, many people may wonder why they should claim ICA. Advice should always be sought, but it is worth noting that ICA does provide a number of further benefits such as Class 1 national insurance contributions, the carer's premium for income support (see Chapter 8 at p.265), and the Christmas bonus.

For how long does ICA continue?

ICA will continue for as long as the person for whom the carer is caring receives attendance allowance. Thus ICA will stop once the disabled person has been an in-patient in hospital for more than four weeks. For further information and assistance regarding the problems of carers, contact:

The Association of Carers, 243 Mortlake Road, Richmond, Surrey TW9 2LS (tel: 081 948 3946). This is an organisation that helps to set up local carer groups and support networks. It also provides information on services and benefits.

The Carers National Association, 29 Chilworth Mews, London W2 3RG (tel: 071 724 7776). This organisation provides information, advice and a newsletter for carers. It gives information about carers' needs to government, local authorities and voluntary organisations and acts as a campaigning pressure group for carers.

Vaccine damage payments

This scheme is designed to compensate victims of vaccine damage, with a lump sum payment of up to £30,000, the amount depending upon the date of claim. It is non-contributory and non-means tested. It does not affect the claimant's rights to pursue independent legal action for negligence. Any damages award in a successful claim will, however, be reduced by the amount of the vaccine damage payment. For further information on the scheme see DSS leaflet HB3 which can be obtained, together with a claim form, from Vaccine Damage Payment Unit, North Fylde Central Office, Norcross, Blackpool FY5 3TA.

EDUCATION

There are four major pieces of legislation that affect the legal rights of disabled children to receive special consideration regarding their education. The first is the Education Act 1981, which has introduced a complex series of procedures whereby the special educational needs of disabled children can be assessed, and provision made for meeting those needs. The second is the Act already referred to above at p.88, the Disabled Persons (Services, Consultation, and Representation) Act 1986. The third is the Children Act 1989, which sets out a series of new provisions regarding local authority responsibility towards 'children in need' (see above at p.89), focusing in particular on the rights of the child. The fourth is the Education Reform Act 1988, which deals with the national curriculum.

Rights of disabled children under the Education Act 1981

The Education Act 1981 was intended to provide a new legal framework for the assessment and placement of children with disabilities in schools up to the age of 19 (though not if they are under 19 and in a college of further education). The Act focuses on children with 'special educational needs', which it defines as a 'learning difficulty which calls for special educational provision to be made'. A learning difficulty means either 'having significantly greater difficulty in learning than the majority of children of the same age or being hindered by a disability from using general educational facilities'. Special educational needs also includes a child under five who *might* have a learning difficulty if they do not have special help before they reach five. The Act specifically excludes from this category children who have a learning difficulty because English is not the main language spoken in their home.

Children who have special educational needs should be identified by the local education authority in which they reside and assessed as to how these needs can be met. The parent of any child aged between 2 and 19 can request that their child is assessed, and this request cannot be unreasonably refused. It is generally recommended that such a request be supported by an expert report by an educational psychologist. Assessment is a long and complex business involving reports from education, health, psychological and social services. It may take as long as a year. Assessment is followed by a complex procedure involving varying levels of responsibility on the part of the local authority and the parents. The most formal outcome of assessment will be the issuing of a Statement by the local education authority in which they will detail their findings as to the child's special educational needs and their proposals for special educational provisions to meet those needs. Once a Statement has been made it must be reviewed annually. Various reforms to the system of statementing have been proposed at the time of going to press, including improving the involvement of parents in the statementing process, extending rights of appeal, and widening the right of parents of children with special educational needs to be educated in the school of their choice. The new rights are contained in the Education Act 1992.

The Education Reform Act 1988

This Act allows children with 'Statements of special educational need' to be excluded from the provisions of the national curriculum.

Any person who believes that an assessment is the appropriate course of action for a child should therefore consult one of the excellent specialist guides to the Education Act 1981, of which the following are particularly recommended:

The *ACE Special Education Handbook*, available from the Advisory Centre for Education, 1B Aberdeen Studios, 22 Highbury Grove, London N5 2EA (tel: 071 354 8321).

RADAR Fact Sheets on the 1981 Education Act (Guide, Assessment, Appeals) available from RADAR (see below, at p.135).

The Centre for Studies on Integration in Education (CSE) provides information and advice about educating children with special educational needs in ordinary schools and can be contacted at 415 Edgware Road, London NW2 2EH (tel: 081 452 8642).

The Voluntary Council for the Handicapped Child, 8 Wakeley St, London EC1V 7QE (tel: 071 278 9441), is concerned with all aspects of disability and special needs in young people and provides a comprehensive advice service to parents and advisers.

Contact a Family, 16 Strutton Ground, London SW1P 2HP (tel: 071 222 2695), is an organisation that brings together families of children with special needs for mutual support and sharing of ideas. Parents in Partnership, 25 Woodnook Road, London SW16 6TZ, is a group campaigning to give more power to the parents of children with special educational needs to participate in the national decision-making process.

The Children's Legal Centre, 20 Compton Terrace, London N1 2UN (tel: 071 359 6251/2), is a campaigning organisation that takes an interest in all aspects of the rights of the child (see Chapter 1 at p.7).

Effects of the DPSCRA 1986 on rights under the Education Act 1981

As mentioned earlier in this chapter (see p.88) the sections of this Act dealing with disabled children are now in force. The sections are designed to place greater responsibility on local authorities to ensure that the needs of disabled children leaving school are properly assessed. The provisions are complex, but in summary they require the following:

- Each local education authority must find out from its local social services department whether a child on whom a Statement has been made following assessment under the Education Act 1981 (see p.130) is disabled at the first annual review after their fourteenth birthday.
- Each local education authority must inform their local social services department of that person's presumed date of leaving full-time education (school or further education) eight months before that date, as long as they are under 19 at the time. Once informed, the social services department must undertake an assessment of the person's needs for any of the services to which the disabled are entitled and in particular to those set out under the CSDPA (see pp.86–7). This assessment must be undertaken within five months of being informed, unless the person (or if under 16, the person's parent or guardian) asks them not to do so.

A useful manual providing employment ideas for disabled school leavers is the *Directory of Opportunities for School Leavers with Disabilities*, available from Queen Elizabeth's Foundation for Disabled People, Leatherhead, Surrey KT22 0BN (tel: 0372 542204).

The Children Act 1989

This Act sets out general duties of local authorities to provide services and other assistance to disabled children, already summarised above at p.89. In addition to these general duties the Act also specifies that local authorities must provide for children in need (see above at p.130) who are attending any school such care or supervised activities as are appropriate outside school hours and in school holidays.

Anybody seeking further information on any of the above should contact the Advisory Centre for Education (ACE) (see p.131 for address).

Special education grants for disabled students in higher education

Disabled students should also be aware that if they are in full-time higher education, and receiving a mandatory grant from their local authority, they can claim a special additional allowance as a supplement to their grant to cover the cost of any extra expenditure 'necessarily incurred' as a result of going on the course. Under this head disabled students have successfully claimed an allowance to cover such things as typewriters, paid helpers, tape recorders, additional heating, and special diets. Normally, extra travel costs are not included under this head. Students who receive only a discretionary grant can also claim this allowance, but in this case it will be entirely within the local authority's discretion whether or not to pay the allowance. For further information on these grants, contact the local education authority for the leaflet *Student Grants and Loans: a Brief Guide* (also obtainable from DES Publications Centre, PO Box 2193, London E15 2EW).

The National Bureau for Handicapped Students, 336 Brixton Rd, London SW9 7AA (tel: 071 274 0565), is a charity specialising in the problems of handicapped and disabled students. They produce a useful leaflet on general financial help to disabled students, called *Financial Assistance for Students with Disabilities*. For further information on the extra financial assistance available to disabled students seeking income support and to those seeking income support with disabled dependants, see Chapter 8, p.265.

The British Students (Educational Assistance) Fund, c/o Dr K. Norbury, University Health Service, Claremont Road, Newcastle upon Tyne NE1 7RU (tel: 091 232 2973), can sometimes provide assistance to students in higher education who have fallen behind in a course of full-time study due to illness, accident or disability, and may also provide help with special aids that are not available from statutory sources, such as the DSS and the NHS.

The Snowdon Award Scheme, c/o Action Research, Vincent House, North Parade, Horsham, West Sussex RH12 2DA, can provide limited financial assistance to disabled students up to a maximum of £1000 per annum.

FURTHER ASSISTANCE

Throughout this chapter, reference has been made to sources of further information that can be obtained from government departments and from other specialist independent bodies. Where appropriate, addresses have also been provided. Two publications in particular have been repeatedly mentioned:

Child Poverty Action Group (CPAG), *Rights Guide to Non-Means Tested Social Security Benefits*.

Disability Alliance, *Disability Rights Handbook* (and *Hospital Patients' Handbook*).

Both these publications are inexpensive and contain highly accurate, reliable accounts of all the financial benefits referred to in this chapter. Both publications are updated annually. It is therefore important to obtain the latest edition. The *Disability Rights Handbook* also contains a range of further information on the wider rights of disabled people, going far beyond legal rights. It is an excellent general source of reference on these matters. It also contains a comprehensive list of addresses of agencies and organisations specialising in particular aspects of disability. The addresses where these two publications may be obtained are as follows:

- Child Poverty Action Group, 1–5 Bath St, London EC1V 9QA (tel: 071 242 9149).
- Disability Alliance, Universal House, 88–94 Wentworth Street, London E1 7SA (tel: 071 253 3406).

Leaflets on benefits for disabled people in Hindi, Punjabi, Urdu, Gujerati, and Bengali are available from ASRA, 155 Kennington Park Road, London SE11 4JJ (tel: 081 820 0155).

Further advice and assistance

The following agencies offer a free, specialised telephone advice service to disabled people or their advisers:

Disability Alliance (tel: 071 247 8776).
Citizens' Rights Office (for advisers only; financial benefits only) (tel: 071 242 9149).
Network (advice on legal action), 16 Princeton Street, London WC1R 4BB (tel: 071 831 8031 or 837 7740).
Disablement Income Group (DIG), Millmead Business Centre, Millmead Road, London N17 9QU (tel: 081 801 8013).
DIG Scotland, 5 Quayside Street, Edinburgh EH6 6EJ (tel: 031 555 2811).

RADAR (research, emphasis, campaigning body, some general advice), 12 City Forum, 250 City Rd, London EC1V 8AF (tel: 071 250 3222).

The British Council of Organisations of Disabled People, Greenlaw St, London, SE18 5AR (tel: 081 854 7289) is a federation of 34 organisations of disabled people concerned to bring about the full integration of disabled people into society through self-help. It provides advice, information, training and counselling services to members.

Dial UK is a nationwide organisation, with some 75 local information offices, that offers an information service to the disabled. Its national headquarters is at Dial House, 117 High St, Clay Cross, Derbyshire (tel: 0246 864498).

NDIP, National Disability Information Project, c/o The Policy Studies Institute, 100 Park Village East, London NW1 3SR (tel: 071 387 2171), produces the Directory of Local Disability Information Providers.

Both the Child Poverty Action Group and Network are willing to provide legal support in cases of exceptional public importance.

In addition to the above national organisations, there are a number of regionally based organisations that may be able to provide assistance. For information on local organisations, consult the Disability Alliance or the local Citizens' Advice Bureau.

Finally, the Union of the Physically Impaired Against Segregation (UPIAS) is a group that aims to oppose all forms of segregation of disabled people and can be contacted at Flat 2, St Giles Court, Diane Road, London W13 9AQ.

POSTSCRIPT

It is worth noting that federal law in both the United States (Americans With Disabilities Act) and Australia (Disability Discrimination Act) make it unlawful to discriminate against people with disabilities across a wide range of activities, including work, education, accommodation, leisure facilities, travel facilities, telecommunications and sports facilities. It remains to be seen when, and if, the government of the United Kingdom is prepared to follow suit.

Chapter 5

Legal rights and mental disability

INTRODUCTION

There are two distinct ways in which a social worker may become professionally involved with the problems of the mentally disabled. The first way is as an Approved Social Worker (ASW), exercising statutory powers to detain patients in a mental institution (usually referred to as a 'section'). Such work is complex, delicate and bound up in detailed legal procedures. There are a number of specialist books that deal with this area: Gostin, L. (1986), *Mental Health Services: Law and Practice* (Shaw and Sons); Jones, R. (1991), *The Mental Health Act Manual* (Sweet and Maxwell); Gostin, L., and Fennell, P. (1992), *Mental Health Tribunal Procedure* (Longman); Hoggett, B. (1990), *Mental Health Law* (Sweet and Maxwell); Gostin, L. et al. (1983), *The Mental Health Act 1983: a Guide for Social Workers* (BASW). A simple but accurate wallchart on the main procedures for detention under the Mental Health Act 1983 is available from MIND: 'Compulsory Detention in Hospital under the Mental Health Act 1983'. A useful general list of the powers and duties of an ASW can be found in the *Social Work Law File on Mental Health* (1987) produced by the University of East Anglia in Norwich.

The second way is through the provision of general social work support – a task that may also be carried out by an ASW – to a client who is suffering from mental disability. This may involve a client in a mental institution, or in the community, or moving between both.

An ASW may often find themselves carrying out both statutory and general social work roles with the same client. This can be both uncomfortable and contradictory for the client, but inevitable in the circumstances. Whatever the difficulties, however, it is essential that the legal rights of the client are at all times safeguarded. This chapter will outline and explain the legal rights of those suffering from mental disability, and will assess the various procedures that exist with a view to safeguarding them. For detailed information on the legal powers and duties of ASWs with respect to detention, the adviser should consult one of the specialist works detailed above.

Definitions

According to a government study, published in 1993:

> Mental illness severe enough to need professional assistance is as common as heart disease and three times as common as cancer. One in ten people suffer from it, and up to one in five children. Over 91 million working days were lost in 1990–1 due to sickness absence certified as mental disorder, compared with 800,000 days lost in 1991 owing to strikes. Over 5500 people commit suicide each year – more than the number who die in road traffic accidents. Most people who commit suicide are suffering from mental illness at the time.

One of the major problems facing anybody helping the mentally disabled is one of definition. What do we mean when we talk of mental disability? The subject is sensitive, as our society all too readily stigmatises victims of mental disability, with little regard for the additional problems such stigma may cause. The problem is compounded by the fact that while the law will grant or withhold a number of legal rights to those who fall within defined legal categories of mental disability, psychiatry is profoundly sceptical of this process of definition, and is frequently unable to agree a definition of a particular condition at all. The problem is made even worse by the desire of those who care for the mentally handicapped (i.e. those with some element of learning disability associated with damage to the brain or genetic malfunction) to distinguish these people quite clearly from the mentally ill. But this distinction also begs further questions about stigma for, by stressing the 'innocence' of the mentally handicapped, whose disability is usually the result of a congenital or an accidental injury, they are implicitly encouraging the assumption that the mentally ill are in some sense less deserving of care and sympathy than the mentally handicapped.

It would not be appropriate to enter into a discussion of the relative merits of these distinctions in this book. An excellent, short and sympathetic introduction to the whole problem of defining mental disability is John Payne's *All in the Mind* (OUP/Chameleon/Ikon, 1976), which can be recommended to the social worker interested in pursuing these themes further. For a useful summary of a wide range of sources in this field, consult Black, J. (1992), *User Involvement in Mental Health Services: an Annotated Bibliography* (Department of Social Policy and Social Work, University of Birmingham). For the purposes of this chapter, the term 'mental disability' will be used throughout to include mental illness, psychopathic disorder, mental handicap and mental impairment so long as the relevant legal rights are identical. Where the rights are affected by the distinction, the text will indicate accordingly.

A distinction that is of more consequence for our purposes, seeking as we are to identify legal rights, is whether a person is living in a mental institution as an in-patient, or alternatively is living in the community. A further distinction is necessary for in-patients, namely, are they *voluntary patients* or are they *detained patients* (i.e. detained by compulsion under a section: see below)?

The in-patient client

In 1982 (the last time a major national survey was conducted) there were 65,000 people resident in mental illness hospitals or psychiatric units in general hospitals, 50,000 people (including 2500 children) in mental handicap hospitals, and 2000 people in high-security special hospitals mainly for offenders and those thought to be a danger to the public. Half the mentally ill population was long-stay, with a large preponderance of elderly patients of whom half were 65 or over. For convenience's sake, all the above institutions will be referred to throughout this section as *mental institutions*. A preliminary distinction has to be drawn between *detained patients* (approximately 10 per cent) and *voluntary patients,* i.e. those not detained under the Mental Health Act 1983 (approximately 90 per cent).

THE DETAINED PATIENT: THEIR RIGHTS IN A MENTAL INSTITUTION

A detained patient is a person resident in a mental institution who has been admitted to, or remains in, the institution by virtue of a section of the Mental Health Act 1983 which allows for such compulsory detention.

There is no minimum age limit for admission to hospital under the Act, but the Code of Practice accompanying the Act stresses that: 'Any intervention in the life of a young person, considered necessary by reason of their mental disorder, should be the least restrictive possible and result in the least possible segregation from family, friends, community and school.'

The detention will either be for up to 72 hours as an emergency (s.4); for up to 28 days for assessment (which can include treatment) (s.2); for up to 6 months for treatment (s.3); by order of a criminal court (usually to a special hospital, see p.140) (Part III); or on transfer from prison by Home Office warrant (usually to a special hospital) (Part III). Because the detention is by compulsion, it is essential that great care is exercised by those involved in their lives to ensure that their legal rights are protected. The Mental Health Act 1983, supported by the Code of Practice (Department of Health, 1990), sets out a number of important legal rights for patients in this category. The following section explains these rights, and outlines the procedures available to detained patients (or their advisers) to protect these rights.

General treatment

The Code of Practice begins with the following important statement of principle: 'Mentally disordered people should be treated with the same respect for their dignity, personal needs, religious and philosophical beliefs, and accorded the same choices, as other people.'

What must the patient be told on arrival?

It is the duty of the managers of the institution where the patient is detained to provide the following information to the patient, both orally and in writing, as soon as is practicable after their detention:

- the provisions under which they are detained;
- their rights concerning any censorship of their correspondence;
- their right to apply to a Mental Health Review Tribunal (MHRT) (see p.157);
- how they might be discharged, either by the institution or by their nearest relative (see p.153);
- their rights to refuse consent to certain types of treatment (see p.143);

- the role of the Mental Health Act Commission (MHAC) (see p.150);
- the Mental Health Act Code of Practice;
- to provide an interpreter to a patient for whom English is not a first language.

In addition to the above, unless the patient requests otherwise, the institution must take all practicable steps to supply the patient's nearest relative with a copy of the information supplied to the patient. Some of the above rights require further clarification.

Can the patient's correspondence be censored in any way?

The answer will depend on whether the patient is in an NHS hospital or a special hospital. A special hospital is one with conditions of special security on account of its patients' 'dangerous, violent or criminal propensities'. The major special hospitals in the UK are Broadmoor, Rampton, and Ashworth hospitals.

Patients in special hospitals

Post sent by a patient may be withheld from the Post Office if either of the following apply:

- the addressee has so requested;
- the hospital managers consider it is likely to cause danger to any person, or distress to any person (excluding, in the latter case, members of the hospital staff).

These powers do not extend to 'privileged' correspondence (see p.141). Post sent to a patient may be withheld if the hospital managers believe it is necessary in the interests of the safety of the patient, or of any other person.

It is clear from the above that the hospital managers have in practice very wide powers to censor the mail of patients in special hospitals, although there is little evidence of abuse of this power. They have the right to open any mail in order to ascertain whether it should be withheld. If mail has been opened, the opener must, however, enclose a note in the packet or envelope stating that this has been done and, if the mail is to be withheld, inform the person who sent it of this decision within seven days. The sender has six months in which to ask the Mental Health Act Commission to review this decision (for the full details see Mental Health Regulations 1983 No. 893 Regs 17–18).

It should be further noted that none of the above restrictions apply to correspondence which can be described as privileged. In this category will be correspondence to or from a Minister, an MP, the Court of Protection or the Lord Chancellor's Visitors (see p.173), the Ombudsman (see p.149 and Chapters 2 and 3), an MHRT, a health or social services authority or Community Health Council (see Chapter 2), the hospital managers, any legally qualified person instructed by the patient, or the European Commission or Court of Human Rights (see Chapter 1).

Patients not in special hospitals

Post sent by a detained person can only be withheld if the addressee has specifically requested. Post sent to a detained person can never be withheld.

What are the patient's voting rights?

As long as a patient remains a detained patient it will be virtually impossible for them to vote. First, in order to vote they must be registered to vote in the constituency where they are resident. If this is a different address from that of the mental institution, and they are detained, they will not be in a position to go out to vote. Second, in order to vote they must be 'of sound mind', which means that at the time of voting they must understand in broad terms what they are doing and the effect of doing it. To be detained a patient must be certified as suffering from a mental disorder. Even if they can get to the polling station where they are registered, they must convince the polling officer that they are 'of sound mind'. The obstacles are thus formidable. The position once a detained patient becomes a voluntary patient is, however, very different (see p.168).

Can the patient ask the institution for any money?

For details of welfare benefits available to patients, see p.176. In addition, it should be noted that the Secretary of State for Social Services does have power under s.122 of the Mental Health Act 1983 to provide hospitals with 'pocket money' for patients who would otherwise be without the resources to meet their personal expenses. For a critical discussion of this whole issue see MIND Policy Paper No. 1, *Money in Hospital*, October 1983 (MIND).

What powers of physical control do the hospital staff have over the patient, in addition to the right to detain them for the prescribed period?

The terms of the order by which a patient is detained will prescribe the period for which such detention may last. This does not, however, give the institution the freedom to detain that person in whatever conditions they choose. The Code of Practice states quite clearly that 'detained patients do not necessarily need physical security. This is only needed for a small number.'

- It is a criminal offence for any member of the hospital staff to ill-treat or wilfully neglect any patient. Alleged criminal offences should always be reported to the police.
- It is the common law duty of any hospital to take all reasonable steps to offer patients the care and treatment they require, and to take reasonable steps to prevent them coming to any harm. In a mental hospital this will include caring for the patients' needs, both mental and physical.
- Solitary confinement (seclusion) should only be used as a 'necessary therapeutic tool' and not as a management and control exercise: see Royal College of Psychiatrists' *Guidelines on Isolation of Patients in Protected Rooms during Psychiatric Treatment* (1980), obtainable from 17 Belgrave Square, London SW1X 8PG (tel: 071 235 2351). The Code of Practice also sets out detailed guidelines on the use of seclusion with the following preamble:

  > Seclusion should only be used where the patient can no longer be managed on the ward and where there is the immediate risk of serious physical harm to self or others. Hospitals using seclusion should have a clear policy and procedure document which seeks to balance safety factors with the dignity of the patient.

- Physical restraint of patients should only be used to prevent them doing harm to themselves or others or to prevent them from unreasonably disrupting the life of the hospital. According to the Code of Practice, restraint 'should be used in accordance with written hospital procedures, always recorded in detail and reviewed by the multi-disciplinary team in the context of the planned programme of care'.

Complaints of any abuse or alleged breaches of good practice should be directed through the complaints procedures outlined below. The Code of Practice also prescribes what should be normal practice for behavioural methods used by staff in hospital wards.

Is a detained patient obliged to consent to any form of treatment?

The law on this subject is precise, but complex. As the patient may often be too befuddled to know what is really happening to them, it is essential that an independent adviser understands the legal position. The answer to the question will depend upon the type of treatment. In every case, however, a preliminary question has to be, what is the meaning of the word 'consent' (see below)?

Note, first of all, that patients detained *either* on an 'emergency 72-hour admission' (under s.4 Mental Health Act 1983), *or* under s.136 Mental Health Act 1983 (which relates to the emergency removal of mentally disordered people to mental institutions or other places of safety, by the police, for up to 72 hours, see p.165), are in the same position as voluntary patients regarding consent to treatment (see p.166), unless their admission is subsequently extended beyond the 72-hour period.

For all other detained patients, the question of consent will depend upon the nature of the proposed treatment. But first, what is 'consent'?

What is 'consent'?

'Consent' in this context is simply agreeing to the particular type of treatment. The Code of Practice makes a number of specific points:

- Detained status does not of itself imply inability to consent.

- Capacity to consent is variable in mental disorder and not everyone is equally capable of understanding the same explanation of a treatment plan.
- Wherever possible, treatment plans should be discussed with the patient both initially and also when changes in the plan are contemplated. A less able person is more likely to be capable of giving valid consent if the explanation offered is appropriate to his level of ability.
- Capacity to consent should be assessed in relationship to the particular treatment proposed.

While these guidelines are clear and should be followed at every stage of a detained patient's treatment, they still do not cover the situation where a patient's condition is so severe that they are quite incapable of giving any informed consent. A High Court judge has directed that in these rare circumstances the following principle applies:

> in exceptional circumstances where there is no provision in law for consent [see p.146] and no one who can give consent [e.g. a parent] and where the patient is suffering such mental abnormality as to be unable ever to give consent then a medical adviser would be justified in taking such steps as good medical practice demands.

Psychosurgery and sex hormone implant treatment

The patient *must* consent (i.e. the above does not apply). The validity of the consent must be confirmed by a certificate signed by three people appointed by the MHAC. One of these three people must be a doctor. They must all certify that the patient has 'understood the nature, purpose and likely effects of the treatment'. The decision to use this form of treatment must be confirmed by a second opinion from an independent doctor. This independent doctor must in turn have consulted two other people concerned with the patient's treatment, one a nurse and the other neither a nurse nor a doctor. The reason for such stringent safeguards is the controversial nature of the treatment and its irreversibility. Although sex hormone implant treatment is very rare in the United Kingdom, psychosurgery is used in between 100 and 200 cases per year in England and Wales. (For comment on this form of treatment, see Gostin, L. (1982), 'Psychosurgery: a Hazardous and Unestablished Treatment? A

Case for the Importation of American Legal Safeguards to Great Britain', *Journal of Social Welfare Law*, no. 83).

Electro-convulsive therapy (ECT) *or* continuing to give medication after it has been administered for three months

There are two *alternative* circumstances in which the above treatment may be permitted:

1. The patient has consented, and the validity of the consent is confirmed by the Responsible Medical Officer (RMO) (i.e. the doctor in charge of the patient's treatment) or a doctor appointed by the MHAC. 'Consent' is the same as above.
2. If the patient refuses to give their consent, or is incapable of doing so, but the doctor's opinion on the appropriateness of the treatment is supported by a second opinion from a doctor appointed by the MHAC (see p.150). Before giving the second opinion, the doctor must consult other people as above. It is the view of one distinguished expert in the field that 'if the patient is competent and expressly refuses the treatment, it should only be imposed when there is substantial justification relating to the patient's health' (see Gostin, L. (1982), 'Compulsory Treatment in Psychiatry: Some Reflections on Self-Determination, Patient Competency and Professional Expertise', *Poly Law Review*, no. 86.

Once consent has been given, can the patient change their mind?

A patient may withdraw their consent at any time before or during the administration of the treatment. Once consent has been withdrawn, the procedures must start afresh as if the patient had never given consent. The only exception is that the RMO has power to continue with treatment even though consent has been withdrawn, if they consider that 'discontinuance would cause serious suffering to the patient'.

Can an open-ended second opinion be given to continue treatment indefinitely against the patient's wishes?

No. To guard against this possibility there is a duty on the RMO to provide the Secretary of State for Social Services with a report on the treatment and the patient's response if the treatment falls under either categories 1 or 2 above. This report must be furbished at 'regular intervals'. As the Secretary of State's supervisory tasks have been delegated to the MHAC, all enquiries and complaints in this respect should be addressed to the MHAC.

Can the provisions regarding consent or second opinions ever be disregarded?

Yes, but only where there is a case of extreme urgency. Urgent treatment is defined as treatment which is:

- immediately necessary to save the patient's life; *or*
- (not being irreversible) immediately necessary to prevent a serious deterioration in the patient's condition; *or*
- (not being irreversible or hazardous) immediately necessary to alleviate serious suffering by the patient; *or*
- (not being irreversible or hazardous) immediately necessary and represents the minimum interference necessary to prevent the patient from behaving violently or being a danger to themselves or others.

Any other treatment for mental disorder administered under the direction of the RMO

As long as the treatment is genuinely treatment for the mental disorder, such treatment can be administered without the patient's consent or a second opinion. Treatment for mental disorder includes nursing, occupational therapy, group therapy and so on, and in practice extends to virtually anything that a Responsible Medical Officer (RMO) deems to be helpful. Whether the treatment is for the mental disorder or for a physical disorder associated with the mental condition may often be difficult to ascertain. This matter does, however, raise an important point of principle associated with the civil liberties and the basic dignity of a detained patient. Under the common law, nobody is obliged to consent to treatment for a physical disorder, and the right to refuse treatment is a fundamental human right. (There may, however, be an exception to the consent rules where the patient is unconscious and delay would be dangerous.) The bodies of the mentally disabled should not be considered less their property than those of the mentally well. At the same time it must be recognised that certain mental conditions lead patients to refuse treatment for unrelated physical ailments. What, for example, should be done about the schizophrenic person who refuses treatment for an abscess or the removal of an appendix, for reasons associated with their mental and not their physical state? Any doctor who carried out treatment in these circumstances would be stretching their legal powers of intervention in a person's life to the very limits, and could probably only justify in law action that alleviated a life-threatening condition. Thus a mental patient who refused treatment for an ulcer, for reasons associated with their mental state, could not have the treatment forced upon them, unless the ulcer became life-threatening, e.g. if septicaemia developed.

If a person is detained for treatment (under section 3 Mental Health Act 1983) can that treatment be administered to them anywhere other than in the hospital to which they are admitted?

No. An important court decision of 1985 decided that the practice of admitting a patient for treatment (under section 3) and then granting leave of absence (see p.154) with the proviso that they should be treated in the community is unlawful, even if that treatment is to be under the auspices of the hospital doctor. If they are admitted for treatment under section 3 (which permits detention for six months) that treatment must be carried out in the hospital. Concern about the restraints of this ruling has led to a campaign by some activists to introduce a new order, the Community Treatment Order (see Gostin, L. (1986), *Mental Health Services Law and Practice* at 11:13).

PATIENTS' COMPLAINTS

If a person wants to complain that any of the rights set out above have been flouted or ignored, what do they do?

It is not enough to know a patient's rights. It is also essential to be familiar with the various procedures that a patient may invoke if they wish to register a complaint that one or more of their rights set out above has been violated. The main procedures for registering complaints by, or on behalf of, mental patients are therefore set out below. For a more detailed account of the procedures, see the *Patients' Rights Handbook* produced by MIND (1983), or Gostin, L. (1984), *Mental Health Services and the Law* (5th edn, Shaw and Sons).

General complaints: using the internal complaints procedures

Both the DSS and health authorities expect every mental institution to have some form of internal procedure for handling complaints by patients about staff. Thus the first avenue of complaint should always be to discover from the hospital or institution administrator how the internal complaints machinery operates. The normal procedure will be as follows:

Stage 1. The complaint should be directed to the person concerned either by the patient or by somebody acting on their behalf. If this is impossible or unsuccessful, the complaint should be made to a senior member of staff.

Stage 2. If Stage 1 does not resolve the matter, or the complaint is too serious or too delicate for Stage 1 to be the appropriate method, the complaint should be made in writing to the hospital, institution or district administrator. The matter will then be investigated either by the local health authority or by the MHAC. If the matter is considered to be very serious (e.g. allegations of brutality by staff, or systematic breaching of the mental health legislation) the health authority or the MHAC can set up an independent inquiry, which may or may not publish its results.

Stage 3. The Secretary of State has the power to order a full-scale inquiry into the most serious allegations under s.84 National Health Service Act 1977 (limited to NHS hospitals) and under s.125 Mental Health Act 1983. As with Stage 2 inquiries, the running of the inquiry will normally be delegated to the MHAC.

Anybody considering invoking the formal inquiry procedures under Stages 2 and 3 above would be well advised to consult with the legal department of MIND before initiating the complaint. If there is no local branch, the central office can always help (for details, see p.176).

Complaints about clinical judgement: using the special procedure

This procedure is the same procedure that is used in other National Health hospitals and is described in detail in Chapter 2, p.51.

Complaints of maladministration within the mental institution: using the Health Service Commissioner (Ombudsman)

The procedure for making complaints to an Ombudsman has already been explained in Chapters 2 and 3 (see pp.52 and 75). In summary, the Ombudsman, who is completely independent of the health services, can investigate any complaint by, or on behalf of, a person who has suffered injustice or hardship caused by their health authority through maladministration, inefficiency, or the failure to provide adequate services which they have a duty to provide. The procedure is initiated by a letter from the patient, or somebody acting on their behalf. The following are areas which the Ombudsman is, however, *not* empowered to investigate:

- matters which are to be the subject of inquiries set up by the Secretary of State (see p.148);
- matters relating to clinical judgement;
- matters which could be taken to a court or a MHRT (see p.157) unless it would be unreasonable to expect the patient to do so (the question of unreasonableness will be decided by the Ombudsman);
- the merits of discretionary decisions unless actual maladministration is demonstrated.

For a fuller account of the general Ombudsman procedures, see Chapter 2. A short leaflet introducing the powers and responsibilities of the Ombudsman in this field entitled *Can the Health Service Ombudsman Help You?* can be obtained together with any further information from:

The Health Service Commissioner for England, Church House, Great Smith St, London SW1P 3BW (tel: 071 276 2035); for Wales, 4th Floor, Pearl Assurance House, Greyfriars Road, Cardiff CF1 3AG (tel: 0222 394621); and for Scotland, Second Floor, 11 Melville Crescent, Edinburgh EH3 7LU (tel: 031 225 7465).

Complaints of professional misconduct of staff

The various procedures for lodging complaints of professional misconduct by doctors, nurses and other paramedical staff are set out in Chapter 2, p.51.

Complaints about detention itself: the lawfulness of detention?

This very important question is considered below in a separate section (see p.152).

Using the Mental Health Act Commission (MHAC)

What is the role and function of the Mental Health Act Commission (MHAC)?

One of the most important changes introduced in the Mental Health Act 1983 was the introduction of the Mental Health Act Commission for England and Wales.

What is the MHAC?

The MHAC is a body of approximately 92 people – doctors, nurses, lawyers, social workers, academics, psychologists, psychiatrists, and lay specialists – with responsibility for reviewing the effective operation of the 1983 Mental Health Act. Most members of the Commission are part-time members. The Commission is principally concerned with the operation of the Act in respect of detained patients, although its jurisdiction may be extended by the Secretary of State to include informal patients.

What are the tasks of the MHAC?

Its principal tasks are as follows:

- To prepare and if necessary update a Code of Practice to stand alongside the Mental Health Act 1983.
- To keep under review the exercise of the compulsory powers and duties under the Act. This clearly gives the MHAC very wide general powers. The MHAC reports directly to the Secretary of State, who in turn has the power to order an inquiry, to declare a health authority in default, and even to dissolve a health authority and reconstitute it with different members. It will be important to monitor the extent to which the MHAC is prepared to use these powers.
- To exercise a number of specific duties as follows:
  a) To arrange for a Commission member to visit all detained patients and interview them in private. Over a 20-month period to 1986 members of the MHAC made 937 visits to 523 mental institutions. During these visits, the MHAC member has the power to inspect any records they wish, and can use the occasion to make probing enquiries.
  b) To review any decision to withhold correspondence (see p.140) if requested to do so.
  c) To appoint the doctors who may provide second opinions and verify patients' consent to treatment (see p.144), and to provide the subsequent review reports on the treatment of such patients.
  d) To publish biannual reports on its activities.
  e) To deal with patients' complaints.

What complaints will the MHAC consider?

The MHAC will consider any complaint made by a detained patient relating to any matter which occurred during the period of their compulsory detention. This procedure exists in addition to the other procedures listed above, although in practice it is likely that the MHAC will make arrangements at a local level to avoid overlap, and double consideration of a complaint. This would be particularly likely in the case of complaints about clinical judgement where the special procedure applies (see p.51), and complaints that fall within the jurisdiction of the Ombudsman (see p.52) which must be made in the first instance to the hospital managers. If the patient remains dissatisfied a complaint to the MHAC may then be considered. The MHAC will also consider a complaint about the exercise by a hospital of their compulsory powers in respect of a detained patient, made by any person. The powers available to the MHAC member who is investigating a complaint are widely drawn, and are broadly similar to those of the Ombudsman. They include the right to visit and interview the patient in private, and to inspect the records relating to the patient's period of detention and treatment. The address of the Mental Health Act Commission is: MHAC, Maid Marian House, 56 Houndsgate, Nottingham NG1 6BG (tel: 0602 504040).

The detained patient's right to sue in the courts

It has been indicated at several points in this text that circumstances may arise where the above procedures are insufficient to satisfy the detained patient, who might thus wish to seek the alternative redress of a court action. This may be, for example, because they are seeking some financial compensation, or because they may wish to obtain a court declaration that a hospital or doctor has acted unlawfully (i.e. beyond their legal powers), as in the case of *Winch* v. *Jones*, in which an award of £27,000 was agreed against doctors and an RMO who made negligent medical recommendations (see Jessel, D. (1991), 'Convenience, compromise and cash', *New Law Journal*, 266–7). They may even wish to initiate a prosecution for a breach of the criminal law.

The use of the courts in any of the above circumstances is feasible but highly problematic. Unfortunately, a patient in these circumstances faces formidable problems, related to the unwillingness of the legal system to allow a person with a mental disorder an unfettered right to apply to the courts without preliminary examination of their state of mind. There is, in addition, a general statutory protection against litigation given to hospital staff in mental institutions who are acting 'with reasonable care and in good faith' (s.139 Mental Health Act 1983). Before being able to start proceedings, the patient will normally have first to satisfy the High Court (civil proceedings) or the Director of Public Prosecutions (criminal proceedings) that there are reasonable grounds for the action. For a wider discussion of this problem see Hoggett, B. (1990), *Mental Health Law*, and White, R. (1975), 'Mental Patients' Rights to Institute Criminal

Proceedings', *Solicitors' Journal,* no. 119, at p.788. It is important to be aware, however, that this preliminary hurdle imposed by s.139 does not apply to applications to the High Court for judicial review of a decision by a doctor, administrator, nearest relative or ASW on the grounds that their decision was either 'illegal' or 'irrational'. In other words, if a detained patient has been admitted to the institution without the correct procedures having been followed, or merely on the basis of a nearest relative's irrational fears, they have the right to apply immediately to the High Court for an order quashing their admission. This right is in addition to the rights of complaint outlined above, and the specific procedures requesting early discharge for detained patients are described in the next sections. Legal aid is available for such actions; thus anybody with a client in this predicament should consult a specialist solicitor or the legal division of MIND (see below) at the earliest opportunity (see also an article by Gunn, M. (1986), 'Judicial Review of Hospital Admissions and Treatment in the Community under the Mental Health Act 1983', *Journal of Social Welfare Law,* 290, and generally Gostin and Fennell, above at p.136).

The procedures for judicial review are described in more detail in Chapter 2.

DETAINED PATIENTS: GETTING OUT

When a patient has been detained in England or Wales under the Mental Health Act 1983 (see p.177 for relevant information on Scotland and Northern Ireland) it will have been as a result of a careful assessment of the patient's condition by a group of professionals, including in most cases an ASW. The Code of Practice provides much detailed guidance for all parties involved in compulsory admissions, and deals in particular with ways of resolving disputes between the parties involved. It is always to be hoped that, at least in the early stages, the detention, however traumatic, will be in the best interests of the patient. Despite this, it is nevertheless undoubtedly true that in the heat of the moment mistakes can be made, especially where relatives are pressurising the professionals involved to take immediate action 'for their protection'. It is also possible that once a patient is detained a process of institutionalisation sets in very quickly, and neither they, nor the staff caring for them, retain as urgent a sense of their rights to be released as the law allows and even, at times, encourages. In this section, the rights of the detained person to get out of the mental institution in which they are detained are examined.

When the prescribed period of detention has ended

Every compulsory admission to a mental institution will be for a prescribed period ranging from a minimum of 72 hours to a maximum of six months (see p.139). Once that period has come to an end the patient is free to leave, unless an application for a further period of detention has been made and been granted, which is a course of action open to the hospital managers if circumstances dictate. (Note, however, that a s.2, (28-day) detention cannot be followed consecutively by a further s.2 detention.) There are two additional sets of circumstances in which the person may be detained for a further short period, which apply to ex-detained and voluntary patients alike (see p.167).

Premature discharge by the RMO or hospital managers

At any time during the period of detention, the RMO or hospital managers have the power of discharge if they feel it is no longer necessary to detain the patient.

Leave of absence granted by the RMO

The RMO has the power to grant a detained patient leave of absence from the mental institution at any time, either for a specified period or indefinitely (i.e. to the end of the period of the detention order). The RMO can place conditions on the leave such as the patient's place of residence, or the attendance by the patient at a hospital for treatment or at an MHRT hearing. Social workers (who do not need to be ASWs) can play an important part in arranging and supervising such leave. A useful booklet on the housing of those discharged from mental institutions is Etherington, S. (1983), *Housing and Mental Health: a Guide for Housing Workers* (MIND/Circle 33). It should, however, be appreciated that the RMO retains the power to recall the patient at any time as long as the patient is subject to a compulsory detention order, if the RMO feels recall is necessary for the 'patient's health or safety' or the 'protection of others'. There are time limits on this power, which should be checked by reference to one of the specialist works detailed above. Furthermore, if the patient remains absent from the hospital for a continuous period of six months, he ceases to be liable to recall. The RMO cannot recall the patient for one night at the end of the six months, either simply to prevent the power from lapsing or to renew the 'section'.

Discharge by the nearest relative

- Admissions under section 3 (six months for treatment) are not permissible if the *nearest relative* (see below) objects, unless a successful application is made to the county court asking for that objection to be overruled on the grounds of its unreasonableness.
- In all cases of detention, other than those for up to 72 hours, the *nearest relative* has the power to discharge any patient who has been detained. The nearest relative must give the relevant hospital managers 72 hours' notice, preferably in writing, of their intention to discharge the patient. In addition, the nearest relative is entitled to instruct an independent doctor to visit the patient at any reasonable time to examine the patient in private, and to inspect the records relating to the patient's detention and treatment, in order to provide independent advice on the question of early discharge. This entitlement is guaranteed by statute and can be insisted upon by the relative. Any refusal to allow this right amounts to a criminal offence.
- If, following an application to discharge by a nearest relative, the RMO raises no objection, the patient will then be discharged after 72 hours. If, however, the RMO during the 72 hours provides the hospital managers with a report expressing the opinion that the patient if discharged 'would be likely to act in a manner dangerous to other persons or her/himself' (known as a Barring Certificate) the nearest relative's 'discharge order' will have no effect.

The *patient* can apply to be discharged by an MHRT within 14 days of an admission for assessment (s.2); the patient or the nearest relative can apply for discharge of the patient by an MHRT within 28 days of the issue of a Barring Certificate if the admission was for assessment and treatment (s.3). If no application for discharge within six months of a s.3 admission for treatment is made, the hospital managers should automatically refer the case to the MHRT for review (see p.157).

Who is the patient's nearest relative?

The law on this subject is a little complicated, and if in any doubt the detailed answer can be found in one of the guides to the Mental Health Act 1983, listed on p.136. In summary, a patient's nearest relative is the person who is highest on the list:

- *Any relative with whom the patient normally resides, or who normally cares for the patient.* If there is more than one such person priority will be given to the person highest on the list below.
- *Husband or wife* (unless permanently or indefinitely separated; this does not have to be a legal separation); or cohabitee of at least six months' cohabitation.
- *Son or daughter.* An adopted child is treated as if they are the child of the adoptive parents. A child whose parents are unmarried is treated as the son or daughter of the mother alone. The child must be 18 or over. A stepchild is not considered a son or daughter. In all these circumstances the oldest takes priority.
- *Father or mother.* Rules on adoptive, unmarried and step-parents are as above. Oldest takes priority.
- *Brother or sister.* Oldest takes priority.
- *Grandparent.* Oldest takes priority.
- *Grandchild.* Oldest takes priority.
- *Uncle or aunt.* Oldest takes priority.
- *Nephew or niece.* Oldest takes priority.
- *Non-related house/flat sharers.* This means any person, not related as above to the patient, but with whom the patient has resided for at least the past 5 years. Oldest takes priority.

If the nearest relative does not wish to exercise their powers under the Act, they may authorise somebody else to do so in writing (Regulation 14). This would be a useful precaution for a nearest relative to take, if they rarely see the patient or if they are anxious that their future relationship is not tainted by taking such action. It may be revoked at any time. If there is no nearest relative, or the nearest relative is incapable of acting as such through mental or other illness, or the nearest relative unreasonably objects to making an application for admission for treatment, an ASW, or any relative or person living with the patient at the time they were admitted to hospital, can apply to the local county court requesting the appointment of an alternative person as a nearest relative. Less than 12 cases per year are taken under this provision. It would, however, be a suitable course of action to take where a social worker is in strong disagreement with the nearest relative who has made the application, and wishes to ensure that a relative more in touch with the patient's needs is appointed in their place. The Code of Practice advises local authorities to have a policy on what they consider might amount to an unreasonable objection by a nearest relative to an application for admission for treatment.

Discharge by a Mental Health Review Tribunal (MHRT)

This section does not deal with the powers of the MHRT in relation to guardianship, as the chapter is limited to patients in mental institutions. The adviser who wishes to learn more about guardianship, which is a procedure whereby a person can be given powers to control the daily activities of a mentally disordered person remaining in the community (similar to the custody rights of a parent over a child), should consult one of the specialist books detailed above: of particular assistance is the *Social Work Law File on Mental Health.* The Code of Practice also contains much guidance on the use of guardianship. An article by Fisher, M. (1989) in the *Journal of Social Welfare Law* (1988), no. 5, provides a useful overview.

What is a Mental Health Review Tribunal (MHRT)?

MHRTs are independent tribunals which were originally established under the 1959 Mental Health Act to hear appeals by or on behalf of detained patients seeking to be discharged. Since 1983 the powers of these tribunals have been considerably enhanced with a corresponding increase in the number of cases brought before them (1006 in 1982, 3888 in 1985, 5834 in 1988). There is an MHRT for every region covered by a regional health authority in England (14) and one for Wales. Four regional tribunal offices provide the tribunals with administrative support. These offices will provide patients, social workers and relatives with information concerning the location of the tribunal for their particular area. Their addresses are as follows:

Clerk to the Tribunal, Mental Health Review Tribunals, Government Buildings, Canons Park, Honeypot Lane, Stanmore, Middlesex HA7 1AY (tel: 071 972 2000). (Tribunals served: NE Thames, NW Thames, East Anglia.)
Clerk to the Tribunal, Mental Health Review Tribunals, 3rd Floor, Cressington House, 249 St Mary's Rd, Garston, Liverpool L19 0NF (tel: 051 469 0095). (Tribunals served: North Western, Mersey, West Midlands; Special Hospital in Region: Ashworth.)
Clerk to the Tribunal, Mental Health Review Tribunals, Spur B, Block 3, Crown Buildings, Kingston Bypass Road, Surbiton, Surrey KT6 5QN (tel: 081 390 4166). (Tribunals served: Oxford, SE Thames, SW Thames, South Western, Wessex; Special Hospital in Region: Broadmoor.)
Clerk to the Tribunal, Mental Health Review Tribunals, Spur A, Block 5, Government Buildings, Chalfont Drive, Western Boulevard, Nottingham NG8 3R2 (tel: 0602 294222). (Tribunals served: Northern, Yorkshire, Trent; Special Hospital in Region: Rampton.)
Clerk to the Tribunal, Mental Health Review Tribunals, 2nd Floor, New Crown Buildings, Cathays Park, Cardiff CF1 3NQ (tel: 0222 825328). (Tribunal served: Wales.)

It has already been stressed earlier in this chapter that hospital managers have a duty to ensure that both patients and nearest relatives are informed at the earliest possible opportunity of the existence of these tribunals and the powers they possess. A useful article explaining the practical steps necessary in preparing an MHRT case is by Sander, A. (1989) in *Legal Action*, July at pp. 11–13.

What powers do MHRTs possess?

The MHRT has broad powers to discharge detained patients. These powers vary according to the circumstances of the detention. Patients detained for 72 hours or less are not entitled to apply to an MHRT. This applies to admission for assessment in cases of emergency (s.4); the doctor's or nurse's holding power (s.5); a warrant to search for and remove patients (s.135); and police powers over persons found in a public place (s.136).

PATIENT DETAINED UNDER AN ORDER IMPOSED BY THE COURT

The legal issues here are complex, as the patient will have committed a criminal offence, which may have been serious, and the MHRT will have a difficult task deciding whether it is safe to release the patient into the community. They have a number of options available to them, and the patient should, if possible, seek skilled legal advice and representation from the MIND/Law Society panel of specialists (see below) before an application to the MHRT is made. If time is pressing, however, it may be advisable to appeal anyway before legal advice can be obtained. For a summary of some recent important decisions on the limits on MHRT powers in restriction order cases, see Harbour, T., in *Legal Action*, October 1988.

PATIENT DETAINED UNDER A RESTRICTION ORDER IMPOSED BY THE COURT

Broadly speaking, the MHRT must discharge the patient if it is satisfied that the grounds for detaining them no longer exist. The burden of proof rests with the patient. Again the legal issues are complex and will vary according to whether the patient is detained for *assessment* (s.2) or detained for *treatment* (s.3). The same advice applies as for Restriction Order patients – obtain expert legal advice before lodging the appeal.

A good study of MHRT decision-making processes is Peay, J. (1989), *A Study of Decision-making under the Mental Health Act 1983* (Clarendon Press).

Are there any helpful further sources of information?

The main text which is useful and up to date is Gostin, L., and Fennell, P. (1992), *Mental Health: Tribunal Procedure* (Longman). This is a detailed guide to effective representation at MHRTs, and is an essential reference source for anybody who is planning an appeal.

Who sits on these tribunals?

Tribunal members are drawn from panels of lawyers (including circuit judges and recorders), medical practitioners and lay people with experience in administration and knowledge of social services, or other relevant qualifications or skills. All appointments are made by the Lord Chancellor. Most tribunals will be composed of three members: a lawyer (who will be the president), a medical practitioner, and a lay person. If the appeal concerns a patient subject to a Restriction Order (see p.159) the president will be a circuit judge or recorder. Research by Fennell suggests that the lawyer is normally the dominant figure on the tribunal (see Fennell (1977), 'The Mental Health Review Tribunal: a Question of Imbalance', *British Journal of Law and Society,* no. 4, p.186). Anybody with a close knowledge of, or involvement with, the patient should not be a member of the tribunal, but a person is not precluded from membership simply because they were on a panel which conducted a previous hearing involving the patient.

How do you apply to a tribunal?

There are four ways in which matters can come before a tribunal:

- application by patient;
- application by nearest relative;
- automatic referral by hospital managers;
- referral by the Secretary of State for Social Services or (if Restricted Order patient) by Home Secretary.

Table 5.1 sets out the circumstances and time limits for these categories. Referrals by government ministers in category four can in theory be made 'at any time if the minister thinks fit'. In practice, such applications are extremely rare and are only likely to be made in exceptional circumstances, where, for example, important new evidence has come to light since an earlier hearing.

The Rules of Procedure governing applications to MHRTs, and the subsequent conduct of the case, are the Mental Health Tribunal Rules 1983 SI 942. A useful, detailed analysis of these rules is contained in Gostin, L., and Fennell, P. (1992), above at p.159.

The procedure whereby a patient or nearest relative can make an application is relatively simple.

Procedure for appeal against admission for assessment (s.2)

Only the patient can appeal against an admission for assessment (although a nearest relative can try to discharge the patient by writing to the

Table 5.1

Category of admission, etc.	Application		Automatic reference by the hospital managers (s.68)
	Patient	Nearest relative	
Admission for assessment (s.2)	Within the first 14 days of admission	—	—
Admission for treatment (s.3)	Within the first 6 months of admission, during the next 6 months, and during each subsequent period of 1 year	Within 28 days after being informed that RMO has issued a report barring nearest relative from discharging patient	If MHRT has not reviewed case within the first 6 months of admission; thereafter, if MHRT has not considered case within period of 3 years (1 year for child under the age of 16)
Hospital order without restrictions (s.37)	Between 6 and 12 months after the making of the order, and during each subsequent period of 1 year	Between 6 and 12 months after the making of the order, and during each subsequent period of 1 year	Reference by managers if a period of 3 years has elapsed since case was last considered by MHRT (1 year for child under the age of 16)
Patient with restriction order or restriction direction (defined s.79) who is in hospital	Between 6 and 12 months after the making of the order or direction, and during each subsequent period of 1 year	—	Reference by Home Secretary in respect of any case not considered by MHRT within the last 3 years
Restricted patient who has been conditionally discharged and is recalled to hospital (s.42, and see s.75)	As if restriction order were made afresh on date of recall	As if restriction order were made afresh on date of recall	Reference by Home Secretary within 1 month after recall
Restricted patient who has been conditionally discharged and not recalled (s.42, and see s.75)	Between 1 and 2 years after conditional discharge, and during each subsequent period of 2 years	—	—

Reproduced from Gostin, L. (1983), *A Practical Guide to the Mental Health Act 1983* (MIND) hospital managers: see p.155). The appeal must be initiated by the patient writing a letter to the offices of the tribunal serving the area of the institution where the patient is detained (see p.158 for addresses). Anybody can write the letter on the patient's behalf. The letter should give the patient's name, the hospital address, the name, address and relationship of the nearest relative (if any), and the name and address of anybody authorised to represent them. As speed is of the essence, the letter should also stress that this is an admission for assessment case. Nothing else need be said in the letter. The letter should be sent by first-class post. An MHRT hearing should then be arranged for a date no later than seven days after the office receives the application. At the hearing the MHRT will have before it the patient's admission documents and medical recommendations, but little else, given the time available. The MHRT will endeavour to inform the nearest relative, the ASW involved in the 'section', and the hospital managers of the hearing, and request their attendance at the hearing.

Procedure in appeals against admission for assessment (long-term cases) (s.3)

The procedure to initiate these appeals is the same as for the first category, except that the nearest relative may also appeal. The initiating letter should set out the section of the Mental Health Act 1983 under which the patient is detained (s.3). All parties will be informed by the tribunal office of the application, and the hospital managers will be asked to provide the tribunal with a Rule 6 Statement within three weeks. The Rule 6 Statement will provide a number of formal details relating to the patient's detention. In addition, the hospital will provide an up-to-date medical report on the patient's condition (drawn up by the RMO), including the RMO's views on the patient's suitability for release and, where practicable, a report on the patient's social circumstances, drawn up either by a hospital social worker or by a social worker from the local social services department. This latter report may have considerable influence on the outcome of the hearing. It should cover the patient's home and family circumstances, the attitude of relatives to the release, opportunities to find employment, accommodation and other support within the community. Those writing the report should not forget that, under s.117 Mental Health Act 1983, both the district health authority and the social services department have a duty to provide, in co-operation with relevant voluntary agencies, after-care services for patients who have been detained for treatment. This point should always be driven home, as tactfully as possible, to the relevant authorities in the patient's home area. At the same time, as the hospital social worker may not have the information or access to the information that the local fieldwork social worker may have, co-operation between the two social workers is an important part of the process of preparing the report. Eventually, once all the information has been obtained, a hearing date will be fixed. It is regrettably often several weeks before this can be done.

What happens at the hearing?

Whenever an application is made there must always be a hearing, unless the application is withdrawn. Before the hearing (normally, though not necessarily, on the same day) the medical member of the tribunal will examine the patient. The hearing will then take place, normally at the institution where the patient is detained. It will be in private unless the patient requests that it be held in public. It is intended to be an informal hearing and it is not uncommon for the applicant to be addressed by a first name, to be allowed to smoke and so forth. Witnesses can be called to the hearing, and the tribunal may ask the patient to leave while others are giving evidence, although it must explain why. The writers of any written reports to the tribunal – e.g. medical reports, social work reports – have the right to request that their reports are not shown to the appellant. They must, however, give a reason for this request, and the tribunal has the right to overrule the request. The tribunal itself has the power to withhold any documents from the patient if it believes 'disclosure would adversely affect the health or welfare of the patient or others'. It cannot, however, withhold any documents from the patient's legal representative, or any other representative that the tribunal has deemed to be 'qualified' to represent them (e.g. a social worker, with the relevant skills). Once a report has been released to a patient it becomes the patient's property. At the end of the hearing the tribunal will give its decision, which may be a majority decision. This will subsequently be committed to writing, which will then be sent to the applicant. The decision must be set out clearly, with proper, intelligible and adequate reasons.

Is there an appeal procedure against an MHRT decision?

The only way of appealing against a decision of an MHRT is through the High Court and even then in very limited circumstances. This will certainly need the assistance of a lawyer. A MIND or Law Society Panel solicitor should be approached for advice on this question.

Who can help the patient with the application?

An applicant is entitled to instruct an independent psychiatrist to visit the patient in the institution where they are detained (unless they are subject to a Restriction Order), to examine them in private, and to inspect any records relating to their detention. The MHAC or MIND can advise on appropriate doctors for this task. The psychiatrist owes a duty of confidence to the patient, with the following exception:

> A consultant psychiatrist who becomes aware, even in the course of a confidential relationship, of information which leads him, in the exercise of what the court considers a sound professional judgement, to fear that ... decisions may be made on the basis of inadequate information and with a real risk of consequential danger to the public, is entitled to take such steps as are reasonable in all the circumstances to communicate the grounds of his concern to the responsible authorities.

Hospital managers should provide patients with as much help as they need in preparing their case. The DSS, MIND and MHRTs provide a series of helpful leaflets. It is, however, perhaps a little unrealistic to expect too much from a hospital in this respect, as they are presumably opposed to the application, and it is their judgement that is being brought into question. At the tribunal the patient can have a person of their choice to represent them at the hearing (so long as it is not another patient in their hospital) and also a friend to accompany them. If this person is a lawyer, the lawyer's fees can be paid for under the Legal Aid Scheme (ABWOR: see p.5). The lawyer, if a solicitor, will be a member of a specialist panel under the overall regulation of the Mental Health and Disability Subcommittee of the Law Society.

Discharge from emergency admissions following arrest by police in a public place

The police have a special power to remove a person from a public place to a place of safety if they reasonably believe that person to be suffering from a mental disorder and in immediate need of care or control. The police are advised that a place of safety under this section should normally be a hospital. A hospital is not, however, legally obliged to admit a person detained in this way, and therefore it is normal practice for the police to take the person to the nearest police station and then seek the immediate assistance of an ASW, who will probably attend the police station personally to assess the person's mental condition. The power of the police to detain a person in this way will lapse as soon as they have been examined and interviewed and, if necessary, suitable arrangements have been made for their care. In any event the police cannot detain a person in this way for more than 72 hours. The Code of Practice states that a record of the person's time of arrival must be made immediately they reach the place of safety. They are also entitled to have another person informed of their arrest and whereabouts, and a right of access to legal advice (see Chapter 6 at p.195). For further information and detailed research on the use made by police of this section, consult Rogers, A., and Faulkner, A. (1987), *A Place of Safety* (MIND), and Bean et al. (1991), *Out of Harm's Way: MIND's Research into Police and Psychiatric Action under s.136 of the Mental Health Act 1983* (MIND).

THE VOLUNTARY PATIENT CLIENT IN A MENTAL INSTITUTION

Voluntary patients account for the vast majority (approximately 90 per cent) of the resident population of mental institutions in the United Kingdom. The Code of Practice specifically states that informal (or voluntary) admission is preferred where possible, but it also suggests that:

> Compulsory admission should be considered where the patient's current mental state, together with reliable evidence of past experience, indicates a strong likelihood that they will change their mind about informal admission prior to actual admission to hospital with a resulting risk to their health or safety or that of other persons.

Social workers will come into contact with voluntary patients far more frequently than with detained patients. It is thus a matter of great importance that the patient client can be given good, clear advice on their legal entitlements during the period of their residence in the institution, which may in some cases be for the rest of their lives.

Does a voluntary patient have to consent to treatment?

A voluntary patient in a mental institution is in exactly the same position as a patient in a general hospital – i.e. the administering of any form of treatment without their consent constitutes an assault or battery (trespass to the person) and is therefore unlawful. Consent can either be express, or inferred by the patient's action, e.g. offering an arm for an injection. The patient must, however, be given sufficient information about the nature of the treatment in order to make a reasoned decision whether to consent or not. Problems will clearly arise where the patient is frail, isolated, confused, or because of their condition simply unable to understand enough to be able to consent at all. In these circumstances, the law is at present very unclear. A number of well-publicised cases in recent years concerning the rights of parents to refuse consent for their children to receive contraceptive advice, or the rights of parents, doctors or courts to decide whether an abortion or a sterilisation operation should be performed on a woman of severe mental handicap, deemed incapable of consenting, have failed to clarify the position. The law on this issue is currently very unsatisfactory (see discussion on p.143 in the context of detained patients). What is clear is that, at all times, every effort should be made by medical staff to ensure that patients should be consulted and kept informed of the nature of their treatment to the fullest extent possible within the constraints imposed by their particular condition. There is one situation where the need for consent can be dispensed with, namely that which the law defines as 'necessity'. 'Necessity' would include circumstances where treatment is necessary to save the patient's life, and they cannot give consent (because, for example, they are unconscious) and are not known to object to the treatment. It would also include the minimum treatment necessary to prevent a patient from injuring themselves, or those around them – e.g. to subdue a violent patient in an emergency. Such treatment should, however, only be administered under the supervision of a medical practitioner.

Can a voluntary patient leave the mental institution whenever they wish?

The answer to this question is a qualified 'yes'. As with consent to treatment, the voluntary patient is in exactly the same position as anybody who is not detained. They are free to leave the institution whenever they wish, and any attempt to restrain them, either physically or by locking the doors, would amount to an unlawful imprisonment for which they could sue for financial compensation. What has to be recognised, however, is that it is always open to the hospital managers to convert the patient's voluntary status into that of a detained patient if they believe that the conditions necessary for detention have been satisfied. Furthermore, because the paperwork necessary to make an application for detention can take a little time, and the personnel involved in the application (supervising doctor, ASW or nearest relative) may not be readily available, the Mental Health Act 1983 has introduced a system of 'holding powers' for both doctors and nurses while the application is being prepared.

Doctor's holding power

If the medical practitioner in charge of a voluntary patient's treatment (or a medical practitioner on the hospital staff to whom they have delegated the task) forms the opinion that an application for the compulsory admission of the patient 'ought to be made', they should furnish a report to the hospital managers explaining why. Once the report is received, the hospital managers have the power to detain the patient for up to 72 hours. This power can also be used to detain an in-patient receiving treatment for a physical illness in a general hospital, provided the criteria for admission under the Mental Health Act 1983 are satisfied.

Nurse's holding power

Sometimes the relevant medical practitioner is not immediately available to make the application and a nurse is faced with the problem of what to do about the voluntary patient who wishes to discharge themselves in circumstances where the nurse considers it dangerous to do so. The Mental Health Act 1983 has provided a limited holding power to nurses in this situation. The limitations are as follows:

- The nurse must be of the 'prescribed class' (a first-level nurse who is qualified in nursing mentally disabled patients as defined in the Mental Health (Nurses) Order 1983).
- The nurse must record in writing on a prescribed form her or his opinion that the patient is mentally disordered to such an extent that it is necessary for the patient's health or safety, or for the protection of others, for them to be immediately restrained from leaving the hospital and it is not practicable to secure the immediate attendance of the relevant medical practitioner. Compulsory detention is permitted only from the time the form is lodged with the hospital managers to the time the relevant medical practitioner arrives to assess the patient, and in any event for no longer than 6 hours. Thereafter, unless the medical practitioner initiates procedures for further detention, the patient is free to leave.

The power is limited to patients receiving in-patient treatment for a mental disorder, i.e. it cannot be used against non-psychiatric patients in general hospitals.

Additional powers under the general law

There is a general power under the common law for anybody to restrain physically a person who is clearly suffering from a mental disorder, and who presents an imminent danger to either themselves or others. This power is, however, severely limited and does not extend to the administering of medication or other treatment. It should only be exercised in an emergency, for as long as it is necessary to call the relevant member of the medical staff to consider the exercise of one of the special powers above.

Can a voluntary patient vote?

It is perfectly possible for a voluntary patient to vote so long as they are registered at their 'place of residence' as a voter. There are two alternative places which they might register as their 'place of residence':

1. The institution where they are in residence, as long as it is not 'maintained wholly or mainly for the reception and treatment of persons suffering from mental disorder'. Patients who can register

under this category must not be mentally disordered and the category normally is limited to those who are living in the institution because they have nowhere else to go. The sorts of institution where registration would be appropriate are old peoples' homes, nursing homes, hostels and psychiatric wings of general hospitals. If in doubt as to the categorisation of the institution or the patient, the second method of registration is likely to be more appropriate.

2. Either the address where they would be residing were they not currently residing in the mental institution or, if this is not possible to provide, any address in the United Kingdom where they have once resided. This address must be provided in an official Declaration on a special form available from HMSO. Hospital managers have a duty to inform any voluntary patient who is not already registered elsewhere as a voter of their right to make such a Declaration. The Declaration must be made annually, on or before the qualifying date for registration. It must be made 'without assistance', which means that the patient must be able to understand the information requested on the form even though they might need physical assistance in filling out the form. Once the Declaration has been completed, the patient has the right to vote either by post or in person.

The issues involved in the voting rights of the mentally disabled are complex and controversial. The Declaration system, for example, effectively prevents mental hospital in-patients from voting for a candidate who represents the constituency in which their hospital is situated, which may in reality be their permanent home. The form itself is written in formal, complex language. An interesting study of the voting rights of mental patients has been written by Linda Ward of the Campaign for People with Mental Handicaps. For those who wish to know more about the issues, this booklet is recommended: Ward (1987) *Talking Points No. 6: The Right to Vote*. For further official assistance see HC (83) 14 Health Services Development – Representation of the People Act 1983: Electoral Registration in Mental Illness and Mental Handicap Hospitals (statement of government policy) and DSS leaflet (MH) *Voting in Elections* which can be obtained from DSS Store, Health Publication Unit, No. 2 Site, Manchester Rd, Heywood, Lancs OL10 2PZ.

Can a voluntary patient's mail be opened or withheld?

Neither the incoming or the outgoing mail of a voluntary patient may be opened or withheld.

Is a voluntary patient's right to sue in the courts subject to the same restrictions as those of a detained patient?

Although the Mental Health Act does not expressly exempt voluntary patients from the provisions and restraints relating to legal action that affect detained patients (see p.152) a court has held in one case, *R* v. *Runighian* 1977, *Criminal Law Review*, 361, that hospital staff do not have the same protection against legal actions by voluntary patients as they do against actions by detained patients. This means, for example, that a voluntary patient has every right to sue a member of the hospital staff who has wrongfully used force against them, or administered treatment without their consent, without recourse to s.139 (see p.152). In these circumstances legal advice from a sympathetic solicitor or MIND should be sought. The right to initiate judicial review proceedings is also available to a voluntary patient (see p.153 and Chapter 3).

Will the mental institution ever give a voluntary patient any financial assistance?

The powers of the Secretary of State to pay 'pocket money' to in-patients who would otherwise be without the resources to meet their personal expenses apply equally to voluntary and detained patients (see p.141). Hospital managers should be approached on behalf of voluntary patients in appropriate cases. See MIND Policy Paper 1 (1983), *Money in Hospital* (MIND).

What complaints procedures exist for voluntary patients?

With the one important exception of access to the MHAC, access to all the complaints procedures described on p.148 for detained patients is available for voluntary patients, with like procedures and remedies as for detained patients. While the Secretary of State for Social Services has, under the Mental Health Act 1983, the power to direct the MHAC to 'keep under review the care and treatment of informal patients', he has not yet directed them to do so. All voluntary patients should see their baseline as stated by Larry Gostin in the following way: 'the rights of voluntary patients should be no different from those of any patient having treatment for a physical illness in a general hospital'. Any lowering of standards by hospitals and mental institutions below this norm should be challenged either directly or indirectly through a complaint to the Health Service Ombudsman (see Chapter 2 at p.52).

GENERAL POWERS OF OTHERS TO MANAGE THE PROPERTY AND AFFAIRS OF THE MENTALLY DISABLED

The majority of mentally disabled people are capable of managing their own affairs, sometimes with the assistance of caring relatives, friends or professionals. It is always desirable that, as long as it remains feasible, this should continue to be the case. There does come a time, however, in the lives of some mentally disabled people when they really cannot manage their affairs at all, and it is necessary to look to alternative solutions. The problem is particularly acute in the case of the very elderly, where the process of mental decline is slow but in some cases can be predicted. According to the Legal Director of MIND, by the end of the century the number of people in the UK over 85 will have doubled to over 1 million. He estimated that 'at present more than 20 per cent of those over 80 suffer from some degree of dementia which to a greater or lesser degree renders them unable to make decisions on their own' (*The Times*, 24 June 1987). There are a number of possible remedies to this problem, the choice of which will depend upon the severity of the problem, of which the most extreme resolution is to vest control of all the person's affairs in the Court of Protection (see p.173). Consistent with the principle of the minimum interference necessary to protect the individual, there is set out below a summary of the options, starting with the least level of interference.

Arranging for the person's income to be paid direct to another, who will manage their affairs for them

Social security benefits (see below and Chapters 8 and 9, p.312) can be paid by the DSS directly to a 'suitable person' if the recipient's mental disability is such that they are unable to manage their property and affairs. The 'suitable person' will then be charged with the job of managing the person's affairs for them. Hospital 'pocket money' (see p.141) can be paid in the same way. There are also provisions under s.142 Mental Health Act whereby the salary, pension or other benefits payable to the employee of a government department (and some other categories of employment) can be paid directly to the person who is managing their affairs.

Setting up a trust for the benefit of the mentally disabled person

Sometimes there are advantages in setting up a trust fund for the benefit of a mentally disabled person, whereby the trustees will administer all the money that is paid into the trust for the benefit of that person. This may well be the most suitable way of managing the affairs of a person suffering from severe mental handicap or long-term mental disorder. There are a number of administrative and fiscal advantages in this method. A solicitor, MIND or MENCAP should be consulted before setting up such a trust.

Guardianship

It has already been mentioned earlier in the chapter that guardianship is an alternative course of action to compulsory detention for dealing with people who are suffering from a mental disorder. If a person has been accepted as the guardian of another who is suffering from mental disorder they have power to require the patient to reside at a particular place (not being a mental hospital), and to attend at places and times specified for medical treatment, occupation, training or education (for further information see p.157).

Enduring power of attorney

Since the coming into force of the Enduring Power of Attorney Act 1985, any person anticipating a deterioration in their mental condition can appoint another person to have power of attorney on their behalf in the event of their subsequently becoming incapable of managing their own affairs. Certain formalities have to be observed when the power is first drawn up, and the power will only become effective if registered with the

Court of Protection (see below), which must first be satisfied that the person is no longer mentally capable, i.e. by reason of mental disorder has become incapable of managing and administering their property and affairs, and also must give close relatives the opportunity to challenge the registration, if they think it inappropriate for any reason. A solicitor's advice should always be sought before creating an enduring power of Attorney. For more information consult Cretney, S. (1989), *Enduring Power of Attorney* (2nd edn) (Family Law: Jordan and Son).

Using the Court of Protection

The Court of Protection (which is an office of the High Court) exists to manage and administer the property and affairs of people who are incapable of doing so themselves by reason of their mental disorder. Its work is under the direction of judges and masters of the High Court, who delegate the work of visiting and interviewing those in its care to a panel of Lord Chancellor's Visitors, a body of lawyers, doctors and civil servants specially selected for this task. Approximately 220 people currently work for the Court of Protection. These people have to manage the affairs of some 23,000 people, which means that, with the best will in the world, their intervention is essentially passive.

Procedure

Anybody can apply to bring another into the Court of Protection: a friend, a relative, a social worker or even a creditor. The application must be supported by the evidence of one doctor, who can be the person's GP and need not be specialised in mental illness. The Court of Protection will supply the forms. The procedure to be followed is formal. The patient will be given notice of the application unless the court feels it to be unnecessary, as the patient will not be capable of understanding what is happening. The procedure is complex. For further information on the procedure and the consequences of the application, consult Gostin, L. (1983), *The Court of Protection* (MIND). Once the application has been accepted, the Court has exclusive control over all the patient's property and affairs. This control will continue until the patient either recovers (which is rare) or dies. It is common for the Court to appoint a person close to the patient (often the person who made the application) as their receiver, with specific powers relating to the affairs of the patient, e.g. to receive their income, to pay certain bills, to effect a property sale. The receiver will, however, be closely monitored by the Court and will normally have to submit regular accounts of their activities in relation to the patient's affairs to the Court. If the matters to be dealt with are very simple and straightforward, and little more than fine tuning of the patient's financial arrangements, the Court of Protection might agree to use their informal procedure, called the Short Procedure, which gives limited authority to an individual over the finances of another, without the necessity of a full-blown application. Advice on this procedure can be obtained in the first instance from the Court of Protection advice line on 071 269 7358. The procedure is free.

Other considerations

There are a number of factors that need to be borne in mind before considering an application to the Court of Protection. First, the Court charges fees for its services which are deducted from the patient's estate (but see above on the 'Short Procedure'). Second, there is no automatic review of the continuing need for the patient to be under the Court of Protection. An application has to be made for discharge, and only around 60 such applications are made annually. Third, the procedure of the Court is slow and impersonal. Fourth, the fact of the application with its consequential removal from the patient of the basic right to manage their own affairs may result in the further alienation of that person from those around them. Fifth, there may be no alternative.

The address of the Court of Protection is as follows: Court of Protection, Stewart House, 24 Kingsway, London WC2B 6HD.

BACK IN THE COMMUNITY: LEGAL DUTIES OF THE LOCAL AUTHORITY

Once a mental patient has returned to the community the legal responsibility for their care shifts from the mental institution to the district health authority and the local social services department. There are several areas of statutory responsibility:

1. *Chronically Sick and Disabled Persons Act 1970*. This states that all the duties imposed on local authorities by this statute towards the

physically disabled extend also to those who are 'substantially or permanently handicapped by illness, injury or congenital deformity' or suffering from mental disorder *of any description* (my emphasis). Thus the scope of this Act is wider than those suffering from mental disorder under the Mental Health Act 1983 and will extend, for example, to episodic disorder and the intervals between disorder. For a detailed account of the nature and extent of these duties, see Chapter 4 at p.86.

2. *National Health Service Act 1977.* This imposes a duty on health authorities to provide facilities for prevention, care and after-care, if appropriate, to those suffering from mental disorder within the Mental Health Act 1983. But this duty has been significantly extended by s.117 of the Mental Health Act 1983 in respect of patients released from hospital following a s.3 detention (i.e. detention for up to six months for treatment) whether their detention was in a mental institution, a 'special hospital' or a prison. Towards this category of ex-patient, both the district health authority and the social services department have a duty, in co-operation with relevant voluntary agencies, to provide after-care services until they are satisfied that the person no longer needs such a service. Such ex-patients will also now almost certainly fall into the group of people for whom care packages have to be designed under the National Health Service and Community Care Act 1990 (see Chapter 4 at p.89).
3. *The Homelessness Legislation* (see generally Chapter 10 at p.320). It can be argued that any person who is homeless and who is mentally disabled is potentially at risk, and therefore 'vulnerable' for the purposes of *priority need* duties. The Code of Guidance on homelessness for local authorities (see Chapter 10 at p.320) states that:

> Many people discharged from psychiatric and mental handicap hospitals and local authority hostels into the community may be regarded as vulnerable. Health authorities have an express duty under advice contained in DOH circulars *HC(90)23* and *LASSL(90)11* to implement a specifically tailored care programme for patients considered for discharge from psychiatric hospitals and all new patients accepted by the specialist psychiatric services.

Because of the danger that the liaison arrangements between housing, health and social services may fall down, local authorities are also directed in the Code to be 'sensitive to direct approaches from discharged patients who are homeless'.

4. *Housing Associations Act 1985*. This Act, together with a number of government circulars, enables registered housing associations to provide special hostel accommodation for mentally disabled people under a variety of joint funding arrangements with local authorities and charities.

SPECIAL FINANCIAL BENEFITS FOR THE MENTALLY DISABLED

Welfare benefit advice for the mentally disabled is a specialised and complex business. Benefits will not be dealt with in any detail at this stage, as most of them are dealt with elsewhere in the book. These include attendance allowance, invalid care allowance (carers), mobility allowance, severe disablement allowance, vaccine damage payments, statutory sick pay, invalidity benefits, income support and housing benefit. For further information, consult the MIND *A–Z of Welfare Benefits for People with a Mental Illness* by Catherine Grimshaw, the two CPAG handbooks, and the *Disability Rights Handbook*. Particular attention should be paid to the chart in the CPAG handbook, setting out which benefits may continue while the claimant is in hospital, and for how long.

SOURCES OF FURTHER ASSISTANCE

Organisations

Mention has been made throughout this chapter of the use of Citizens Advice Bureaux, and specialist solicitors whose names can be obtained from MIND and the Legal Aid Solicitors Referral Lists. There are also three specialist organisations that offer skilled advice and assistance:

MIND, 22 Harley St, London W1N 2ED (tel: 071 637 0741) (National HQ)

North-west: 21 Ribblesdale Place, Preston PR1 3NA;
North: 158 Durham Rd, Gateshead NE8 4EL;

South-east: 4th Floor, 24–32 Stephenson Way, London NW1 2HD;
South-west: Bluecoat House, Saw Close, Bath BA1 1EY;
Trent and Yorkshire: The White Building, Fitzalan Square, Sheffield S1 2AY;
Wales: 23 St Mary St, Cardiff CFI 2AA;
West Midlands: Princess Chambers (3rd Floor), 52–4 Lichfield St, Wolverhampton WV1 1DG.

MIND is a campaigning body which seeks to promote the rights of people suffering from mental disability. MIND has a national headquarters, seven regional offices and nearly 200 affiliated local groups. It offers advice and information on all aspects of mental health, runs courses and conferences, and issues a wide range of publications. It has its own legal department which offers an MHRT representation service, and is occasionally willing to take test cases on issues of general importance in the higher courts. It will also offer advice, information and skilled specialist referral. If possible, enquiries should be in writing because of the great pressure on the telephone service. All the MIND publications referred to in this chapter can be obtained direct from the MIND Bookshop, 071 608 3752.

MENCAP, 123 Golden Lane, London EC1Y ORT (tel: 071 454 0454).

MENCAP offers an extensive range of services for mentally handicapped people and their families through its 12 regional offices, 500 local societies and central London office. It supports research into the causes of mental handicap, and runs a specialist bookshop.

Scotland and Northern Ireland

Surprisingly little of the material in this chapter is of direct application to Scotland or Northern Ireland. The mental health legislation in each country is different in a number of key respects from that in England and Wales.

Scotland

In Scotland the relevant legislation is the Mental Health (Scotland) Act 1984. For a guide to the contents of this legislation and other related advice, contact: The Scottish Association for Mental Health (tel: 031 229

9687). This association is an independent voluntary body devoted to broad issues of mental disability and mental health.

The statutory body in Scotland charged with responsibility for exercising 'protective functions in respect of persons who may by reason of mental disorder be incapable of adequately protecting their persons or their interests' is: The Mental Welfare Commission (tel: 031 225 7034).

Northern Ireland

In Northern Ireland the relevant legislation is contained in the Mental Health (Northern Ireland) Order 1986. A detailed guide to this legislation can be obtained from the Department of Mental Health (tel: 0232 520000). A shorter summary of the law can be obtained from: The Northern Ireland Association for Mental Health (tel: 0232 328274). This organisation is an independent voluntary body devoted to promoting mental health in the community through information and education and works towards improvements in services for the psychiatric patient and ex-patient. The rough equivalent body in Northern Ireland to the Scottish Mental Welfare Commission and the MHAC for England and Wales is: The Mental Health Commission (tel: 0232 651157). Finally, although a little out of date, the MIND *Mental Health Yearbook* of 1981–2 still provides a massive and unrivalled data bank of addresses and other sources of help and information on mental health issues throughout the United Kingdom.

Chapter 6

Civil rights and the police

Relationships between clients and the police can be a critical element in the practice of many engaged in social work. There are, of course, a number of circumstances in which co-operation between social workers and the police is normal, and indeed essential, to the effective carrying out of the social worker's tasks, e.g. seeking place of safety orders, exchanging information regarding child abuse, seeking protection from violence in the course of daily work, etc. There will also inevitably be a number of circumstances where the social worker's client may be in conflict with the police. In these circumstances, it is essential that the social worker has a clear and accurate knowledge of the precise legal rights and duties both of themselves and of their client. As there will invariably be a sense of drama and urgency wherever there is police intervention, a vague and woolly notion of legal rights will be useless. Precise, accurate knowledge is essential to counter the tendency of some over-zealous police officers to ride roughshod over proper procedures in their anxiety to obtain a conviction, and to give a client the detached, professional advice they need at such moments of crisis.

There are three particular sets of circumstances in which the social worker may be pulled into a situation of potential conflict with the police, in the interests of their client:

- A social worker may be asked in an emergency to advise a client, in conflict with the police, on their civil rights relating to such matters as search, arrest, or detention.
- A social worker may be called to a police station to sit in on an interview with a juvenile, or mentally ill or mentally handicapped suspect.

- A social worker may be asked to hand over to the police confidential records regarding a client.

In the course of this chapter, each of these three situations will be closely examined. The chapter will also examine a wide range of questions that may face the client or the social worker in those dramatic moments of conflict that characterise the early contacts between a police officer and a suspect.*

SOURCES OF INFORMATION

Most of the law relating to police powers and duties is to be found in the Police and Criminal Evidence Act 1984 (commonly abbreviated to PACE). The Act is supplemented by five Codes of Practice which have been regularly amended since their introduction. In addition, there has also been in existence since 1988 a Code of Practice for Police Computer Systems (see Chapter 2, p.32). The Codes can be obtained in full from HMSO, and are also reproduced in full in several of the main texts. They are very useful documents in any social worker's library. Although a Code of Practice contains guidelines, and not law, a failure to follow any aspect of the Codes is treated by senior police officers as a serious matter that may lead to disciplinary proceedings. A failure to follow the Codes can in some circumstances provide a defendant with a defence against a charge of assaulting a police officer in the execution of his duty, and can lead to confession evidence being deemed inadmissible (see p.203). Anybody who believes that the police have failed to follow PACE or the Codes of Practice in any material detail should always inform their solicitor of the fact, as it might be relevant to their defence. In addition, there is a Complaints Procedure that allows an aggrieved person to lodge a complaint against a particular police officer (see Chapter 2 at p.31).

Here, in alphabetical order, are a number of useful texts that provide more detail on every aspect of this chapter as follows:

*The information contained in this chapter only relates to England and Wales. Police powers and responsibilities in both Scotland and Northern Ireland, while broadly similar, are also sufficiently different in detail for them to be regrettably excluded from the chapter.

Bevan, V., and Lidstone, K. (1991), *The Investigation of Crime: a Guide to Police Powers* (Butterworth).
Cape, E. (1993), *Defending Suspects at Police Stations* (Legal Action Group).
Heavens, L (1993), *Calvert's Powers of Arrest and Charges* (Butterworth).
English, J., and Card, R. (1991), *Butterworths Police Law* (Butterworth).
Levenson, H., and Fairweather, F. (1992), *Police Powers: a Practitioner's Guide* (Legal Action Group).
Littlechild, B. (ed.) (1987), *Social Work Guidelines to the Police and Criminal Evidence Act 1984* (BASW Publications).
Zander, M. (1990), *The Police and Criminal Evidence Act 1984* (Sweet and Maxwell).

DETENTION BY THE POLICE*

Does a person have to help police with their enquiries?

Technically speaking, nobody is under any duty to help police officers with their enquiries and refusal to do so cannot lead to any action or penalty, unless a person is guilty of wasting police time by giving them false or misleading information. A good citizen may, however, feel that as the main role of the police force is to assist in the prevention and detection of crime, co-operation with *bona fide* police enquiries is generally desirable, all other things being equal.

Can a person be arrested for refusing to co-operate with police enquiries?

It follows from the above that a person cannot be arrested for refusing to co-operate with the police (but see p.193 on 'General arrest conditions').

In what circumstances can a police officer detain a person?

There are only two general circumstances in which a police officer may detain a person:

*All advisers should note that many of the rights and safeguards described below do not apply in cases where terrorist offences are suspected.

1. limited detention to stop and search;
2. detention following arrest.

Both of these circumstances are carefully defined and limited by law, and are the subject of detailed treatment in the various Codes of Practice that govern police behaviour and practice (see p.180). In addition to these two general circumstances, the police also have powers to order motor vehicles to stop for specific purposes (see p.187).

LIMITED DETENTION TO STOP AND SEARCH A PERSON

If a police officer wishes to search a person it will clearly be necessary to detain them for the limited period of the search. A public search can be intimidating or humiliating. It amounts at face value to an infringement of the liberty of the individual, and is liable to abuse, and thus it is a matter of some importance that the boundaries between what is, and is not, permitted are clearly understood. The Code of Practice recognises quite explicitly that the exercise of stop and search powers by police officers is a matter of some sensitivity. For example, the original Code stated:

> There is strong evidence that on many occasions [stop and search] powers have been used where reasonable grounds to suspect the individual concerned of having the article in question on him did not in fact exist. There is also strong evidence that such misuse plays an important part in mistrust of the police among some sections of the community.

All those engaged in social work should ensure that the details both of the Act and of the Codes of Practice are scrupulously observed in day-to-day practice, for if a police officer exceeds his or her powers, a citizen is entitled to resist these powers and to register a subsequent complaint (see Chapter 2, p.30). In addition, it is worth noting that any court has a discretion to exclude any evidence that has been obtained unlawfully (e.g. by police officers acting in excess of their powers), even though in practice it may sometimes be difficult to persuade a court to do so. See p.203 on 'Inadmissible evidence'.

Which police officers have power to stop and search?

Any police officer has the power to stop and search a person. The term 'police officer' includes all ordinary police officers (though not cadets), special constables, and police officers acting for a particular statutory body, e.g. Transport Police, Ministry of Defence Police, Harbour Police, Atomic Energy Authority Police, Civil Aviation and Airport Police, etc. (For a full account of all the powers of special police forces see Levenson and Fairweather p.181 or *Halsbury's Laws of England*, 36, paras 211–19.)

What must the officer do before carrying out the search?

The police officer must inform the person about to be searched of:

- the officer's name, and the name of the station to which they are attached;
- the object of the search;
- the grounds for undertaking the search.

If the officer is not in uniform, identification in the form of a warrant card must be produced.

What happens if the suspect ignores the police officer, e.g. walks away?

Police officers have no power to force a person to stop in order to investigate an offence. It has, however, been established that the touching of a person in order to engage their attention is lawful. If, in addition, the police officer already has reasonable grounds for the search (see p.184) it would be lawful to use 'reasonable force' to detain the subject for the limited period for the search (see p.187).

Must the police officer make a record of the search?

The police officer making the search must (unless it is impractical to do so at the time, e.g. there is a riot going on) make a written record of the search. The person to be searched must also be informed (unless it is impractical to do so) of their right to be given a copy of the record of the search if they request it within a year. This record must contain the following information:

- the object of the search;
- the grounds of the search;
- the name of the person searched, or if not known, a brief description of them;
- the date and time the search was made;
- the place the search was made;
- whether anything, and if so what, was found;
- whether, and if so, what injury to a person or damage to property appeared to the officer to have resulted from the search.

Where can a police officer stop and search a person?

A police officer can stop and search any person in a public place, which includes a place to which the public have ready access such as a pub car park, a cinema foyer or a shop (during opening times). It may also extend to a yard or garden that is actually private property, if the police believe that the person they wish to search has no lawful right to be in such a place. (On football match powers, see p.191.) The power to stop and search does not otherwise extend to a person on private property (for police rights to enter private property, see p.198). The search should be carried out speedily. If the search involves only superficial examination of outer clothing, then 'it is an unusual search that cannot be completed within a minute or so'.

A police officer may, however, ask the person to be searched to accompany them to a nearby police van or police station if they feel it appropriate that the search be carried out in a more private place. This might occur, for example, if the police feel they must ask the suspect to remove more than outer clothing (see p.186). The Code of Practice states quite specifically on this point that: 'every reasonable effort must be made to reduce to the minimum the embarrassment that a person being searched may experience'.

Can the police stop and search anybody they like?

The whole system of searching is underpinned by the concept of *reasonable grounds*. The Code of Practice accompanying the Act is intended to provide the safeguards to the Act's abuse by unscrupulous or heavy-handed police activity in public. The Code of Practice contains the following broad philosophy:

- There is no power to stop and detain a person against his or her will in order to find grounds for a search.
- In some circumstances preparatory questioning may be unnecessary, but in general a brief conversation or exchange will be desirable as a means of avoiding unsuccessful searches.
- The fact that a person refuses to answer a question put to them in a public place is not, in itself, reasonable grounds for a search.

Reasonable grounds to suspect what?

The police can only stop and search a person whom they have reasonable grounds to suspect is carrying one or more of the following:

- illegal drugs (this power arises under the Misuse of Drugs Act 1971 s.23);
- stolen goods;
- a prohibited article. By this is meant an article made or adapted to commit burglary (e.g. a jemmy); deception (e.g. a false credit card); theft; or taking and driving away a car without the owner's permission (e.g. a master set of keys);
- firearms or any other offensive weapon. This category can include articles intended to be used as an offensive weapon such as kitchen knives, spanners, coshes, knuckledusters, or Stanley knives, or articles that have been converted for use as offensive weapons, such as sharpened sticks or coins. The police may decide that the item is suspicious because of the circumstances in which the suspect is found to be carrying it and carry out a search accordingly;
- items connected with terrorism;
- items linked to certain offences in connection with game and wildlife.

In addition to the above, police have special statutory powers to stop and search people in proximity to certain 'statutory undertakings', e.g. nuclear power stations and military bases. They also have power to stop and search coaches and trains and people travelling to and inside certain designated football grounds, for intoxicating liquor.

'Reasonable grounds' are never defined as a matter of policy in statutes. The test should, however, be an objective one. As the issue of police searches in a public place is a sensitive one, the first Code of Practice does, however, go out of its way to comment on what good police practice ought to be in this respect.

However, even this first Code was so heavily criticised from a number of quarters that the revised Code was far more explicit in this respect:

> Whether reasonable grounds for suspicion exist will depend on the circumstances in each case, but there must be some objective basis for it. Reasonable suspicion can never be supported on the basis of personal factors alone. For example, a person's age, colour, hairstyle or manner of dress, or the fact that he is known to have a previous conviction for possession of an unlawful article, cannot be used alone or in combination with each other as the sole basis on which to search that person. Nor may it be founded on the basis of stereotyped images of certain persons or groups as more likely to be committing offences.

Can a police officer remove any of the suspect's clothing in the course of the search?

If the search takes place in a public place, the police officer carrying out the search has the power to request the removal of the suspect's jacket, gloves or outer coat. It is not permitted to request the removal of any other clothing, including headgear and footwear, in public. The searching officer may, however, ask the suspect to go to a nearby police vehicle or station, or somewhere else out of the public view, in order to carry out a fuller search which may require the removal of further clothing. This is only permissible if the search is intended to find an object whose presence has already been suspected. If the suspect refuses to remove the item of clothing voluntarily the police officer can remove it, using reasonable force.

Can a suspect be searched by a police officer of the opposite gender?

Any search involving the removal of more than an outer coat, jacket, gloves, headgear or footwear may only be made by an officer of the same gender as the person searched and may not be made in the presence of anyone of the opposite gender.

Can a police officer use force to carry out the search?

Force can be used by a police officer carrying out a search but only 'as a last resort'. Before force is used, the unwillingness of the suspect to co-operate voluntarily must first be established. The amount of force that can be used is the minimum that is reasonably necessary to complete the search.

What happens once the search has been completed?

Once the search has been completed the police powers of limited detention come to an end. The suspect must either be released or arrested.

STOP AND SEARCH: A VEHICLE

General powers to stop and search vehicles

General powers under the Road Traffic Act 1988

A police officer has a general power under the Road Traffic Act 1988 to require anybody driving a motor vehicle or riding a bicycle on a road to stop, if the officer making the request is in uniform. Failure to stop following such a request is an offence. Once a vehicle has been stopped a police officer (including one not in uniform) may search that vehicle for the same general reasons that they may search a person, subject to the same preliminaries (p.183).

Specific powers to mount road checks (as circumscribed by the Police and Criminal Evidence Act 1984)

In addition to the above powers, a police officer of the rank of superintendent or above (or in an emergency, any officer) can authorise the setting up of a special road check that can be maintained for up to seven days for any of the following reasons:

- to discover whether there is an escaped prisoner in the vehicle;
- if an officer has reasonable grounds for believing that a *serious arrestable offence* (see p.197) has been committed in the area, to discover whether the person who committed the offence, or might have been witness to the offence, is in the vehicle. This power extends to any suspicion on the part of the officer that there might be in the vehicle some person intending to commit such an offence.

In all the above cases, the grounds for suspicion must be reasonable enough to justify the road check though, once the check is justified, any vehicle may be checked without needing to prove suspicion relating to that particular vehicle.

All the above procedures must be recorded, and any person stopped in a road check can apply for a written statement of the purpose of the check up to 12 months from the date of the check.

ARREST AND DETENTION FOLLOWING ARREST

Arrest

Arrest constitutes the second circumstance in which a person may be detained without their consent by a police officer. Again, it is necessary to stress the distinction between voluntary attendance at a police station, to assist police officers with their investigations, and detention following arrest. According to the Code of Practice, any person attending a police station voluntarily for the purpose of assisting with an investigation may leave at will, unless placed under arrest.

What is an arrest?

An arrest is the taking of a person, if necessary by force, into custody. Every member of the public has the power to arrest another in certain very limited circumstances (e.g. if they have just seen that person commit a serious crime). Police officers have wider powers of arrest. If an arrest is unlawful (i.e. it is outside the officer's legal powers) the arrested person has a right to resist the arrest using reasonable force, and to take subsequent action in the civil courts for assault and wrongful imprisonment. There is an increase in the number of cases that are being taken against the police for assault and unlawful arrest. A very detailed and comprehensive book on the subject is Clayton, R., and Tomlinson, H. (1987), *Civil Actions Against the Police* (Sweet and Maxwell).

Is physical contact with the arrested person necessary to constitute the arrest?

No. As long as the arrested person is informed that he or she is under arrest, then the arrest has taken place, even without physical contact. The fact of the arrest must, however, be made clear to the arrested person. A court has decided, for example, that the words, 'I shall have to ask you to come with me to the police station', are insufficient to amount to an arrest. A police officer may use such force as is reasonable to effect the arrest. It follows that serious attempts to resist arrest by force can be met by the arresting officer with equal force in return.

Must the arrested person be told why they have been arrested?

The arrested person must be made aware, in general terms, of the reason for the arrest at the time of the arrest.

In what circumstances can a police officer carry out an arrest?

This question has to be answered in two parts as the circumstances will differ accordingly:

- arrest with a warrant;
- arrest without a warrant.

Arrest with a warrant

A warrant is a document that has to be issued by a Justice of the Peace on the basis of sworn evidence from a police officer. The arrest warrant will name the person to be arrested and specify in general terms the reasons for issuing the warrant. The sorts of offences for which arrest warrants will be issued are as follows:

- an indictable or imprisonable offence has been committed and the person named in the warrant is suspected of having committed that offence;
- a summary offence has been committed, and the address of the suspect is insufficiently established to issue a summons;
- failure to pay money due under a maintenance order, fine or compensation order. (Note that a civilian enforcement officer, employed by the court to collect such sums due, does not have the same powers of arrest and entry as a police officer);
- failure to appear in court at the time and place specified in an earlier summons (limited to specified circumstances set out in the Magistrates' Courts Act 1980);
- to arrest a bankrupt.

Arrest without a warrant

There are a number of circumstances in which a police officer may arrest a person without an arrest warrant, as follows:

- in connection with arrestable offences;
- to prevent breaches of the peace;
- under a specific statute;
- where the 'General Arrest Conditions' apply;
- to fingerprint a convicted person.

Arrest in connection with arrestable offences

A police officer may arrest any person whom they have reasonable grounds to suspect has committed, is committing, or is about to commit an arrestable offence.

WHAT IS AN ARRESTABLE OFFENCE?

An *arrestable offence* is one which carries a sentence of at least five years' imprisonment. Examples of arrestable offences are murder, manslaughter, rape, robbery, blackmail, theft, burglary, most offences of violence, criminal damage, causing death by dangerous driving, and many drugs offences; included here also are attempts or conspiracies to commit any of these offences. The important point is that the offence carries such a sentence, not that the sentence is likely to be imposed. In addition to the above type of arrestable offence there are a number of other offences listed in PACE as arrestable offences even though they do not carry the possibility of long sentences. The most important of these are:

- taking a motor vehicle without authority, or being driven in such a vehicle;
- certain sexual offences;
- certain offences relating to official secrets and customs and excise;
- going equipped for burglary, theft or cheat.

For the full list, see s.24 Police and Criminal Evidence Act.

Although juveniles cannot be sent to prison, they can be arrested for arrestable offences. Recent legislation has extended the power of arrest without a warrant to two new and important areas. First, in connection with certain sporting events (e.g. major football matches), police can arrest a person in possession of intoxicating liquor at the ground, or on certain vehicles travelling to the ground (Sporting Events [Control of Alcohol] Act 1985). Second, when public order is threatened, police can arrest for such offences as acting in a manner likely to stir up racial hatred, causing fear or provoking violence (Public Order Act 1986).

Arrest to prevent breaches of the peace

This is an ancient power given to the police to arrest any person they believe to be breaking or about to break the peace in a public place. It is a very general power and very hard to define. According to Professor Leigh of the London School of Economics:

> A [police officer] has power at common law to arrest without warrant any person whom he sees breaking the peace or who so conducts himself that he causes a breach of the peace to be reasonably apprehended. If no breach of the peace is imminent the most that a [police officer] can do is to admonish the persons concerned to keep the peace.

There have been a number of cases which have sought to define, extend or limit the concept of breach of the peace over many centuries. Fighting is clearly a breach of the peace. Threats that are not related to violence are probably not. Noisy demonstrations with no threat of violence would not constitute a breach of the peace. Demonstrations at which violence is anticipated would allow the police to justify arrests. The best recent judicial summary of the state of the law in this area is probably that of Lord Justice Watkins in 1982 as follows:

> We cannot accept that there can be a breach of the peace unless there has been an act done or threatened to be done which either actually harms a person, or in his presence his property, or is likely to cause such harm, or which puts someone in fear of such harm being done.

Arrest under a specific statute

A number of statutes grant police officers a specific power of arrest without warrant for that particular offence. The full list of such offences is contained in Schedule 2 of PACE. The most important of these offences relate to drunken driving, criminal trespass, persons unlawfully at large (on the run), immigration offences, and offences against animals.

Arrest where the General Arrest Conditions apply

Generally speaking, the police are encouraged to proceed by way of a summons, rather than by arrest, in all minor alleged breaches of the criminal code. A summons is merely a court document ordering the suspected person to appear before a designated magistrates' court on a particular date to answer the charges laid against them. Almost all driving offences, for example, proceed by way of a summons. There are some circumstances, however, where, even though the offence would normally best be dealt with by summons, the police nevertheless have the power to arrest the subject. These circumstances are as follows:

- the police officer believes the suspect to have committed, be committing or be about to commit any offence, however trivial; and
- the police officer has reasonable grounds for such belief. This means that a reasonable person, acting without passion or prejudice, would fairly have suspected the suspect; and
- the police officer forms the view that service of a summons on the suspect is either impractical or inappropriate because one of the General Arrest Conditions applies.

WHAT ARE THE GENERAL ARREST CONDITIONS?

The General Arrest Conditions fall into three categories:

1. The police officer does not know the suspect's name or does not believe the name that has been given by the suspect or has not been given a satisfactory address at which to serve the subsequent summons. The address need not be the suspect's home: it can be that of a place of work or study, or that of a friend, social worker or solicitor, for example. As there is no power to detain the suspect, in order to check the address, a doubting police officer is left with the stark choice of believing the suspect or arresting them. The doubt must, however, be reasonable.
   or
2. The police officer believes that an arrest is necessary to prevent the suspect from harming themselves or another, or from suffering an injury, or from causing loss or damage to property, or from committing an offence against public decency, or from causing an unlawful obstruction to the highway (if the unlawful obstructor has been asked to move and has refused). This could include the arrest of a helpless drunk, of an aggressive person, of people behaving in a sexually explicit and 'grossly indecent' way in public.
   or
3. The police officer believes that arrest is necessary to protect a child or other vulnerable person from the arrested person. Protection here extends beyond physical protection, and could include protection from sexual abuse. A 'vulnerable person' is not defined, but according to a Home Office Minister it is 'someone who is particularly susceptible to injury, somebody who is ... particularly at risk. Someone in need of protection.' This power exists in addition to those already in existence under various mental health (see Chapter 5 at p.165) and child care provisions.

It is clear that the powers of arrest under this head are very wide indeed, and it is this width that has given civil liberties groups cause for much concern. At the same time it must be stressed that we are talking here about powers of arrest and not about new criminal offences. If arrests under these provisions do not lead to charges, the suspect must be released (see p.196).

Arrest for fingerprinting a convicted person

This power of arrest is very limited. It will only arise when:

- the person has been convicted of a 'recordable offence' (i.e. one which is kept on police records);
- the person was never detained in custody at a police station;
- the person's fingerprints were never taken at the time;
- within one month of the conviction the person was asked by a police officer to attend a police station for fingerprinting and after seven days has failed to do so (on fingerprinting, see p.208).

What must happen to the suspect once they have been lawfully arrested?

After a person has been arrested (and any arrest that is not carried out in one of the above ways is unlawful) the police have to follow a very strict procedure. Although police statistics demonstrate the average time that a suspect remains in a police station following arrest is only $1^1/_2$ hours, it is nevertheless important that the procedures are followed to the letter, however short the period of detention, if civil liberties are to be maintained. Evidence obtained in breach of any of these procedures may be subsequently deemed inadmissible evidence at a trial (see p.203).

Detention at police station following arrest

For a more detailed practical guide to practice and procedures at the police station, see Cape (1993) above at p.181.

- *Stage 1.* The suspect must be taken to a police station 'as soon as is practicable'.
- *Stage 2.* The suspect must be cautioned before being asked any further questions. Nobody is ever obliged to answer any questions, either before or after arrest. The right of silence is absolute although at the time of writing the government is seeking to change this. If questions are put to a suspect after arrest, the suspect should be told: 'You do not have to say anything unless you wish to do so, but what you say may be given in evidence.' Failure to caution the suspect can render any statement inadmissible evidence. In any

subsequent trial the prosecution do not at present have the right to question a suspect on the reason for exercising the right to silence.

- *Stage 3.* On arrival at the police station the suspect must be told both orally and in writing of their rights both to have someone informed of their detention and to see a solicitor. If the suspect is a juvenile, i.e. under 17, their parent or guardian must be informed as soon as possible of their presence at the police station.

These two rights can only be denied a suspect in very exceptional circumstances and then only on the authority of a senior police officer. The exceptional circumstances would be that:

a) the suspected offence is a *serious arrestable offence* (see p.197); and the senior police officer believes that the immediate exercise of the rights will either interfere with the evidence or will alert other unarrested suspects, or will hinder the recovery of stolen property or the intervention of police in certain offences relating to drug trafficking, sex establishments or video pirating.

b) the solicitor cannot be contacted, or is unwilling to attend, and the suspect has turned down the offer of access to the Duty Solicitor Scheme (see p.214).

For full details of the above provision see Code C of the PACE Codes of Practice. In addition, it should be noted that the Court of Appeal has held that where a senior police officer denies access to a solicitor on one of the above grounds this is tantamount to believing that the solicitor is going to do something grossly unprofessional and almost certainly criminal. A more sympathetic view was set out in another Court of Appeal case where Hodgson J. said as follows:

> Solicitors are intelligent, professional people; persons detained by the police are frequently not very clever and the expectations [that the situation at a) above] will occur, contemplates a degree of *naïveté* and lack of common sense in solicitors which we doubt often occurs.

In the light of this decision it should be very rare indeed for a senior police officer to deny rights of access of a suspect to a solicitor. It is important to note, however, that, in any case, a senior police officer may proceed with questioning before a solicitor arrives if 'awaiting the arrival of a solicitor would cause unreasonable delay to the processes of the investigation'. It is thus a good idea for social work advisers always to have open quick channels of access to a sympathetic solicitor. Given the existence of the nationwide Duty Solicitor Scheme (see p.214) a decision to question a suspect in the absence of a solicitor on these grounds should always be challenged. If the person denied access is a legal executive or a solicitor's clerk the police may take a tougher line and remain intransigent, particularly if they have reason to believe that the clerk is not of suitable character to give advice, but in these circumstances they must inform the solicitor's office immediately that the clerk has been denied access.

For further details on the above see the *Law Society Guidelines for Solicitors Advising Suspects in a Police Station* (1988), and Cape (1993) *Defending Suspects at Police Stations* (Legal Action Group).

- *Stage 4.* The suspected person must either be charged or released within 24 hours, unless the suspected offence is a serious arrestable offence in which case see *Stage 5*. The time begins to run from the moment of arrival at the police station.
- *Stage 5.* In the case of a serious arrestable offence a senior police officer may extend the period of detention to 36 hours, so long as s/he is satisfied of the following:
  a) The questioning is progressing diligently and speedily.
  b) Further time is necessary to secure or preserve evidence, or to obtain evidence from the suspect.
- *Stage 6.* After 36 hours have expired the suspect must either be released, charged or a further extension of the detention time obtained from a magistrate. The magistrate may extend the time to a maximum of 72 hours, but may choose to order a shorter extension, after which further applications can be made up to the 72 hours maximum. The magistrate is not allowed to hear the application to extend the detention unless the suspect has been given a copy of the documents applying for the extension and is brought personally before the magistrate. The suspect is entitled to be legally represented. After this a suspect can only be detained a further 24 hours (up to a maximum of 96 hours, on the authority of a magistrates' court).

- *Stage 7*. If charged, the suspect must be brought before a magistrates' court at the earliest possible time, or bailed by the police to appear at a later date. Otherwise the suspect must be released.

What is a 'serious arrestable offence'?

It will have been seen from the above that a distinction is made between an 'arrestable offence' and a 'serious arrestable offence'. If a suspect is being held in connection with the latter, the police have far greater powers. So what is a serious arrestable offence?

Essentially, it is an arrestable offence which was intended or likely to lead to any one of the following:

- serious harm to the security of the state or to public order;
- serious interference with the administration of justice or with the investigation of offences or a particular offence;
- the death of any person;
- substantial injury to any person;
- substantial financial gain to any person;
- serious financial loss to any person.

Some offences are always serious arrestable offences regardless of intention or outcome.

Who checks that the above procedures are followed?

By law every police station will have on duty at all times a police officer, not below the rank of sergeant, called the Custody Officer, whose sole responsibility will be to ensure that all these procedures are followed. The Custody Officer will not be involved in the suspect's case, will always be in uniform, and will have responsibility for keeping the custody record, the document that records every detail of the detention from the moment of the suspect's arrest. If there is a conflict between the Custody Officer and the officer who carried out the arrest, it must be referred to an independent senior officer. All suspects must be provided with a copy of their custody record, 'as soon as is practicable' after they leave the police station, if they so request.

Are there any other safeguards to protect the suspect?

The job of the Custody Officer, ensuring that correct procedures are followed, is supplemented by a further Review Procedure. If the suspect has been charged, the Review Procedure will be carried out by the Custody Officer. If the suspect has been arrested, but not yet charged, the Review Procedure will be carried out by an officer of at least the rank of inspector, who has not at any stage been involved in the investigation. The Review must take place at the following times:

- first Review not later than six hours after detention first authorised;
- subsequent Reviews at intervals of no more than nine hours.

The purpose of the Review is to ensure that all the procedures have been followed, and to decide whether further detention of the suspect can be justified.

POLICE POWERS TO ENTER AND SEARCH PREMISES*

What exactly are premises?

The definition of premises is very broad and general. According to PACE, premises 'includes any place, and in particular includes any vehicle, vessel, aircraft, hovercraft, offshore installation, tent or movable object'. There are numerous reasons why a police officer might wish to enter premises, e.g. to make enquiries, to look for a suspect, to carry out an arrest, to look for evidence of a crime, or in an emergency to protect somebody who is in some way at risk. But because the entering of private premises by police officers raises fundamental questions about the privacy of the citizen and other civil rights, the law has laid down with great care the following rights.

*For a very detailed account of the law in this area consult Stone, R. (1989), *Entry, Search and Seizure*, (2nd edn, Sweet and Maxwell).

In what circumstances can a police officer enter premises?

There are three alternative legal methods by which a police officer may enter premises. Whatever method is used the police must provide the occupier with a Notice of Powers setting out their rights.

Entering with the consent of the person able to grant permission to enter

Consent can only be given by the person with the immediate right of occupation, e.g. a landlord cannot consent to police officers entering and searching the premises of their tenant. The Code of Practice states:

> If it is proposed to search premises with the consent of a person entitled to grant entry to the premises the consent must be given in writing before the search begins. Before seeking consent the officer in charge shall state the purpose of the proposed search and inform the person concerned that s/he is not obliged to consent and that anything seized may be produced in evidence. If at the time, the person is not suspected of an offence, the officer shall tell them so when stating the purpose of the search.

If consent is subsequently withdrawn, even when the police are on the premises, they must leave or they will be trespassers.

Entering without consent and without a warrant

A police officer may only enter premises without consent and without a warrant, in the following circumstances:

- To arrest somebody or to recapture an escaped prisoner. Naturally, a power of arrest must also exist (see p.188). The police officer must in these circumstances have reasonable grounds to suspect that the person they wish to arrest is on the premises.
- In an emergency to save life, limb, or prevent serious damage to property. This power could therefore be used in domestic violence emergencies.
- They can also enter the premises controlled or occupied by a person they have arrested for an arrestable offence (see p.190) if

they have reasonable grounds to suspect they might find evidence related either to the offence for which the person was arrested, or evidence of a related or similar offence. The police cannot enter the premises of an arrested person for any other reason. It would, for example, be unlawful for the police to enter the premises of a person arrested for a public order offence, to search for stolen goods. When entering premises under this power the police officers must have with them a written authorisation for the search from a police inspector (or above).

- There are a number of statutes that give the police specific powers of entry for particular offences, e.g. to execute an arrest warrant issued by a magistrate for non-payment of a fine (see p.190); to look for drugs; under the gaming laws, etc. The full list of such offences can be found in Levenson and Fairweather (see p.181).

If a police officer does have lawful grounds to enter premises, and such entry is resisted, reasonable force may be used to secure entry.

IF THE POLICE ENTRY WAS UNLAWFUL CAN THEY USE ANY MATERIAL THEY SEIZE AS EVIDENCE IN A SUBSEQUENT TRIAL?

See p.203 under 'Inadmissible evidence'.

Entering without consent but with a warrant

If a police officer wishes to search premises, and none of the above conditions apply, it will be necessary to obtain a search warrant from a magistrate. The application will be made *ex parte,* i.e. there will be no access to the hearing for the person whose premises are to be searched. The application will be supported by sworn evidence given by a police officer. The magistrate must be satisfied that it is not possible or desirable to seek the owner's consent to the search (because, for example, the owner might try to conceal the evidence) and that it is likely that evidence of substantial value will be found on the premises. The warrant will only be issued if a serious arrestable offence (see p.197) is believed to have been committed. The warrant can be used on one occasion only, a copy of the warrant must be given to the occupier of the premises to be searched, and once the search has been carried out the warrant must be returned to the court that issued it.

Can a warrant be issued to search premises of somebody other than the suspect?

The premises to be searched under the warrant need not be those of the suspect. They may belong to any person. What matters is that the police believe they will find on the premises evidence relating to the particular offence. The warrant will, however, only relate to particular named premises.

What can a police officer seize once lawfully on the premises?

The answer to this question is particularly complex, and cannot be dealt with in any great detail in a chapter of this limited length. It is important, however, that the social work adviser has a general understanding of the broad limits of police powers to seize material for two reasons:

1. In order to challenge any police officer who appears to be acting unlawfully at the time of the search.
2. Because there is always the possibility that evidence unlawfully obtained will not be admitted at any subsequent trial (see p.203 under 'Inadmissible evidence'). It is particularly important, therefore, that a social worker involved in a case at the time of the search keeps a record of exactly what is said by the police.

If a police officer has entered premises lawfully, by one of the above methods, it has already been made clear that he or she may seize any evidence of any offence, subject only to the exceptions set out below. This power extends to the lawful entry by a police officer of premises which have nothing to do with the suspect, but where the police hope to find evidence of crime. Thus the power may extend to a search of the premises of a social worker or social work adviser. It is for this reason that the following section is of particular importance to the social worker.

What evidence can a police officer *never* seize?

A police officer can never seize the following:

1. *Any item subject to legal privilege.* This basically means any correspondence with a solicitor, or other documents relating to some legal action, but the question is complex and advisers seeking more detailed information should consult one of the principal texts mentioned at p.181.
2. *Excluded material.* This is defined as any of the following:
   - human tissue or fluid held confidentially for diagnosis or treatment;
   - journalistic material in the form of documents, or records, and held confidentially;
   - personal records of a trade, business or other profession or office, held confidentially. This will clearly extend to all client records held by social workers, probation officers, advice workers, etc., and anybody engaged in social work, or holding office, e.g. as a councillor, so long as such records are genuinely confidential (see Chapter 3 on 'confidentiality of records').

Can a court give a police officer special authority to seize any evidence that could not normally be seized?

Yes. There are certain categories of potential evidence of which a circuit judge may authorise seizure after a special application by the police. Normally, but not always, the person in possession of the evidence has the right to appear at the hearing of the application. These categories are as follows:

- *Journalistic material not held confidentially.* Generally speaking, the courts will hold that such material must be released to the police if the benefit to the course of justice would outweigh the importance of ensuring the independence and safety of the press.
- *Items other than personal records of a trade, business or other profession, that are nevertheless held confidentially.* This will presumably extend to all communications of a confidential nature between colleagues in a department that are not personal records, and will also include such items as company accounts, and stock records held on behalf of a client.

Inadmissible evidence

It will never be certain that evidence obtained after an unlawful police action will be excluded in any subsequent trial. Unlawfully obtained evidence may include evidence unlawfully seized during a search, or following an unlawful arrest or entry. It may also include evidence obtained by confessions, when special procedures are not followed (see p.213 under 'Confession evidence'). All that the law says is that a judge can refuse to allow the evidence if 'it would have such an adverse effect on the fairness of the proceedings that the court ought not to admit it'. In one case, for example, the High Court held that they had a discretion to exclude evidence of possession of cannabis against a suspect whose house had been unlawfully searched, following his arrest for stealing a sandwich in a public house. The fact that he had allegedly stolen a sandwich did not reasonably lead to the suspicion that he was a cannabis smoker. In another case, a man confessed to committing arson having been told (falsely) by the police that his fingerprints had been found on a fragment of a bottle containing inflammable liquid, close to the scene of the crime. Excluding the confession evidence, the Court of Appeal said, 'We hope never again to hear of deceit such as this being practised on an accused person.' The discretion of the judge in these circumstances is very wide. Examples in recent years of courts excluding evidence wrongfully obtained include confessions obtained by a trap (though not if obtained through an *agent provocateur*), confessions made after access to a solicitor had been wrongfully denied, and a confession obtained by deceit, and close to the scene of the crime.

POLICE POWERS AND SUSPECT'S RIGHTS AT THE POLICE STATION

Having reviewed the general circumstances in which a police officer may detain a suspect at a police station, and the detailed procedures that must be followed by a police officer throughout the period between arrest and release, or appearance before a magistrate, a number of subsidiary questions remain to be addressed regarding the rights of individuals while in police custody at a police station. The particular issues to be addressed here are the special procedures concerning arrested juveniles, and those suffering from illness, physical or mental handicap or disability; arrangements for the suspect to consult a solicitor in private; rights of the suspect and the police concerning search, and taking of fingerprints, photographs and body samples; identification parade procedures; recording of interviews; confession evidence; complaints about the police; the Duty Solicitor Scheme.

A breach of any of these procedures by the police could render them liable to disciplinary procedures or to official complaints procedures, and could render evidence thereby obtained inadmissible (see p.203 under 'Inadmissible evidence').

Juvenile suspect

These procedures apply to anybody who is, or appears to be, under 17. There are a number of special procedures laid down concerning the treatment of juveniles while in police custody.

The procedures are as follows:

1. If anyone in police custody appears to be under the age of 17, then s/he shall be treated as a juvenile in the absence of clear evidence to show they are over 17.
2. If a person under paragraph 1 ('the suspect') arrives at a police station in police custody, the Custody Officer must as soon as is practicable inform an appropriate adult of the detention and of the reasons for the detention, and invite that person to come to the police station where they are being held.
3. An appropriate adult is one of the following:
   - The suspect's parents or guardian (unless also a suspect) or, if unobtainable, a social worker. BASW has produced a helpful publication called *Social Work Guidelines to the PACE 1987* which can be of great assistance to social workers called upon to assume the role of appropriate adult in these circumstances.
   - If in care, the relevant care authority or organisation. In these circumstances, if the suspect is living with their parents or foster parents, steps should also be taken to inform them, although this is not a legal obligation.
   - Failing the above, another responsible adult who is not a police officer or employed by the police.
4. If the suspect is known to be the subject of a supervision order, reasonable steps must be taken to notify their supervisor of the detention.

5. Interviewing of the suspect should not normally begin until the appropriate adult has arrived. Nor should the suspect be asked to provide or sign any written statement in the absence of the appropriate adult. A senior police officer may, however, authorise that questioning may begin in the absence of an appropriate adult if they have a genuine belief that delay will involve an immediate risk of harm to persons or serious loss of or damage to property, or if they believe that awaiting the arrival of that person will cause 'unreasonable delay' in the investigation of the crime. Such delay is, however, only permissible where the suspect is suspected of committing a 'serious arrestable offence'.
6. The suspect should not be placed in a police cell, unless no other secure accommodation is available and the custody officer considers that it is not practicable to supervise them if they are not placed in a police cell.
7. If either of the exceptional courses allowed at items 5 or 6 above are taken, the facts must be recorded in the custody record (see pp. 197 and 213).

Suspect with mental handicap or physical or mental illness

The procedures concerning the treatment while in police custody of a suspect who is, or appears to be, suffering from some mental handicap or illness are very similar to those of the person appearing to be a juvenile. Failure to follow the correct procedures may lead to similar consequences as for juveniles. For suspects in this category, the appropriate adult will be one of the following:

- a relative or guardian; *or*
- some other person who is responsible for their care or custody; *or*
- another responsible person, who if possible is known and trusted by the suspect and if possible has experience in dealing with people with mental handicap or illness. This person cannot be a police officer or employed by the police, and must be 18 or over.

For further assistance, see *Social Work Guidelines to the PACE 1987* (BASW).

What is the appropriate adult supposed to do, once they arrive at the police station?

Once at the police station, the role of the appropriate adult is more than one of mere observer status. The appropriate adult is there to advise the suspect, to ensure that the suspect is given orally and in writing a list of their rights, including in particular the right to a solicitor, to observe that the interview is conducted fairly, and to facilitate communication with the suspect. Advising the suspect, for example, to 'be careful what they say' is a perfectly legitimate role of the appropriate adult.

Are there special procedures for suspects who cannot understand what is being said to them for other reasons, e.g. they are deaf, or do not understand English?

Yes. The Code of Practice states as follows: 'If the [suspect] does not understand English or appears to be deaf then the custody officer must as soon as is practicable call an interpreter and ask her/him to [help].'

What happens if the suspect is, or appears to be, ill?

The Code of Practice states (in summary) that:

> If a [suspect] appears to be suffering from physical or mental illness, or is injured, or is incoherent or somnolent, or is thought to be a drug addict or otherwise to need medical attention, or if [they] become injured or ill the Custody Officer must immediately call the police surgeon, or in urgent cases send the person to hospital or call the nearest available medical practitioner. This applies even if the person makes no complaint and whether or not s/he has recently had medical treatment elsewhere.

Suspect's access to a solictor

As stated above, all suspects have a right to consult a solicitor once they have been detained at a police station (subject to delays, see p.195). The right is to consult, if wished, a specific solicitor, in private. Alternatively, the suspect must be given the opportunity to consult either the duty solicitor (see p.214) or to choose a solicitor from a list provided by the

Custody Officer. As the right of access is only to a solicitor it may be denied to a solicitor's clerk, or a legal executive, but good reasons for denial must be communicated immediately to the solicitor.

Search of the suspect at the police station

Can a police officer ever retain a suspect's clothes or personal effects unrelated to the crime following any search?

Yes, if the Custody Officer believes that the person from whom they have been removed would otherwise use them to cause physical injury either to themselves or to another person, to interfere with evidence, to damage property or to assist in their escape. Otherwise, the police officer may only retain items that may be evidence of the crime suspected.

Types of search

We have already dealt with the general powers of the police to search a person in a public place (see p.182). These same powers extend to a suspect who is voluntarily at a police station without having been arrested. Once a suspect has been arrested, wider powers of search arise. These are as follows, in order of extent:

1. *Basic search* to ascertain what possessions the suspect has with them. This will only become necessary if the arrested suspect refuses to submit voluntarily to a request of this nature. All items found on the suspect must be recorded in writing, which the suspect must then sign. The search may only be carried out by a police officer of the same sex as the suspect.
2. *Strip search.* This is a far more controversial power that has led to much criticism and bad feeling between the police and certain categories of suspect. A strip search is 'a search involving the removal of more than outer clothing'. Such a search can only be carried out by a police officer of the same sex as the suspect, and should not be performed in the presence of a member of the opposite sex, unless that person is a doctor. Reasons for such a search must be given and recorded in the custody record. The reasons must be of a compelling kind – for example, the very reasonable suspicion that the suspect is concealing on their person evidence of the crime of which they are

suspected. The courts have made some attempts to define the limits of such searches, the Court of Appeal finding, for example, that the removal of a suspect's brassiere would require 'considerable justification'. For, in the words of the Court of Appeal, 'strip searches involve an affront to the dignity and privacy of the individual'. It is 'the duty of the courts to be ever zealous to protect the personal freedom and dignity of all'. For a brief description of a successful action suing the police for an unlawful strip search near Greenham Common (£2000 damages), see *Legal Action*, September 1988, and for an example of damages being awarded in excess of £10,000 for wrongful strip searching of prison visitors, see *Legal Action*, February 1993.

3. *Intimate body search.* This is naturally the most controversial power of all, and is therefore the power subject to the closest regulation. An intimate body search is a search of a suspect's body orifices, e.g. anus, rectum, vagina, nose, mouth or ear. A police officer of at least the rank of superintendent must authorise an intimate body search. If the authorisation is verbal it must be translated into writing as soon as is practicable. Such a search can be authorised in only one of two circumstances, namely that the authorising officer has reasonable grounds to believe that the suspect has concealed in a body orifice something which could cause physical injury or a class A dangerous drug (e.g. heroin, cocaine).

Who may carry out such a search?

A drugs search must be carried out by a doctor or nurse either in a hospital, or at other suitable medical premises. The search for something that may cause physical injury (but is not a dangerous drug) should also be carried out by a similarly qualified person in similar circumstances. In an emergency, however, a senior police officer may authorise a police officer of the same gender as the suspect to carry out the latter type of search. Presumably, however, the suspicion that the suspect has a weapon concealed in a body orifice creates, by definition, an emergency.

Fingerprinting

It has already been explained earlier (see p.194) that a police officer can arrest a person simply to take their fingerprints, but in very limited circumstances. A police officer may also take a suspect's fingerprints in the following circumstances:

- At any time with the suspect's consent. If the fingerprints are taken in the police station, the consent must be in writing and details will appear on the custody report. If the suspect is mentally ill or mentally handicapped, the consent is only valid if given in the presence of an appropriate adult (see p.205). If the suspect is aged between 14 and 17, the consent of a parent or guardian must be given in addition to the suspect's consent. If the suspect is between 10 and 14, the consent of a parent or guardian is sufficient.
- Without consent and using, if necessary, reasonable force. This may be authorised by a police officer of superintendent rank or above who has reasonable grounds to believe that the suspect has committed an offence, and that the taking of fingerprints will tend to confirm or disprove their involvement in the offence. This power applies to any suspect over the age of 10.

What happens to fingerprints if the suspect is either not charged, or is charged and acquitted? (Applies also to fingerprints of those not suspected, e.g. the prints of the victim of a burglary)

All fingerprints of suspects in the above categories (and any copies of those prints) must subsequently be destroyed by the police. This must happen as soon as is practicable after the termination of the relevant proceedings or once they have fulfilled their purpose. When fingerprints are destroyed, access to the relevant computer data should be made impossible as soon as practicable. Any person to whose fingerprints the data relates may ask for a certificate that this duty has been performed from the chief officer and must be given such a certificate within three months of asking. If anyone asks to witness the destruction of their prints, they must be allowed to do so.

Taking of body samples

Body samples fall into two categories as follows:

1. *Non-intimate body samples.* These are defined as hair (except pubic hair); sample taken from a nail or under a nail; a swab taken from

any part of a person's body; a footprint, or impression of any part of a person's body (including teeth) other than part of the hand.
2. *Intimate body samples*. These are defined as samples of blood, semen or other tissue fluid, urine, saliva, pubic hair, and a swab taken from a body orifice.

In what circumstances may a police officer take a non-intimate body sample?

The taking of such a sample will normally require the suspect's written consent. However, a police officer of at least the rank of superintendent can authorise the taking of such a sample, without the suspect's consent, and if necessary using reasonable force, if they believe:

- the suspect has committed a serious arrestable offence, and
- the sample will tend to prove or disprove their involvement.

In what circumstances may a police officer take an intimate body sample?

An intimate body sample may only be taken from a suspect if they provide their written consent. The consent provisions for juveniles and the mentally ill or handicapped are the same as for fingerprinting (see p.209). In addition, a sample can only be requested by a police officer of like rank and in like circumstances to those for the taking of non-intimate body samples without the suspect's consent. The difference is that if the suspect refuses permission to take an intimate body sample, the police have no power to take it. There is, however, a powerful sanction which operates against the suspect who refuses an intimate body sample 'without good cause', e.g. religious grounds. The court in any subsequent trial will be told of the refusal, and will be allowed to 'draw such inferences as they think fit'.

Who takes the samples?

Only a registered medical practitioner may take intimate body samples, except urine or saliva. Failure to comply with this provision will render the taking of the sample unlawful. Non-intimate samples may be taken by police officers. If any clothing other than outer clothing is removed, there must be no officers of the opposite gender present.

Photographing a suspect

A suspect at a police station may only be photographed in one of three circumstances:

1. With their written consent; *or*
2. Under the Public Order Act 1986 a court making an exclusion order which excludes offenders from football grounds on their conviction of an offence connected with football may also make an order that the defendant should be photographed; *or*
3. In the special circumstances set out in the Code of Practice. In every case the police must destroy the photographs together with any copies and negatives, if the suspect is either released without charge, or is tried for the offence and acquitted. The suspect must be allowed to witness the destruction of the photographic material, so long as they make such a request within two days of the decision not to proceed or the acquittal.

What are the special circumstances?

There are three categories of special circumstances:

- the suspect has been charged with or reported for a recordable offence (i.e. offences for which a conviction is recorded in national police records), and has not yet been released or brought before a court; *or*
- the suspect has been convicted of a recordable offence and no photograph has been taken of them already (there is no power of arrest for this purpose, as there is for fingerprinting) (see p.194); *or*
- the suspect is arrested at the same time as other persons or at a time when it is likely that other persons will be arrested (e.g. at a demonstration), and a photograph is necessary to establish who has been arrested, at what time and at what place.

It is important to realise, however, that, unlike the taking of a fingerprint, the mere taking of a photograph does not constitute an assault and therefore there is little that a person can do to prevent police officers from taking photographs in public places, where they are not generally subject to these tighter controls.

Identification parades

Identification parades *must* be held if identification evidence is disputed and if the suspect asks for one. They *may* also be held if the officer in charge of the case requests one, but then only with the suspect's consent. If the suspect refuses to participate, either in an identification parade or in a controlled appearance with a more general group of people (e.g. outside a tube station), the police may decide to arrange for a direct confrontation between the suspect and the victim. A suspect going before an identification parade must always be given reasonable opportunity to have a friend or solicitor present.The rules governing identification parades are very tightly drawn and are normally followed with scrupulous care by the police. Any social worker called to attend an identification parade as a 'friend' should consult Annexe A to PACE 1984, Code of Practice D.

Recording the interview

We have already looked at the procedure that a police officer must follow when interviewing a suspect, noting in particular that the interview should be recorded in writing, and signed by the suspect as a fair statement of what was said by all parties. Because of the risk of interviews being wrongfully conducted, there was introduced in 1988 a further Code of Practice governing the tape recording by police of their interviews in police stations, which must be done in most cases where a person has been cautioned in respect of an indictable offence. The Code is Code E of the PACE Codes of Practice. If the police wish to make a videotape of a confession, including a reconstruction of a crime, they must inform the suspect that participation in such a video recording is voluntary, and the suspect is also entitled to record their own comments on the film, once it is made.

Confession evidence

Any 'confession' that is obtained by oppression (defined as the use of actual or threatened violence, or indirect threats or inhuman treatment) will be considered inadmissible in any subsequent court hearing. This provision is a special provision relating to 'confessions' and is in addition to the provision on 'inadmissible evidence' (see p.203). Examples of 'oppression' that have been considered sufficient to allow a court to render the evidence inadmissible have been 'confessions' made by a suspect held overnight merely because his story was disbelieved; by a suspect held for 50 hours without charge during which time 700 questions were asked; by a suspect kept alone in a cold cell for 4½ hours with no refreshments and no watch, interspersed with two periods of rigorous questioning; and a suspect denied access to a solicitor and kept in custody for seven days without charge.

The custody record

Mention has already been made of the custody record kept by the Custody Officer (see p.197) and of the suspect's right to receive a copy. The record will contain details of the following:

- the grounds for the detention;
- the time of the detention;
- a record of any property taken from the suspect and the reason why it was taken;
- the suspect's signed acknowledgement that they were given written notice of their right to obtain legal advice, and to have a person of their choice informed of their detention;
- details of any complaints the suspect made about their treatment;
- details of any food or drink taken, of any visits, or messages received;
- details of any medical treatment given to the suspect, and any medical examinations or searches conducted on the suspect;
- details of any times that the suspect was not with the Custody Officer, e.g. because they were being questioned;
- records of all reviews of detention;
- records of fingerprinting, of any strip search or intimate body search;

- details of the time of release, of any applications to continue detention, and finally of any charges, and bail conditions.

The Duty Solicitor Scheme

There is now in existence in many police stations in the country a Duty Solicitor Scheme whereby local solicitors run a 24-hour rota to ensure that any suspect arriving at a police station has access to a solicitor should they request it. The Scheme is financed by the government, and the suspect will not therefore have to pay for the service. The suspect is under no obligation to accept the solicitor offered by the Scheme. Since April 1992, however, all solicitors who participate in the Duty Solicitor Scheme must have completed some training accredited by the Law Society. Arrestees are always at liberty to choose their own solicitor, providing that the solicitor is willing to act for them. The Custody Officer should bring the Scheme to the attention of every detained suspect. The Criminal Law Committee of the Law Society (p.38) has produced a useful leaflet called *Advising a Suspect at The Police Station.* The Legal Aid Board (p.6) has produced a pamphlet *Duty Solicitor Arrangements 1990.* For detailed assistance, consult Cape, E. (1993), *Defending Suspects at Police Stations* (Legal Action Group).

Complaints about the police

Throughout this chapter allusion has been made to the strict regulation of police powers both by the Police and Criminal Evidence Act 1984 and within the Codes of Practice. This chapter has not, however, dealt with the problem of what to do if a police officer appears to the client or the adviser to have acted either unlawfully or in breach of the Codes of Practice. Essentially, there are two remedies:

1. Filing a complaint under the Police Complaints Procedure (see Chapter 2 at p.31).
2. Suing the police officer, but only if the victim has suffered some injury, e.g. as a result of assault or false imprisonment following wrongful arrest (see p.188).

Chapter 7

Legal rights and the workplace

written by David Lewis*

This chapter will look at the legal rights of employees in their place of work. It would be impossible to cover the whole range of employment law in such a short space, and any adviser or client who wishes more detailed information on the law should consult one of the recommended reference works set out in the bibliography at the end of the chapter. What the chapter seeks to do is to identify a number of the most important areas in which disputes may arise and in which the adviser's assistance may be sought. The themes that the chapter will cover are as follows:

1. Getting a job: discrimination at the hiring stage.
2. Employment contracts (types and contents).
3. Discrimination in employment (on grounds of gender, race or trade union activity).
4. Maternity rights.
5. Health and safety at work.
6. Losing employment.
7. The enforcement of employment rights.

In addition to the bibliography at the end of the chapter, there is a list of some of the most useful or important organisations where the adviser or their client can go for more detailed advice and assistance.

*Reader in Employment Law, Middlesex University.

GETTING A JOB: DISCRIMINATION AT THE HIRING STAGE

This section does not deal with the problem of finding work but outlines the legal constraints imposed on employers at the hiring stage.

What matters must an employer ignore when deciding whether or not to employ somebody?

Ex-offenders

Normally the law does not require applicants to disclose facts about themselves which could hinder them in getting jobs, unless their silence amounts to fraud. Under the Rehabilitation of Offenders Act 1974 certain persons are relieved from the obligation to disclose 'spent' convictions to a prospective employer and it is unlawful for an employer to deny employment on the grounds that the applicant had a conviction which was 'spent'. However, this protection is not afforded to those applying for a whole range of jobs: for example, social workers, probation officers, teachers or nurses. (For the full list of jobs that are exempted from protection the Act and its accompanying Statutory Instrument should be consulted.)

WHAT IS A 'SPENT CONVICTION'?

Sentences of over $2^1/2$ years' imprisonment never become 'spent', otherwise convictions become 'spent' after periods which are related to the sentence imposed. Thus a sentence of imprisonment for a period of between 6 months and $2^1/2$ years is 'spent' after 10 years. Imprisonment for less than 6 months requires a 7-year rehabilitation period, and fines and community service orders take 5 years to become 'spent'. A probation order, conditional discharge or binding over will be 'spent' after a year or when the order expires, whichever is the longer. Absolute discharges are 'spent' if 6 months have elapsed since sentence. Unfortunately, the courts cannot compel an employer to engage a rehabilitated offender, they can only declare the exclusion of the applicant to be unlawful.

Disabled persons

The law relating to the employment of disabled people is set out in detail in Chapter 4 at p.95.

Anti-discrimination legislation

It is unlawful to refuse employment to people because they are or are not members of a trade union. In addition, the Sex Discrimination Act 1975 (SDA) and the Race Relations Act 1975 (RRA) make it unlawful to discriminate in any of the following ways when offering employment:

- in the arrangements made for the purpose of determining who should be offered employment;
- in the terms on which employment is offered;
- by refusing or deliberately omitting to offer employment.

It is equally unlawful to refuse to employ a person simply because they have given evidence in connection with proceedings, or have brought, or are about to bring, proceedings against a previous employer under the Equal Pay Act 1970 (EPA), the SDA or RRA. It is important to note that the titles of the SDA and the RRA do not fully reflect the matters that they cover. The SDA, for example, also outlaws discrimination against married persons on the grounds of marital status, while 'racial grounds' extend much wider than pure racial discrimination to include discrimination on grounds of colour, nationality, and ethnic or national origins. Although the RRA covers religious discrimination, it has been decided that Sikhs but not Rastafarians are protected, on the grounds of ethnic origins.

Can discrimination on grounds of race or gender ever be lawful?

In certain limited circumstances gender or race discrimination at the recruitment stage is permitted by law, if there is a genuine occupational qualification (GOQ). In the case of discrimination on grounds of gender, there are several types of GOQ, of which the most important are as follows:

- The essential nature of the job demands a particular physiology (excluding physical strength): for example, when acting a particular role.
- The job needs to be held by a particular gender in order to preserve decency or privacy: for example, searching for security purposes.
- The nature of the establishment demands a person of a particular gender because it is an establishment for persons requiring specialised care or attention: for example, in a single-gender institution.
- The job holder provides personal services which can most effectively be provided by a person of a particular gender: for example, in a team of social workers providing specialised services.

The only GOQs allowed for under the RRA are:

- where discrimination is necessary in order to allow authenticity in the provision of food and drink, in entertainment or in modelling;
- where the job holder provides personal welfare services which can be most effectively provided by a person of a particular racial group.

Finally, it should be noted that an employer cannot rely on the existence of a GOQ if the organisation already has sufficient workers capable of carrying out those duties whom it would be reasonable to employ in that way.

On the enforcement of rights under the SDA and RRA, see p.226.

EMPLOYMENT CONTRACTS (TYPES AND CONTENTS)

It is very important to be able to distinguish the type of contract that an employee has been given as many of their rights will depend upon this initial decision. It may often be the case that a contract is not in law what it is described to be by the employer.

What are the main types of contract found in the workplace?

Contracts of service and contracts for services

There are significant legal differences drawn between workers who are engaged under contracts of service (employees) and those who are engaged under contracts for services (self-employed or independent contractors). Employees gain the benefit of a number of individual rights under employment protection legislation, and are subject to the unwritten general obligations implied in all contracts of employment (see p.222). When employees, as opposed to self-employed persons, are engaged, employers are required to deduct social security contributions and tax. Unfortunately, it is sometimes difficult to determine whether someone works under a contract of service or for services. It is the operation of the contract in practice rather than its appearance that is crucial. Thus a person may be described as self-employed but be treated by the law as an employee. If there is a dispute, it will ultimately be for the court or tribunal to decide whether the person was carrying on a business on his or her own account. The fact that workers pay their own social security contributions and tax is not conclusive. Indeed, people who work at home may be classed as employees so long as there is a degree of mutual obligation to continue the relationship with the person for whom they are working. Although individuals engaged under special employment schemes may not be categorised as employees, for certain purposes they are to be treated as such, for example under health and safety regulations (see p.233).

Indefinite and fixed-term contracts

Employees may be hired for an indefinite period or for a fixed term (i.e. on a contract which has a defined beginning and a defined end). Provided it is for a specified period, a fixed-term contract exists even though it may be terminable by the giving of notice within that period (see p.241). From an employee's point of view the main disadvantage of a fixed-term contract is that it is possible for the employer, by means of an exclusion clause, to remove the right to claim unfair dismissal (if the contract is for a year or more) or a redundancy payment (if the contract is for two years or more).

Temporary and part-time employees

Since Parliament has not provided a definition of temporary status, an employee described as 'temporary' who has satisfied any necessary qualifying period of service and worked the requisite number of hours (see below) will have exactly the same statutory rights as other employees.

'Part-time employment' is only indirectly defined by legislation and the statutory provisions are frequently at variance with the boundaries drawn in practice by employers and trade unions. The law stipulates that any person who has a contract of employment for more than 16 hours per week, or who has been continuously employed for the previous 5 years under a contract for more than 8 hours per week, can qualify for the full range of statutory protection.

The contractual rights of 'temporary' and 'part-time' workers will be determined by their individual contracts.

How can an employee work out their terms and conditions of employment if they have not been given them in a written contract?

Apart from apprentices, who can only be employed under written deeds, contracts of employment may be oral or in writing. In theory, the parties to a contract of employment are free to negotiate the terms and conditions that suit them. However, in practice, about 50 per cent of employees do not negotiate on an individual basis but are engaged on such terms and conditions as are laid down in currently operative collective agreements. Express terms are those which are expressly agreed as forming part of the contract. An express term takes precedence over an implied term (see p.222). The exception is where the implied term derives from statute.

What information must be supplied to an employee about the terms and conditions of their employment?

Not later than two months after the start of employment of a person working eight hours a week or more, and whose employment continues for a month or more, the employer must supply a written statement which provides the following particulars:

1. The identity of the parties.
2. The date on which the employee's period of continuous employment began.
3. The scale or rate of remuneration, and the intervals at which remuneration is paid. Additionally, there is a right to receive an itemised pay statement.

4. Any terms and conditions relating to hours of work and normal hours of work.*
5. Any terms and conditions relating to holidays and holiday pay. It should be noted that there is no general statutory right to any holiday.
6. Any terms and conditions relating to incapacity for work owing to sickness or injury, including any provision for sick pay.*
7. Any terms and conditions relating to pensions and a statement as to whether a contracting-out certificate is in force.*
8. The length of notice that an employee is entitled to receive and obliged to give (see p.239).*
9. The title of the job, or a brief description of the employee's work.
10. Where the employment is temporary, the period for which it is expected to continue, or, if it is for a fixed term, the date when it is to end.*
11. The place of work, or, if the employee is permitted or required to work at various places, an indication of that fact and the employer's address.
12. Any collective agreements which directly affect the terms and conditions of employment, including, where the employer is not a party, the person by whom they were made.*
13. Where the employee is required to work outside the UK for more than a month:
    - (i) the period of work outside the UK;
    - (ii) the currency in which payment will be made;
    - (iii) any additional pay and benefits to be provided by reason of the work being outside the UK;
    - (iv) any terms and conditions relating to the employee's return to the UK.*
14. The name or description of the person to whom employees can apply if they are dissatisfied with any disciplinary decision, or wish to pursue or redress a grievance. Where there are further steps consequent upon any such application, the employee must receive details explaining those steps or be referred to a reasonably accessible document which explains them. These requirements do not apply in relation to discipline if the employer has less than 20 employees.*
15. Whether a contracting-out certificate is in force for the employee's employment.*

It should also be noted that for particulars of any of the matters mentioned in 6, 7 and 8, the statement may refer the employee to some other reasonably accessible document. The matters marked with an asterisk may be given in instalments but must still be supplied within two months of the start of employment.

Changes cannot be made to a contract of employment without the consent of the employee but, where agreement is reached to alter the terms, the employee must receive a written statement detailing the changes within one month. It is important to understand that the statement issued does not constitute a contract. It is merely the employer's version of what has been agreed. Nevertheless, if an employee confirms that what has been issued is an accurate summary of the main employment terms the particulars may be treated by the courts as having contractual status. Where there is no written statement, or an incomplete or inaccurate statement is issued, the employee can complain to an industrial tribunal.

What terms are implied into all contracts of employment?

Certain terms are regarded by the law as being inherent in all contracts of employment. In the remainder of this section the major obligations which are imposed automatically on the parties to a contract of employment will be outlined.

The duties of the employer

The duty to pay wages

This is the most basic obligation of the employer and is normally dealt with by an express term. However, in certain circumstances the law does not leave the parties entirely free to determine the amount of remuneration payable, for example, if an equality clause operates (see p.229). The normal rule is that wages must be paid if an employee is available for work. Thus, if employees voluntarily absent themselves from work (for example, by taking strike action) an employer is entitled to withhold wages for the period of the absence. As regards deductions from wages for any other reason, the law provides that a deduction will be unlawful unless it is required by statute – for example, PAYE or social security contributions, or if the worker has agreed to it.

A useful organisation to contact in connection with problems associated with low pay is the Low Pay Unit, a campaigning advice and research organisation concerned with the problems of low pay. The Unit runs a rights and advice service, and produces a large number of pamphlets relating to issues of low pay. The address of the Low Pay Unit is: Low Pay Unit, 9 Upper Berkeley St, London W1H 8BY (tel: 071 262 7278).

The duty to provide work

Employers are not usually obliged to provide work and most employees who receive their full contractual remuneration cannot complain if they are left idle. Nevertheless, in exceptional circumstances the failure to provide work may amount to a breach of contract, as for example in the case of a pieceworker whose earnings depend on work being provided.

The duty to co-operate with the employee

One effect of the unfair dismissal provisions (see p.240) has been that the courts have frequently stated that employers must not destroy the mutual trust and confidence upon which co-operation in the workplace is built. Although each case depends on its particular set of facts, it may be interesting to note that employers have been held to be in breach of contract in the following situations:

- where an applicant for transfer had not been treated fairly;
- where there was a failure to investigate a genuine safety grievance;
- where there was a false accusation of theft on the basis of flimsy evidence;
- where an employer has persistently attempted to vary an employee's conditions of service.

The duty to take reasonable care of the employee

This is detailed at p.233.

The duties of the employee

THE DUTY TO CO-OPERATE WITH THE EMPLOYER

For convenience this can be divided into:

- The duty to obey lawful and reasonable orders.
- The duty not to impede the employer's business.

THE DUTY TO OBEY LAWFUL AND REASONABLE ORDERS

The obligation to carry out lawful orders has two distinct aspects. First, it means that employees are not required to obey an order if to do so would break the law – for example, falsifying accounts. Second, it also means that employees are not obliged to obey orders which fall outside the scope of the contract. This is consistent with the view that, at least in theory, the terms of a contract cannot be unilaterally varied. Unfortunately, this does not prevent employees from being *fairly* dismissed for refusing to follow instructions which are outside their contractual obligations.

THE DUTY NOT TO IMPEDE THE EMPLOYER'S BUSINESS

Since the essence of the employment relationship is that the employee is ready and willing to work in exchange for remuneration, it follows that going on strike breaches a fundamental term of the contract. Indeed, it would seem that even industrial action falling short of a strike is likely to be unlawful.

THE DUTY OF FIDELITY

Employees must avoid putting themselves in a position whereby their own interests conflict with those of their employer. Thus employees must not accept any reward for their work other than from their employer: for example, a secret gift or commission. It is worth noting that there are three particular aspects to this duty: the obligation not to compete with the employer, the duty not to disclose confidential information, and the law relating to inventions and copyright. The duty not to disclose information may apply even where the employment has ceased, if the information could reasonably be regarded as a trade secret. Additionally, employees who have access to confidential information may be restricted by express clauses in their contracts, which can set precise limits on their future employment, at least for a reasonable period. Arguably, however, an employee will not be bound by such clauses when he or she has been wrongfully dismissed by their employer (see p.240).

THE DUTY TO TAKE REASONABLE CARE

This is detailed at p.236.

What can be done if either party breaks the contract of employment?

The choices available to the innocent party will depend on whether the breach is of a minor or serious nature. An innocent party may choose to continue with the contract as if nothing had happened, they may sue for damages or, in the case of a serious breach, they may treat the contract as at an end. In most cases, however, employers will prefer to take disciplinary rather than legal action.

Traditionally, the law has placed great emphasis on the personal nature of the contract of employment and courts have been reluctant to order a defaulting party to continue to perform the contract of employment. Thus, although an injunction (an order restraining a particular act) may sometimes be available, in most cases where there has been a breach of contract damages will be the normal remedy. Those who get damages will be compensated for the direct and likely consequences of the breach. This is a complicated legal formula that tries to take into account the loss to the innocent party that arises as a result of the breach of contract and express this in financial terms.

Finally, it should be noted that ordinary breach of contract cases (for example, failure to pay wages or holiday money that is due) are currently heard by the ordinary civil courts (in most cases the local county court) and not by industrial tribunals. However, the jurisdiction of industrial tribunals is likely to be extended in 1994.

DISCRIMINATION IN EMPLOYMENT

Sex and race discrimination

These issues will be dealt with together since the relevant statutes are drafted in virtually identical terms. The definitions of sex and race discrimination were considered on p.217.

What is the difference between direct and indirect discrimination?

Both the SDA and the RRA draw a distinction between *direct* and *indirect* discrimination. Direct discrimination occurs when a person is treated less favourably than a person of the opposite gender, a single person, or a person not of the same racial group* would be treated. A person can complain of indirect discrimination where an employer applies a requirement or condition which would apply equally to a person of the opposite gender (single person or person not of the same racial group) but which is such that the proportion of the applicant's gender (marital status or racial group) who can comply with it is considerably smaller than the proportion of persons of the opposite gender (single people or persons not of the same racial group). For example, a height requirement might have a disproportionate impact. The applicant must also show that he or she suffered a detriment as a result of being unable to comply with the requirement. Employers can escape liability by demonstrating that the requirement or condition was justifiable irrespective of the gender (marital status or race) of the person to whom it is applied. A number of points need to be made about the above definitions:

1. Both statutes stipulate that, when drawing comparisons, the relevant circumstances of the complainant and the person with whom they compare themself (known as the *comparator*) must be the same or not materially different.
2. The statutory definitions cover cases where the reason for the discrimination was a generalised assumption that people of a particular sex, marital status or race (see footnote below) possess or lack cer-

*Wherever the term 'racial group' is used hereafter, it includes 'colour, nationality, ethnic or national origins'. See above at p.217.

tain characteristics (for example, the assumption that married men rather than married women are the principal breadwinners).

3. The words 'requirement or condition' refer to something that has to be complied with.
4. The words 'can comply' have been interpreted to mean 'can in practice comply' rather than physically or theoretically comply. Thus it has been held that an age limit of 28 for recruitment could amount to indirect discrimination against women, since they are less likely than men to be available for work below that age due to child-rearing.
5. The courts have ruled that a person only suffers detrimental treatment where its effect is such that a reasonable employee could justifiably complain about his or her working conditions or environment.
6. Indirect discrimination will only be justifiable if an industrial tribunal is satisfied that there were objectively justified grounds for the requirements or condition.

What would amount to unequal treatment in the course of employment?

It is unlawful for employers to discriminate:

- under the RRA, in the *terms* of employment afforded (terms which discriminate on the grounds of gender are covered by the EPA – see p.229).
- in the way they afford access to opportunities for promotion, transfer or training, or access to any other benefits, facilities or services, or by refusing or deliberately omitting to afford access to them.

  However, special arrangements are permitted for the training of persons of a particular gender or racial group if it can be shown that within the previous 12 months only a small minority of that gender or racial group was performing a particular type of work in Great Britain.
- by dismissing or subjecting the employee to any other detriment.
- by victimising people simply because they have given evidence in connection with proceedings, have brought proceedings, or intend to do so against someone under the anti-discrimination legislation.

It should also be noted that detrimental treatment on the grounds of pregnancy or maternity is capable of amounting to sex discrimination.

How is the anti-discrimination legislation enforced?

If the provisions of the SDA or RRA are not complied with, both the employing body and named individuals can be sued. Individuals may be liable for instructing or putting pressure on someone to perform an unlawful act and for knowingly aiding another person to do an unlawful act. Employers will be liable for the acts of employees in the course of employment, whether or not they were done with the employer's knowledge or approval, unless it can be proved that the employer took such steps as were reasonably practicable to prevent the employee doing that act. Indirect discrimination is unlawful whether it is intentional or not, but no compensation can be awarded for indirect discrimination if employers can show that they did not intend to discriminate.

To whom should complaints be made?

Both statutes permit individuals to bring complaints before an industrial tribunal within three months of a discriminatory act occurring, although out-of-time claims can sometimes be heard. The Equal Opportunities Commission (EOC) and the Commission for Racial Equality (CRE) can provide financial support for complainants and, if they think it desirable, can instigate formal investigations of anyone believed to be discriminating unlawfully. While the burden of proof is on the complainant to show unlawful discrimination, once an initial (*prima facie*) case of indirect discrimination has been established, the employer will have to satisfy the tribunal that the discriminatory requirement or condition was justifiable. Both statutes provide that customer or union preferences cannot constitute a defence.

What remedies are available to the complainant?

If no settlement is reached and the complaint is upheld, three possible remedies are available. First, the tribunal can make a declaration of the complainant's rights, i.e. make a simple declaration that discrimination has occurred, which might be of sufficient symbolic importance to satisfy an applicant in some cases. Second, the person who has been sued (the respondent) can be required to pay compensation, which may include an element to cover hurt feelings. Finally, there may be a recommendation that the employer takes action within a specified period designed to reduce the effect of the discrimination that has taken place. It should be observed that where a discriminatory dismissal is alleged to have occurred the remedies available for unfair dismissal are likely to prove more attractive to the employee. Not only does the employer have to show a fair reason for dismissal but reinstatement or re-engagement can be ordered.

The two Commissions mentioned above can be contacted for further assistance as follows:

Commission for Racial Equality (CRE), Elliot House, 10–12 Allington St, London SW1 5EH (tel: 071 828 7022).
Equal Opportunities Commission (EOC), Overseas House, Quay Street, Manchester, M3 3HM (tel: 061 833 9244).

Equal pay

When is an employee entitled to equal pay?

An *equality clause* operates when a person is employed on any of the following:

- 'like work';
- 'work rated as equivalent';
- work of 'equal value' to that of a person of the opposite sex in the same employment.

The effect of the equality clause is that any term in a person's contract (whether concerned with pay or not) which is less favourable than in the contract of a person of the opposite gender must be modified so as to be not less favourable.

What is *like work*?

This concept focuses on the job rather than the person performing it. Once a person has shown that her or his work is of the same or broadly similar nature as that of a person of the opposite gender, unless the employer can prove that any differences are of practical importance in relation to terms and conditions of employment – for example, the performance of supervisory duties – that person is to be regarded as employed on like work. Attention must be paid to the frequency with which any differences occur in practice as well as to their nature and extent. Thus tribunals investigate the actual work done rather than rely on theoretical contractual obligations.

What is *work rated as equivalent?*

A person's work will only be regarded as rated as equivalent to that of a person of the opposite gender if it has been given equal value under a properly conducted job evaluation scheme. If the work has been rated as equivalent there is no need to show that a similar job is performed.

When can an *equal value* claim be brought?

Because of the complexities involved in bringing an equal value claim it is likely that this procedure will only be invoked where it cannot be shown that like work or work rated as equivalent is being performed. Indeed, where work has been given different ratings under a job evaluation study, an equal value claim cannot proceed unless a tribunal is satisfied that there are reasonable grounds for concluding that the evaluation study was discriminatory.

What defence is available to the employer?

An employer can defeat a claim for equal pay by proving that the variation between the woman's and the man's contract was 'genuinely due to a material factor which is not the difference of gender' – for example, if the variation is due to differences in length of service or geographical location. However, the burden of proof will only be discharged if the employer can demonstrate objectively justified grounds for any difference in pay.

How is the equal pay legislation enforced?

Employees can apply to an industrial tribunal and claim arrears of pay. However, under United Kingdom law, a tribunal cannot make an award in respect of any employment earlier than two years before the date on which the proceedings were commenced. Complainants must identify a comparable person of the opposite sex in the same employment, i.e. a person employed at the same establishment or at another of the employer's establishments where broadly similar terms and conditions are observed. Although comparisons cannot be made with a hypothetical person, a complainant can compare her/himself with a previous job incumbent.

Victimisation on trade union grounds

Action short of dismissal

This is a negative right. Employees have the right not to have action short of dismissal taken against them as individuals by their employer for the purpose of:

either

- preventing or deterring them from being, or seeking to become, a member of any independent trade union or penalising them for doing so;

or

- preventing or deterring them from taking part in the activities of an independent trade union at any appropriate time, or penalising them for doing so;

or

- compelling them to become a member of any trade union or of a particular trade union or of one of a number of particular trade unions.

Several points must be made about the nature of this protection.

1. 'Action' is defined as including omissions. Thus a *failure to promote,* as well as more positive acts, like segregation, is covered.
2. Tribunals have the task of determining what are 'activities of an independent trade union'. The following have been accepted as such:
    - attempting to recruit new members or form a workplace union branch.
    - taking part in union meetings and consulting a union official.
3. 'Appropriate time' is defined as being outside working hours or within working hours in accordance with arrangements agreed with the employer. The employer's consent may be express, for example

in a collective agreement, or it may be implied from the conduct of the parties.

Dismissal on trade union grounds is dealt with below on p.243.

MATERNITY RIGHTS

Since the law is both detailed and complicated, this section will merely list the maternity rights that exist. The reader seeking more detailed information is advised to refer to the specialist publications listed at the end of this chapter.

1. It is unfair to dismiss an employee if:
   a) the reason, or principal reason, for dismissal is that she is pregnant, or is any other reason connected with her pregnancy; or
   b) her maternity leave is ended by dismissal and the reason, or principal reason, for dismissal is that she has given birth, or is any other reason connected with her having given birth; or
   c) her contract was terminated after the maternity leave period and the reason for dismissal is that she had taken maternity leave; or
   d) the reason, or principal reason, for dismissal is a requirement or recommendation relating to suspension on health and safety grounds; or
   e) her maternity leave period is ended by dismissal and the principal reason for it is redundancy, but the duty to offer alternative employment has not been complied with.
2. A woman who is dismissed at any time while she is pregnant, or after childbirth in circumstances in which her maternity leave ends by reason of dismissal, is entitled to written particulars of the reason for dismissal.
3. If an employer has available suitable alternative work for an employee who cannot continue her usual job because of a relevant health and safety provision, she is entitled to be offered that job. Where a woman is suspended on maternity grounds she is entitled to be paid unless she has unreasonably refused an offer of suitable alternative employment.
4. A pregnant woman who, on the advice of a registered medical practitioner, midwife or health visitor, has made an appointment to receive

ante-natal care, has the statutory right not to be unreasonably refused time off during working hours to keep the appointment.

5. Women who are absent from work wholly or partly because of pregnancy or confinement are entitled to either statutory maternity pay or maternity allowance depending on their length of service and level of earnings.
6. Irrespective of the hours they work, or their length of service, women will be entitled to 14 weeks' maternity leave. However, a woman with two years' continuous service of 16 hours a week or more has the right to return to work with her employer at any time before the end of 29 weeks, beginning with the week in which the confinement occurred.

HEALTH AND SAFETY AT WORK

What precautions must an employer take to ensure that an employee is reasonably safe from injury?

Recognising that employers cannot guarantee that no employee will be injured at work, the standard of care which the law demands is that which 'an ordinary prudent employer would take in the circumstances'. Thus it is accepted that employers should only be held liable if they fail to safeguard against something which was reasonably foreseeable. Employers are entitled to follow recognised practices in their industry, unless they are obviously unsafe, but must make arrangements to ensure that they are kept abreast of current developments. Once an employer knows of a source of danger, or could have been expected to know of it, it is necessary to take all reasonable steps to protect employees from risks which hitherto have been unforeseeable. The duty is to assess the likelihood of injury and to weigh the risk against the cost and inconvenience of taking effective precautions to eliminate it. The duty is owed to each individual employee. Thus employers will be expected to take special precautions in respect of disabled, untrained or inexperienced workers, together with those who have language difficulties.

The duty of care may be divided into the following headings:

- Safe premises, for example non-slippery floors.
- Safe plant, equipment and tools.

- Safe system of working. Under this heading are all the matters which relate to the manner in which the work is performed, job design, working methods, the provision of protective clothing, training and supervision. There is no reason in law why this should not apply equally to the proper protection of social workers from violence from clients, or health workers from illness and disease.
- Safe and competent colleagues. This means that employers must engage competent staff, instruct employees in safe working methods and then provide adequate supervision to check that these methods are being adhered to.

What has been the effect of the Health and Safety at Work Act 1974 (HASAW)?

With the exception of domestic workers, all employed persons are covered by the HASAW. The Act also seeks to protect persons other than those at work, i.e. members of the general public, against risks to their health and safety arising out of, or in connection with, work activities.

The general duties under HASAW

It is the duty of every employer to 'ensure, so far as is reasonably practicable, the health, safety and welfare at work of all his employees'. The matters to which this duty extends include:

- The provision and maintenance of plant and systems of work that are, so far as is reasonably practicable, safe and without risks to health.
- Arrangements for ensuring, so far as is reasonably practicable, safety and absence from risks to health in connection with the use, handling, storage and transport of articles and substances.
- The provision of such information, instruction, training and supervision as is necessary to ensure, so far as is reasonably practicable, the health and safety at work of employees.
- So far as is reasonably practicable as regards any place of work under the employer's control, to maintain it in a condition which is safe and without risks to health and to provide and maintain means of access to and egress from it that are safe and without such risks.

- The provision and maintenance of a working environment for employees that is, so far as is reasonably practicable, safe, without risks to health and adequate as regards facilities and arrangements for their welfare at work.

What does *so far as is reasonably practicable* mean?

While the standard of care owed is similar to that imposed by the implied duty to take reasonable care (see p.233), the defendant in any legal proceedings for a failure to comply with the HASAW has to prove that it was not reasonably practicable to do more than was in fact done.

Do employers have to have safety policies?

Except where fewer than five employees are employed at any one time in an undertaking, every employer must: 'prepare and as often as may be appropriate revise a written statement of his general policy with respect to the health and safety at work of his employees, and the organisation and arrangements for the time being in force for carrying out that policy, and to bring the statement and any revision of it to the notice of all of his employees'.

What are the functions of safety representatives and safety committees?

The HASAW provides for the appointment by recognised trade unions of safety representatives from among the employees. Where such representatives are appointed, employers have a duty to consult with them with a view to the making and maintenance of arrangements which will enable the employer and employees to co-operate effectively in promoting and developing measures to ensure the health and safety at work of the employees, and in checking the effectiveness of such measures. Where at least two safety representatives submit a written request, employers must establish a safety committee. Before doing so they must consult with the safety representatives who made the request and with the representatives of recognised trade unions. The function of safety committees is to keep under review the measures taken to ensure the health and safety at work of employees.

What are the responsibilities of employees under HASAW?

Two general duties are imposed on employees while they are at work:

1. to take reasonable care of the health and safety of themselves and of others who may be affected by their acts or omissions;
2. to co-operate with employers to enable them to fulfil their statutory duties.

Clearly it could be argued that employees who refuse to wear protective clothing or fail to observe safety procedures are in breach of this statutory duty. Finally, it is stated that nobody should intentionally or recklessly interfere with or misuse anything provided in the interests of health, safety or welfare in pursuance of any statutory provision.

What has been the impact of European safety laws?

Regulations have been adopted in the UK which implement European Community directives covering a wide range of issues. In brief these cover:

1. *Management of health and safety.* Employers must make a 'suitable and sufficient' assessment of the health and safety risks in their workplaces, identify the preventative and protective measures which need to be taken, and establish systems for their management. Employers must appoint a 'competent' person to assist them in complying with their health and safety obligations, and procedures must be established for health surveillance and dealing with emergencies.
2. *Workplace requirements.* Certain requirements must be met in relation to ventilation, temperature, lighting, workstation design and rest facilities.
3. *Work equipment.* Employers are under a specific obligation to ensure that all work equipment is suitable and well maintained. Workers must be provided with information and training on the use of equipment. More specific requirements must be met in relation to a range of issues, for example, dangerous parts of machinery and maintenance operations.
4. *Personal protective equipment.* Employers must provide protective equipment where necessary. In addition, they must ensure that it is

suitable and well maintained and that workers are given information and training on its use.

5. *Manual handling operations.* Employees should not be required to undertake manual handling operations which involve a risk of injury where it is reasonably practicable to avoid this. The approach is ergonomic, i.e. employers should make the job suitable for the employee rather than vice versa, by using principles of physics and so forth in reducing lifting stresses. Where it is not practicable entirely to remove risk of injury, the employer must make a 'suitable and sufficient assessment' of the risk involved and take 'appropriate steps' to reduce it as far as is reasonably practicable. Employees must also be given certain information on the loads they are now required to handle. An excellent booklet on this issue is *Health and Safety Executive: Manual Handling Operations Regulations 1992: Guidance on Regulations* (HMSO, 1992).
6. *Display screens equipment.* Employers must assess workstations and take steps to reduce any safety risks that are identified. Work on display screen equipment must be planned to allow breaks, and users must be provided with free eye tests and information on the use of their workstations.

How are health and safety laws enforced?

While a breach of the HASAW or Regulations issued under it amounts to a criminal offence, civil liability only arises if there is a failure to comply with Regulations. A failure to observe any provision of an approved Code of Practice does not of itself render a person liable to any proceedings, but such a Code is admissible in evidence and proof of a failure to meet its requirements will be sufficient to establish a contravention of a statutory provision unless a court is satisfied that the provision was complied with in some other way.

Apart from the Crown and most of the National Health Service, any person or corporate body can be prosecuted for an offence under the HASAW. However, if an offence is proved to have been committed with the consent or connivance of, or to have been attributable to neglect on the part of, any director, manager, company secretary or other similar officer, that person as well as the corporate body may be found guilty of an offence. Where the commission of an offence by any person is due to the act or default of some other person, that other person may be charged whether or not proceedings are taken against the first-mentioned person. Thus Crown servants may be prosecuted despite the immunity of the Crown itself. If people are convicted of offences in respect of any matters which appear to the court to be within their power to remedy, the court may, in addition to, or instead of, imposing any punishment, order them to take such steps as may be specified to remedy those matters.

Except for the enforcement responsibilities of local authorities (the Regulations impose certain inspection duties on local authorities), the HASAW is enforced by the Health and Safety Executive (HSE). Where an inspector from the HSE is of the opinion that a person is contravening (or has contravened) a statutory provision in circumstances that make it likely that the contravention will be repeated, he or she may issue an improvement notice stating that opinion. If an inspector believes that activities are being carried on (or are about to be carried on) which will involve a risk of serious personal injury, the inspector may issue a *prohibition notice*. Such a notice may take effect immediately, although ordinarily it will take effect at the end of a period specified in the notice. A person on whom an enforcement notice (whether an improvement or a prohibition notice) is served may appeal to an industrial tribunal, which has the power to cancel, affirm or modify the notice. Failure to comply with a notice is an offence.

How often does the HSE take action through the courts?

The number of recorded convictions as a result of HSE prosecutions in 1992/3 was 1843, with an average penalty of £1384. The number of enforcement notices issued in 1990–1was 25,768, of which 19,079 were improvement notices, 6222 were *immediate* prohibition notices, and 467 were *deferred* prohibition notices.

The address of the Health and Safety Executive is: HSE, Baynards House, 1–13 Chepstow Place, London W2 4TF (tel: 071 243 6000). The enquiry point of the HSE is able to deal with urgent questions.

LOSING EMPLOYMENT

Although the bulk of this section deals with the statutory rights to claim unfair dismissal and redundancy payments it might be helpful to begin by outlining the basis on which an action for breach of contract can be brought.

Dismissal in breach of contract

The first distinction to be made is that between dismissal without notice and dismissal with notice.

Dismissal without notice

Where the employer terminates the contract without giving notice the employee is said to be summarily dismissed. In order to justify a summary dismissal the employee must be in breach of an important express or implied term of the contract, i.e. guilty of gross misconduct. Although certain terms are always regarded as important, for example the duty not to steal or damage the employer's property, the significance of other terms will depend on the nature of the employer's business and the employee's position in it. If employers do not invoke the right to summarily dismiss within a reasonable period of the conduct occurring it will be assumed that they have waived this right (although they may be able to dismiss fairly with notice, see below). What is a reasonable period will depend on the facts of the particular case.

Dismissal with notice

Usually either party is entitled to terminate a contract of employment by giving notice and once notice has been given it cannot be unilaterally withdrawn. For notice to be effective it must be possible to ascertain the date of termination, and not infrequently employees have confused an advance warning of closure with notice of dismissal. The length of notice will be determined by the express or implied terms of the contract. Apart from the situation where the employee is guilty of gross misconduct, the law provides that certain minimum periods of notice must be given. After a month's service an employee is entitled to a week's notice and this applies until the employment has lasted for two years. At this point two weeks' notice is owed and from then on the employee must receive an extra week's notice for each year of service up to a maximum of 12 weeks. An employee with a month's service or more need only give one week's notice to terminate, but there is nothing to prevent the parties agreeing that both should receive more than the statutory minimum.

What are the remedies for wrongful dismissal?

Basically, a wrongful dismissal is one without notice or with inadequate notice in circumstances where proper notice should have been given. The expression also covers dismissals which are in breach of agreed procedures. Thus, where there is a contractual disciplinary procedure an employee may be able to obtain an injunction or declaration from the courts to prevent a dismissal or declare a dismissal void if the procedure has not been followed. However, in the vast majority of cases the employee's remedy will be damages for breach of contract. Since damages are not available for hurt feelings or the manner in which the dismissal took place, an employee will normally only recover the amount of wages lost.

Unfair dismissal

Who can claim unfair dismissal?

While the law grants many employees the right not to be unfairly dismissed, and the right to seek reinstatement and compensation if they are unfairly dismissed, there are nevertheless a number of general exclusions from and qualifications upon this right. First, no claim can be made if, on or before the effective date of termination, the individual had attained the normal retiring age for an employee in his or her position or, if there is no normal retiring age, was 65 years old. Second, two years' continuous service is required before the right arises. However, neither the age limit nor the service qualification apply if the reason for dismissal is 'inadmissible' (see p.243). Third, while Crown employees are covered by the legislation, those who ordinarily work outside Great Britain are excluded.

What is a dismissal?

For both unfair dismissal and redundancy purposes an employee is to be treated as dismissed if:

1. The contract under which he or she is employed is terminated by the employer with or without notice. It should be noted that where an

employer has given notice to terminate, an employee who gives counter-notice indicating that he or she wishes to leave before the employer's notice has expired is still to be regarded as dismissed. Obviously, if people resign of their own volition there is no dismissal at law, although if pressure has been applied the situation will be different, for example where the employee is given the choice of resigning or being dismissed. A mutually agreed termination does not amount to a dismissal.

2. A fixed-term contract expires without being renewed under the same contract (see p.219 for exclusion clauses in fixed-term contracts).
3. The employee terminates the contract with or without notice in circumstances such that he or she is entitled to terminate it without notice by reason of the employer's conduct. This is commonly referred to as a constructive dismissal. Employees are only entitled to treat themselves as constructively dismissed if the employer is guilty of conduct which is a fundamental breach of contract, for example where the employee is demoted or given a significant change of job duties without their consent. If employees continue for a lengthy period after such a breach without leaving, they will be regarded as having elected to affirm the contract and will lose the right to treat themselves as discharged.

Must an employer give a reason for a dismissal?

Yes, and if not the employee can apply to an industrial tribunal (see p.251). Once an employee has proved that there has been a dismissal the tribunal will require the employer to show the reason, or if there was more than one, the principal reason for dismissal and that it falls within one of the following categories:

1. It related to the capability or qualifications of the employee for performing work of the kind which he or she was employed to do.
2. It related to the conduct of the employee.
3. The employee was redundant.
4. The employee could not continue to work in the position held without contravention of a duty or restriction imposed by statute – for example, where a person loses a driving licence.
5. There was some other substantial reason of a kind such as to justify the dismissal of an employee holding his or her particular position.

In all the above cases the reason for dismissal must have existed and been known to the employer at the time of dismissal. This makes it impossible for an employer to rely on subsequently discovered misconduct.

Must the employer put the reasons for the dismissal in writing?

A person who has been continuously employed for two years, or a pregnant woman who has been dismissed, has the right to be supplied with a written statement giving particulars of the reason for dismissal. The employer must provide the statement within 14 days of a request being made. If it is alleged that the employer unreasonably failed to provide such a statement, or that the particulars given were inadequate or untrue, a claim may be presented to an industrial tribunal (see p.251). If the complaint is well founded the tribunal may make a declaration as to what it finds the employer's reasons for dismissing were, and must order that the employee receive two weeks' pay from the employer.

What reasons for dismissal are potentially fair?

Capability or qualifications

Capability is to be assessed by reference to 'skill, aptitude, health or any other physical or mental quality' (on pregnancy and maternity, see above at p.232). Qualifications means 'any degree, diploma or other academic, technical or professional qualification relevant to the position which the employee held'. For our purposes it is convenient to consider capability in terms of competence and ill health.

As regards incompetence, unless it can be shown that a warning would have been 'utterly useless', for example where the inadequacy of the employee's performance is extreme or the actual or potential consequences of a mistake are grave, employees should not be dismissed unless warnings have been issued. In relation to ill health, it should be emphasised that the decision to dismiss is not a medical one but a matter to be determined by employers in the light of the medical evidence available. The basic question is whether in all the circumstances the employer could have been expected to wait any longer for the employee to recover. Clearly, where there has been long-term absence due to illness a discussion of the position with the employee will be more appropriate than a warning.

Conduct

In this context conduct means behaviour of such a nature, whether done inside or outside the course of employment, which has an impact in some way on the employer/employee relationship. It is not the function of tribunals to decide whether misconduct is gross or criminal but whether the employer has, in the circumstances of the case, acted reasonably in dismissing.

Redundancy

It is well established that employers have a duty to consider the alternatives to compulsory redundancy, and the ACAS Advisory Booklet, *Redundancy Handling*, suggests methods of avoiding such redundancies. If compulsory redundancies cannot be avoided, in the absence of an agreed procedure or customary arrangement, the personal circumstances of employees must be taken into account. While an employer will be expected to show some special reason for not consulting it should be observed that the absence of consultation does not render a dismissal automatically unfair (see p.247 on the circumstances in which an employee is redundant, and see below on automatically unfair dismissals).

Some other substantial reason (SOSR)

This was included in the legislation so as to give tribunals the discretion to accept as a fair reason for dismissal something that would not conveniently fit into any of the other categories. It covers such diverse matters as dismissal for failing to obtain a fidelity bond, refusing to sign an undertaking not to compete, and personality clashes between employees. SOSR has frequently provided a convenient peg where employees have been dismissed as a result of a reorganisation of the business.

Will a dismissal ever be automatically unfair?

A dismissal will be automatically unfair if the reason for it (or, if more than one, the principal reason) was one of the following. That the employee:

1. Was or proposed to become a member of an independent trade union.

2. Has taken, or has proposed to take, part in the activities of an independent trade union at any appropriate time (see p.231).
3. Was not a member of any trade union or of a particular trade union, or had refused or proposed to refuse to become or remain a member.
4. Left, or proposed to leave, their place of work or any dangerous part of the workplace in circumstances of serious or imminent danger which the employee could not reasonably be expected to have averted.
5. Took, or proposed to take, appropriate steps to protect themselves or other employees in circumstances of serious or imminent danger. Employers will have a defence in these circumstances if they can show that the employee's action was so negligent that a reasonable employer would have treated the employee in a similar way.
6. Brought to the employer's attention, by reasonable means, work circumstances which the employee reasonably believed were harmful to health or safety, where it was not reasonably practicable for the matter to be raised by a safety representative or committee.
7. Carried out, or proposed to carry out, activities designated by the employer in connection with preventing or reducing risks to the health and safety of employees.
8. Performed, or proposed to perform, any of their functions as a safety representative or a member of a safety committee.
9. See p.232 in connection with 'inadmissible' reasons and maternity rights.
10. 'Inadmissible reasons' in connection with redundancy. If the reason a person was selected for redundancy related to any of the above, or if a person was selected in contravention of a customary or agreed procedure and there were no special reasons justifying a departure from that arrangement or procedure, dismissal will be unfair. Selection for redundancy on the grounds of pregnancy or maternity will also be unfair.
11. Had brought proceedings against the employer to enforce a statutory right or alleged that the employer had infringed such a right.
12. Where the transfer of an undertaking (see below), or a reason connected with it, is the reason or principal reason for dismissal then the dismissal is to be treated as unfair, unless there is an economic, technical or organisational reason entailing changes in the workforce. For these purposes a distinction is drawn between a

business which is transferred while it is a going concern, and the mere sale of assets. An 'undertaking' includes a trade or business.

NB Where at the date of dismissal the employee was locked out or taking part in a strike or other industrial action, a tribunal has no jurisdiction to determine whether a dismissal was fair or unfair unless it can be shown that one or more 'relevant' employees of the same employer were not dismissed in the circumstances or that, within three months of the complainant's dismissal, any such employee has been offered re-engagement and the complainant has not. If, at the time of the dismissal, the employee was taking part in unofficial action no complaint of unfair dismissal can be made.

Note that there is no service qualification for any of 1–11 above (i.e. no need to serve two years to claim unfairness).

In what circumstances will a dismissal be reasonable?

Where the employer has given a valid reason for dismissal the determination of the question whether the dismissal was fair or unfair depends on whether, in the circumstances (including the size and administrative resources of the employer's undertaking), the employer acted reasonably or unreasonably in treating it as a *sufficient* reason for dismissing the employee; that question shall be determined in accordance with equity and the substantial merits of the case.

Thus, at this stage, tribunals must take account of the wider circumstances. In addition to the employer's business needs, attention must be paid to the personal attributes of the employee, for example seniority and previous work record. The words 'equity and the substantial merits' also allow tribunals to apply their knowledge of good industrial relations practice and to ensure that there has been procedural fairness. However, it is not the function of tribunals to ask themselves whether they would have done what the employer did in the circumstances; their function is merely to assess the employer's decision to dismiss to see if it falls within a range of responses which a reasonable employer could have taken. Finally, it should be noted that the ACAS Code of Practice does not have the force of law and therefore a failure to comply with it does not make a dismissal automatically unfair.

What are the remedies for unfair dismissal?

Re-employment

When applicants are found to be unfairly dismissed tribunals must explain their powers to order reinstatement or re-engagement and ask employees if they wish such an order to be made. Only if such a wish is expressed can an order be made and if no order is made the tribunal must turn to the question of compensation.

Where re-employment is sought a tribunal must first consider whether reinstatement is appropriate, i.e. should the complainant be treated in all respects as if he or she had not been dismissed. If reinstatement is not ordered the tribunal must then decide whether to order re-engagement and, if so, on what terms.

Where a person is re-employed following a tribunal order but the terms are not fully complied with, if the matter is referred again to the tribunal the employee can be compensated for the loss caused by the non-compliance. If a complainant is not re-employed in accordance with such an order compensation will be awarded, together with an additional or special award, unless the employer satisfies the tribunal that it was not practicable to comply with the order.

Awards of compensation

Compensation will be calculated in accordance with the following formula:

Basic award. Normally this will be calculated in the same way as a redundancy payment and will be reduced by the amount of any redundancy payment received. Where the reason or principal reason for dismissal related to any of the reasons listed at 1–3 or 7–8 on pp. 243–4 there is a current minimum award of £2700. The basic award can be reduced by such proportion as the tribunal considers just and equitable on two grounds: a) the complainant unreasonably refused an offer of reinstatement; b) any conduct of the complainant before the dismissal.
Compensatory award. The amount of this award is that which a tribunal 'considers just and equitable in all the circumstances having regard to the loss sustained by the complainant in consequence of the dismissal in so far as that loss is attributable to action taken by the employer'. However,

it should be noted that a complainant cannot be reimbursed for the cost of pursuing an unfair dismissal claim. The compensatory award can be reduced where the employee's action caused or contributed to the dismissal and where the employee failed to mitigate his or her loss. The maximum compensatory award is currently £11,000. The legislation aims to reimburse the employee rather than to punish the employer. Thus employees who appear to have lost nothing, for example where it can be said that irrespective of the procedural unfairness that occurred they would have been dismissed anyway, may not qualify for a compensatory award.

Redundancy

In what circumstances is an employee redundant?

Employees are redundant if their dismissals are attributable to:

1. The fact that the employer has ceased, or intends to cease, to carry on the business for the purposes for which the employees were employed, or to carry on that business in the place where the employees were so employed.
2. The fact that the requirements of that business for employees to carry out work of a particular kind, or for employees to carry out work of a particular kind in the place where they were so employed, have ceased or diminished or are expected to cease or diminish.

In this context, 'cease' or 'diminish' mean either permanently or temporarily and from whatever cause. Thus employees will be entitled to a payment notwithstanding that it could be seen from the commencement of the contract that they would be dismissed for redundancy. It is also important to note that dismissed employees are presumed to have been dismissed by reason of redundancy unless the contrary is proved.

What is the effect of an offer of alternative employment?

If before the ending of a person's employment an employer makes an offer to renew the contract or to re-engage under a new contract which is to take effect either on the ending of the old one or within four weeks afterwards, the law states as follows:

1. if the provisions of the new or renewed contract as to the capacity and place in which the person will be employed, together with the other terms and conditions, do not differ from the corresponding terms of the previous contract;

or

2. the terms and conditions differ but the offer constitutes an offer of suitable employment (for example work at another location);

and

3. in either case the employee unreasonably refuses that offer, he or she will *not* be entitled to a redundancy payment.

The burden is on the employer to prove both the suitability of the offer and the unreasonableness of the employee's refusal.

Where the terms and conditions will differ from those of the previous contract a trial period may be invoked. This will last for four calendar weeks unless a longer period has been agreed for the purpose of retraining. If during the trial period the employee for any reason terminates the contract, or the employer terminates the contract for a reason connected with or arising out of the change (as, for example, when the employer terminates the contract because the employee is incapable of doing the new job), the employee is to be treated for redundancy purposes as having been dismissed on the date the previous contract ended.

Who can claim a redundancy payment?

Employees who have two years' continuous service over the age of 18 qualify for a payment. Certain categories are specifically excluded, for example civil servants and National Health Service employees. Also ineligible are employees who ordinarily work outside Great Britain and those who are 65 years old (or reach a normal pensionable age (see Chapter 9 at p.302) of less than 65). On exclusion clauses in fixed-term contracts, see p.219.

Workers will normally only be entitled to make a claim if within six months of their employment terminating they have:

either

- given notice to the employer that they want a payment;

or

- referred a question as to their right to a payment, or its amount, to a tribunal;

or

- presented a complaint of unfair dismissal to a tribunal.

How is a redundancy payment calculated?

Redundancy payments are calculated according to the following formula, with a maximum of 20 years being taken into account. Starting at the end of the employee's period of continuous service and reckoning backwards:

- $1\frac{1}{2}$ weeks' pay is allowed for each year of employment in which the employee was between the ages of 41 and 64. Those who are aged 64 have their entitlement reduced by one-twelfth in respect of each month they remain in employment. A week's pay for each year of employment in which the employee was between the ages of 22 and 40. Half a week's pay for each year of employment between the ages of 18 and 21. A week's pay is calculated on a gross basis but the reckonable maximum is currently £205 per week.

Can an employee get time off to look for work when facing redundancy?

A person who has been continuously employed for two years or more and is under notice of dismissal by reason of redundancy is entitled to reasonable time off during working hours to look for new employment or to make arrangements for training. Such an employee should be paid at the normal hourly rate throughout the period of absence. A complaint that an employer has unreasonably refused time off, or has failed to pay the whole or part of any amount to which the employee is entitled, must be presented to an industrial tribunal within three months of the day on which it is alleged that the time off should have been allowed. If the complaint is well founded the tribunal must make a declaration to that effect and order the employer to pay the amount which it finds due to the employee. However, the maximum that can be awarded is two-fifths of a week's pay.

THE ENFORCEMENT OF EMPLOYMENT RIGHTS

Having dealt with a number of the most important issues in the workplace where the employee has legal rights, this chapter will conclude by reference to the various methods whereby an employee can seek to enforce these rights, and will also suggest sources of further advice and assistance.

Where to get specialist advice and assistance

Apart from general advice agencies like CABs and law centres and specialist bodies like the Equal Opportunities Commission, Commission for Racial Equality and the Health and Safety Executive (see above at pp. 229, 238), there are two main sources of employment advice and assistance.

Trade unions

Those who are members of a trade union should approach their local union representative for assistance. Most employment problems can be resolved without recourse to the law, but if legal proceedings are necessary trade unionists are often entitled to representation and financial support.

Advisory, Conciliation and Arbitration Service (ACAS)

ACAS is an independent body with the general duty of promoting the improvement of industrial relations. One of its functions is to provide advice to workers, trade unions and employers on any matter concerned with employment. In addition, ACAS has the task of conciliating in industrial tribunal cases (other than claims for redundancy payments). When a claim is received by an industrial tribunal a copy of it will be sent to a conciliation officer who has the duty to promote, if possible, a settlement without the matter having to go to a tribunal hearing. Conciliation officers can intervene if requested to do so by the employee or employer or where they believe they could act with a reasonable prospect of success. Most importantly, the conciliation officer can act before a complaint has been made to the tribunal if there is a dispute which could be the subject of tribunal proceedings. Where a settlement is reached after the involvement of a conciliation officer the employee is prevented from taking the case to a tribunal hearing.

What are industrial tribunals?

Although ordinary breach of contract cases are heard in the county court or High Court (see Chapter 1), most employment protection rights are enforced at industrial tribunals. Tribunal cases are usually heard by legally qualified chairpersons and two other persons, known as lay members, who are nominated by organisations of workers and employers. Hearings at industrial tribunals are relatively informal. The parties can represent themselves or be represented by a lawyer, trade union official or any other person. While legal aid is not available for tribunal hearings, it is possible to obtain advice and assistance in preparing a case under the Legal Aid Scheme.

Complaints, known as originating applications, must normally arrive at an industrial tribunal within three months of the action complained about – for example, the date of the termination of employment in a claim for unfair dismissal. Each party has to bear their own costs unless it can be shown that the other party behaved frivolously, vexatiously, abusively, disruptively or otherwise unreasonably in bringing or conducting the proceedings.

SOME USEFUL ADDRESSES

ACAS (central office), 27 Wilton Street, London, SW1X 7AZ (tel: 071 210 3000). ACAS also has a number of regional offices situated in London (tel: 071 388 5100), Birmingham, Nottingham, Newcastle upon Tyne, Manchester, Liverpool, Bristol, Leeds, Glasgow and Cardiff.

The addresses of the central offices of the industrial tribunals in the United Kingdom are as follows:

England and Wales: Government Buildings, 100 Southgate Street, Bury St Edmonds, Suffolk IP33 2AQ (tel: 0284 762300).
Scotland: St Andrews House, 141 West Nile St, Glasgow G1 2RU (tel: 041 331 1601).
Northern Ireland: 2nd Floor, Bedford House, Bedford St, Belfast BT2 7NR (tel: 0232 327666).

Industrial tribunals are located in London, Ashford (Kent), Birmingham, Bristol, Bury St Edmunds, Cardiff, Leeds, Liverpool, Manchester, Newcastle upon Tyne, Nottingham, Sheffield, Southampton, Aberdeen, Dundee, Edinburgh and Glasgow. Applicants should contact the nearest office to their home or place of work. For the full address, consult the local telephone directory or local CAB.

The Employment Appeal Tribunal (EAT) has a central office in London but can sit anywhere in England, Wales or Scotland. It hears appeals on points of law from industrial tribunals, and consists of High Court judges and a panel of lay members nominated by employers' and workers' organisations. Its decisions are binding on industrial tribunals. Legal aid is available for representation before the EAT. The address of the Employment Appeal Tribunal is: EAT, 4 St James's Square, London SW1 4JU (tel: 071 210 3000).

The Trades Union Congress (TUC) can also be contacted by anybody who wishes either to join a trade union or is seeking information as to which unions cover their particular workplace. The address is: TUC, Congress House, Great Russell St, London WC1B 3LS (tel: 071 636 4030).

BIBLIOGRAPHY

Barrett, B., and Howells, R. (1993), *Health and Safety Law* (M and E Handbook, Pitman).
Outlines the legal framework for occupational health and safety.

Bowers, J., and Honeyball, S. (1993), *Textbook on Labour Law* (2nd edn, Blackstone).
In this book employment rights are explained without recourse to legal jargon, and the discussion of everyday problems gives an insight into how the law works in practice.

Greenhalgh, R. (1992), *Industrial Tribunals* (IPM).
This is a highly practical guide for anyone who may be involved in an industrial tribunal case.

Hepple, R., and Fredman, S. (1992), *Labour Law and Industrial Relations in Great Britain* (Kluwer).
This book provides an introduction to employment law in its industrial relations context. It assumes no prior knowledge of law and is aimed primarily at students.

Kibling, T., and Lewis, T. (1991), *Employment Law: An Adviser's Handbook* (Legal Action Group).
Provides a step-by-step guide to employment law and evidence.

Lewis, D. (1994), *Essentials of Employment Law* (4th edn, IPM).
A practical guide for managers and a textbook for students of personnel management.
Selwyn, A. I. (1993), *Law of Employment* (Butterworths).
A detailed handbook for someone dealing with employment law on a daily basis.
Smith, I., and Wood, I. (1993), *Industrial Law* (Butterworths).
A well-written textbook for students of employment law.
TUC Guide to Maternity Benefits and Rights (TUC Publications).
Provides details of state maternity benefits and assesses their impact.
Wedderburn, Lord (1986), *The Worker and the Law* (Pelican).
Discusses the present state of employment law in terms which the intelligent non-lawyer will be able to appreciate and also explains the social, economic and political background.

The Labour Research Department regularly publishes inexpensive guides to changes in employment legislation. For details of full publication list, contact: Labour Research Department, 78 Blackfriars Rd, London SE1 8HF (tel: 081 928 3649).

The Department of Employment produces a number of guides to employment law which are available free of charge from local offices. The central office is at Caxton House, Tothill St, London SW1H 9NF (tel: 071 273 3000). The Department has eight regional offices.

Chapter 8

Welfare benefits

GENERAL INTRODUCTION

The need for those engaged in social work and advice work to have a basic working knowledge of welfare benefits cannot be overstressed. Most social work clients are entitled to some form of welfare benefit, and the statistics confirming low take-up rates are truly alarming. Furthermore, the links between low take-up and other forms of social stress and deprivation are well documented. For example, the Social Security Advisory Committee Research Paper No. 1 (HMSO, 1989) clearly demonstrated the parallel (and interlinked) sharp rises in serious debt, mortgage repossession and homelessness (see Chapter 10). It is unfortunately the case that the initial assessments by the DSS of client entitlements are frequently defective, the 1987 Annual Report of the Chief Adjudication Officer suggesting that as many as one-third of social security decisions are wrong! A report entitled *Quality of Service to the Public at DHSS Offices*, HC 491 (HMSO 1988), published at the same time, found that DSS offices were widely failing to provide the public with sufficient information on benefit entitlement. In these circumstances, advisers have a duty to be accurate and vigilant in the advice they give to their clients. In a book of this length it is only possible to provide an outline of the system of welfare benefits that is currently in operation in this country. (For the purposes of this chapter we are talking about the unified system that operates throughout England, Wales and Scotland, though not Northern Ireland, which has its own social security system.) There are, however, a number of excellent guides to welfare benefits of which the Child Poverty Action Group (CPAG) guides are the most detailed and best value for money. No adviser should be without these guides, published annually under the titles *Rights Guide to Non-Means Tested Benefits* and

National Welfare Benefits Handbook. There is in addition a series of detailed and specialised texts as follows:

Bonner, D., Hooker, L., and White, R. (1993), *Non-Means Tested Benefits: The Legislation* (Sweet and Maxwell).
The Disability Rights Handbook (Disability Alliance, annual edition).
Jacobs, E., and Douglas, G. (1993), *Child Support: The Legislation* (Sweet and Maxwell).
Rowland, M. (1993), *Medical and Disability Appeal Tribunals: The Legislation* (Sweet and Maxwell).
Mesher, J. (1993), *CPAG's Income-Related Benefits: The Legislation* (Sweet and Maxwell).
Findlay, L., and Ward, M. (1993), *CPAG's Housing Benefit and Council Tax Benefit Legislation* (CPAG).

All relevant DSS leaflets are referred to individually in the appropriate section of the chapter. They can all be obtained from: Benefits Agency Information Division, Leaflets Unit, Block 4, Government Buildings, Honeypot Lane, Stanmore HA7 1AY, or ISCO5, DSS, The Paddocks, Frizinghall, Bradford BD9 4HD. To put your name on the mailing list for new leaflets, write to Social Security Mailing List, Room 607, Benefits Agency, Ray House, St Andrew's Street, London EC4A 3AD. There is also a free benefits advice hotline on 0800 666 555.

Note that, although the DHSS was in 1989 split into two sections, the Department of Health (DOH) and the Department of Social Security (DSS), many of the leaflets currently in circulation still emanate from the DHSS, having been published before the division was made. For the real specialist, the definitive annotated guide to all the means tested social security legislation is Mesher, J. (1993), *Income-Related Benefits* (Sweet and Maxwell), and to the non-means tested social security legislation is Bonner et al. (1993), see above.

The chapter is divided into two sections to reflect the two basic categories of benefit. The first section deals with benefits to which claimants who satisfy the relevant criteria will be entitled without a means test. The second section deals with benefits that are subject to a means test. The two CPAG guides also reflect this same broad division.

Two further general points should be made to welfare rights advisers. First, always claim as early as possible. Many benefits can only be backdated for a limited period unless 'good cause' can be shown for the delay. For detailed advice on this issue, consult Partington, M. (1989), *Claim in Time* (2nd edn, Legal Action Group). Second, advisers should familiarise themselves with the concept of 'passporting', i.e. entitlement to one benefit (e.g. income support) will often give the claimant access to further benefits, so it is worth claiming the first benefit, however small the amount. The latest edition (third) of Ogus and Barendt (1988), *Law of Social Security* (Butterworths), provides detailed assistance in this area, but most welfare rights guides address the problem in outline. Finally, note that some of these benefits will be significantly altered from April 1995.

NON-MEANS TESTED WELFARE BENEFITS

Benefits for people incapable of work

What does *incapable of work* mean?

This means that the claimant is unable to go to work either because they are ill, injured, disabled or convalescing after illness, or because they may be the carrier of an infectious disease. Evidence from the claimant alone is normally sufficient for the first week of incapacity, after which a medical certificate should be obtained from the claimant's GP. Any disputes as to whether the claimant is in fact incapable of work as a result of their condition can be referred by the DSS to the DSS Regional Medical Service.

The benefits that may be claimed in these circumstances will depend upon the length of the incapacity and the cause of the incapacity. A claimant in receipt of any of these benefits may also 'top up' their income with income support if their means are sufficiently low (see p.263). The sequence of entitlements is broadly as follows:

1. statutory sick pay or sickness benefit for the first 28 weeks of incapacity during the period of entitlement (see p.257);
2. invalidity benefit (pension and allowance) thereafter (see p.258);
3. severe disablement allowance (for severely disabled claimants: see Chapter 4, p.124);
4. industrial injuries benefits if the incapacity is the result of a work-induced accident or illness; see Chapter 4, p.109 and the DSS leaflet,

Injured at Work? A more detailed source of reference is Lewis, *Compensation for Industrial Injury* (Professional Books).

For specialists, the definitive annotated guide to non-means tested social security legislation is Bonner, D. et al. (see above at p.255).

Statutory Sick Pay (SSP)

Most employees who are incapable of work will be entitled to receive SSP from their employers after four days' incapacity. The maximum amount of SSP payable is 28 times the current weekly rate in any one period of entitlement, after which time the employee will claim invalidity benefit if still incapable of work. Periods of incapacity of four or more consecutive days are joined in one period of entitlement if there are less than eight weeks between them. As long as the employee informs their employer of their incapacity they will automatically receive SSP without having to claim it. Many employees will find that in their contract of employment (see Chapter 7, p.218) their employer has agreed to pay them more than the current rate of SSP during a period of incapacity. There are two rates of SSP which are related to the earnings of the claimant at the time of the incapacity. PAYE tax and NI contributions will be deducted from SSP. A few categories of employee are excluded from the scheme, in which case they will have to rely upon sickness benefit. For further information, see: DSS leaflet NI 244, *Statutory Sick Pay*; DSS leaflet NI 270, *Employer's Manual on SSP;* DSS leaflet NI 268, *Employer's Key: a Quick Guide to NI and SSP.*

Sickness Benefit (SB)

A person who is incapable of work but is not entitled to receive SSP (see above) can claim sickness benefit (SB) if they have paid sufficient NI contributions (see Chapter 9, p.306 on how to find out how many NI contributions you have paid). SB may thus be an alternative benefit to people who are incapable of work but are in an excluded SSP category (see above) or are unemployed or self-employed but have paid sufficient NI contributions. It should be noted, however, that even the lower rate of SSP (see above) is higher than the current rate of SB. SB is not taxable. It has to be claimed on DSS Form SC1. For further information, see DSS leaflet NI 16, *Sickness Benefit.*

Invalidity Benefit (IB)[1]

If a claimant is still incapable of work after 28 weeks in receipt of either SSP or SB they will normally automatically receive invalidity benefit (IB), as long as they have made the right number of NI contributions (see p.306). IB is made up of a basic invalidity pension, which is higher than the SB rate but lower than the higher rate of SSP, and, if the claimant was under 55 (women) or 60 (men) when their incapacity began, an additional invalidity allowance. The amount of the invalidity allowance will depend upon the age at which the incapacity began. In both cases there will be additional payments for any adult or child dependants of the claimant. An additional payment will be made to reflect any contribution by the claimant to SERPS (see Chapter 9, p.305). IB is not taxable. Subject to means testing, receipt of invalidity benefit provides a 'passport' to a disability premium to the claimant in receipt of income support (p.265). For further information, see DSS leaflet NI 16A, *Invalidity Benefit.*

Unemployment Benefit (UB)[2]

This is a benefit paid to people who are available for work but have no job. It is payable for a period of up to one year in fortnightly payments. To claim UB a claimant must have paid the appropriate number of NI contributions (see p.306), they must be available for work and actively seeking work (see below), and must not be disqualified. UB is not payable for the first three days of interruption of employment, and is taxable.

What does *available for work* mean?

A claimant of UB has to be actively seeking work (which is more than mere 'availability'), and available and ready for any suitable work that is offered to them. This does not mean:

- that they must accept work that involves self-employment;
- that they must accept work that it would be unreasonable to expect them to do, i.e. a claimant can restrict their availability to work requiring their particular skills or in a particular place at reasonable

[1]To be replaced in April 1995 by a new benefit – Incapacity Benefit.
[2]To be replaced in April 1995 by a new benefit – Job Seeker's Allowance.

hours or at a certain level of pay. These restrictions must, however, be 'reasonable'. This power to restrict the range of suitable work becomes more limited after a period has lapsed during which no work has been found. Eventually, a claimant will have to be willing to accept work at a lower rate, and agree to attend 'restart interviews' for different types of employment to maintain their continuing eligibility for this benefit.

There are a number of special rules regarding studying and the taking of holidays while receiving UB, and doing part-time or seasonal work. On part-time work, see DSS leaflet FB 26, and on seasonal work, see DSS leaflet NI 55. For details of the position regarding those affected directly or indirectly by a strike or other industrial action, consult the CPAG *Rights Guide*.

What does *disqualified* mean?

A claimant may be disqualified from receiving UB for up to 26 weeks if:

either

- They lost their previous job through misconduct. Whether this is the case is often a matter of dispute between the claimant and their ex-employer. A claimant has the right to appeal to a social security appeal tribunal against any decision regarding misconduct (see p.260).

or

- They voluntarily left their previous employment without just cause. The precise meaning of this phrase has been the subject of many cases before appeal tribunals and its interpretation will ultimately depend upon the facts of each particular case. The general rule is that an employee should not voluntarily give up their employment without first making a serious attempt to secure another job, no matter how unsuitable their current employment may be. A person who volunteers for redundancy will not, however, be disqualified. If a job is vacated in order that the employee can live with a relative who lives in another area, a period of disqualification may be imposed unless that relative is the employee's spouse, or in need of care, etc. The test is, 'was there just cause in vacating the job in the circumstances?'

A claimant who feels that they have been unfairly disqualified from claiming UB, even for a short period, should seek advice on the possibility of an appeal to the SSAT (see below).

UB is claimed by 'signing on' for work at the local Unemployment Benefit Office. When 'signing on' a claimant should take with them their NI Number card and their P45 form from their previous employer, if they have one. The claim is made on Forms UB 461 and UB 671.

For further information on benefits for people doing voluntary or part-time work, consult DSS leaflet FB 26, *Voluntary and Part-Time Workers*. Those who have been made redundant should consult DSS leaflet NI 231, *Made Redundant?* Specialist advisers should refer to *The Adjudication Officers' Guide*, Chapter 10, which contains useful summaries of relevant case law. A series of useful pamphlets on all the above issues can be obtained free (enclose sae) from the Unemployment Unit, 409 Brixton Road, London SW9 7DQ.

Social Security Appeal Tribunals (SSATs)

All the decisions regarding claims for the welfare benefits listed above are made either by adjudication officers working for the DSS Benefits Agency or for the Department of Employment. Adjudication officers are human and can make mistakes. If a claimant or their adviser believes that a mistake has been made they should consider an appeal to the local Social Security Appeal Tribunal (SSAT).

It is a simple procedure to lodge an appeal. The claimant, or a person acting on their behalf, merely writes a letter to their local SSAT within three months of receiving written notification of the adjudication officer's decision, explaining the reasons why they wish to appeal against the decision. In exceptional circumstances a chairperson may allow an appeal outside the three-month period. The addresses of the SSAT offices are listed at the end of this chapter. The letter of appeal should be as detailed as possible, as it is normally this letter that will form the basis of the arguments when the appeal is heard. If the grounds for the appeal are strong, the adjudication officer may review the matter in the claimant's favour before the appeal is heard, otherwise a date will be fixed for the hearing which will normally be some weeks after the application for appeal is first filed.

The hearing

An SSAT hearing is relatively informal. The SSAT will consist of three (or occasionally two) members of whom the chairperson will be a lawyer with experience in the area of social security law. Hearings often take place in such informal venues as church or town halls. A claimant has the right to be represented by a person of their choice, and research suggests that representation increases their chance of success. Legal aid is not, however, available for representation, although a solicitor can give the claimant general advice under the Green Form Scheme prior to the hearing (see Chapter 1), and any relatively articulate person with a sound knowledge of welfare rights should be perfectly able to put a claimant's case for them if they are unable or anxious about doing it themselves. Particular organisations which specialise in the provision of free advice and representation to claimants in this situation are the Free Representation Unit (FRU), the Claimants and Unemployed Workers Union and local claimants' unions (addresses from the Federation of Claimants' Unions). For details of all these, see p.262. In addition, a local CAB may be able to advise on any independent advice service that operates in their area.

At the hearing the presenting officer will rely upon the written statement that will have been circulated to the claimant prior to the hearing date. The claimant or their representative will be given the opportunity to question the presenting officer on any part of the statement with which they disagree. The claimant will also be given the chance to put their case to the tribunal. When all the evidence has been heard the members of the tribunal will discuss the appeal in private. They will normally give their decision to the claimant that day and will send the claimant a more detailed written account of their reasons for reaching this decision.

Is there any further appeal?

It is possible in some circumstances for a claimant to appeal against an unfavourable decision by an SSAT. These circumstances are limited to where it is alleged by the claimant that the tribunal made an error of law. This means in broad terms that the tribunal did one or more of the following:

- It made a decision based on a misunderstanding of the relevant law.
- It failed to give an adequate statement of the facts on which it reached its decision and the reasons for that decision.
- It had no evidence on which it could have reached its decision.
- It broke the rules of natural justice (see Chapter 3, p.82).

An appeal in these circumstances is to the Social Security Commissioners, who are professional judges with specialist knowledge in the area of social security law. Again, legal aid is not available, but the local CAB will be able to advise a claimant if there are any specialist agencies in their area who are willing to take up such cases. Anybody considering an appeal against a tribunal decision must write to the clerk to the tribunal within three months of that decision requesting 'leave' (permission) to appeal and explaining the reasons why they wish to do so.

In some circumstances, and especially in London and south-east England, a claimant might be able to use the free services of an organisation called the Free Representation Unit (FRU), a group of young barristers and solicitors who offer free representation in a number of tribunals. They can be contacted at 49–51 Bedford Row, London WC1R 4LR (tel: 071 831 0692). Other possible sources of free representation are the Claimants and Unemployed Workers Union, 120 Standhill Crescent, Barnsley, South Yorkshire (tel: 0226 28776) and a local claimants' union. Further information can be obtained from The Unwaged Centre, 72 West Green Road, Haringey, London N15 (tel: 081 802 9804).

The addresses of the Social Security Commissioners are listed at the end of this chapter. For further information on reviews and appeals, consult *DSS Guide to Reviews and Appeals*, leaflet NI 260.

MEANS TESTED BENEFITS

Since the reorganisation of the system of means tested benefits introduced in April 1988 there are now three principal categories of benefit: income support, family credit and housing/council tax benefit. In addition, there is a discretionary fund of money available to give out loans and occasionally grants to meet exceptional difficulties and emergency needs which is called the Social Fund. Housing benefit/council tax benefit subsidy towards the cost of rent and council tax is dealt with in Chapter 11, p.404). The other means tested benefits are dealt with below.

Income Support (IS)

Income support (IS) is a welfare benefit to help people who do not have enough to live on. The minimum amount of money that a person requires to live on is, however, defined by law. It is only if a person's means do not reach this minimum amount that they may become entitled to claim IS. IS is administered by adjudication officers and DSS staff operating from the local branch office of the Benefits Agency. It is paid either by girocheque or through a weekly benefit book.

Who is eligible for IS?

To be eligible for IS a claimant must meet all the following conditions:

- They must normally be aged 18 or over. Between 16 and 18, to receive a small benefit a young person has to enrol on a government-sponsored Youth Training Scheme (YTS). There are very few exceptions to this rule.
- They must be resident in Great Britain (although temporary periods abroad for up to four weeks can be ignored).
- Their capital must not exceed £8000. Some capital items are, however, ignored, of which the most important are the value of the claimant's home (and the capital they hold as a result of selling the home if it is to be used to purchase a new home in the next six months); the whole of the surrender value of a life insurance policy; and the value of a trust fund arising from a personal injury claim payment for a period of at least two years (for full details, see the *National Welfare Benefits Handbook*).
- Their income must not exceed the relevant applicable amount (see p.265).
- Neither the claimant nor their partner (see p.264) must be engaged in *full-time remunerative work* (see p.267).
- The claimant must be *available for work and actively seeking work* (see p.258) unless they are exempted from these provisions (see p.267).

- If the claimant is aged under 19 they must *not be in relevant education*. This provision is complex. It excludes most students under 19 who are attending courses of study of 12 or more hours per week from claiming IS. For details of the exceptions to this rule, see the *National Welfare Benefits Handbook*.
- If the claimant is a student aged 19 or over, they will not normally be eligible to claim IS if their course is a full-time course (single parents and disabled students can be exempted from this provision). A student in these circumstances should approach their local education authority for an education grant.

Can a claim be made on behalf of more than one person?

If a claimant is living with a partner, whether married or unmarried, with whom they share a common household, the claim is considered to be made by the 'family'. An unmarried couple is treated as a 'family' where the two are 'cohabiting', i.e. living together as man and wife. A gay or lesbian couple would not, therefore, be treated as a 'family'. This concept of 'family' extends to include any child or young person who is a member of that household for whom the claimant and/or their partner are responsible.

A couple can choose which partner makes the claim for both of them. The term 'household' is not defined by law, but it is generally expected that in order to establish a separate 'household' while living under the same roof as the claimant (and thereby not be relevant to the calculation of their claim) it will be necessary to demonstrate considerable independence from the claimant in such matters as financial arrangements, eating and cooking arrangements, responsibility for individual housing costs, and some separate living quarters within the property.

The phrase 'living together as man and wife' or 'cohabitee' has caused an immense amount of debate, and generated much case law. Gone are the days of the social security snooper counting the number of shoes under the bed. The decision will derive from the answers to the following collection of questions, which will not necessarily be put directly to the claimant, but which might be deduced by the adjudication officer from circumstantial evidence. The questions will be:

- Are the couple living in the same 'household'?
- Is the relationship stable?

- How are money matters handled in the relationship?
- Is there a sexual relationship?
- Are there any children?
- Do the people 'behave like a couple' in public?

What is the claimant's *applicable amount*?

This is the key concept for the calculation of IS. Each claimant's applicable amount is made up of three components:

1. Their *personal allowance* plus (if relevant) the personal allowance of their partner. The amount of the personal allowance is fixed annually by the Secretary of State for Social Services (see latest edition of the *National Welfare Benefits Handbook* or DSS leaflet NI 196 *Social Security Benefit Rates* for current rates. The amount of the personal allowance will differ according to the age of the claimant and the number (if any) of their dependent children.

plus

2. Any *premium* to which they might be entitled in addition to their personal allowance. Premiums are payable to a claimant in any of the following categories:
    - A *family premium* and *lone parent premium*, both of which are paid if the claimant has a child for whom they are responsible and who is a member of their household. There is a maximum of one such premium per household. 'Child' includes a person under 16 and a person under 19 who is in full-time education.
    - A *pensioner premium* (Rate 1, aged 60–74; Rate 2, aged 75–79) and a *higher pensioner premium* (over 80, or over 60 and in receipt of a disability benefit or blind).
    - A *disability premium* for the long-term invalid or disabled claimant under 60 (see also Invalidity Benefit at p.258). For full details of this complicated provision, consult *The National Welfare Benefits Handbook*.
    - A *disabled child premium* in respect of any dependent child in receipt of attendance allowance, or disabled living allowance, or who is blind.
    - A *carer's premium,* payable to a claimant if they or their partner is receiving invalid care allowance, or would get it but for the overlapping benefit rules.

- A *severe disability premium* which is available to a single claimant living alone in receipt of attendance allowance or disabled living allowance where nobody is receiving invalid care allowance in respect of their care, or to a couple when they both satisfy this condition (for details on attendance allowance and invalid care allowance, see Chapter 4, pp. 123, 126). For fuller details of these premiums, see the *National Welfare Benefits Handbook* or the *Disability Rights Handbook*. If a claimant qualifies for more than one premium they will normally be entitled to claim only one such premium, whichever is the highest. There are three exceptions to this rule:
    - The *family premium* is awarded in addition to any other premium.
    - The *disabled child premium* is awarded to each child who qualifies and in addition to any other premium.
    - The *severe disability premium* is awarded in addition to either the disability premium or the higher pensioner premium.

plus

3. Any *eligible housing costs*. Most housing costs, e.g. rent and council tax, will be met through housing benefit. If the claimant owns their own home, however, certain housing costs are an eligible addition to their applicable amount. The following are the principal housing costs that are eligible, wholly or in part, as an addition to the applicable amount (for fuller details see the *National Welfare Benefits Handbook*).
    - Mortgage interest payments. But if the claimant or their partner is under 60 the DSS will pay only 50 per cent of the interest payments for the first 16 weeks.
    - Interest on a home repairs or improvements loan.
    - Rent or ground rent on a lease in excess of 21 years.
    - Any payments under a co-ownership scheme.
    - Service charges (though deductions will be made from the eligible service charge should it include any amounts for heating, hot water, cooking or lighting, as these are supposed to be paid for out of IS).

NB A claimant is expected to pay their water rates out of their IS.

What is *full-time remunerative work*?

IS cannot be claimed if either the claimant or (if claiming as a couple) their spouse or partner is working for 16 hours or more each week. The work must be work for payment or in expectation of payment. If the hours fluctuate from week to week the adjudicating officer can average them over a 'recognisable cycle'. Certain claimants will not be treated as being in full-time remunerative work for the purposes of IS even though they may be working in excess of 24 hours. They are:

- Disabled people whose disability has reduced their earning capacity by 25 per cent or more.
- Childminders working at home.
- Claimants on certain government training schemes.
- Claimants involved in a trade dispute after the first seven days of the dispute have passed. But there are numerous restrictions on claiming welfare benefits during a trade dispute (see the *National Welfare Benefits Handbook* and Webb, I. (1988), 'Income support and the trade dispute disqualification' in *Legal Action,* December).
- Voluntary workers receiving expenses only.
- Carers looking after a person in receipt of disabled living allowance or attendance allowance or someone who has claimed such an allowance and is awaiting the decision.

Who is exempted from the need to be *available for work/actively seeking work*?

The following categories of claimant are exempted from the need to be available for work. Any claimant who is:

- aged 60 or over;
- a lone parent or lone foster-parent caring for a child under 16;
- incapable of work through disease or mental or physical disablement;
- suffering a mental or physical disability that has reduced their earning capacity by 25 per cent or more;
- registered as blind;
- in receipt of *invalid care allowance*;

- pregnant, *and* unable to work *or* in the period 11 weeks before birth to 7 weeks after birth;
- caring for an invalid receiving disabled living allowance (higher/middle rate) or attendance allowance or who has applied for attendance allowance in the last six months;
- engaged in temporary child care because the parent or normal carer is ill or temporarily absent;
- receiving a government training allowance.

These are the main exemptions. For the complete list, see Income Support (General) Regulations 1987 SI 1987/1967.

Any claimant who is not in an exempted category must be available for work in order to be eligible to claim IS.

If a person believes they may be eligible to claim income support, how do they work out how much they will receive?

The formula for calculating IS is relatively straightforward:

Applicable amount minus *income* = IS.

What is meant by *income* for these purposes?

The following is only a summary account. For full details, consult the *National Welfare Benefits Handbook.* Income for these purposes is worked out in the following way:

- Total net weekly income of claimant and, if relevant, of their partner or spouse (i.e. income after stoppages such as tax and national insurance). If the claimant and/or their partner or spouse pay anything towards an occupational or personal pension scheme, only 50 per cent of that payment will be deductible from their gross income.

plus

- If the claimant has any capital in excess of £3000 every £250 of that capital in excess of £3000 is deemed to generate £1 of income per week.

plus

- A claimant may also be treated as having further 'notional' income if they have deprived themselves of income in order to claim or increase their benefit or if they are working without claiming the going rate for the job, unless the work is genuinely voluntary.

All the following sources of income are ignored:

(In full)

- disabled living allowance, and attendance allowance (see Chapter 4, pp. 114, 123);
- education maintenance allowance;
- any grant for non-advanced education;
- any fostering allowance;
- payments from a local authority, health authority or voluntary organisation for looking after somebody on a temporary basis;
- the Pensioners' Christmas Bonus (DSS);
- Housing benefit (see Chapter 11).
- Payments under the Social Fund (see p.275).

(In part)

- earnings (called the *earnings disregard*, the level of which is fixed each year by the Secretary of State for Social Services). Some categories of claimant, e.g. lone parents, are allowed a higher level of earnings disregard: for full details, see the *National Welfare Benefits Handbook*;
- two-thirds of any earnings from childminding;
- the first part of any of the following sources of income: weekly payments from boarders and sub-tenants; regular charitable or voluntary payments (unless from the McFarlane Trust, in which case they are ignored); war disablement pension or war widow's pension. For precise details on the ways in which deductions are calculated, see the *National Welfare Benefits Handbook.*

Special rules on income support for people living in *special accommodation*

This section deals with a claimant who lives in any of the following types of accommodation (special accommodation):

Those living in local authority (Part III) accommodation

Local authority residential accommodation is a means tested service and the local authority will assess the applicant for a contribution according to their income and capital (see Chapter 9 at p.295). Each year a level of personal allowance for those in residential accommodation is fixed by law.

Those living in other types of residential care or nursing homes (see Chapter 9 at p.295)

1. Those already in the accommodation on 1 April 1993.
   People in this category have *preserved rights* under the old system as follows: the *applicable amount* for any claimant in this category is calculated in a wholly different way from other claimants and is made up of two components:
   - An amount for *personal expenses* (which is fixed annually by the Secretary of State for Social Services and will vary according to the type of accommodation) plus extra sums for dependants.
   - An *accommodation allowance.* The DSS sets a maximum ceiling for the allowance in each type of property which is published annually and which will vary according to the part of the country in which the accommodation is situated. There are provisions to allow claimants to receive payments in excess of the maximum in exceptional circumstances. They are complex. For full details, consult the *National Welfare Benefits Handbook.* There are no extra premiums payable to claimants in special accommodation.
2. Those moving into residential care or nursing homes on or after 1 April 1993.
   People in this category are paid under the new rules. Their applicable amount is calculated by adding together the following:
   - the applicant's *personal allowance*;
   - any *premiums* to which they are entitled;
   - a *residential allowance* to cover accommodation charges.

People without accommodation

People of 'no fixed abode' (NFA) can claim income support, either at the special NFA section of the local Benefits Agency, or at a normal office. The *applicable amount* for such claimants is simply the basic age-related personal allowance (see above at p.265).

How is IS claimed?

IS is claimed by filling out DSS Form A1 which can be obtained from any post office or filling out an Income Support leaflet obtainable from any Benefits Agency branch or social security centre. Some people can claim IS through an interview without having to fill in the form themselves.

How is IS paid?

People who are unemployed are usually paid IS by girocheque at the end of each two-week period of the claim. The giros are usually sent out by the Unemployment Benefit Office and they can be cashed at a post office. Other claimants are normally paid by an order book that can be cashed every week at a post office.

Can a claim for IS be backdated?

IS is normally paid from the date the claim is first received, although it can be backdated if the claimant shows continuing 'good cause' why they failed to claim earlier (see Partington, above at p.256).

If a claimant is paid too much IS do they have to repay the overpayment?

The answer to this question will depend upon the reason for the overpayment. If the claimant revealed all material facts in their claim and the overpayment was an office error the claimant is under no obligation to repay it. If the claimant failed to reveal or misrepresented a material fact in their claim form they can be ordered to repay the overpayment even if their failure to disclose the fact was completely innocent and not intended to deceive.

Is there an appeal against any decision regarding IS?

The same procedure for appealing against IS decisions is available as for the non-means tested benefits outlined above on p.260.

Further assistance

In addition to the *National Welfare Benefits Handbook* (CPAG), advisers can obtain further information from the *DHSS Guide to Income Support*, SB 20. The IS and family credit (FC) laws are available in a looseleaf manual called *The Law Relating to Social Security* ('The Blue Book') which can also be obtained for use by the specialist. The DSS produces its own *Adjudication Officers' Guide* which contains a mass of information and guidance about the law in this area.

Single people without a permanent home should consult *Benefits*, which is a detailed manual explaining how to claim IS and housing benefit (see Chapter 11) when living in a nightshelter, bed and breakfast accommodation, a lodgings house, a bedsit, a hotel, a hostel, a resettlement unit, a women's refuge, or with a relative or squatting. It is available from CHAR, Room 11, 5–15 Cromer Street, London WC1H 8LS (tel: 071 833 2071).

Family Credit (FC)

This is a means tested benefit for claimants who are employed or self-employed and who have at least one child. It is designed to help low-earning families where at least one member of the family is in full-time work. Its principal purpose is to keep low-earning families out of the poverty trap whereby the move from unemployment to employment results in a decrease in income. For a broad and general guide to welfare benefits for families with a young child, see Rowe, T., and Trelogan-Dunn, C., *Social Security Benefits for Families with a Young Child*, available from Voluntary Organisations Liaison Council for Under-Fives, 77 Holloway Road, London, N7 8JZ.

Who is eligible for FC?

To be eligible for FC a claimant must meet the following conditions:

- They must be resident in Great Britain.
- They must support at least one child who normally lives with them, whether as part of a married couple, with a cohabitee or as a lone parent.
- Their capital must not exceed £8000 (see p.263).
- They must be *engaged and normally engaged in remunerative work,* i.e. not less than 16 hours per week of work that is paid or is done in the expectation of payment, e.g. on a commission basis: for more detail, see p.267. *Work* includes self-employment.

Where the claimant is living as part of a couple (see p.264) the claim must normally be by the woman, although both partners must sign the claim form.

How is FC claimed?

FC is claimed by filling out DSS Form FC1 which can be obtained from a post office or a Benefits Agency office. Once completed, the form has to be despatched to the DSS central office that administers FC. The claim will be treated as made on the day it is received by that office. The claim can be backdated for up to a year as long as there is 'good cause' for the delay, e.g. the claimant was ill, preoccupied by other major concerns and so forth. Mere ignorance of the right to claim FC is not 'good cause' for backdating. For the address of FC Central Office (known as the Family Credit Unit), see p.275.

How is entitlement to FC calculated?

The following formula will be applied when calculating the claimant's entitlement, if any, to FC:

Stage 1: Calculate the claimant's maximum payable FC according to the rates currently fixed by the DSS (these will vary according to the number and ages of dependent children).
Stage 2: Calculate the claimant's *income*. The same general principles apply for calculating income as for IS (see p.268), i.e. it is net joint income that is used, including estimated income from capital between £3000 and £8000 and notional income. Any income will be averaged out over five weeks before the date of the claim or two months if the claim-

ant is paid monthly. If self-employed the calculation will be based upon the claimant's average net profit over the preceding six months. There are also a number of categories of income that are ignored either in full or in part. Some of these are the same as for IS; others differ. For a full list of these categories, consult the *National Welfare Benefits Handbook.*
Stage 3: Compare the claimant's income with the applicable amount for FC (otherwise known as the threshold level). This is fixed each year by the Secretary of State for Social Services. Unlike the applicable amount for IS, the threshold level does not vary according to the size of the claimant's family:

- If the claimant's income is below the threshold level they will be entitled to maximum FC.
- If the claimant's income is above the threshold level the following formula will be applied in calculating their entitlement:
  Maximum FC minus 70 per cent difference between claimant's income and threshold level = claimant's FC.

How is FC paid?

Once the DSS has processed the claimant's application it will inform them in writing of its decision. If favourable, FC will be paid to the claimant for 26 weeks regardless of any change in their circumstances. It can be paid *either* directly into a bank or building society account every four weeks *or* by order book that can be cashed weekly at a post office. If the claimant wishes to continue receiving FC after 26 weeks they should make a fresh claim within the last four weeks of the period. If a claimant is dissatisfied with the decision regarding their claim they may appeal to a Social Security Appeal Tribunal (SSAT) (see p.260).

Does receipt of FC entitle the claimant to any further benefits?

A person in receipt of FC will not have to pay for any of the following either for themselves or for their partner or children:

- NHS prescriptions;
- NHS dental treatment;
- travel to hospital for NHS treatment;
- part of the cost of purchasing glasses.

For further information on FC, consult the *National Welfare Benefits Handbook* or DSS leaflets NI 261, *A Guide to Family Credit;* FB 4, *Help While You Are Working*, and FB 27, *Bringing Up Children.* The Family Credit Unit can be contacted directly at DSS, Government Buildings, Warbreck Hill, Blackpool FY2 0YF (tel: 0253 500050 or 0253 856123).

The Social Fund

The Social Fund is described by the DSS as 'a scheme to help people with exceptional expenses which are difficult for them to pay from their regular weekly income'. It has a *non-discretionary* and a *discretionary* part. The Social Fund is 'cash limited' which means that no local DSS office will be able to spend more than its annual allocation from central government. The national allocation for the discretionary fund in 1993–4 is £340m. This figure should be compared with the £350m paid out in single payments in 1986, the system that the Social Fund has replaced. Furthermore, over two-thirds of the total budget is for loans which must be paid back, and there is no right of appeal against a decision to an independent tribunal. It thus seems inevitable that many claimants will not receive the help they require from the state and will be obliged to seek alternative forms of financial assistance. For further analysis of this problem, see *The Social Fund and Voluntary Organisations: How Do You Respond?* (1988), which can be obtained from the Social Security Consortium, c/o NCVO, 26 Bedford Square, London WC1B 3HU.

What follows below is merely a summary of the two schemes to provide advisers with a preliminary idea of the circumstances in which an application to the Social Fund might be considered and a sense of the severe constraints that operate upon the Social Fund. Those seeking a more detailed appraisal of the detail and scope of the Social Fund should consult Becker, S., Hannam, I., and Hyde, D. (1988), *Guide to the Social Fund Manual* (Nottingham Welfare Rights Service), which can be obtained from County Hall, West Bridgford, Nottingham NG2 7QP, or the latest edition of the *National Welfare Benefits Handbook* (CPAG). The *Guide to the Social Fund Manual* does not contain reference to the regulated scheme but it provides a detailed and compact technical summary of the *Social Fund Manual* which is the official handbook of DSS staff in this matter. The Association of Metropolitan Authorities, 35 Great Smith Street, London SW1P 3BJ, has produced its own *Social Fund Position Statement and Practice Guide for Local Authority Associations* and BASW has produced advice to members in *Social Fund Guidelines*. The DSS produce, free of charge, their own *Guide to the Social Fund*, SB 16, which can be obtained from any DSS office. A short study of the problems with the Social Fund in London by Carol Sexty of the Social Policy and Service Development Unit of NACAB, which also recommends extending mandatory elements of the fund, ending the system of loans and introducing an independent right of appeal, is *Getting Nowhere: the Social Fund and Housing Problems in London* (NACAB). Both the SSAC and the Audit Office have also published reports on the working of the Social Fund.

How does the Social Fund operate?

Payments made under the Social Fund are based on directions and guidelines issued by the Secretary of State, which are summarised in the *Guide to the Social Fund Manual* (see p.275). Decisions are made by special DSS officials called Social Fund Officers (SFOs). The Social Fund is divided into two segments:

1. *The Regulated Scheme:* which provides legal entitlement to payments for maternity needs, funeral expenses and fuel costs in cold weather.
2. *The Discretionary Scheme:* which provides the possibility of loans and grants to cover certain defined crises.

The Regulated Scheme (i.e. non-discretionary)

Maternity Expenses Payment

A flat-rate maternity expenses payment is payable to a person if they or their partner is in receipt of income support, disability working allowance or family credit (see pp. 263, 113, and 272) for each baby expected, born or adopted. The payment will be reduced by the amount of any capital that the claimant has in excess of £500 unless the capital was in the form of a widow's payment (see Chapter 9, p.306) in which case it is ignored. For further advice and claim form, see DSS leaflet NI 17A.

FUNERAL EXPENSES PAYMENT

A graduated funeral expenses payment is payable to a person if they or their partner are in receipt of income support, disability working allowance, housing benefit, council tax benefit, or family credit (see pp. 263, 113, 404–11, and 272) and they, or a member of their family, take responsibility for the cost of a funeral. A 'member of the family' means partner or child of claimant (or partner) for whom they have responsibility and who is a member of their household. The same rule regarding capital applies as for a maternity expenses payment (see p.276). The payment should cover most of the costs of the funeral. For full details of amount, see the *National Welfare Benefits Handbook*. For further advice and claim form, see DSS leaflet D49 and Form SF 200.

FUEL COSTS IN COLD WEATHER

In certain circumstances a person in receipt of income support may be able to claim a grant from the Social Fund to help towards the cost of extra fuel used during a period of exceptionally cold weather, currently defined as seven consecutive days with a 0°C mean daily temperature. For further details on this, contact the local DSS office.

IS THERE ANY APPEAL AGAINST DECISIONS UNDER THE REGULATED SCHEME?

An appeal against a decision of an adjudication officer to an SSAT lies in the same way as for any other social security benefit (see p.260).

The Discretionary Scheme (budgeting loans, crisis loans and community care grants)

Although the overall nature of this fund is discretionary, advisers should nevertheless distinguish between directions, which must be followed, and guidance, which is no more than that.

BUDGETING LOANS

These loans are designed to help a claimant spread the cost of exceptional expenses over a longer period. To be eligible a claimant (or their partner) must have been in receipt of income support (see p.263) for at least six months. The loan is interest free but it has to be repaid by weekly deductions from income support. Regulations describe the various normal rates of repayment. Each applicant will be required to sign and return an acknowledgement of the terms of the loan and agree that, should benefit cease, repayments will continue. Loans can be recovered from the benefit of a claimant's partner. If the claimant has capital in excess of £500 it will be deducted from the amount of the loan.

For what items or services can a budgeting loan be given?

The guidance to SFOs, contained in two volumes, the *Social Fund Guide* and the *Social Fund Administration Guide* (which is not binding but which will normally be followed), sets three categories of applications described as high priority, medium priority and low priority. There is also a long list of directions concerning matters for which a budgeting loan is not payable, which includes school uniforms or sports clothing, travelling expenses to and from school, school meals, work-related expenses and any educational or training need including clothing and tools. Local education authorities (LEAs) do, however, meet a number of the costs connected with education outlined above and should be approached directly.

A *high priority* must be given to an application where refusal could cause 'hardship or damage or risk to the health or safety of the applicant or the family'. In addition, applications for any of the following items or services are to be considered high priority: essential items of furniture or household equipment, bedclothes, essential home repairs and maintenance for owner-occupiers if a bank loan or mortgage is not available, fuel meter installation and reconnection charges and non-mains fuel costs, e.g. oil, paraffin or bottled gas. Examples of *medium priority* items and services are non-essential items of furniture and household equipment, redecoration where the applicant is responsible, HP and other debts, and clothing. Examples of *low priority* items and services are rent in advance where the applicant already has secure accommodation and a move is not essential (but see *crisis loans* on p.279) and leisure items.

All decisions regarding budgeting loans are made by the Social Fund Officer (SFO) operating from the local DSS office. The SFO cannot exceed their local budget. Each payment will be stored and monitored on an office microcomputer. SFOs are instructed to 'take care to identify circumstances which might give the application a higher priority' but they must always look at the least expensive means of meeting a need, such as repair rather than replacement or whether the need can be better or partly met from another source.

This provision has great implications for local authority social workers as the SFO may feel that the local social services department (or, indeed, a charity) is the most appropriate source of assistance. Claims should normally be decided within 28 days (see p.283).

For more detail on the amount and extent of budgeting loans, consult the *Guide to the Social Fund Manual* or the *National Welfare Benefits Handbook* (see p.275). A claim for a budgeting loan should be made on DSS Form SF 300, but if sufficient information is contained in a letter this can be accepted instead.

Crisis Loans

Any person aged 16 or over can apply to the DSS for a crisis loan (i.e. they do not need to be in receipt of income support) if they are without sufficient resources to meet the immediate short-term needs of their family or themselves and they are involved in an emergency or a disaster (e.g. fire or flood; emergency travel expenses; emergency board and lodging expenses; down payments for rented accommodation if the claimant is leaving institutional or residential care). The list is illustrative and is not exhaustive, which means that the SFO must consider any circumstances that are alleged to constitute a crisis. In addition, unless the loan is a down payment of rent (see above) it must be shown that the loan is the 'only means by which serious damage to the health or safety of the claimant or a member of their family can be prevented'. The SFO guidance states that when deciding whether a crisis loan claimant has 'sufficient resources' a wide range of resources should be considered including credit facilities, money available through bank and building society facilities and other loan sources. A number of the claimant's resources will, however, be disregarded, including housing benefit, the assets of any business owned by the claimant, and the value of their home. For full list, see the *Guide to the Social Fund Manual* or the *National Welfare Benefits Handbook.* A person on IS should not be required to use credit facilities.

The need for help will normally be for a specific item or service or for immediate living expenses for a period not normally exceeding 14 days.

Loans are interest free but will have to be repaid at a rate agreed in advance. The same items and services are excluded as for budgeting loans (see p.278) and in addition a number of other items are excluded, including installation, rental and call charges for a telephone; mobility needs; holidays; TV licence, rental or aerial charges; and housing costs. Crisis loans cannot be paid to people in Part III residential accommodation (see Chapter 9), nursing homes, residential care homes, hospital, or prison.

Consult handbooks for more detail on the amount and extent of crisis loans. An application for a crisis loan should be made in writing on DSS Form SF 400 either at an office interview or, exceptionally, in the course of a home visit.

Community Care Grants (CCGs)

CCGs form the only payments in the discretionary sector of the Social Fund that are not repayable. They are intended to help promote community care by complementing health and personal social services provision to eligible applicants.

Who is eligible for a CCG?

To be eligible for a CCG a claimant must be:

1. *Either* in receipt of income support (see p.263) *or* be hoping to be discharged from an institution within six weeks and then to claim income support;

and

2. seeking assistance with expenses in connection with one of the four specified 'community care needs' as follows:
   - *Situation A:* help to re-establish themselves in the community following a stay in institutional or residential care.
   - *Situation B:* help to remain in the community rather than enter institutional or residential care.
   - *Situation C:* help in easing 'exceptional pressures' on themselves and their family.
   - *Situation D:* help to provide assistance with expenses of travel within the UK in order to visit someone who is ill, or attend a relative's funeral, or ease a domestic crisis, or visit a child who

is with the other parent pending a custody decision, or move to suitable accommodation.

Exceptionally, a CCG may be considered for an ineligible applicant in considerable need if there is a serious risk to health or safety. The same rules regarding capital apply as for the Social Fund loans (see p.275).

Priority groups

The DSS has identified 10 groups of potential eligible applicants to whom priority for CCGs may be given as follows:

1. elderly people, in particular those with restricted mobility or having difficulty performing personal tasks;
2. people with a learning difficulty;
3. people with mental illness;
4. people with physical disability (this includes those with sensory impairment);
5. chronically sick people, in particular the terminally ill;
6. people who have misused alcohol or drugs;
7. ex-offenders requiring resettlement;
8. people without a settled way of life undergoing resettlement;
9. families under stress;
10. young people leaving local authority care.

The regulations make it clear that there may be applicants who do not exactly match a priority group but whose personal circumstances nevertheless require that they be treated as a priority applicant. SFOs should meet the highest priority need first wherever it arises. These are specifically described as:

- people setting up home in the community after a stay in residential or institutional care;
- people who are likely to go into institutional or residential care unless they receive a CCG;
- children being boarded-out for a short period prior to adoption.

For what expenses might assistance be given where an eligible applicant applies for a CCG?

The SFO guidance makes it clear that the nature of the assistance that might be funded by a CCG will vary depending upon which of the situations (see p.280) is relevant to the application. In addition, it makes it clear that within each of the four situations consideration will be given primarily to claimants in the relevant priority groups for that particular situation.

The types of assistance (grants) available in the form of CCGs are as follows:

1. Start-up grants.
2. Cost of one change of clothing, sufficient protective clothing and footwear.
3. Removal expenses when travelling to take up a new tenancy (lower of two estimates) and if necessary cost of furniture storage.
4. Fares when moving home: normally the cheapest means available.
5. Connection charges, including, where reasonable, disconnection and reconnection of domestic appliances.
6. Furniture and furnishings, although this is subject to rigorous and detailed guidelines and only covers such extreme situations as, for example, where previous furniture has been damaged by the prevailing housing conditions, such as damp.
7. Minor structural repairs and maintenance costs, where the claimant is the person responsible for the repairs and the property does not belong to a local authority or a housing association.
8. Internal redecoration and refurbishment if the claimant is the person responsible for the work. The grant normally only covers the cost of materials.
9. Bedding, washing machines and heaters, but only in exceptional circumstances, e.g. where the claimant is bedridden and incontinent or chronically sick.
10. Fuel costs, which are limited to reconnection charges if the supply has been disconnected and the claimant is going on to fuel direct payments; re-siting meters if a disabled person needs easier access, and installation of prepayment meters for claimants who have difficulty in budgeting for quarterly bills.
11. Heavy laundry needs, limited to the incontinent.

12. Furniture: this only covers very limited circumstances as follows: where an elderly person needs special furniture which the local authority have no duty to provide; where a claimant has a chronic medical condition requiring them to sleep in a separate bed from their partner; and where a claimant or their partner has damaged existing furniture as a result of a behavioural condition. All other claims should be treated as an application for a budgeting loan (see p.277).
13. Excessive wear and tear of clothing and footwear caused by a particular condition or illness.
14. Boarding-out fees if a claimant's child is being placed for a short and limited period with specialist foster parents while adoption is arranged and is not in local authority care and boarded-out by them.
15. Other circumstances: not defined but described as 'low priority'.

How to work out which types of assistance might be relevant to which applicants

See Table 8.1 overleaf.

Is it possible to challenge a decision of an SFO regarding payments under the Social Fund?

There is no appeal procedure for challenging the decision of an SFO as there is to challenge the decision of an adjudication officer regarding other benefits. There is, however, an internal review procedure. Applications requesting that an SFO decision be internally reviewed must normally be made within 28 days from the date the challenged decision was issued or posted. A detailed formal procedure must then be followed, at the end of which the decision will either be altered or confirmed. At this stage a dissatisfied claimant can request a further review by a Social Fund Inspector (SFI) (all currently based in the DSS regional office in Birmingham). Again, this request must be made within 28 days of the SFO decision. If the claimant is still dissatisfied they can complain to the Social Fund Commissioner (SFC), whose task it is to monitor the quality of decisions of SFIs and help them to improve the standard of their decision-making by giving any appropriate advice and assistance. The SFC can be contacted at Millbank Tower, 21–24 Millbank, London SW1P 4QU (tel: 071 217 4799). In very limited circumstances (see Chapter 3,

Table 8.1

Situation A	Situation B	Situation C	Situation D
Setting up home (priority 1–6; grants 1–5)	*People moving to more suitable accommodation* (priority 1–5; grants, 3, 4, 5, 6)	*Breakdown of the relationship* (priority 9, especially where domestic violence; grants 1, 2, 3, 5)	Fares to visit patient in hospital or home
Discharge from hospital (priority 1–6; grants 1–5)	*Applicants moving nearer relatives/close friends who will provide support (includes applicants moving into another household)* (priority 1–5; grants 3, 4, 5, 6)	*Reconciliation of the relationship* (priority 9, grants 3)	Fares to visit critically ill relatives
People leaving homes or hospitals (part of a planned programme) (priority 1–8; grants 1–5)	*Applicants moving nearer to or into the house of vulnerable groups to provide greater support* (priority 1–5; grants 3, 4, 5, 6)	*High washing costs because of a disabled child* (priority 9 – with disabled child; grants 5, 11 – washing and drying machine)	Fares to attend funerals or cremations
Discharge from prison and youth centres (priority 1–7 and young people unable to live with parents; grants 1–5)	*Applicants moving within the community to set up home for the first time* (priority 1–5; grants 1, 3, 4, 5)	*Families needing to move house* (priority 9; grants 3, 5, essential furniture (12))	Domestic crisis
Home leave for prisoners and young offenders (priority – NA; grants – living expenses)	*Vulnerable groups (others than families) improving living conditions* (priority 1–5; grants 7, 8, 9, 10, 11, furniture)	*Repair/replacement of items damaged by behavioural problems within the family* (priority 9 – with mentally handicapped ill child; grants 2, 8, essential household items, security items)	Custody proceedings
Young people (16 plus) leaving Local Authority Care (priority 10 and young people who left care in last 12 months; grants 1, 4, 5)		*Minor structural repair to keep home habitable or for safety of child* (priority 9 – with disabled child; grants 3, 7)	Fares when moving house
Moving house to look after a person moving from institutional care (priority 1–8; grants 3, 4, 5, 6)		*Excessive wear and tear on clothing* (priority 9, grants 2)	
Child or young person rejoining the household after a period in care or special residential school (priority – children under 16 and young people 16–19 returning to their families; grants 2, essential furniture (12))		*Short-term boarding out prior to adoption* (priority 9; grants 14, boarding out fees for up to 8 weeks)	
		Fuel costs (priority 9 – child disabled or under 5; grants 5, 10 – installation of prepayment meter)	

Reproduced with the permission of Benefits Research Unit (Service) Ltd, from *Guide to the Social Fund Manual* (Nottinghamshire Welfare Rights Service).

p.81) it may be possible to apply to the High Court for judicial review of the SFO/I decision. For further detail on how to challenge Social Fund decisions, see Luba, I. (1988), 'Challenging Social Fund Decisions' in *Legal Action*, May 1988.

Further assistance

The best sources of information on the Social Fund are the *National Welfare Benefits Handbook* and the *Guide to the Social Fund Manual* detailed on p.275. The adviser who has regular dealings with the Social Fund should also obtain from the DSS the more detailed (and more expensive) *Social Fund Manual* (DSS). The DSS also produce a *Social Fund Factsheet: Fig. 4*, which is only an outline, and the more substantial *Guide to the Social Fund*, SB 16. Those who prefer to seek alternative help from charities should consult the *Directory of Charities* (1988, Charities Aid Foundation) which provides details of a wide range of charities, and the types of applicants for which they cater (see p.106).

Chapter 9

Law and older people

This chapter examines the needs of older people by looking at various ways in which the law entitles them to special assistance over and above that provided to the rest of the population. For a large variety of reasons, the number of older people in the United Kingdom is rising rapidly, both in absolute terms and as a proportion of the population as a whole. Official government projections suggest that there will be a million more older people in 30 years' time than today. What is of particular significance for social work is the increase in the number of older people aged 75 and over, which is likely to rise from 32 per cent of those of pensionable age in 1981 to 38 per cent in 2011. While many of the themes dealt with elsewhere in this book may also be relevant to older people, with like rights and entitlements, this chapter will focus on three areas where special provision is available for them: housing, state benefits, and the management of personal affairs.

HOUSING AND OLDER PEOPLE

Older people at home

According to the Centre for Policy on Ageing, 'over 90 per cent of old people stay in their own homes until they die'. The ideological movement away from residential care towards community care for older people over the past two decades, culminating in the National Health Service and Community Care Act 1990 (see Chapter 4 at p.89), has guaranteed that this figure will remain as high, if not higher, even though the ideological shift from residential care towards community care has not been accompanied by anything like sufficient resources to fund the new initiative.

Whatever the political arguments for or against caring for older people in their own homes, the fact remains that this is where the majority of them will remain for the foreseeable future and it is therefore important to see the alternative possibility of accommodation in a residential home in its correct perspective. The bulk of social work carried out with older clients will be with those who are still living in their own homes, whether they be owner-occupiers, renting, or living on an informal basis with relatives. There is ample evidence that older people living at home suffer disproportionately from bad housing conditions (see in particular Smith, K. (1986), *I'm Not Complaining: the Housing Conditions of Elderly Private Tenants* (SHAC) and Taylor, H. (1987), *Growing Old Together: Elderly Owner-Occupiers and their Housing* (Centre for Policy on Ageing)). Other chapters in this book also address specific issues relating to legal rights and housing. These chapters should be consulted in addition to this chapter, in relation to the housing problems of older people at home, as follows:

- Detail on ways in which the law might assist older people to improve the conditions of their homes, see Chapter 11.
- Detail on the rights of the older homeless, see Chapter 10.
- Detail on security from eviction for both private and public tenants, licensees and defaulting mortgages, see Chapter 10.
- Detail on rent registration and assistance in paying rents and council tax: see Chapters 8 and 11.
- Detail on the rights of chronically sick and disabled older people to receive special assistance from their local authority in adapting their homes for their more convenient use, see Chapter 4 and see also: *Care and Repair: a Guide to Setting Up Care and Repair Agency Services for Elderly People* (1988, Shelter).

Age Concern produces the following very useful publications which may also be of interest and assistance to the older person who wishes to remain in their home:

Bookbinder, D. (1991), *Housing Options for Older People* considers a number of options, include special housing schemes, special mortgage schemes for older people, financial help with improvements and repairs, and home income plans.

Hinton, C., and Bookbinder D. (1993), *Using Your Home as Capital* is a practical guide to ways in which older people can free the capital tied up in their home to produce income but remain living there.
An Owner's Guide: Your Home in Retirement (1990) provides advice on routine maintenance, alterations and extensions, labour-saving fixtures and adaptations and home security measures.
A Buyer's Guide to Sheltered Housing (1993) provides comprehensive practical advice on the purchase of a flat or bungalow in a sheltered scheme.

All these publications are obtainable from Age Concern (for address, see p.317). *Not Rich, Not Poor* (Bull, J. and Poole, L., 1989) is a guide to housing options for older people on middle incomes produced by SHAC/ Anchor Housing Trust.

Residential accommodation for older people

We shall define the accommodation that is provided for those who do not live in their own homes as *residential accommodation.* This is distinct from, for example, hotel accommodation in that the term *residential accommodation* includes both board and personal care for persons in need of personal care by reason of old age. Residential accommodation for older people is provided from three different sectors, local authorities, voluntary (non-profit-making) organisations and the private sector. Although the sources of funding of each category of home will clearly differ, there is considerable overlap in practice between the three sectors, with each sector being subject to statutory regulation, and many older people being placed by local authorities in one of the other two sectors, either because there is no available space in any local authority home or because the home in question is more suitable to the needs and wishes of the older person. In fact, since the coming into force on 1 April 1993 of the new community care legislation (see above at p.286), local authorities are obliged to ensure that 85 per cent of the total residential accommodation budget at their disposal is spent in the independent sector, which could be either residential or domiciliary care.

Which department in the local authority should be approached for assistance in finding residential accommodation for older people?

If the person is *homeless* or *threatened with homelessness* (for explanation of these terms, see Chapter 10 at p.321) the local housing department should be contacted. Most housing departments have special units to deal with applications from homeless people. In all other cases, responsibility rests with the social services department.

Does a local authority have a duty to provide or find residential accommodation for every older person who requests it?

In general, a local authority cannot be *forced* to find or provide residential accommodation for an older person who requests it. In other words, the provision of residential accommodation for older people is a power and not a duty. But the whole issue also has to be looked at in the context of the community care legislation, introduced in 1993, and the duties and responsibilities that this legislation has placed upon local authorities towards older people. Under the National Health Service and Community Care Act 1990 (NHSCCA), if it appears to a local authority that a person for whom they provide, or arrange for the provision of community care services (e.g. older residents of their area), may be in need of such services, they must:

1. Carry out an assessment of that person's needs for those services;

and

2. Decide whether these needs should be met by such services, in the light of the assessment.

The provision of residential accommodation for older people, under Part III of the National Assistance Act 1948, is now incorporated within the definition of community care services, and it therefore follows that local authorities have clear statutory responsibilities to ensure that accommodation requirements of needy older people in their area are met, either through direct provision or more likely through referral to the voluntary and private sectors (see further above, Chapter 4 at p.86).

Are there any circumstances in which an older person can be forced into residential accommodation (including a hospital) against their will?

There are three circumstances in which action may be taken to compel an older person to enter residential accommodation (which can include a hospital) without their consent:

1. Where the older person is deemed to be suffering from a mental disability or disorder under the Mental Health Act 1983, and one of the procedures for committing a mentally disabled person to a mental institution is followed (see Chapter 5).
2. Where an older person is considered by a local authority to be in the above category, but the alternative of Guardianship Proceedings is chosen, and the local authority as guardian wishes to place the older person in a particular home (see Chapter 5, at 'Guardianship'). This procedure is currently rarely used (less than 200 cases per year) but may become a more attractive option if the current emphasis on 'community care' is strengthened by further allocation of resources.
3. There is a procedure under section 47 of the National Assistance Act 1948 (used in practice in only about 200 cases per year) whereby a magistrate can make an order to remove an older person to a residential home (or hospital) for up to three months at a time if s/he is satisfied, on the evidence of the District Community Physician, that the older person is:
   - suffering from grave chronic illness;

   and
   - living in insanitary conditions;

   and
   - not receiving proper care and attention;

   and
   - it is in the interests of that person to be detained, either for their own good or because they are a serious nuisance to other people.

Seven days' notice of the application must be given either to the older person direct or to some person in charge of them, unless the District Community Physician and one other doctor certify that removal of the person without delay is necessary, in their own interests, in which case written notice is not required. If written notice is not given, however, an order can only be made with a maximum duration of three weeks, although it is open to the local authority to apply, on notice, to extend that order to three months during that period. In addition, the person managing the premises to which it is intended to remove the older person must be given seven days' notice of the hearing to give them the opportunity to explain their position to the magistrate and express any objections that they may have to receiving the person – objections which may influence the decision. After the three months have expired the local authority can apply to extend the detention for further three-month periods, and further periods thereafter, for a seemingly indefinite number of times. Legal aid is not available to a person who wishes to contest the application (see Chapter 1). The section does not permit compulsory medical treatment of any person thus removed (see further Chapter 5 at p.143).

The British Geriatric Society (BGS) and the British Association of Social Workers (BASW) have produced guidelines for the use of Section 47 applications which can be obtained from either organisation. BASW, for example, recommends that any decision under this section should only be made following a case conference, and the authority must be satisfied that the physical, emotional and psychological well-being of the person would be improved by compulsory removal from their home, given the distress this involves. There is further useful discussion on the issues involved, with case histories, in Age Concern (1986), *The Law and the Vulnerable Elderly* (see below).

Use of the section remains controversial and there is wide regional variation in its use: some local authorities never use the section as a matter of policy. Only 15 per cent of those admitted under Section 47 ever return to their homes, and the average survival rate once admitted is only two years.

For further information, contact the British Geriatric Society, 1 St Andrew's Place, London NW1 4LB (tel: 071 935 4004), or BASW, 16 Kent St, Birmingham B5 6RD (tel: 021 622 3911).

What sort of people will a local authority consider eligible for a place in their own residential accommodation for the older person (Part III accommodation)?

Under the NHSCCA, every local authority must have a care plan for those in need of care. In relation to the accommodation needs of older people, the Department of Health, in its 1990 publication *Community Care in the Next Decade and Beyond*, has suggested that the following order of preference should normally be adopted:

1. Support for the older person in their own home, including day and domiciliary care, respite care, the provision of disability equipment, and adaptations to accommodation as necessary (for more information on these procedures, see Chapter 4 at p.87).
2. A move to more suitable accommodation which might be sheltered housing, plus social services support.
3. A move to another private household, to live with relatives or friends, or as part of an adult fostering scheme.
4. Residential care.
5. Nursing home care.
6. Long-stay care in hospital.

The circumstances in which a local authority might offer their own residential accommodation to older people are broadly set out in Part III of the National Assistance Act 1948 (NAA). The primary test is one of need. The NAA states that 'Part III accommodation' may be provided to those who are 'in need of care or attention by reason of age, infirmity or any other circumstances and for whom such care or attention is not otherwise available'. It is thus not strictly necessary for the applicant to have reached retirement age. There is continuing controversy over the adequacy of current assessment procedures prior to the acceptance of older people into Part III accommodation. There are no standard procedures, although there is a basic approach that the government believes should be universal and which is described in a document produced by the DSS Social Services Inspectorate Development Group (1985), *Assessment Procedures for Elderly People Referred for Local Authority Residential Care* (DSS). The new procedures being introduced at local levels to ensure the proper implementation of community care packages are likely to converge to standard models as time progresses, but at present there is little uniformity of approach.

Is the applicant given a choice of home?

If, following assessment, the local authority decides to offer residential accommodation to the applicant they will normally offer a particular home, or choice of homes. However, if the applicant does not like the home offered, or wishes to be given a place in an alternative home, they have a right to request such an alternative, which the local authority must provide, as long as the accommodation is suitable to the person's assessed needs, a place is available, the accommodation in question is willing to enter into a contract on the authority's usual terms and conditions, and the accommodation does not cost more than the authority would usually expect to pay for someone with similar needs. The High Court has stressed the importance of this provision, stating that where the needs assessment is clear about the type of home necessary to meet the applicant's particular needs, it is not open to the local authority to offer accommodation that does not meet the fully assessed needs, simply on the grounds that it is cheaper. If a third party is willing to pay the additional costs of a more expensive home, the local authority is obliged to accept this offer and to arrange a place in the more expensive home, recouping the difference from the third party.

For further information on these issues see National Assistance Act 1948 (Choice of Accommodation) Directions 1992 – Local Authority Circular (LAC) (92) 27.

Must the applicant satisfy any residence requirements before the local authority will consider the application?

Yes. Applicants must fall within *one* of the following categories:

- They must be *either* ordinarily resident in the area of the local authority,

or

- be in that area with no settled residence anywhere,

or

- be ordinarily resident elsewhere but nevertheless in the area at the time of application and in urgent need of residential care.

In addition, the local authority can offer accommodation to any other persons provided that the local authority in whose area they normally reside consents (it seems unlikely that many local authorities would be likely to refuse such an offer).

If the local authority decides to offer the applicant residential accommodation, does it have to be in one of its own homes?

No. The accommodation may be in a home run by the local authority in its own area, or in another area. It may be in a home run by a voluntary organisation but under the general management responsibility of the local authority, or it may be in the fully voluntary sector, or in the private sector. Under the NHSCCA, it is the responsibility of the local authority 'care manager' to 'purchase' whatever services are necessary to meet the needs of the applicant, under the care package. This may include 'purchasing' a place for the applicant in a private residential home. Indeed, local authorities are obliged by government policy to spend at least 85 per cent of their allocated community care budget on 'purchasing' private sector accommodation for applicants in need of residential accommodation. The mechanics of the word 'purchase' are explored in more detail below at p.295.

Advisers seeking information on particular nursing homes in the London area can consult Counsel and Care, Twyman House, 16 Bonny St, London NW1 9PG (tel: 071 485 1566). Another organisation, Elderly Accommodation Counsel Ltd, 46a Chiswick High Rd, London W8, operates a computer register of all forms of accommodation for older people but does not visit. GRACE LINK, Upper Chambers, 7 Derby St, Leek, Staffordshire ST13 6HN (tel: 0345 023330) is an organisation which visits and provides advice about private residential or nursing home accommodation to applicants and seeks to match them with their needs, for a reasonable fee.

If a place is available and offered in a particular home, how can its suitability be assessed?

This is clearly a question of critical importance as the home is likely to be that person's home for the rest of their life. A number of helpful publications are available to assist in making this choice:

Young, P. (1988), *At Home in a Home* (Age Concern) is a cheap and practical guide to what to think about and investigate when choosing a home.

Home Life: a Code of Practice for Residential Care (1986, Centre for Policy on Ageing). This is a cheap, widely available, definitive work that is essential reading for all those running or selecting a home for an older person. It covers every type of residential care home, and sets standards for physical and social care, covering such things as admission procedures, privacy, medical care, financial affairs, diet, environment, and management and training of staff. It is available, together with all other Centre for Policy on Ageing publications, from Bailey Distribution Ltd (see p.317).

A series of pamphlet checklists for people inspecting homes is available from the Consumers' Association, Castlemead, Gascoyne Way, Hertford SG14 1LH (tel: 0992 589031).

The major reference work (though not advised for individual purchase as it is expensive) on private homes is the *Handbook on the Registration and Inspection of Nursing Homes* produced by the National Association of Health Authorities and Trusts (NAHA) and available in the reference section of a good public library. For the address of NAHA, see Chapter 2 at p.54.

Who pays for the accommodation?

Anybody entering residential accommodation since 1 April 1993 is subject to a new charging regime, in the light of the community care legislation. The new regime also applies to those placed in homes by a local authority (mostly Part III accommodation) prior to 1 April 1993. Those already in place in registered care homes (private sector) on that date are not affected by these changes and will have had their existing charging and social security benefit regime 'preserved' (for further information on 'preserved rights' to social security benefits, see DSS leaflet SSCC1). Under the new system if, following a community care assessment (see above at p.289), a local authority agrees to arrange a place for the applicant in residential accommodation, the local authority will be responsible for paying the full fee to the home. The local authority will then be able to recoup all or some of the fees from the applicant under the charging assessment procedure set out below. This procedure applies regardless of the type of accommodation (i.e. council, voluntary or private).

The charging assessment procedure

The charging assessment procedure is carried out according to national rules, roughly similar to the rules for determining income support (see

Chapter 8 at p.263). Firstly, the local authority must set a 'standard rate' for the accommodation, which in the case of their own accommodation is the full cost of providing a place, and in the case of other homes is the gross cost of paying for the accommodation under the contract with the home. An applicant with more than £8000 in savings will pay the full 'standard rate' until their capital falls below that £8000. If the applicant owns their own home, this will be treated as capital, unless to do so would cause hardship to somebody with whom they had previously been sharing the home on a long-term basis. Those with capital below £8000 are means tested, and a check is also made to ensure they are receiving all the state benefits to which they are entitled. Applicants in private or voluntary homes are entitled to receive income support, plus a residential allowance, towards the costs of their care and accommodation, together with a personal allowance of (in 1994) £12.65 per week. Applicants in local authority homes cannot claim income support or residential allowance, unless their income is below the basic pension (see below at p.301). For full details of the scheme, which is complex, see Age Concern England *Factsheet 10: Local Authority Charging Procedures for Residential and Nursing Home Care* or the *Disability Rights Handbook* (18th edn, Chapter 35).

NB. Transfer of assets prior to moving into residential accommodation

It is not possible for an older person who anticipates going into residential accommodation to avoid this charge on their capital by transferring the house to another person shortly before moving into the residential accommodation. In these circumstances, the law will allow the local authority to recover payment from anyone to whom a person in residential accommodation has transferred assets (including a house) less than six months before entering the home if they did so 'knowingly and with the intention of avoiding charges for the residential accommodation'. If the transfer was blatantly to avoid payment, recovery can in fact be enforced even if the transfer was more than six months prior to entering accommodation (for more details, see *Disability Rights Handbook*, 16th edn, J4 at 181).

While a local authority cannot force a person to sell their home in order to meet the charge that is levied by the local authority to cover the cost of the residential accommodation, it can protect its interest by insisting that a legal charge is placed on the property. This legal charge will enable it to recover any unpaid fees at a later date, when the property is transferred either by will, or on intestacy or sale. This factor is one of great importance to consider, if an older person wishes to leave their home to a relative, as a long-accumulating debt expressed as a charge on that property will substantially reduce the value of the legacy to the relative. Most residents will also be in receipt of some form of social security assistance from the state to help them with their costs. For details on this, see p.301 and Chapter 8.

What method can the local authority use to recover the residential accommodation charges if the resident does not pay?

It has already been explained that the local authority can place a charge on the resident's house to protect its financial position in the event of non-payment of the fees. In addition, the local authority can issue proceedings in any court for the recovery of any outstanding debts (but see pp. 173 and 315 on the role of the Court of Protection and at p.314 on the enduring power of attorney). It may also issue proceedings against the resident's spouse, but not against any other member of their family.

Can a resident ever be evicted from the residential home in which they are living?

PART III ACCOMMODATION

There are a number of safeguards to the security of tenure of a Part III resident:

1. The older person will have the status of a secure tenant even though they only hold a licence to occupy (see Chapter 10, p.345). In these circumstances they can only be evicted if the managers of the home can establish grounds for possession as set out in Chapter 10, p.349.
2. The National Assistance Act 1948 allows the Secretary of State to intervene in any situation where s/he thinks fit to do so, if satisfied that the local authority has failed to carry out its responsibilities to provide Part III accommodation. While this power is rarely used, it is a useful fallback position for a dissatisfied person to adopt if they feel they have been wrongfully deprived of their residential accom-

modation. Even if this formal power is not used, a complaint to the DSS can always be considered in cases of serious concern about the conduct in question. The right to complain to the DSS has the effect, however, of precluding any right to complain to the courts. Finally, once the new inspection and complaints procedures set out in the NHSCCA are in place a further tier of monitoring and scrutiny will be available.

3. The Local Ombudsman can always be brought in where maladministration or bias is suspected (for details on this procedure, see Chapter 3 at p.75).

PRIVATE SECTOR ACCOMMODATION

As the status of the resident will almost invariably be that of a licensee and not a tenant (see Chapter 10) it will always be legally possible for the owners or managers of the home to evict the resident, although it will be necessary to do so through court proceedings (see Chapter 10 at p.347).

Can an older occupant of residential accommodation be locked in their room against their will?

The only circumstances in which the managers of a residential home can deprive an occupant of freedom of movement by locking them in their room is where the occupant is the subject of a compulsory detention order under the Mental Health Act 1983 (a 'section'), in which case they are subject to the same laws as any other person committed under that Act (see Chapter 5 at p.138). Otherwise, any attempt to regulate the freedom of movement of residents within the parts of the premises to which they have legal access will amount to an infringement of their civil liberties and should be resisted.

For further information on the problem and scale of elder abuse, and strategies for confronting it, see the SSI London Region Survey (1992), *Confronting Elder Abuse* (HMSO), and De Calmer and Glendinning (1993), *Mistreatment of Older People* (Sage).

What controls operate on residential homes to ensure that they are properly run?

Part III accommodation

Part III residential accommodation is the responsibility of the local authority social services department and thus any controls that operate on these homes are those which the local authority itself imposes. This also means that all the complaints procedures outlined in connection with eviction and also those procedures outlined in Chapter 3 at p.71 are available in connection with Part III accommodation. If the complaint amounts, however, to an allegation by a member of staff about patient care, and the home is part of the National Health Service, there is a procedure available that has been devised by the National Association of Health Authorities (NAHA) and is contained in a 1985 publication called *Protecting Patients: Guidelines for Handling Staff Complaints about Patients' Care* (see Chapter 2, p.53). Also, since April 1993 local authorities have started to put in place a system of monitoring and inspection of their homes, together with a mechanism for making complaints about homes. The government wishes free-standing inspection units to be set up in local authorities that will eventually take responsibility for the inspection and monitoring of voluntary, private and public sector homes. For further information, see also *Inspecting for Quality: Social Services Inspectorate Guidance on Practice for Inspection Units in Social Services Departments and Other Agencies* (SSI).

Private sector accommodation

Most of these homes are regulated by the Registered Homes Act 1984 which is a long, complex, but comprehensive piece of legislation. Anybody who is engaged in social work with older people in residential settings would be well advised to familiarise themselves with its general provisions. For a detailed but readily comprehensible book about the Act, consult Jones, R. (1989), *Registered Homes Act Manual* (Sweet and Maxwell). In summary, the Act provides a system of registration for a whole range of residential homes, including any home providing 'residential accommodation with both board and personal care for persons in need of personal care by reason of old age'. If the residential home also provides either physical or mental nursing care, it will be subject to a further set of detailed regulations governing the conduct of the institution, and the services and facilities it provides. Local authorities are required to inspect the home at least twice a year, and one of the visits should be unannounced.

Any home covered by the Act cannot operate unless it has been registered. Operating a residential home covered by the Act without registration is a criminal offence. Applications for registration are considered by the social services department of the local authority in which the home is situated. An application may be refused, accepted, or accepted with conditions. There is a right of appeal to a registered homes tribunal. Detailed information regarding registration can be found in *Home Life: a Code of Practice for Residential Care* referred to on p.294. Registration officers should also consult the *BASW Practice Notes for Social Workers and Residential Officers Working with the Private and Voluntary Residential Sector*.

The registers of a registration authority must be made available to the public for inspection at all reasonable times, and members of the public are entitled to take copies of entries on payment of an appropriate fee. Any complaints about a particular home should be addressed in the first instance to the registration authority, and if the complainant alleges maladministration by the registration authority in its registration, then the Local Ombudsman (see Chapter 3 at p.75). Guidance on the Act is provided by DHSS Circulars Nos. LAC (84)15, HC(84)21, LAC(86)6, HC(86)5 and LAC(90)13. See also *Inspecting for Quality: Social Services Inspectorate Guidance on Practice for Inspection Units in Social Services Departments and Other Agencies* (SSI).

Are there any special social security benefits to assist people living in residential accommodation?

For information on these benefits, see Chapter 8 at p.269.

Are there any special grants available to older people to help them to carry out improvements in their home?

See Chapter 4 at p.101.

STATE BENEFITS FOR OLDER PEOPLE

State benefits for older people are complex and many involve making careful choices which should be based on sound advice. This section will summarise the most important benefits. For more detailed information, advisers should consult two excellent manuals produced by Age Concern: *Your Rights: a Guide to Money Benefits for Retired People* and *Your Taxes and Savings*. New editions of each of these manuals appear annually. For quick advice on a particular state benefit, ring DSS Freephone: 0800 666555.

State benefits for older people can be divided into two categories:

1. Those to which an older person is entitled as of right.
2. Those which are discretionary, that is to say, they are subject to need, to means, or to both. This section will consequently be divided into two parts to reflect these two general categories.

Benefits as of right

Pensions

A more detailed guide to pensions is the *Pensions Handbook*, published in 1993 by Age Concern. Set out below is a summary of the law on pensions, which is generally quite complex.

Rights to pensions are closely linked to the number of national insurance contributions that a person, or their spouse, has paid during their working life. Every employee and employer have a duty to pay national insurance contributions if the employee's earnings are above the legal 'lower earnings limit' (see DSS leaflet NI 208). The amount of the contribution will be a percentage of the employee's wage.

Pensions can be divided into two broad categories, the *basic state retirement pension* and the *additional pension,* of which there are several categories.

THE RETIREMENT PENSION (TAXABLE)

Who can claim a retirement pension?

Any person of pensionable age (65 for men, 60 for women) who has paid a sufficient number of national insurance contributions during their working life is entitled to claim a retirement pension. To achieve a 'sufficient number' the person must have paid or been credited with national insurance contributions during approximately 90 per cent of their working life. (Working people should therefore take care to ensure that they are credited with national insurance contributions during periods of unemployment, sickness, or child/older person care: see p.306 on how to check your national insurance contribution record.)

Some married women may have paid national insurance contributions at a reduced rate, which will affect their entitlement to a full retirement pension. Anybody in these circumstances should consult DSS leaflet *Married Women: Your National Insurance Position*. Divorced or separated women should consult DSS leaflet NI 95, *Divorced Women National Insurance Guide*.

Whether or not a person chooses to claim their retirement pension from the moment they become entitled to it (see below) will require a careful assessment of their overall financial position, including in particular an assessment of the level of their future earnings upon which expert financial advice from a CAB or other adviser might well be sought. A retirement pension can normally be backdated for only three months, though claims can in fact be made up to four months in advance of eligibility. Once a claim has been processed, and the level of payment agreed (see below), the claimant will either be sent a book of money orders, to be cashed weekly in advance, or, if preferred, arrangements can be made with the DSS for the person to be paid monthly or quarterly in arrears (for further information, see DSS leaflet NI 105).

Does everybody in receipt of a retirement pension receive the same amount?

No. The amount will depend upon the category into which the claimant falls (see p.303).

When can you get retirement pension?

A person can claim retirement pension once they have reached 'pensionable age' (see p.301), or they can defer claiming their pension for up to five years. If they go on working to 'retirement age' (65 for women, 70 for men) and do not claim all or part of their pension until they retire, they will be entitled to claim extra pension upon retirement. This 'enhancement' of the pension will amount to about 7.5 per cent for each year of deferment up to retirement age. If a person begins claiming their retirement pension and subsequently decides to defer claiming until 'retirement age' they can do so, but this can be done only once. When a person works after pensionable age their earnings will be counted together with any pension they are claiming as 'taxable income'. They will not, however, have to pay national insurance contributions, and should receive from the DSS a certificate of exemption to this effect.

What are the various categories of retirement pension?

The amount of the retirement pension that a claimant will receive will depend upon which of the following categories the claimant falls into. The higher the category the larger the pension. The current rates of payment are given in DSS leaflet NI 184.

Category A. This pension will be payable if the claimant has satisfied the national insurance contribution requirement on the basis of their own record (for full details, see the CPAG *Rights Guide to Non-Means-Tested Social Security Benefits* or DSS leaflets NP 32, NI 42 and NI 48, or Age Concern *Factsheets*, see p.305). For details on how to obtain information on national insurance contributions, see p.306. This pension may also be supplemented by further amounts to reflect any adult or child dependant of the pensioner (unless the adult dependant is claiming a Category B pension, or earning money which amounts to the same sum: see below).

NB In addition to the above, it should be noted that certain widows and widowers are also entitled to receive Category A pensions, although the claim is not based on their own contributions. The rules for such claims are complex. For full details, consult the CPAG *Rights Guide* (see p.305).

Category B. This pension will be payable to married women over pensionable age whose husbands are entitled to Category A retirement pensions, but who are not themselves entitled to Category A pensions. (For further information see DSS leaflet NP 32, *Retirement Benefits for Married Women*.)

Category B (Widow or Widower). This pension will be payable to the widow or widower of a person who was entitled to receive a Category A pension. This pension is subject to a number of qualifications regarding the age and entitlements of both the claimant and the deceased (see

CPAG Rights Guide and DSS leaflet NP 45, *Your Retirement Pension if you are Widowed or Divorced*). Although this is called a Category B pension it is paid at the Category A rate!
Category C and Category D. These pensions are non-contributory retirement pensions and are rare. They are only available to the very much older person, or to the widow or widower of a very much older person (see CPAG *Rights Guide* and DSS leaflet 184).

Is a retirement pension reduced if the recipient is in hospital?

Retirement pensions are reduced after the pensioner has spent six weeks in hospital for in-patient treatment on the National Health Service, and are reduced still further if the recipient remains in hospital for over a year (see DSS leaflets NI 9 and SF 300). The pension is reduced immediately if the recipient was living in residential accommodation at the time of their admission to hospital. Sometimes part of the reduced amount can be set aside as 'resettlement money' but this will not be the case if the recipient remains in hospital for 2 years. It is worth noting that some hospitals and some social work departments have befriending schemes for volunteers to visit and advise pensioners who are in hospital for a long time.

Can a person who cannot work regularly because of home care responsibilities protect their retirement pension rights?

Since 1978 there has been a scheme in operation to protect the pension rights of a person who has been unable to work regularly because they have had to stay at home to care for an older or disabled person or children. It is called Home Responsibilities Protection (HRP). The effect of eligibility is to reduce the number of 'working years' that person will have to establish in order to be eligible for a retirement pension. A person who is looking after:

- a child for whom they receive child benefit;

or

- who is receiving income support to enable them to stay at home to look after a sick or disabled person;

or

- who spends at least 35 hours a week for 48 weeks a year looking after a person who is getting attendance allowance, DLA care component at the middle or higher rate (see p.114) or constant attendance allowance and who is not themselves in receipt of invalid care allowance (see p.126)

should claim HRP to protect their future pension rights on DSS leaflet and form HP 27.

Further sources of information on retirement pensions

DSS leaflet NI 32, *Your Retirement Pension.*
CPAG *Rights Guide to Non-Means Tested Benefits* (latest edition), published annually in April.
Consumers' Association booklet, *What will my pension be?*
Age Concern *Factsheets*: *National Insurance Contributions and Retirement Pensions (up to 1948); National Insurance Contributions and Retirement Pensions (1948–75); National Insurance Contributions and Basic Retirement Pensions (1975 onwards).* Help the Aged also produce a free information sheet on pensions.
Your Rights (Age Concern) and *Your Taxes and Savings* (Age Concern).

ADDITIONAL PENSIONS (TAXABLE) (SEE DSS LEAFLET NI 38)

State Earnings-Related Pension Scheme (SERPS)

Many employees are entitled to an additional pension to supplement their state retirement pension. The first of these is administered by the DSS and is earnings related. It is commonly known as SERPS. Under SERPS the DSS calculate an earnings factor for every year that the claimant has worked since 1978, based on the claimant's income which is then adjusted upwards to take account of inflation. On retirement an additional pension is paid to the pensioner on the basis of this figure. Anybody in this scheme and of pre-retirement age can obtain from the DSS a statement of the current value of their additional pension by filling out a form contained in DSS leaflet NI 38, *Your Future Pension.*

Changes will be occurring to the scheme in the coming years, but will not affect anyone reaching state pension age before 6 April 1999.

Occupational pensions and personal pensions

All employees have the right to contract out of the SERPS pension scheme, and take the alternative of either an *occupational pension scheme* (if one is operated by their employer) which is salary related (COSR), i.e. based on the person's earnings, or a *money purchase scheme* (COMP), which is based on the value of a fund the individual builds up. The options may be complex, and the choice critical. All employees are strongly advised to seek independent advice on this issue before deciding which scheme to choose, as once a decision has been made it will be difficult, if not impossible, to switch. Detailed information packs on the pension choices can be obtained from the Central Pensions Branch of the DSS, Newcastle upon Tyne, NE98 1YX (tel: 091 213 5000). A number of private insurance companies also now offer a range of alternative personal pension schemes in a bid to encourage people away from the occupational pensions. They should be considered with great care and on their merits, having taken independent advice. For further specialist advice on occupational pensions, contact: The Occupational Pensions Advisory Service (OPAS), 11 Belgrave Road, London SW1V 1RB (tel: 071 233 8080). In some circumstances it is also possible to complain to the newly created Pensions Ombudsman.

WIDOWS' BENEFITS

Although this chapter is primarily designed to provide advice on the legal rights of older people, it seems the most appropriate place to include details of widows' benefits. It is of course possible that a woman may be widowed before she becomes old, in which case she may be entitled to further benefits which are not available to the older widow. Any woman who is widowed before the age of 40, or while she still has dependent children, should consult the CPAG *Rights Guide to Non-Means Tested Social Security Benefits* for full details on any available extra entitlements, or obtain DSS leaflets NI 29, *Help When Someone Dies*, and NI 45, *A Guide to Widow's Benefits*.

A note on national insurance contributions

All the benefits below depend upon accurate information concerning national insurance contributions. In order to obtain this information a letter should be sent to the local office of the DSS enclosing the national insurance number of the deceased and, if appropriate, the widow, requesting a written statement of their national insurance contribution record (see DSS leaflets NI 42 and NI 48). The same applies when checking your own contributions.

If the woman was still married to her husband (not cohabitee) at the time of his death (even if they were separated, or were in the process of obtaining a divorce which had not yet been finalised) she is able to claim the following widow's benefits:

1. Widow's payment, a one-off tax-free sum of £1000 payable if
   either
   - she was under 60 when he died

   or
   - he was under 65

   or
   - he was 65 or over and was not receiving a state retirement pension and he had paid a sufficient number of national insurance contributions.
2. Widow's pension, a weekly, taxable benefit which will continue until she is entitled to receive a retirement pension (see p.301) or until she remarries, which is payable as long as the woman was 55 or over when her husband died. The amount will depend upon the level of national insurance contributions paid by her husband. In limited circumstances women between 40 and 45 on their husband's death can apply; on changes in the law in this respect, consult the local CAB.

Claims for either or both of the above benefits should be made within 12 months of the death on Form BW1, which can be obtained from any DSS office. Widow's payment is paid by girocheque. Widow's pension can be paid either in an order book cashable weekly at a post office, or by credit transfer into a bank account, every 4 or 13 weeks.

NB All pensions can be topped up by the means tested income support (described in detail in Chapter 8) where the person's means are less than their legally defined needs.

For further information on retirement pension for widows, consult DSS leaflet NI 32A, *Your Retirement Pension if You are Widowed or Divorced.* For further advice, information and friendly support, widows can contact the National Association of Widows, 1st Floor, Neville House, 14 Waterloo St, Birmingham, B2 5TX (tel: 021 643 8348).

Benefits payable on proof of need

These benefits can be grouped into two distinct categories: those which are subject to proof of special disability but are not means tested, and those which are subject to proof of special need and are in addition means tested.

Special needs benefits which are not means tested

The most important benefits in this category are disability living allowance, attendance allowance, invalid care allowance, mobility allowance and benefits arising from injury, illness or disablement at work. As none of these benefits relate exclusively to older people, they are all dealt with in detail in other parts of the book as indicated. In summary, however, the benefits relate to the following circumstances:

- DLA care component or attendance allowance is payable to a severely disabled person who needs very frequent attention either in connection with their bodily functions or to prevent them from injuring themselves. For full details of this benefit, see Chapter 4 at p.114 and DSS leaflet NI 205.
- Invalid care allowance is payable to a person of working age who is unable to work because they are engaged in the full-time home care of a severely disabled person. For full details of this benefit, see Chapter 4 at p.126 and DSS leaflet NI 212.
- DLA mobility component or mobility allowance is payable to a person who is so severely disabled that they are virtually unable to walk. For full details of this benefit, see Chapter 4 p.117 and DSS leaflet NI 211.
- Benefits arising from injury, illness or disablement at work. These benefits are all dealt with in Chapter 4 at p.109 and Chapter 8 at p.256. They cover circumstances where a person is no longer able to work through illness, industrial accident or industrial disease, or where their capacity to work has been removed or limited as a result of disablement caused by an accident at work.

Means tested special needs benefits for older people

All the benefits in this category, relating to such things as extra heating, warm clothing, special diets, fares to hospital and so forth, are covered by the Social Security Act 1986 and are mostly only available to a person in receipt of income support. For full details on the income support system and the Social Fund from which special payments are drawn, see Chapter 8. Those who do not get income support may still qualify for free or subsidised treatment if they obtain Certificate AG2 or AG3, which certifies they have something called 'low-income entitlement', i.e. not in receipt of income support but have less than £8000 in savings (see DOH leaflet AB11). With either of these certificates, the older person can obtain free dental treatment, provided they attend for regular treatment ('continuing care') (see Age Concern England *Factsheet 5, Dental Care in Retirement*, and DOH leaflet D11); free eye treatment and help towards the cost of glasses (DOH leaflet G11). All people of pensionable age receive free prescriptions. Applications for assistance in the cost of travel to and from hospital for treatment can be made on a hospital claim form AG1. The form can be obtained from a hospital or social security office. Once filled out it should be sent to the Agency Benefit Unit, Longbenton, Benton Park Road, Newcastle upon Tyne NE98 1YX (tel: 091 213 5000).

Fuel costs

There is a special code of conduct regarding the disconnection of the gas or electricity supply to a house in which there are older or sick residents which is described in detail in Chapter 2 at p.16. The Electricity Consumer's Council (see Chapter 2 at p.16 for address) has produced a special leaflet for older people called *Electricity and You: Advice for Older People*. Guides on keeping down heating costs are available from the Department of Energy (Room 1312, Thames House South, 310 Millbank, London SW1 4AU (tel: 071 211 3000), in particular *A Guide to Home Heating Costs and Handy Hints to Save Energy: Help with your Winter Heating*. For information on *draught-proofing* grants (only available in certain parts of the country), contact Neighbourhood Energy Action, 2 Bigg Market, Newcastle upon Tyne, NE1 1UW (tel: 091 261 5677). For information on *insulation grants* ('minor works grants'), see Chapter 4 at p.105). The most comprehensive general guide on all questions relating to fuel cost management is the *Fuel Rights Handbook* (SHAC). Finally, Shelter (1988) produces some very useful *Hard to Heat Packs* written by the Nottingham Heating Project. If a person is receiving one of the pensioner or disability premiums with income support (see Chapter 8 at p.265) they will automatically receive a further Cold Weather Payment, for each period of seven consecutive days when the average temperature in their area has been, or is expected to be, 0°C, or below (see DSS leaflet CWP 1).

Tax planning

It is clear from the complex range of benefits set out above that older people may need specialist advice on their tax planning. The first source of assistance should be the Inland Revenue leaflet, *Income Tax and Pensioners*, Inland Revenue leaflet IR 4, which is available from any local tax office.

Other useful sources of advice are as follows:

1. The most up-to-date and comprehensive specialist guide on the market at present is the Age Concern booklet *Your Taxes and Savings*, which is produced annually. It explains in simple terms the complexities of the tax system, how to work out a tax bill and how to minimise tax payments. It also advises on the great range of investment opportunities that are of special interest to older people.
2. *Income Tax and Widows*, Inland Revenue booklet IR 23.
3. *Approaching Retirement*, *What will my pension be?*, and *'Which?' Tax Savings Guide* (all published by the Consumers' Association).
4. Free *Factsheets* provided by Help the Aged (enclose large sae).
5. *PEP Guide* (1993), Chase de Vere Investments plc.
6. Lysons, K., *Earning Money in Retirement* (Age Concern/ACE Books).

THE MANAGEMENT OF PERSONAL AFFAIRS

The majority of older people are perfectly capable of continuing to manage their personal affairs right up to the time of their death, with perhaps little more than the occasional assistance of a relative, friend or trusted family adviser, like the family solicitor. Sometimes, however, the onset of old age brings with it a real or perceived anxiety in the minds of older people that they may no longer be able to manage their own affairs. This section looks at some of the commonest problems facing older people who are feeling unable to manage their affairs and sets out the possible courses of action that are available.

Making a will

A person who makes a will is described as a testator. Everybody should make a will regardless of their age, but many do not contemplate such matters until they are older. There are good reasons for making a will, the most obvious being that a will enables a person to decide to whom they would like their property to pass on their death. If a person dies without making a will (intestate) the law takes over and applies a series of rules which determine to whom any property will pass, which may not be what the deceased person would have wished. It is advisable to consult a solicitor, bank, building society or insurance company, all of whom have the legal ability and expertise to advise on the making of a will. Alternatively, a person can use the Age Concern will writing service, for a small fee. The legalities of will writing are complicated and precise, and it is better that any problems are sorted out in the testator's lifetime rather than after death. A solicitor will charge a fee for this assistance, which should be discussed in advance. It is almost certainly a worthwhile investment. See further, *Making a Will* and *Making a Will Won't Kill You*, available for a small fee from the Law Society (see p.38).

Is the legality of a will affected by the testator's mental state at the time when the will is made?

A will is not valid if at the time of making it the testator was incapable of understanding what they were doing, or the nature and effect of the will. If any relatives or dependants, on the death of the testator, are aggrieved by the testator's failure to leave them anything, the law permits them in certain defined circumstances to apply to the court for the will to be rewritten. In practice this is rarely done, and legal advice should be sought before any such action is contemplated. Even if a person's affairs are under the general supervision of the Court of Protection (see pp. 173 and 315), they can still make a valid will, although the Court of Protection does have the power to override that will at a later date, on proof that the testator was incapable of knowing what they were doing.

For further detailed information and advice on the making of wills, consult the Consumers' Association booklet *Wills and Probate*. A will form can be obtained from any large stationers.

How can a person leave instructions concerning funeral arrangements and other personal matters following their death?

It is perfectly in order to leave any instructions in a will in the hope and expectation that the executors will carry them out. Alternatively, there are more private ways of dealing with such matters, which may be more appropriate in some circumstances. Age Concern produces a useful form called *Instructions for my Next of Kin and Executors upon my Death* which can be used to sort out these personal details. The form is not a will, and can be kept separate and private from the will.

Giving legal power to another to manage your affairs

There are a number of ways in which older people may grant legal powers to allow others to manage some or all of their affairs for them during their lifetime.

Agency

An older person may nominate or instruct another to act on their behalf as their agent. This procedure is commonly used by an older person who wishes somebody else to collect their pension or other benefits from the post office for them, because they are unable to go there themselves. The DSS have a standard procedure whereby such a nomination may be made. If the practice is to continue for a long time, it is advisable to obtain an agency card from the DSS which the agent can produce as authority for the payment to be made to them. If the older person is in Part III residential accommodation (see p.292) they can alternatively nominate an official of the local authority as their 'signing agent' who will cash all their benefits for them on their behalf. It seems that in 80 per cent of local authority homes it is official policy to use this procedure as a way of ensuring that the 'standard payment' is made. This clearly has certain quite disturbing civil liberty implications and advisers should be alert to detect any abuse of this power by over zealous officials, particularly where the older person might also be mentally disordered. (For further information, see the 1985 report by the Social Services Inspectorate of the DSS, *Inspection of Local Authority Care for Older Mentally Disordered People* (DSS).) Finally, if the older person is too ill to be disturbed or to understand what is happening, and an agent has not previously been appointed, there is a special procedure whereby the DSS can take a statement of the circumstances from any 'responsible person' and appoint a temporary agent who may well be that same 'responsible person' who will be empowered to cash benefits as the older person's agent until they are well enough to issue instructions personally.

Appointee

An alternative to agency is to appoint another person who will not only collect a benefit on the older person's behalf but will also be entitled to spend it. This person is described as an appointee. This power only relates to social security benefits, but it does therefore include pensions. An appointee has to be appointed by the DSS who will only make such an appointment where it is satisfied that the claimant is unable to act personally and is not under the Court of Protection (see pp. 173 and 315). About 45,000 such appointments are made each year (they are by no means limited to older people). The DSS has a detailed checking procedure that must be followed to confirm the suitability of a prospective appointee. Generally, the ideal appointee would be a close relative who lives with the claimant. If the older person is in a residential home or hospital, a member of the staff of that institution will normally be made an appointee. The DSS stipulates that when an appointee is appointed 'any benefit received must be used in the interests of the claimant'. If the claimant is in hospital, the appointee should ensure that, from the amount of benefit granted, a sufficient weekly sum is provided to the claimant to meet personal needs. In an emergency, and only if there is no appointee, the DSS has the power to pay a claimant's benefit to any person it thinks fit, e.g. to a public utility or landlord, if it believes that the claimant is incapable of budgeting, or wilfully refusing to budget for any item of normal, additional or household requirements applicable to them.

Power of attorney

It is always open to any adult person to grant a power of attorney to another adult person to act on their behalf in the management of all their personal affairs if, for example, they are going abroad for a substantial period or are going into hospital. The power of attorney is granted by filling out a simple form (with the help of a solicitor if necessary). A power of attorney ceases, however, if the grantor ceases to be mentally capable of knowing what they are doing. This is because a power of attorney implies a continuing clear and conscious awareness on the part of the grantor of what the grantee is doing. In reality, however, it is likely that powers of attorney continue to be used long after the grantor remains mentally capable, despite the fact that this is in effect an illegal use of the power. In order to combat this problem, there has been in existence since 1985 an alternative power of attorney known as the 'enduring power of attorney'.

Enduring power of attorney

If a person has the ability to grant a power of attorney, and is worried that at some time in the future they may lose their mental capabilities, there is the alternative choice of granting an enduring power of attorney. The mental capacity to grant such a power is the same as that for making a will (see p.311). The procedure for granting such a power is similar to the ordinary power of attorney. The difference is that if the donor loses mental capability the donee can continue to exercise the power of attorney, but only if the Court of Protection subsequently registers the enduring power of attorney, on the application of the donee. Notice of any application to the Court of Protection to register the enduring power of attorney must be given to specified relatives, although this notice may be waived if such relatives cannot be reasonably ascertained, or are under 18, or are mentally incapacitated, or no useful purpose would be served by contacting them.. Any relative with notice of the application has 28 days in which to lodge an objection to the proposed registration on such grounds as undue pressure on the donor, or the unsuitability of the donee, given, for example, the nature of their relationship with the donee. It is often only when notice of a wish to register is circulated in a family that the existence of the enduring power first comes to light, as prior to registration it is a private and not a public arrangement. If a social worker or other adviser is unhappy about the proposed registration they are quite entitled to express these reservations in a letter to the Court of Protection before a final decision on registration is made. The Court will only register the enduring power of attorney when it is satisfied with the evidence of the donor's mental incapability, and if all the procedures regarding notice have been followed. For a general outline of the system, see *Enduring Power of Attorney*, available from the Public Trust Office, Court of Protection (see p.173). For more detailed information, consult Cretney, S. (1989), *Enduring Power of Attorney* (2nd edn; Family Law, Jordan and Son).

Having the power to manage your own affairs taken away

If it becomes necessary to take away an older person's legal powers to manage their own affairs it is not because of their age but because of their mental capacity (see Chapter 5, p.171). The two possible procedures are to put the older person's affairs into Receivership under the Control of the Court of Protection, or to make them the subject of Guardianship Proceedings. Full details of these procedures can be found in Chapter 5 at pp. 172–3 (see also *Handbook for Receivers*, Public Trust Office). While the powers conferred by the Court of Protection are very wide indeed, those conferred by guardianship are far more limited and confined to three, namely the power to require the person to reside at a specified place, the power to require the person to attend at any given time for treatment, and the power to insist that the person provides access to named individuals, e.g. a doctor or a social worker. Guardianship is only likely to be a success, however, if local authorities are prepared to use it, and more importantly to commit the necessary resources to make it work.

NB The equivalent of the Court of Protection in Scotland is the Curator Bonis, where a person is nominated to take over the affairs of a mentally incapacitated person. A Scottish lawyer should be consulted in the drawing up of the relevant documentation. In Northern Ireland the Office of Care and Protection has similar powers for citizens of Northern Ireland to those of the Court of Protection.

What to do when someone dies

It is an unfortunate fact that in addition to coping with the pain and stress of losing a close relative, there also remain many formalities that have to be complied with, normally the responsibility of the nearest surviving relative. There is set out below a checklist of the matters that will have to be dealt with. For a more detailed account of what has to be done, consult the relevant section of the *Penguin Guide to the Law* by John Pritchard.

- The death must be registered with the local Registrar of Births, Marriages and Deaths within five days of the death. The Registrar's address will be in the local telephone book. In order to register the death the Registrar will require a death certificate from a doctor (or if the matter was reported to the coroner, a coroner's form), and basic details of the time and place of death. The Registrar will then issue a certificate of registration of death (necessary in order to claim widow's benefit: see p.306), and a certificate to enable disposal of the body to take place.
- The funeral must be arranged. This can be done by an undertaker (funeral director) – if possible, a funeral director who is a member of the National Association of Funeral Directors (NAFD) should be used, as their members are bound by a Code of Practice agreed with the Office of Fair Trading. (On the status of Codes of Practice generally, see Chapter 2.) A copy of the Code can be obtained from the NAFD, 618 Warwick Road, Solihull B91 1AA (tel: 021 711 1343). An NAFD undertaker must give a full estimate of the cost of the funeral in advance. Advice on the choice of burial or cremation, and the location of the funeral, can also be obtained from the funeral director.
- All persons or agencies with whom the deceased held current accounts or investments must be notified of the death by the executors (or the administrators if no will has been written) so that, where appropriate, accounts can be closed or transferred to the names of the executors or administrators or the relevant beneficiaries.
- Where the deceased has left a will it is the duty of the executors, if appointed by the will, to carry out the terms of the will. Where the assets are substantial, the executors will need to obtain probate of the will from the Probate Registry. This can be done personally by the executors, but a solicitor should be consulted in case of difficulty. Where the deceased has not left a will the distribution of the assets is the responsibility of the nearest relative (called the administrator) according to the law of intestacy. It is necessary to apply for Letters of Administration from the Probate Registry where the assets are considerable. For further information on the procedures

to follow, consult the Consumers' Association booklet *Wills and Probate*, the Consumers' Association pamphlet *What to do when Someone Dies*, the DSS leaflet *What to do after a Death* (DSS leaflet D49), or the *Penguin Guide to the Law*.

The address of the Probate Registry is South Wing, Somerset House, Strand, London WC2R 1LP (tel: 071 936 6000) or for personal applications Probate Personal Applications Dept, Registry of Family Division, 2nd Floor, Somerset House (as above) (tel: 071 936 6983).

SOURCES OF FURTHER ASSISTANCE

Much prominence has been given in this chapter to a leading charity that is devoted to assisting older people, Age Concern. Age Concern has a large number of local offices, but its national headquarters are as follows:

Age Concern England, Astral House, 1268 London Road, SW16 4ER (tel: 081 679 8000).
Age Concern Northern Ireland, 6 Lower Crescent, Belfast, BI7 1NR (tel: 0232 2454729).
Age Concern Scotland, 33 Castle St, Edinburgh EH2 3DN (tel: 031 225 5000).
Age Concern Wales, 1 Park Grove, Cardiff CF1 3FJ (tel: 0222 371821 and 0222 371566).

An organisation with a research and policy-making role with reference to the needs of older people is:

The Centre for Policy on Ageing, 2–31 Ironmonger Row, London EC1V 3QP (tel: 071 253 1787).

In addition to a large publications list, the Centre provides advice and information to professionals working with older people. The Centre has a substantial reference library and is actively engaged in initiatives aimed at the integration of all older people into the community. For the publications of the Centre for Policy on Ageing, write to Bailey Distribution Ltd, Warner House, Units 1A and 1B, Mountfield Independent Estate, Learoyd Road, New Romney, Kent TN28 8XU (tel: 0679 66905).

A further organisation that is London-based but is an excellent source of referral information on a wide range of problems affecting older people is Help The Aged, whose address is:

Help The Aged, St James's Walk, London EC1R 0BE (tel: 071 253 0253).

This organisation provides a telephone advice and referral service, a range of free pamphlets giving advice to older people, and a number of reasonably priced guides on specific areas of concern, including some of those mentioned in this chapter.

There are several excellent sources of further information on a whole range of issues relating to older people:

1. Griffiths, A., Grimes, R., and Roberts, G. (1990), *The Law and Elderly People* (Routledge). This is a very comprehensive account of all aspects of law relating to work with older people with extensive footnotes. A fairly academic text.
2. McDonald, A., and Taylor, M. (1993), *Elders and the Law* (Pepar). This is a slender, clearly written and concise account of law covering older people with sections on services in the community, residential care, finance and business affairs, and death and family provision.
3. The Longman Self-Help Guide by Gill Manthorpe (1986), *Elderly People – Rights and Opportunities*, sets out in clear terms the rights of older people in a range of areas including retirement, money, housing, health, families, local and legal services, and holidays, and provides a mass of information on further sources of assistance.
4. The Age Concern publication (1986) *The Law and Vulnerable Older People* combines an accurate account of the law relating to accommodation, money management, consent to treatment, and compulsion of older people, with many ideas for reform, well backed-up with informed comment and statistics.
5. *Daily Mail Retirement Guide* is a concise, cheap, readable guide covering a wide range of problems.

A recent journal, covering a wide range of issues designed to inform those who work with older people, called *Elders: The Journal of Care and Practice*, is available from Pepar Publications, Southside, 249 Ladypool Road, Sparkbrook, Birmingham, B12 8LF.

Chapter 10

Finding and keeping a home

This chapter will take a look at the various ways in which the law can be used as a tool to assist in finding or keeping a home.* Wherever there is a problem demanding social work intervention, there is a high probability that the absence of a decent home, or a state of uncertainty concerning the client's existing home, will form a direct or indirect part of that problem. Many legal rights and responsibilities will operate upon such problems. This chapter will illuminate the most important of these. It is arranged as follows:

1. Getting council accommodation (whether homeless or already housed).
2. Buying council accommodation from the council.
3. Retaining council accommodation as a tenant.
4. Rights to housing association accommodation.
5. Seeking and keeping privately rented accommodation.
6. Retaining mortgaged accommodation.
7. The criminal law and the protection of accommodation rights.

GETTING COUNCIL ACCOMMODATION

The rights of an individual to obtain council accommodation will depend upon whether, at the time of their application, they are homeless.

*The chapter will deal only with the position in England and Wales. Housing rights in both Scotland and Northern Ireland, while broadly similar to those in England and Wales, do differ in significant points of detail and anybody advising clients in those countries should take local advice to clarify exactly where those differences lie. (For a summary of the content of the Housing (Scotland) Act 1988, see *Roof*, January–February 1989.)

Rights to council accommodation if homeless

Homelessness is a problem of major proportions in the United Kingdom. Estimates of the numbers of homeless people at present in the United Kingdom rise as high as 250,000. In these circumstances, it is easy to understand how hard-pressed council housing departments have adopted very rigorous procedures to try to ensure that priority is given to the most deserving cases. Not only is the pressure on resources immense, but it is disproportionately directed towards inner-city councils with large, fluid populations. In these stressful circumstances it is clearly a matter of considerable importance that the adviser has a good understanding of the legal obligations that lie with councils to provide accommodation to those who request it. (For contemporary research on the causes, the impact and ways of reducing homelessness, advisers should read *Your Place or Mine?*, published in 1993 by NCH, 85 Highbury Park, London N5 1UD (tel: 071 226 2033.) On single homelessness, see *Counted Out* (CHAR/Crisis, 1992), and *Single Homelessness: Illustrating the Crisis* (CHAR). Details about CHAR appear on p.329.

What duties do councils have to provide accommodation to homeless persons?

The answer to this question is to be found in an important piece of legislation that began its life in 1977 as the Housing (Homeless Persons) Act and is now Part III of the Housing Act 1985. This Act is supplemented by a Code of Guidance, and a Local Authority Agreement. All Homeless Persons Units attached to councils in England and Wales are supposed to operate strictly according to the terms of the Act. The Act has in turn been much scrutinised and modified by a number of important cases. What follows is a summary of the position; those seeking more detailed information should consult Moroney, L., and Goodwin, J. (1992), *Homelessness: a Good Practice Guide* (Shelter); Hunter, C., and McGrath, S. (1992), *Homeless Persons* (Legal Action Group); or *In on the Act: An Introductory Guide to the Homelessness Legislation and Single People* (1993, CHAR).

The basic position under this legislation is that a council has a legal duty to provide permanent accommodation to certain categories of people who are either homeless or threatened with homelessness and to provide temporary accommodation or advice and assistance to certain other categories. As would be expected, each one of these words has been exhaustively analysed and defined by the courts. In addition, official reports demonstrate that the ways in which local authorities in practice interpret their responsibilities differ widely; see *Responding to Homelessness: Local Authority Policy and Practice* (1988, HMSO).

What does *homeless* mean?

The law considers a person to be homeless if they have 'no accommodation' in England, Wales or Scotland. 'They' extends to any person who might normally be expected to live with the homeless person as a member of their family, for example a caring relative, a child or a spouse. The phrase 'no accommodation' is a legal term and means something different from a 'roof over your head'. It means accommodation that the occupier has a legal right to occupy, i.e. which they own, rent, occupy under a trust, have a licence to occupy, or which they have a special legal right to occupy, for example as a result of a post-divorce settlement or pending a court possession order hearing. It also extends to accommodation that is legally available to the homeless person to occupy but which they are prevented from occupying through fear of domestic violence or because the landlord has illegally locked them out. In addition to the above, it must be reasonable to expect them to occupy the premises in question (see below at p.322). There are special rules about owners of mobile homes and houseboats with nowhere to site them. See Letall, M. (1988), *Mobile Homes: An Occupier's Guide* (Shelter).

A person is 'threatened with homelessness' if they are likely to become homeless within 28 days. Thus a person who has received a possession order, or a person in temporary hostel accommodation with a maximum stay period of less than 28 days, is 'threatened with homelessness'.

Must the accommodation be of a certain standard?

The accommodation must be 'available' to live in, but must it be of any particular standard? In the past few years there have been a number of important cases that have tried to set down some coherent answer to this question, without much success. In 1986 Parliament amended the relevant section of the 1985 Housing Act in an effort to clarify the position. The law now states that a person will be treated as having 'no accommodation' unless they are in accommodation which it is reasonable to expect them to continue to occupy. But in deciding what is 'reasonable', a council can take into account the general standard of accommodation in their area, i.e. if housing is generally bad in the area, the standard of the accommodation need be no better than the prevailing standard. This amendment therefore does nothing to assist the development of uniform housing standards, which is unfortunate, as it is in the areas of the poorest housing conditions that the highest levels of homelessness are also to be found: 70 per cent of local authority expenditure on bed and breakfast accommodation for homeless families is in London. Case law in this respect is not encouraging, as it is only in the most extreme cases that the courts have accepted arguments of 'unreasonableness' (as in one case where it was deemed unreasonable to describe as 'accommodation' a rat-infested hut 10 ft by 20 ft, with no mains services, inhabited by a couple with three children, including a young baby).

Is a person homeless if they are in temporary accommodation?

The answer to this question will depend on how 'temporary' the accommodation is. A woman given temporary accommodation in a women's refuge is certainly homeless. Similarly, a person given temporary accommodation in a night shelter is homeless. If the legal rights of the occupant are slightly more strong, e.g. they have a temporary licence to be there, they will not be homeless, but they may well be 'threatened with homelessness' if the notice period necessary to remove them is less than 28 days.

What happens if the homeless person has accommodation outside England, Wales or Scotland?

The fact that an applicant may have accommodation in another country is not a relevant consideration in deciding whether they are homeless, although it may be a relevant factor in deciding if they are intentionally homeless, which will enable the local authority to refuse to house them (see p.325). This factor is of particular importance to new immigrants and refugees. Some particularly hard-pressed local authorities have refused to house applicants precisely because they have accommodation in another country that, in the view of the council, they should not have left. In a particular series of cases concerning homeless families in Tower Hamlets, the court was prepared to hold that inadequate accommodation in Bangladesh was *available* to the applicants as it had in fact provided them with occasional homes in the previous 18 months. By giving it up they were consequently intentionally homeless.

What happens when a person claiming to be homeless presents themselves to a council?

Any person who considers themselves homeless can present themselves as such to any council homeless person's unit. They must, however, have sufficient mental capacity to understand the concept of being offered accommodation, which means that adults without mental capacity cannot apply for accommodation in their own right. Similarly, dependant children cannot apply in their own right. The adults on whom both the above categories depend must apply on their collective behalf. Subject to the above paragraph, a council has a legal responsibility towards any person who presents themselves to the council as 'homeless' or 'threatened with homelessness' to make any necessary enquiries to establish whether this is true. The enquiries do not have to be 'CID type', but they must be sufficient to come to a rapid and fair decision. If in addition to claiming homelessness the applicant appears to be in 'priority need' (see below at p.324), the council must provide the applicant(s) with temporary accommodation pending the outcome of their enquiries. In hard-pressed inner-city areas this will normally be 'bed and breakfast' accommodation.

If after initial enquiries the council accepts that the applicant is homeless or threatened with homelessness, what happens next?

The answer to this question will depend upon whether the applicant is 'homeless' or 'threatened with homelessness'.

Homeless

If the applicant is homeless the council officers must then carry out a number of further enquiries to establish the following:

- Does the applicant have a priority need?
- Did the applicant become homeless intentionally?
- Does the applicant have a local connection with another housing authority in England, Wales or Scotland? (They will only make

this third enquiry if the applicant appears to have no local connection with them, and even then they are not obliged to follow this third procedure.)

What is priority need?

The law defines priority need as a person in any one or more of the following categories:

- A pregnant woman, or a person with dependant children either living with them or who ought reasonably to be living with them, e.g. the children are in voluntary care because the parents are unable to accommodate them. Grandchildren, foster-children and adopted children all come in this category, but dependency is normally deemed to end at 16 (19 if the child is in full-time education or training and not otherwise able to support him- or herself).
- Anybody who ought reasonably to be living with the above people, e.g. spouse, cohabitee or dependant children.
- A person who is homeless through flood, fire or other disaster.
- A person who is vulnerable either as a result of old age (near or over normal retirement age) or for some other special reason such as physical or mental disability (including illness). Councils are not normally willing to include what they term self-imposed disabilities, e.g. alcoholism and drug addiction, unless other disabilities are also manifested.

Young people aged 16–18

The Children Act 1989 imposes a further set of legal duties on local authorities in respect of 'children in need' between the ages of 16 and 18. The Act states:

> Every local authority shall provide accommodation for any child in need within their area who has reached the age of 16 and whose welfare the authority considers is likely to be seriously prejudiced if they do not provide him with accommodation.

A graphic account of the extent of young homelessness, called *Young Homelessness*, can be obtained from YHG, 5th Floor, 140A Gloucester Mansions, Cambridge Circus, London WC2H 8HD. For an initial study of the ways in which local authorities are (or are not) responding to this new provision, see *Plans, No Action: the Children Act and Homeless Young People*, which is available from CHAR, 5–15 Cromer Street, London WC1H 8LS (tel: 071 833 2071). An organisation called Children Act Housing Action Group (CAHAG) has been established, working from the same office, with the following aims:

1. To ensure that the sections of the Children Act 1989 which relate to young homeless people, and specifically 16- and 17-year-olds, are interpreted and fully implemented to benefit this group.
2. To enable groups working with young homeless people to have access to remedies at a local level, if clients are not receiving the appropriate services due to local policies relating to the Act.
3. To act as a pool of expertise for groups working with young homeless people wanting to take a grievance procedure forward, and to assess key cases for judicial review [see Chapter 3 at p.81].

Finally, a guide to good practice for social services departments in this particular area is Hilken, A., and Laws, S. (1992), *In on the Act: Homeless Families and the Children Act*, obtainable from London Homelessness Forum, Jadwin House, 205–11 Kentish Town Road, London NW5 2JU.

What is intentional homelessness?

This is the part of the legislation that has caused the most difficulty and controversy. The idea behind this part of the legislation is to disqualify from eligibility for immediate accommodation anybody who has deliberately given up their existing accommodation. Sadly, many councils have exploited this loophole in the legislation as a way of avoiding responsibility to house people who are often in a desperate plight. Case law has tended to come out on the side of councils in this area and a line of restrictive decisions has resulted in many homeless people never getting beyond this hurdle.

In claiming 'intentional homelessness' and thereby avoiding the need to provide permanent accommodation, councils may rely upon either the applicant's deliberate acts or the applicant's failure to do something.

Thus not only is an applicant intentionally homeless if they deliberately give up accommodation they have a right to occupy, they are also intentionally homeless if they fail to do whatever is necessary to keep their existing accommodation, e.g. wilfully refuse to pay rent, fail to keep their family or lodgers under control, or illegally sublet, resulting in their own eviction. The case law in this area is prolific, and legal advice from an expert should always be sought if there is any suggestion by the council of 'intentional homelessness'. The Code of Guidance to the Act is also very important because although it is not legally binding it should normally be followed. The Code emphasises the fact that the disqualifying conduct of the applicant, whether by an act or a failure to act, must be shown to have been in bad faith and not just the result of a genuine lack of understanding. Thus non-payment of rent in ignorance of the availability of housing benefit (see Chapter 11) or the acceptance of temporary accommodation in the belief it was permanent would be examples of behaviour that may lead to homelessness, but would be unlikely to give rise to a successful allegation of 'intentional homelessness'.

Some further points need to be made regarding 'intentional homelessness':

- The deliberate giving up of accommodation that remains available to occupy in another country has been construed as 'intentional homelessness'.
- The giving up of accommodation that cannot accommodate those with whom the applicant reasonably expects to share the accommodation, e.g. his or her children, does not amount to 'intentional homelessness' even though the accommodation may remain available to the applicant if living alone.
- Councils may look beyond the immediate cause of the applicant's homelessness for an earlier act that amounted to 'intentional homelessness' and thereby avoid any liability to provide accommodation. This is called the 'chain of causation', which is best illustrated by an example. A and B voluntarily move out of their accommodation to live in a squat when A becomes pregnant. They did not have to move, although the accommodation they had been living in was squalid and inappropriate for a young baby. After several more squats they are finally evicted and they present themselves at the local council as homeless. Although they are clearly homeless and in priority need, the council will be able to argue that

they are 'intentionally homeless' because they voluntarily left the first accommodation. Once a person is thus 'tainted' with 'intentional homelessness' it is very difficult for them to break the causation chain. It can only be done if they manage to secure for themselves some 'settled accommodation' in which they spend a period of time. This will have the effect of breaking the chain so that if they have the misfortune to become homeless at some date in the future the council will no longer be able to refer back to the earlier act of 'intentional homelessness'. 'Settled accommodation' means accommodation in which the occupant has a 'reasonable degree of security' and will not therefore be established by a period in temporary hostel accommodation, or a holiday let.

- Where homeless applicants were previously living with relatives but were asked to leave by those relatives it is sufficient for the relatives to have given the applicant written notice to leave within a reasonable period, and for that period to have passed for the applicant to be deemed homeless. Despite statements by some councils to the contrary, it is not necessary for the relatives to take court proceedings to avoid the charge of intentionality. A number of decisions by Ombudsmen in recent years have put this matter beyond any doubt. Once the relatives have ended their guest's licence to remain, the guest is homeless.

What happens if the applicant has a local connection with another housing authority?

In some circumstances the local authority will also enquire whether the applicant has a 'local connection' with another housing authority in England, Wales or Scotland, in order to pass the responsibility to house the applicant to that authority. But this can only be done in very limited circumstances. The local authority can only invoke this line of enquiry if neither the applicant, nor anybody who might reasonably be expected to live with them, has any 'local connection' with them.

By 'local connection' is meant a connection with the local authority because of one or more factors: employment in the area; past or present voluntary residence in the area; family associations in the area; or for any other special reason. Thus if a person gets off a train in London and presents themselves as 'homeless' and they have no 'local connection' with that authority it is legitimate for that local authority to contact an area with which they do have a 'local connection', providing one exists. There is a Local Authority Agreement which states that a period of residence of less than 6 months in the 12 months immediately prior to the application will not normally be sufficient to establish a 'local connection'. This Agreement is *policy*, however, and not law, and if an applicant has established a 'local connection' after a shorter period the policy need not be applied, particularly where a local connection is argued also on the basis of, say, family associations.

If a local authority does use the 'local connection' provision and that other authority accepts responsibility for the applicant the first authority must provide them with temporary accommodation whilst their transport back to the other authority is being negotiated. It follows from the above that if the applicant has no 'local connection' with any other authority in England, Wales or Scotland, e.g. they are a political refugee from another country, or they have just got off a boat from Belfast or Dublin, the provisions are of no relevance. (But note the alternative possibility of an argument of 'intentional homelessness', see p.322.)

The 'local connection' provisions will also not apply if the applicant runs the risk of domestic violence should they be returned to the housing authority with which they have a 'local connection' and which area they have presumably left because of this risk.

What are the council's duties once it has carried out all the above enquiries?

The enquries may take anything from a few days to many weeks, depending on their complexity. The applicant should co-operate with the council as far as they are able (giving false information is a criminal offence – see p.331) but should also seek the help and support of an experienced adviser, particularly before signing any forms or statements. The help of a social worker could be very significant at this stage. The applicant should be given copies of any forms that they sign (On 'Access to Personal Files' see Chapter 3 at p.68.) Once the decision has been taken it must be communicated to the applicant in writing. It has already been stated that if the applicant is homeless and in priority need the council must provide them with temporary accommodation pending the completion of any other enquiries. The following is a list of the council's duties to the homeless applicant once the enquiries are completed:

1. If it finds that the applicant is homeless but without priority need the council's duty is limited to providing 'such advice and assistance as the council considers appropriate'. This may in practice mean no more than a list of accommodation agencies, hostels and bed and breakfast hotels. For assistance in the London area, consult the *London Hostels Directory* (Resource Information Service). The applicant should always check whether the council has any special schemes offering accommodation to people like themselves. There are also a number of charities and pressure groups that try to provide advice and assistance to homeless people who fall in this category, including: Campaign for the Homeless and Rootless (CHAR), 5–15 Cromer St, London WC1H 8LS (tel: 071 833 2071); IYSH, 1–9 Woburn Place, London WC1H 0LY (tel: 071 837 7151); YHG, 5th Floor, 140A Gloucester Mansions, Cambridge Circus, London WC2H 8HD (tel: 071 836 0494).
2. If it finds that the applicant is homeless, has priority need but is intentionally homeless, its duty is to provide the applicant with temporary accommodation for a reasonable period to enable them to find accommodation of their own. There is no fixed period, and it will depend upon the facts of the individual case, but the applicant cannot expect to be allowed more than a few weeks as a maximum.
3. If it finds that the applicant is homeless, has priority need and is not intentionally homeless, it has a duty to ensure that the applicant, together with those reasonably expected to live with the applicant, are provided with 'suitable accommodation'. This can be provided by themselves or somebody else, for example housing associations, which in 1991–2 gave 17 per cent of their total allocations to statutorily homeless people. The deliberate insertion of the word 'suitable' is an explicit recognition by Parliament that the particular needs of the applicant, and if necessary their family unit, must be taken into account. Thus, for example, the courts have held that such matters as the particular psychological need of an applicant to be housed near a parent, and the likelihood of racial harassment occuring to a black applicant in a particular area, are the types of factor that a local authority *cannot* ignore in deciding whether particular accommodation is suitable.

Can the applicant appeal against the council's decision?

There are three possible ways in which an applicant might appeal against an unfavourable decision:

1. Use any appeals procedure that exists within the council itself (see Chapter 3 at p.71). Alternatively, appeal to a senior officer, to a councillor or to the relevant subcommittee (see Chapter 3 at pp. 72–3).
2. Complain to the Local Ombudsman (see Chapter 3 at p.75). This will only be possible if the applicant is alleging bias or maladministration. There have been a number of complaints upheld by Ombudsmen in connection with the administration of homelessness applications. For example, when a Homeless Persons Unit failed to make adequate enquiries in the case of applicants being made homeless by their own housing department; or when a council provided inadequate temporary accommodation pending the outcome of their enquiries; or when councils insist that relatives evict their families through the courts before the council will accept them as homeless. (NB. The government is proposing to make the latter procedure compulsory.)
3. Apply for judicial review of the decision. This is a complicated and lengthy procedure that involves making an application to the High Court, and will inevitably require the use of lawyers. Legal aid would be available for such an application (see Chapter 1). For further details on judicial review, see Chapter 3 at p.81. Successes for applicants under this procedure are not very common. It is thus of the greatest importance for the applicant to be sure that their original application argues their case as strongly as possible. It is at this early stage that social work intervention could prove invaluable.

Threatened with homelessness

If the applicant is not homeless, but is threatened with homelessness, the duties of the council officers are more straightforward. First, they must establish whether the applicant and/or their dependants are in priority need. If they are not in priority need the council's duty rests at 1 above. If, on the other hand, the applicant and/or their dependants are in priority need the council has a duty to take steps to try to prevent the threatened homelessness coming about. This could mean, for example, advising the person of their rights to obtain housing benefit and other welfare rights if the homelessness is threatened as a result of rent arrears. Or it could mean taking action against a landlord who is threatening illegal action to evict a tenant.

Are there any criminal offences associated with homelessness?

It is a criminal offence for an applicant to lie to the council about their circumstances in an attempt to be classified as eligible for housing as homeless. It is also a criminal offence for an applicant to withhold from the council any changes in their circumstances that occur before the application is determined that might affect the council's decision. It is a criminal offence for anybody else to lie to the council to try to help the applicant obtain housing. Lying includes making statements without any idea whether or not they are true, e.g. saying that the applicant has always lived in the area, or that they have children, without knowing one way or another. All these offences are triable in the magistrates' court and are punishable with a fine.

Will the council look after the applicant's property while their application is being examined?

The council will have a duty to take reasonable steps to protect the property of an applicant who is homeless or threatened with homelessness while they are processing the application, if they believe it is in danger of being lost or damaged, that no other suitable arrangements to protect it are being made and the applicant is unable to look after it.

Rights to council accommodation if not homeless

Despite the fact that there are over 1.5m people on the waiting lists for council housing in the United Kingdom, government policy in the past decade has concentrated on the deliberate attrition of the council housing stock as part of its wider philosophy of privatisation. This attrition has been stimulated in two ways. First, the introduction in 1980 of the right of a council tenant to buy their home from the council, which has resulted in the sale of over 1 million council homes into the private sector since 1981. Second, in the steep decline in the number of new council houses built each year, meaning that the council housing stock has fallen to its lowest level since the war. Further decline took place in the wake of the

Housing Act 1988 with the extension of the Right to Buy provisions, the facilitation by the government of the voluntary disposal by local authority of their housing stock to the private sector, the creation of Housing Action Trusts, and the introduction of the right of council tenants to vote for a private landlord takeover.

Despite the developments outlined in the previous paragraph, the allocation of council houses to new tenants still continues, albeit on a far more limited scale than in the past. This section will examine the legal framework within which the allocation of council homes operates.

Is a council obliged to inform the public of its council house allocations policy?

Yes. Every council housing department is obliged by law to publish a summary of the rules and procedures they adopt in allocating their housing stock to tenants. This summary will normally be in the form of a short pamphlet available in housing offices and the Town Hall. It must be free of charge. It will describe the system that the council uses in establishing its priorities, but it does not have to state how long an applicant will normally have to wait before being offered a home. A more detailed description of the rules and procedures must also be made available to anybody on request, normally for a small charge. In addition, anybody who has actually applied for council accommodation (e.g. by putting their name on the waiting list) is entitled to a free copy of their application form, in order to check that the details are correct.

One of the most important ways of improving cross-communication between local authorities, tenants and the general public is to develop forums for exchanges of views and some element of collective management. For more ideas and information on this approach, see Bell, T. (1991), *Joining Forces: Estate Management Boards. A Practical Guide for Councils and Residents* (PEP Publications) and Barran, S. (1992), *Creating Co-operative Working Relations between Housing Staff and Tenants* (PEP Publications). Consult also TPAS (see p.370 for details).

Is a council obliged by law to adopt any particular type of allocations policy?

There are very few legal constraints on the type of allocations policy that a council must adopt. The law makes the general statement that a council must give 'reasonable preference to applicants who are occupying insanitary or overcrowded houses, have large families or are living in unsatisfactory housing conditions', but it is very difficult in practice to make much use of this statement to further the claim of a particular individual. In practice, a council is likely to adopt one of three different types of scheme: a *date order scheme* whereby tenancies are allocated to the person who is top of the waiting list on a 'first come first served' basis; a *merit scheme* whereby tenancies are allocated according to the views of councillors as to the merit of each particular case; or a *points scheme* whereby points are allocated to each applicant on a complicated scale of need and tenancies are granted to those who achieve the highest number of points. The third scheme has become the most widely used in recent years, but the factors for which points are awarded vary considerably between councils. They may include such factors as length of time on the waiting list, existing housing conditions, age, number of children, overcrowding in current accommodation and health factors. Any council adopting a points scheme should explain its rules and procedures for allocation in the information pamphlet that it makes available to the public.

There are two circumstances where a council must provide a person with accommodation regardless of their own procedures:

1. If they have a legal obligation under the homelessness legislation (see p.320).
2. If they have displaced that person from their existing home by a compulsory purchase order, a closing order, a clearance or demolition order, or the service of an improvement notice. For full details about this provison, see Arden, A. and Hunter, C. 1992, *Manual of Housing Law* (5th edn; Sweet and Maxwell).

What kind of council allocation policy might be unlawful?

There are certain things which a council cannot do lawfully in connection with its housing allocations policy:

1. A council cannot impose a blanket condition that prevents it from considering the merits of a particular case. For example, a council cannot impose a policy condition that it will never offer accommodation to a person who still has the joint tenancy of another home, but who needs new accommodation because of domestic breakdown, or

it cannot impose blanket conditions on the type of property allocated to homeless families, e.g. that it will always be of the minimum size legally permissible.

2. A council cannot discriminate either directly or indirectly against an applicant on the grounds of their colour, race, nationality, sex or ethnic origins. This means that any policy to encourage a reasonable black/white balance on council estates is unlawful, whatever the merits of its intentions. The Commission for Racial Equality (CRE) has, however, approved the practice adopted by many housing authorities of recording the ethnic origin of all applicants for their housing as long as this is used constructively to improve the circumstances of ethnic communities and not in order to bring in discriminatory policies (for further information, see Chapter 3 at p.80).

Examples of indirect discrimination (see Chapter 3 at p.80 and Chapter 7 at p.226) might be a requirement that housing points can only be given for children actually living with their parents, as this might discriminate against an immigrant applicant whose family is waiting to join him; or even a residence requirement, as many members of new immigrant communities might be disadvantaged by such a requirement.

What can an applicant do to complain about the way in which their application has been handled?

The procedures for complaining about a council service, or lack of it, are fully explained in Chapter 3 at p.71. An applicant who alleges maladministration in the handling of their application can lodge a complaint with the Local Ombudsman (see p.75). If there is a serious possibility of discrimination on the grounds of race or sex, the applicant should contact the Commission for Racial Equality (CRE) or the Equal Opportunities Commission (EOC) for further advice or assistance.

BUYING ACCOMMODATION FROM THE COUNCIL

Since 1980 it has been possible for secure tenants, i.e. council tenants with security of tenure (see p.336) and certain types of housing association tenants (see p.343), to buy their home from the council on very favourable terms. Not surprisingly, this right has proved very popular and over a million tenants have taken advantage of it. The law governing the right to buy is complex, as is the general law governing the purchase of property. A tenant is strongly advised to consult a solicitor or licensed conveyancer before embarking upon the purchase of their council home. A summary of the general principles governing council house sales is set out below.

- The tenants must have been *secure tenants* (see p.336) for at least two years before they can claim the right to buy. The two years need not have been continuous, nor in the same property. The tenancy must be secure at the moment of completion; thus, if the tenant dies between exchange of contracts and completion, the deceased tenant's personal representative cannot enforce the sale.
- The property can be a house or a flat but it must not be in one of the list of exempted categories (the council will soon inform the applicant if their property is exempted!). The list includes sheltered accommodation for frail or older people, but accommodation which has been adapted for a physically disabled occupant, and is not in a group of specially adapted dwellings with special facilities, retains the right to buy. The distinction is sometimes difficult to draw. Thus, in a case where an elderly tenant wanted to buy his council flat in a warden-assisted block in which individual flats were connected to a resident warden call system, he was allowed to do so on the grounds that *his* flat was not connected to the warden call service. Conversely, a tenant who lived in a council block where her flat *was* connected to a warden call system was not allowed to buy her flat, despite the fact that she was neither frail nor an older person, and she was totally unaware of the warden call system!
- The purchase may be of a freehold or a long leasehold, depending upon the nature of the property.
- The tenant will be entitled to a discount off the market value of the property, depending on the length of time they have been a 'public tenant'. It will vary from 32 per cent for two years to a maximum of 60 per cent for 30 years or more if the property is a house, and from 44 per cent to 70 per cent if the property is a flat. The maximum discount is now £50,000.
- If, having purchased the property, the tenant (now owner) resells it within three years they will have to pay back the discount less 20 per cent for each full year of occupation since the purchase. There

are limited exceptions to this rule, e.g. where the resale is a 'family transaction' such as a transfer on death or divorce.

- A secure tenant who has the right to buy also has the right to obtain a mortgage to finance the purchase either from the local authority or, where the landlord is a housing association (see below at p.342), from the Housing Corporation.

Those interested in reading a full account of the background, operation and effects of the introduction of the right to buy should consult Forrest, R., and Murie, A. (1988), *Selling the Welfare State: the Privatisation of Housing* (Routledge).

RETAINING COUNCIL ACCOMMODATION AS A TENANT

How secure from eviction is a council tenant?

Since 1980 most council tenants have had security of tenure, which means that they cannot be evicted unless the council takes them to court and proves legal grounds for the eviction. The legal term used to describe such tenants is a logical one: they are described as *secure tenants*. The term 'secure tenant' extends wider than tenants, however, to include, among others, council licensees (for the distinction between a *licensee* and a *tenant*, see p.346). The only exception is a licensee who entered the property initially as a trespasser (or squatter) to whom the council has subsequently granted a licence to remain in occupation. A person in this situation cannot become a secure tenant. Some council tenancies are specifically excluded from being secure tenancies. The most important of these exceptions are service tenancies (i.e. where the tenant is required to occupy the premises for the better performance of their duties, as in the case of a resident caretaker), and various forms of temporary accommodation, e.g. temporary accommodation given to homeless people unless they have occupied it for more than a year from the date the council informed them they would only be given temporary accommodation; temporary accommodation given to a person for up to a year when they have been offered employment in the area of the council and are looking for accommodation in the area; and temporary accommodation given to a person by a council while repairs are being carried out on their main home. If there is any doubt as to the status of the tenancy a letter to the council requesting clarification should be sufficient to resolve the problem. For a full list of the exemptions see Arden, A. and Hunter, C. 1992, *Manual of Housing Law* (5th edn; Sweet and Maxwell).

Must the council have grounds to evict a secure tenant?

A council cannot evict a secure tenant unless it can prove one of the *grounds for eviction* set out in Group A, B or C below.

Group A (Grounds 1–8)

In addition to proving one or more of these grounds the council must also satisfy the judge that it is reasonable to evict the tenant, i.e. the judge retains a discretion not to evict the tenant, despite the existence of grounds for possession, because he or she believes that it would be an unjust decision to make.

Group B (Grounds 9–10)

In addition to proving one or more of these grounds the council must satisfy the judge that suitable alternative accommodation will be provided to the secure tenant if they are evicted. Suitable alternative accommodation is accommodation which is reasonably suited to the needs of the tenant, bearing in mind:

- their income;
- their existing accommodation;
- the size of their family;
- the proximity of the accommodation to their work and to any schools or relatives whom they might need to visit regularly.

If the secure tenant does not feel that the accommodation being offered is suitable, they should defend the court action on this basis.

Group C (Grounds 12, 13, 15 and 16)

In addition to proving one or more of these grounds the council must also prove both that it is reasonable to evict the secure tenant (see A) and that suitable alternative accommodation is available (see B).

The Grounds (the numbers relate to those used in the Housing Act 1985)

Grounds 1–4: These are identical to the Discretionary Grounds for Possession against Protected Private Tenants (see p.352). They relate broadly to circumstances in which the secure tenant has either breached a term in the tenancy agreement, e.g. by falling into arrears of rent, or been in some other way at fault, e.g. by causing a nuisance to neighbours. In the recent past some progressive councils have been using these grounds in an attempt to evict tenants who engage in systematic racial harassment of other tenants on their estate, with some success. For a detailed guide to the ways in which councils can take action against tenants who indulge in racial harassment, see Forbes, D. (1993), *Action on Racial Harassment* (2nd edn, Legal Action Group).
Ground 5: The tenant obtained the tenancy by making a false statement.
Ground 6: The tenant obtained the tenancy by an exchange during which money, or money's worth (goods), changed hands.
Ground 7: The tenancy was tied to a particular job and the tenant has been guilty of unacceptable behaviour, making it impossible for them to remain on the premises.
Ground 8: The tenant is the secure tenant of 'other premises' but was granted temporary accommodation in these premises while repair work was carried out on the 'other premises'. The work is finished but the tenant refuses to move back.
Ground 9: The premises are illegally overcrowded. This is a legal phrase that is very carefully defined either by reference to the ratio between the total number of occupants and the total room size, or by the fact that two or more people of the opposite sex, aged 10 or over, who are not living together as man and wife, are obliged to sleep in the same room. The local Environmental Health Officer will confirm whether or not premises are illegally overcrowded.
Ground 10: The council needs to move the tenant in order to demolish, or carry out major structural alterations on, the property. The council must, however, prove both that it intends to carry out works and that the works could not be reasonably carried out without first obtaining possession, i.e. it would not be possible to move the tenant to temporary accommodation pending completion of the works. This ground will also operate if the premises form part of an 'approved development area' (the council will provide details of what this is), and the council,

having obtained possession, intend to sell the property with vacant possession.

Ground 11: Only applies to tenants of a charity.

Ground 12: This relates to certain types of tenancy tied to employment when the employee's replacement needs to move into the premises.

Ground 13: The premises are specially adapted for a physically disabled person and there is no longer such a person residing on the premises.

Ground 14: Only relevant to housing associations and trusts (see below at p.342).

Ground 15: The premises form part of a group of dwellings for people with special needs (e.g. the mentally ill or elderly) with special facilities nearby (e.g. resident wardens or social services day centres) and there is no longer anybody living on the premises with special needs.

Ground 16: The tenant became a secure tenant of the premises by succeeding to the tenancy on the death of a family member, and the council considers that the property is too large for them.

If the council have grounds to evict a secure tenant what procedure must it follow?

If a council wishes to evict a secure tenant it has to follow a set procedure. First, in the case of the majority of secure tenancies it has to serve on the secure tenant a document called a Notice of Intention to Seek Possession (NISP). This document will set out the grounds on which the council is intending to seek possession against the tenant (e.g. rent arrears, nuisance, demolition of property and so forth). It will also state the earliest date on which it might commence court proceedings against the tenant to put its intentions into effect. If a secure tenant receives an NISP it is always advisable for them to seek immediate specialist advice from a law centre, a solicitor or a housing aid centre.

At the second stage of the procedure, once the date specified in the NISP has passed, the council can apply to the local county court for a possession summons to be issued against the secure tenant. This summons will inform the secure tenant of the date set for the hearing of the summons and will provide more detail of the grounds upon which possession is being sought. If they have not done so already, at this stage, the secure tenant should certainly consult a housing specialist law centre, housing aid centre or solicitor. A solicitor may decide to apply for legal aid on behalf of the secure tenant to represent them at the hearing (see Chapter 1).

The third stage of the procedure takes place at the County Court on the day of the hearing. The council will have to prove its case to the court. To do this it must provide evidence of one or more of the legal grounds described above.

What will happen to the secure tenant if the council wins the case?

If the council proves its case to the satisfaction of the judge an order for possession will be made. Unless the grounds fall in Group B above, however, the court will have a wide discretion as to what sort of order to make and it is important for the tenant to try to persuade the judge to make the most lenient order possible. If, for example, the grounds for possession are rent arrears, the court may suspend execution of the order indefinitely as long as the tenant pays back the arrears at a regular agreed rate. Alternatively, if the tenant has breached some other term of the agreement, the court may accept an undertaking by the tenant to make good any damage, and will suspend the order accordingly. If the court makes an absolute order for possession, because they consider the grounds to be sufficiently serious, the judge can still order that it should not be executed until a date fixed some weeks ahead. The tenant will, however, remain liable for rent throughout that period. Only a court bailiff (or sheriff if the hearing was in the High Court) has the power to carry out the eviction. It is a criminal offence to resist the eviction by force.

Will the council rehouse the tenant after the eviction?

It is extremely unlikely that a council will offer to rehouse a tenant whom they have evicted. However, if the tenant or any other people evicted from the property qualify as 'homeless people to whom the council has a legal obligation' (see p.320) they will be given further accommodation, although it is likely to be inferior to the accommodation from which they have been evicted. It should be noted that it is open to councils to treat as intentionally homeless tenants who are evicted for rent arrears that they could and should have paid, or for unacceptably anti-social behaviour.

What is a Housing Action Trust (HAT)?

In 1988, as part of a major overhaul of housing provision in England and Wales, the government introduced Housing Action Trusts (HATs) which were intended to take over the running of large, carefully selected estates of a particularly dilapidated and run-down nature, and run them for a fixed period, injecting new life and capital into the area. Before a HAT can come into existence there must be a ballot of all the affected tenants, and the HAT cannot be set up if a majority of those tenants who vote are opposed to the scheme. In all six areas where HATs were initially proposed, the tenants voted against the idea. The first HATs to come into existence were in Waltham Forest, East London and in Hull. Tenants of a HAT remain secure tenants (see above at p.336). For further information, see the DOE booklet *Housing Action Trusts* (1988) from HPS Division, DOE Room N11/20, 2 Marsham St, London SW1P 3EB, and two articles in the Shelter Journal *Roof* by Dwelly, T. (1991), vol. 16(2), 22–4, and Owens, R. (1992), 17(1), 17–19.

For an account of alternative approaches to the problems of difficult-to-let estates through the use of local management techniques, see Power, A. (1991), *Running to Stand Still* (PEP Publications).

Can local authorities sell off their entire housing stock?

Since 1985, local authorities can, with the consent of the Secretary of State, sell off their entire housing stock, either to the Housing Corporation, to a housing association or, as in the case of Rochester DC in Kent, to a private sector landlord. There is also a new provision, loosely described as Tenants' Choice, giving secure tenants the opportunity, with or without the support of their council, to opt out of the council sector and pick a new landlord, subject to a ballot. These procedures are beyond the scope of this book, and are set out in detail in *Tenants' Choice: Criteria for Landlord Approval and Guidance Notes for Applicants* (1989) which is available from the Housing Corporation (see p.342). For a detailed analysis of the procedures, see Rodgers, C. (1989), *Housing Act 1988: The New Law* (Butterworths).

RIGHTS TO HOUSING ASSOCIATION ACCOMMODATION AND CO-OPERATIVE HOUSING

Housing associations are organisations that provide subsidised housing for rent in very similar ways to councils. They receive grants from both central and local government to purchase, administer and maintain their properties. Although they employ full-time officials, each one is under the general control of its elected management committee which will often include tenant representatives. Housing associations are either registered with the Housing Corporation, or unregistered. A simple telephone call to the Housing Corporation (tel: 071 387 9466) will ascertain whether or not a particular association is registered. If the housing association is not registered, the position of the tenant is exactly the same as if they were tenants of a private landlord (see 'Licences in the private sector' below).

How do housing associations allocate their houses?

Every housing association has to have an allocations policy, the details of which it must provide to anybody who asks to see it. The policy will vary widely according to the particular area and purposes of the association. Many associations have been set up to cater for a specific target group, e.g. the elderly, the disabled or the single homeless, in which case these people will form the basis of their allocations policy. Details of a particular policy can be obtained from the registered address of each association, details of which may be obtained from the Housing Corporation, 149 Tottenham Court Road, London W1P 0BN (tel: 071 387 9466).

What security of tenure do tenants of registered housing associations have?

Housing association law is complex. The key text which contains all you need to know about HAs is Alder, J., and Handy, C. (1991), *Housing Association Law* (2nd edn, Sweet and Maxwell). It costs £75, but is worth the money. Another useful source of information of how housing associations operate is the National Federation of Housing Associations' *Committee Members' Handbook* which can be obtained from 175 Gray's Inn Road, London WC1X 8UP (tel: 071 278 6571). The most comprehensive source of data on all aspects of housing association activity, size, distribution and so forth is probably the Housing Corporations' own publication, *Housing Associations in 1992*.

In summary, housing associations fall into the following categories for the purposes of security of tenure:

- Tenancies granted before 15 January 1989 by the Housing Corporation, housing trusts and most registered housing associations are secure tenancies under the Housing Act 1985 (i.e. under the same regime as council tenancies as regards security of tenures, see p.336). Any tenancies granted by housing associations in this period which were not secure tenancies are likely to be protected tenancies under the Rent Act 1977.
- Tenancies granted on or after 15 January 1989 by housing associations (other than fully mutual housing associations), housing trusts, and the Housing Corporation are either *assured tenancies* (see p.357) or *assured shorthold tenancies* (see p.360).

Certain 'approved' housing associations were also able to grant 'assured tenancies' between 1980 and 1988, under the Housing Act 1980. All such tenancies are now assured tenancies under the Housing Act 1988.

Does a housing association tenant have the same right to buy their property as a council tenant?

Although the right to buy (see p.334) is granted by legislation to secure tenants (which definition, as we have seen, includes some housing association tenants) whose tenancy began prior to 15 January 1989, it should be noted that the major exemptions from this right are secure tenants of a housing association which is a charity, or a co-operative housing association. For further detail on this complex area, consult Alder and Handy (see p.342) or the Housing Corporation. Note also that a number of housing associations operate a range of alternative schemes to assist tenants in the purchase of their own or another flat, details of which can be obtained from the relevant management officer within the association.

Housing co-operatives

The idea of the housing co-operative (or co-op), in which a group of people share the expense and organisation of obtaining and running a property or group of properties, is fast gaining in popularity, particularly among younger people living in the big cities. The subject is complex, with a wide range of possibilities. Those interested in setting up a co-op should write to the Housing Corporation, 149 Tottenham Court Rd, London W1P 0BN (tel: 071 387 9466), which produces a series of helpful booklets explaining exactly what is involved. Those interested in buying co-operatively (as compared to renting) should read Treanor, D. (1988), *Buying Your Home with Other People* (Shelter Publications). A very useful text, published in 1992, which sets out the history, achievements and prospects of the housing co-op movement in Britain, together with a detailed bibliography for further reading, is by Clapham, D., and Kintrea, K., *Housing Co-operatives in Britain* (Longman). For further information generally about housing co-ops, contact the National Federation of Housing Co-operatives, 175 Gray's Inn Road, London WC1X 8UP (tel: 071 278 6571).

SEEKING AND KEEPING PRIVATELY RENTED PRIVATE ACCOMMODATION*

Although private renting has seen a steep decline since the beginning of the century (from 90 per cent of the housing stock to around 10 per cent in 1993), it remains an important source of accommodation for certain types of people such as young house sharers, recently divorced or separated couples, and new immigrants to Britain. It is part of the policy of the current government to seek to restimulate the private rented sector by deregulating private rents and easing the restrictions on eviction of certain private tenants. To this end it has introduced a range of new measures designed to encourage an increase in private renting which affect all tenancies in the private sector which commenced on or after 15 January 1989.

There are a large number of legal problems associated with private renting that seem out of all proportion to the relative size of the private rented sector in the housing market. This section will concentrate on the most common legal problems facing tenants of rented property in the search for a property to rent and in the struggle to remain in that property if the landlord wants to evict the tenant.

*For more detailed information on private renting, consult Campbell, R., and Gallagher, J. (1993), *Security of Tenure in the Private Rented Sector* (looseleaf, SHAC Publications).

How much can an accommodation agency legally charge a prospective tenant for its services?

There is a law which controls the way in which accommodation agencies may ask for commission for their services from prospective tenants. It is part of the criminal law, which means that in theory any accommodation agency that breaks this law can be reported to the police and be prosecuted. In practice this is very rare, although it is possible for the Director of Fair Trading to prohibit estate agents convicted of this offence from further carrying out such work, and the threat of such a loss of livelihood can be effective in resolving any disputes of this nature. Prosecution aside, it is clearly a matter of some importance to people who use accommodation agencies in their search for privately rented accommodation to know how much the agency can legally charge them for their services. Any illegal charge will not have to be paid by the client.

In summary the position regarding accommodation agency charges is as follows:

- The agency cannot charge the client for registering the client's name and requirements on their lists, nor can they charge for providing the client with particulars of a place that is available for renting.
- The agency can charge for other services for which they have genuinely incurred cost, providing this was made clear to the client at the outset. This means, for example, that they can charge for the work involved in matching available accommodation to the client's needs, letters, telephone calls, introductions and so forth, as long as the charge does not include any of the work for which they are prohibited from charging.

LICENCES IN THE PRIVATE SECTOR

For many years it was common practice for a landlord letting property to offer prospective tenants an agreement called a licence rather than a tenancy, as a licensee has considerably fewer legal rights than a tenant. In recent years, however, it has become considerably harder for landlords to offer a licence as a legitimate alternative to a tenancy, following two important decisions of the House of Lords (*Street* v. *Mountford* 1985 and

Antoniades v. *Villiers* 1988). In both these cases the House of Lords decided that what a landlord calls the letting should be treated as of little importance. What matters is what it actually is, and they said that when deciding what the letting actually is 'a court should be astute to detect and frustrate sham devices whose only object is to disguise the grant of a tenancy'. In other words, since these decisions we can safely say that if a letting amounts to the grant of a tenancy it matters little that the parties to the agreement have signed a document calling it a licence. This will apply regardless of whether there is a single tenant or two or more people sharing. These two cases should not, however, be taken to mean that it is no longer possible for a genuine licence to be created. There still exist situations in which a licence rather than a tenancy is created: the following are some examples:

- If two or more people are sharing accommodation in which they each occupy some part of the premises that is their own, e.g. bedroom, but share the use of other rooms, e.g. living room, kitchen and bathroom, and the landlord has made it clear that *a*) they are each only liable for a proportion of the rent and *b*) should one occupant leave, the landlord reserves the right to choose their replacement, then the occupants are licensees. The reason for this is that the occupants cannot be said to exercise *exclusive possession* of the premises against the landlord (see p.348).
- If the arrangement is one of extreme informality, as for example where a member of one's family or a close friend is given accommodation to help them through a difficult period, it is likely that a court will also describe such accommodation as a licence.
- Most hostel and hotel arrangements.

What are the consequences of having a licence and not a tenancy?

A licence is a contract granting the licensee permission to live in the premises for the period set out in the licence, in the same way that a theatre ticket is a contract allowing the holder to remain in the theatre for the duration of the play in exchange for money. But whereas the theatre owner normally reserves the right to end the contract prematurely, as for example in the case where the ticketholder is drunk or misbehaves, the legal position of a residential licensee is a little stronger.

Most residential licensees (but see the note below) cannot be legally evicted unless the landlord obtains a court order in the local county court. Any eviction that does not follow this procedure is almost certainly unlawful and could lead to the prosecution of the landlord under s.6 Criminal Law Act 1977 and an action for compensation by the tenant for illegal eviction.

NB The position of some licensees ('excluded licensees') whose licence was created on or after 15 January 1989 is not as secure, as the need for a landlord to obtain a court order does not apply in some circumstances (including where the licence was granted to a person previously squatting on the premises; where the landlord is resident, it is his only or principal home, and s/he is sharing with the licensee more than just the common parts or storage areas; and where the premises are a hostel). If in any doubt as to whether a licence is excluded from protection in this way, consult a solicitor. It should further be noted that if a landlord threatens violence in the absence of a court order it is likely that they are committing a criminal offence under s.6 of the Criminal Law Act 1977. The police should be called.

How can a licensee be evicted?

Licences created before 15 January 1989

A very simple procedure exists whereby a landlord can seek a court order against a licensee. All the landlord needs to do is give the licensee four weeks' notice to vacate the premises by a certain date. The notice can be written or verbal. If it is given in the form of a notice to quit it must be in the form of a proper legal document (see p.354). The landlord need not give any reason for the notice. If the licensee has not vacated by the given date, the landlord can immediately apply to the court for a possession order, and also ask that the licensee pay the costs of the application. In practice, the pressures of time on county courts mean that it may be some weeks, or even months, before the matter comes before the court, although procedures are being streamlined for this type of application. At court the licensee will have no defence to the action unless it can be established either that the notice period was inadequate or that the letting was not a licence at all but a tenancy (see p.348). If the licensee loses the case, they can be ordered to pay the costs of the hearing including a contribution to the landlord's legal costs. A possession order will be issued which will enable the court bailiff to evict the licensee within a fairly short period.

Licences created on or after 15 January 1989

The only circumstance in which the same procedure as above need not be followed is if the licensee forms an 'excluded letting' (see p.365).

TENANCIES

What is a tenancy?

There are three features of a tenancy, namely exclusive possession, a fixed or periodic term, and rent. Let us examine each of these features in turn.

Exclusive possession

This simply means that the tenant is granted the right to exclude all others from the premises including the landlord. If the tenant is a sole tenant this right is personal to the tenant. If the tenant holds the tenancy jointly with others it is their collective right. Whether or not exclusive possession had been granted is often hard to establish. The sort of question to ask is: Do the parties act as if (for the duration of the letting) the tenant owns the property with all the formal responsibilities that that entails, or is the arrangment somehow more informal, with the landlord coming and going at will? The former tends to suggest exclusive possession, the latter not. The fact that a landlord may visit the premises by arrangement to collect rent, carry out repairs and so forth does not mean there is no exclusive possession vested in the tenant. But if the letting genuinely allows the landlord to shift the tenant(s) from room to room, as in the hostel arrangement, exclusive possession cannot be said to exist.

Fixed or periodic term

This refers to the necessity that the letting is for an identified period of time such as a week, a month or a year. The letting may also allow for automatic renewal of that period by use of such words as 'weekly' or 'monthly', in which case the tenancy is called a 'periodic tenancy'.

Rent

This is defined as money, or quantifiable goods or services, and will extend to rent that is deducted from wages if the letting comes with a particular job.

In what circumstances can a landlord evict a tenant?

The answer to this question is complicated by the fact that there are a number of different categories of tenancy with differing consequences. A tenant's rights will differ according to the category of the tenancy. In the event of any threatened eviction proceedings it is therefore always sensible to seek expert advice from an adviser trained in housing law, in, for example, a law centre, a housing aid centre, or a solicitor's office. A summary of the position is set out below.

Position for tenancies created before 15 January 1989

If the letting is a tenancy and not a licence (see above), the next question to decide is whether the tenancy is protected by the Rent Act 1977 (as amended), because such a tenant has far more extensive rights than one who is not protected.

Tenancies fully protected by the Rent Act (protected/statutory tenancies)

A tenancy is fully protected by the Rent Act if it is a tenancy of residential premises (which may be no more than a room in a house) and it does *not* fall into the stated list of exceptions, of which the following are the most common:

- The landlord lives in the same building as the tenant and has lived there continuously since the tenancy began. This exception will apply even if the part of the building that the landlord occupies is an entirely separate dwelling, e.g. a self-contained flat, but will not apply if the building is a purpose-built block of flats. The landlord must genuinely reside there as a 'home' although s/he may own another home. There are complicated provisions covering the situation where a resident landlord dies, on which further advice should be sought.

- The letting is for a holiday, as long as this is a genuine holiday and not a sham.
- The letting includes the provision of 'board' which was a genuine part of the agreement between the landlord and the tenant when the tenancy was first created. 'Board' is not clearly defined, but basically amounts to the regular provision of some meals which have been prepared for the tenant on behalf of the landlord, e.g. a substantial daily breakfast or evening meal would amount to 'board'.
- The cost of the letting includes a substantial proportion to cover the provision by the landlord of personal services to the tenant, e.g. room cleaning and linen change.
- The letting amounts to college accommodation provided to a student by a university or other college of further or higher education.
- The tenant uses the property for business purposes instead of or in addition to a residence. This covers the situation where a tenant works from home, or starts to run a business involving the property, e.g. taking in lodgers for profit. The exception will not be established if the business use is very trivial or marginal.
- The rent is very low, i.e. less than two-thirds of the rateable value of the property. This exception is normally limited to tenancies of long leases where the tenant pays a large capital sum to acquire the lease and a small annual ground rent thereafter. Such tenancies are not intended to come within the protection of the Rent Act.
- The rateable value of the property is exceptionally high (this relates to luxury lets and is unlikely to be of concern to most social work clients).

What is the advantage to the tenant of a fully protected/statutory tenancy?

There are two outstanding advantages that the fully protected tenancy has over other tenancies. First, the tenant can register a fair rent at the local Rent Officer Service which will be binding on the property for the next two years (see Chapter 11 at p.398). Second, the tenant cannot be evicted from their tenancy unless the landlord proves grounds for eviction to the satisfaction of the local county court. These grounds are limited and are set out in various pieces of legislation. In summary, the grounds are as follows:

Mandatory grounds

Grounds where, if the facts are proved to the court, the judge must make a possession order, i.e. there is no discretion.

Protected shorthold tenancies. The tenancy was described at the outset as a protected shorthold tenancy, the period of the shorthold has come to an end, and the landlord has served the correct notice indicating an intention not to continue the tenancy any longer. Since 15 January 1989 such tenancies have been supplanted by *assured shorthold tenancies* (see p.360).
Returning owner-occupier. The tenancy is of a property that the owner once lived in (as a freeholder or a tenant) and the owner now wants it back as a home either for themselves or for a member of their 'family' (not defined) who had previously lived there. The need must be 'genuine' though it does not have to be 'reasonable'. The intention may only be to live there intermittently. That will be sufficient to gain possession. This provision also applies if the returning owner-occupier wants to sell in order to purchase another home more suited to the owner's work needs (e.g. closer to a new job).

These grounds will typically cover the situation of the homeowner who wants to rent out their home for a period while they are working abroad but at the same time wants to be sure that they can regain their home on their return. Normally the court will only allow possession if the owner *made it quite clear in writing before the tenancy began* that this was the situation (but see note, p.352). These grounds can also be used by people who inherit homes and want to live in them or sell them with vacant possession, and by mortgage companies who want to sell the house with vacant possession because the mortgagor has defaulted on the mortgage payments. This latter provision only applies, however, if the mortgage was in existence before the tenancy began. It can thus be seen that the grounds are potentially very extensive and can be abused. The equivalent provisions for tenancies created after 15 January 1989 are different and less complex (see p.356). Where there are joint owners of the property it will be sufficient to demonstrate that the grounds apply to at least one of the owners, i.e. they do not all need to demonstrate a desire to live there.

Retirement homes. Sometimes people buy themselves a retirement home some way in advance of their projected retirement date and in the interim wish to rent it out to a tenant. As long as they inform the tenant in writing at the beginning of the tenancy that they will wish to repossess the home as their retirement home, they will have grounds for possession against the tenant when that time arrives. Should they die before that date, or should they default on a mortgage in force on the property at the outset of the tenancy, similar provisions apply regarding repossession as for properties let by owner-occupiers (see p.351). Likewise, the same provisions apply regarding the 'genuine' (though not 'reasonable') need of the landlord, and regarding joint owners of the property.

NB In the case of both returning owner-occupiers and retirement homes it seems to be the case that a court will sometimes be willing to grant possession even if the tenant was *not* given full notice of the intention to repossess at the time the tenancy began. There would have to be special reasons for this oversight, however, such as the failure of a letter to arrive or the belief on the landlord's part that verbal oral notice was sufficient.

Miscellaneous grounds. There are a number of other miscellaneous mandatory grounds for possession that are unusual and are therefore not treated here in any detail. They cover such situations as out-of-season lettings of holiday homes or student lettings, lettings by servicemen abroad, and lettings to certain types of agricultural worker.

Discretionary grounds

These are the grounds where the judge retains the discretion whether or not to grant a possession order. There are a number of situations where a landlord wishes to regain possession of a fully protected tenancy but the mandatory grounds set out above do not exist. In these circumstances, the landlord first has to prove one or more of the discretionary grounds set out below, and second has to satisfy the judge that it would be reasonable to make the order for possession. Even then the judge has wide discretionary powers to suspend the execution of the order on condition that, for example, the tenant clears outstanding rent arrears within a reasonable time, or to give the tenant a lengthy period to find alternative accommodation before the landlord can execute the order. The discretionary grounds are as follows:

- Suitable alternative accommodation is available to the tenant. There have been a number of cases which have tried to define exactly what amounts to suitable alternative accommodation. Essentially, the accommodation must be roughly the same size, same price and in an area that is reasonably suitable to the needs of the tenant. The 'character' of the area is a factor that can be taken into account in rejecting the accommodation as unsuitable, if it differs significantly from the area where the tenant currently lives. The courts have held that 'character' does not extend to ethnic character or the proximity of friends.
- The tenant has breached a term of the tenancy agreement, e.g. non-payment of rent, or breach of some other term of the agreement.
- The tenant has allowed the property or furniture in the property to become seriously damaged or neglected.
- The tenant or any other occupier has been found guilty of using the premises for illegal or immoral purposes or has caused serious annoyance or nuisance to nearby residents, e.g. by persistent noise at anti-social hours.
- The tenant has sublet the whole of the premises without the landlord's consent.
- The tenant has given the landlord notice to quit the tenancy, as a result of which the landlord has made a commitment to sell the property to another person with vacant possession.
- The tenancy was originally a service tenancy, i.e. it came with a full-time job offered by the landlord, the tenant is no longer employed to do that job and the landlord needs the property for another full-time employee of the landlord.
- The landlord needs the property as a residence for him/herself, or any son or daughter over 18 years of age, or his/her mother or father, or a father-in-law or mother-in-law. This particular ground will be defeated if the tenant can show that they, or anybody living with them, will suffer greater hardship by losing the tenancy than the landlord/relative will suffer by not acquiring the property.

If a landlord successfully obtains possession under either of the above two grounds and it subsequently transpires that this was under false pretences, the tenant has a right to sue the landlord in the same court for financial compensation for the loss of the tenancy.

- The tenant has sublet part of the property at a rent which is in excess of any registered rent operating on the property (see Chapter 11 at p.398).

WHAT PROCEDURE MUST A LANDLORD FOLLOW IN ORDER TO OBTAIN POSSESSION UNDER ANY OF THE ABOVE GROUNDS?

Possession proceedings against fully protected tenants are subject to rigorous procedures that must be followed to the letter. The adviser who needs a detailed account of every aspect of these procedures should consult Luba, J., Madge, N., and McConnell, D. (1993), *Defending Possession Proceedings* (Legal Action Group). The procedure is the same whether grounds are mandatory or subject to the judge's discretion. In summary it is as follows:

- The landlord must begin the procedure by bringing the contractual tenancy to an end. This means either waiting for the lease to expire, if the tenancy was for a fixed term, or serving the tenant with a detailed legal document that is either a forfeiture notice or a notice to quit. If the contractual tenancy has not been brought to an end by one of the above methods any possession proceedings will be struck out as null and void. It is always worth asking a housing expert to scrutinise the document to check that it has been correctly drafted. For example, a notice to quit must give the tenant at least four weeks' notice, and the notice must end on a day when rent is due. It must also contain certain information about a tenant's rights, once the notice to quit has been served. A letter from a landlord merely giving the tenant a month's notice is not a notice to quit.
- Once the contractual tenancy has ended, the landlord has to serve the tenant with a possession summons which will be issued from the local county court. This summons will set out the details of the grounds on which the landlord is seeking possession and fix a date for the hearing. At this stage the tenant should consult a solicitor or other housing adviser in order to consider the drafting of a defence, which must normally be submitted to the court within 14 days and certainly in advance of the hearing date. Legal aid is available to a tenant to defend possession proceedings subject to a means test (see Chapter 1) provided the legal adviser believes that the tenant

has an arguable defence. It should be noted that where certain of the mandatory grounds are being argued (returning owner-occupier, retirement home, service personnel lettings) a special quick procedure is available to landlords to bring the matter more rapidly before the courts.

- Assuming that no settlement is reached between the parties the matter will have to be heard by a judge sitting in the county court where the summons was issued. Some county courts nowadays have a duty advocate who will be prepared to assist unrepresented parties, but it is strongly advisable to obtain legal advice and representation in advance of the hearing. At the hearing the judge will listen to evidence from both sides, plus any witnesses either side wishes to call, and will then make a decision. If s/he decides that mandatory grounds for possession have been proved an order will be made for possession to take effect in 14 days. It is also possible that the tenant will be ordered to contribute towards the landlord's costs. In cases of grave hardship the 14 days can be extended to 6 weeks. If s/he decides that discretionary grounds have been proved, s/he has a further discretion as to what action if any to take. The normal order, however, is for possession to be granted in 28 days, and it is unusual for a judge to exercise a wider discretion than this except in cases of rent arrears where there are mitigating factors to be taken into account and it seems likely that the tenant will be able to pay off the arrears over an extended period.

Tenancies partially protected by the Rent Act

Some tenancies may not be fully protected by the Rent Act despite their being tenancies and not licences, because they are expressly exempted from such protection (see p.349), e.g. where there is a resident landlord. A few of these tenancies do, however, qualify for very limited protection as *restricted contracts.* A restricted contract is a private tenancy or licence that is not fully protected but which includes the payment of rent and the provision by the landlord of furniture or services. It will thus extend to most lettings by resident landlords (unless unfurnished), educational establishments, lettings providing some board or substantial personal services, and many licences. Certain tenancies are expressly excluded from being restricted contracts, in particular holiday lettings and those where board is substantial (such as half/full-board hotels/hostels).

An occupier (whether tenant or licensee) who has a restricted contract has certain limited rights not available to an occupier who does not have a restricted contract. These rights relate to the length of time for which a judge may suspend any possession order that is made in the county court. In the case of a restricted contract, if entered into after 28 November 1980, the court may suspend the order for up to three months. Before this stage is reached, however, the landlord must go through exactly the same process as for an action against a fully protected tenant (see p.350), first bringing to an end the contractual tenancy, then serving a possession summons. The only difference is that the landlord will not have to prove any grounds for possession.

Tenancies without any Rent Act protection

It follows from the above that there remains a small residue of private tenancies that are completely unprotected by the Rent Act. These will principally be genuine holiday lettings and lettings where substantial board is provided. The position of the tenant in these circumstances is exactly the same as that of a licensee (see p.347). The law states that it is unlawful to evict any tenant or residential licensee without a court order. Any such eviction can lead to prosecution with the possibility of a substantial fine, compensation order and even imprisonment (see p.366). Any threats suggesting eviction without a court order should be reported to the local authority legal department or the police. Unreasonable refusal to leave the premises will, however, increase the likelihood of the tenant being ordered to contribute towards the landlord's costs at the court hearing.

Position for tenancies coming into existence on or after 15 January 1989

The Housing Act 1988 introduced two new types of tenancy. It is no longer possible to create a protected tenancy of the type described above. The two new types of tenancy are the *assured tenancy* and the *assured shorthold tenancy.* Both types of tenancy are regulated by the Housing Act 1988. They have less security of tenure than enjoyed by previous protected tenancies and little regulation of the rent by law.

Assured tenancies

Assured tenancies are lettings at market rents with some security of tenure. There is no control over the rent at which an assured tenancy is initially let and subsequent rent regulation is minimal (see Chapter 11 at p.403). The security of tenure provided is different to that granted to Rent Act tenants (see below) and the grounds for possession are more widely drafted.

What is an assured tenancy?

An assured tenancy is one in which the tenant is an individual tenant (or tenants), i.e. not a company, of residential premises (which may be just a room) occupying the premises as their only or principal home and the tenancy does not fall within one of the stated exceptions. The most important exceptions are as follows:

- The tenancy is an assured shorthold tenancy (see p.360).
- The landlord is a resident landlord (see p.349 but note that, in addition, the home must be the landlord's only or principal home for this exemption to apply).
- College/university letting (see p.350).
- Tenant uses the property for business purposes in addition to or instead of as a residence (see p.350).
- The rent is very low (see p.350) or the rateable value of the premises is very high (see p.350).
- The letting is for a holiday (as long as it is a genuine holiday and not a sham).

If the tenancy falls within one of the above exemptions it is unprotected except that in most cases (see p.365) the landlord will have to obtain an order of the court to evict the tenant. There is no 'halfway house' equivalent to the restricted contract under the 1977 Rent Act (see p.355).

How can an assured tenant be evicted?

A landlord can only evict an assured tenant by following the detailed procedure laid down in the Housing Act 1988. It is complex and what is set out below is no more than an outline. Advisers seeking more detailed information should consult a specialist work. The landlord must first serve on the tenant a notice in prescribed form (similar to the NISP for secure tenants: see p.339) which must set out the grounds for possession (see below) and specify the detail of those grounds, e.g. the precise amount of arrears, the detail of any tenant's alleged misbehaviour and so forth. An old-style notice to quit (see p.347) is of no effect on an assured tenancy. The period of the notice will depend upon the grounds. Advice should always be sought as to whether sufficient notice has been granted. The court does have power to dispense with the need to serve a notice if it considers that it would be 'just and equitable' to do so. It cannot dispense with the need to serve a notice, however, where the grounds for possession are that the tenant has three months arrears of rent (see p.359). Once a notice has been served the landlord has one year in which to commence possession proceedings against the tenant.

If possession proceedings are served a date for a court hearing will be fixed. The procedure thereafter is very similar to the procedure for Rent Act possession actions (see p.354). At court the landlord will have to satisfy the judge that grounds for possession exist against the tenant. In summary the grounds are as follows:

Mandatory grounds

Grounds where, if the facts are proved to the court, the judge must make a possession order, i.e. the judge has no discretion.

Ground 1: returning owner-occupier. The landlord must prove that before the tenancy began, written notice was served on the tenant(s) stating that possession might be recovered under this ground, although the court has power to dispense with the notice requirement if it feels that it would be 'just and equitable' to do so, for example where it is proved that a notice was sent by post and did not arrive. In addition, the landlord must prove that either at some time before the tenancy began they occupied the dwelling as their 'only or principal home' or that they now require the premises to become the 'only or principal residence' for themselves or their spouse. A landlord cannot use the latter case if they became landlord by purchasing the property after the tenancy had already begun.
Ground 2: applies where the property was mortgaged at the time the Ground 1 tenancy was created, and the morgagee wishes to exercise their power of sale over the property (e.g. because the mortgagor has defaulted

on the mortgage) and sell the property with vacant possession. This ground is subject to the same provisions concerning notice as Ground 1.
Ground 3: applies to 'holiday property' let out of season by landlords for a period of up to eight months. For this ground to be used the landlord must have served notice of intent not later than the beginning of the tenancy.
Ground 4: applies to 'college property' let out of term. The same notice provisions apply as for Ground 3.
Ground 5: applies to residences for ministers of religion.
Ground 6: applies where the landlord intends to demolish or reconstruct the whole or a substantial part of the dwelling house or carry out substantial works. Reconstruction means 'a substantial interference with the structure of the premises and then a rebuilding in probably a different form, of such part of the premises as has been demolished by reason of interference with the structure'. In addition, the landlord must satisfy the court that the work cannot reasonably be carried out without the tenant giving up possession and must pay the tenant's reasonable removal expenses. Like Ground 1, this ground cannot be used by a landlord who bought the property after the tenancy had begun.
Ground 7: allows a landlord to obtain possession against a person who inherits the tenancy from the deceased tenant unless they are a spouse succeeding to the tenancy (see p.362). Proceedings must commence within 12 months of the landlord becoming aware of the death.
Ground 8: allows a landlord to obtain possession where there are three months' rent arrears (13 weeks if a weekly tenancy) both at the time notice is served and at the date of the court hearing. Delays in paying housing benefit on the part of the DSS or local authority provide no defence.

Discretionary grounds

Grounds where once the facts are proved to the court the judge still retains a discretion not to make a possession order.

Ground 9: suitable alternative accommodation is available to the tenant. For what constitutes 'suitable alternative accommodation', see p.353.
Ground 10: rent arrears both at the time of the notice and the date of the hearing.
Ground 11: persistent delay in paying rent, whether or not there are arrears at the date proceedings are commenced.

Ground 12: breach of any other term of the tenancy.
Grounds 13–14: similar to Rent Act 1977 grounds (see p.353) regarding nuisance to neighbours, illegal or immoral use of the premises, and allowing the premises or the furniture to fall into significant neglect.
Ground 16: the premises were let to the tenant by the landlord (or previous landlord) in consequence of the tenant's employment which has now come to an end.

Once a judge has made an order for possession the power to suspend the order and the time limits for making an order are the same as for Rent Act tenants (see p.355). A special fast procedure has also been introduced to enable landlords to obtain possession against certain types of defaulting assured tenants, without the need to attend court. A solicitor or housing adviser should be consulted for details of the scope of this procedure.

Assured shorthold tenancies

What is an assured shorthold tenancy?

The *assured shorthold tenancy* replaces the protected shorthold tenancy under the Rent Act 1977 (see p.351) and provides a tenant with no long-term security of tenure. It is also subject to minimal rent control (see Chapter 11 at p.403). For an assured shorthold tenancy to come into effect:

- The tenancy must be for a fixed term of not less than six months.
- The tenancy must not contain any provision enabling the landlord to terminate the tenancy within six months of the beginning of the tenancy.
- Notice in the prescribed form must have been served on the tenant prior to the commencement of the tenancy. The court has no power to dispense with this provision, and even an incorrectly drafted notice has been held to be invalid.
- The tenancy would have been an assured tenancy, had the above three conditions not been met.

WHAT IS THE SECURITY OF TENURE OF AN ASSURED SHORTHOLD TENANT?

During the fixed term of an assured shorthold tenancy a landlord can recover possession against the tenant in the same way as against a fixed-term assured tenant under Grounds 2, 8, 10, 11, 12, 13, 14 or 15. At the end of the fixed term the landlord has the right to obtain possession through a court order subject to the need to give at least two months' notice to the tenant. Notice can be given before the tenancy comes to an end as long as the expiry date is not earlier than the end of the fixed term. A special fast procedure has been introduced to enable landlords to obtain possession against expired assured shorthold tenants without the need to attend court, as long as all paper procedures are followed.

For the position regarding rent regulation under an assured shorthold tenancy, see Chapter 11, p.403).

Other ways to end a tenancy

There are a number of other ways in which a tenancy can be ended which are listed below in summary form. For further information consult Arden (1993), Martin (1986), and Campbell and Gallagher (1992) (see 'Further sources of reference', p.368).

1. *Surrender by the tenant.* This occurs when the tenant and landlord come to an agreement that the tenancy will end and the tenant leaves the property and returns the key. This sometimes occurs in exchange for a lump sum of money paid by the landlord to the tenant to vacate the property without court proceedings and is a perfectly legitimate and legal practice. If a landlord offers a tenant a lump sum in exchange for vacant possession, however, the tenant should always take advice before accepting the money and also must be certain that they have new accommodation available. They will not be rehoused by the council as they will be considered as 'intentionally homeless' (see p.325). As a general rule, a tenant in this situation should be seeking to negotiate a sum that represents the difference to the landlord between the value of the tenanted property and its value with vacant possession. This often amounts to several thousand pounds or more.
2. *Declaration as unfit.* If a local authority declares a house to be unfit for human habitation (see Chapter 11 at p.386) they may place a

closing order on the property, at which stage they are obliged by law to provide the occupants with alternative accommodation and the tenancy of the property will end. The occupants may also be entitled to financial compensation (see Chapter 11 at p.395).

3. *Overcrowding.* If the tenanted property is overcrowded, the landlord can seek possession against the tenant. Overcrowding exists if the number of people sleeping in the premises exceeds levels set down in Part IX of the Housing Act 1985, or if two people of different sex over 10 (not married or cohabiting) are sleeping in the same bedroom.
4. *Transfer to another tenant.* Unless there is something written in the tenancy agreement expressly forbidding transfer (known technically as assignment) it is possible for a tenant to end their tenancy by transferring it in writing to another tenant. This should never be done, however, without first consulting a solicitor or expert housing adviser, as there are a number of possible complications, depending upon the type of tenancy.
5. *Succession to another family member on death of tenant.* On the death of a Rent Act protected tenant (see p.349) the tenancy will pass automatically to their spouse providing the spouse was living with them at their death. The spouse will become the new tenant of the landlord on the same terms. This right also applies to a cohabitee who was living with the tenant in a stable relationship at the time of the tenant's death. If there is no spouse or cohabitee in this position the right of succession passes to any member of the deceased tenant's family who had been living with them for at least two years at the time of the death. There is no fixed rule as to who qualifies as a 'member of the tenant's family' for these purposes, and any dispute, if unresolved, will ultimately have to be resolved by the local county court. If succession is to a member of the deceased tenant's family (and only one such succession is permitted) the new tenancy will be an assured tenancy. On the death of an assured tenant (unless they became the tenant by succession) who was living in the premises as their only or principal home, any spouse or cohabitee living with them at the time of the death will succeed to the tenancy as the new assured tenant. If the tenancy was an unprotected tenancy, while the tenant may make provision in their will to leave their tenancy to a named person – and if not it will pass to their next of kin – the inheritor will remain as vulnerable to eviction

proceedings as their predecessor (see p.356). For further detail on this complex area of law, consult a specialist manual or seek the advice of a solicitor.

RETAINING MORTGAGED ACCOMMODATION

What is the effect of a mortgage?

When a building society or finance company lends money to a home-owner either to help buy or to help improve property it will invariably enter into a parallel agreement with the borrower, setting out the terms for the repayment of the loan. By far the commonest arrangement is a scheme whereby the borrower agrees to make a monthly payment to the lender over a period of many years. It is not uncommon for these schemes to be linked to life or endowment insurance policies. The general term to describe such arrangements is a *mortgage*. As long as the borrower keeps up the payments there should be no problems. (If the borrower is in receipt of income support it may also be possible for them to receive assistance in repaying the interest on the loan: see Chapter 8 at p.266). Naturally, the lender (the mortgagee) will seek more security from the borrower (the mortgagor) in the event of the mortgagor failing to keep up the repayments. This security will normally take the form of a charge on the property. A charge has two effects. First, it gives the mortgagee the right to sell the property in the event of the mortgagor failing to keep up the payments; and second, it ensures that any prospective purchaser of the property is aware of the existence of the loan, which will have to be repaid before they can acquire the property.

What will the mortgagee do if the mortgagor fails to keep up with their repayments?

Repossession proceedings

If a mortgagor falls behind on their payments, the following procedure will probably be adopted by the mortgagee.

Stage 1: the mortgagee will write a letter asking the mortgagor to make arrangements to get the payments up to date.

Stage 2: if the payments are not restored the mortgagee will write to threaten legal proceedings, and will pass the matter to their solicitor. Eventually, a summons may be issued in the local county court setting out the details of the arrears, of any steps taken by the mortgagee to recover arrears, and details of any relevant information about the defendant's financial position known to the mortgagee. The mortgagor will be asked to return a form to the court stating whether the details of the claim are correct. A date will be fixed for the hearing of the case.
Stage 3: if the matter has still not been settled, the court hearing will take place. If the mortgagor makes a satisfactory proposal to the court for clearing the arrears, this will probably end the matter. If they fail to do this, the court can make an order allowing the mortgagee to repossess the property, and sell it, in order to recover the loan. They can also make an order for possession, against the wishes of the mortgagee, if they consider it would be unfair on the mortgagor to postpone the sale. Even at this stage, however, the court can suspend the execution of the order to allow the mortgagor time to find the money to pay off the loan, in which case no eviction will occur. Legal aid will normally be available to help the mortgagor defend the proceedings (see Chapter 1).

For further information both on the above and also on various ways in which a mortgagor in this position can obtain financial assistance, consult an excellent handbook by McKenny, J., and Thompson, L. (1993), *Rights Guide for Home-Owners* (CPAG/SHAC). See also Meadowcroft, C. (1987), *The Homeowner's Guide to the Law* (Fourmat) and (1989), *Owning your own Flat: a Practical Guide to Problems with your Lease and Landlord* (SHAC).

NB There is also in existence a Building Societies Ombudsman with the specific task of investigating actions taken by a building society in respect, *inter alia*, of repossession proceedings, mortgages, loans and overdrafts, current accounts, automatic cash dispensers, and foreign exchange. The office of the Building Societies Ombudsman is at 35–7 Grosvenor Gardens, London SW1X 7AW (tel: 071 931 0044). See also James, R., and Seneviratne, M. (1992), 'The Building Societies Ombudsman Scheme', *Civil Justice Quarterly*, vol. 11, 157–74.

THE CRIMINAL LAW AND THE PROTECTION OF ACCOMMODATION RIGHTS

There are a number of criminal offences that a landlord can commit. If a tenant believes that their landlord has committed or is about to commit any of these offences they should seek the assistance of the Tenancy Relations Officer of their local council, whose job it is to try to ensure that these offences are not committed, and to consider prosecution of offenders. In the case of the most serious of these offences, illegal eviction, the police should be immediately involved, as they are more likely to be able to influence a landlord to restore the tenant immediately, and if not, may proceed to prosecute. It is possible for a landlord to be sent to prison if found guilty of a serious illegal eviction, even for a first offence. For a full study of the practical experience of this type of criminal activity, see Burrows, L., and Hunter, N. (1991), *Forced Out: Harassment and Illegal Eviction* (Shelter).

What are the criminal offences associated with accommodation rights?

Illegal eviction

It is a criminal offence for anybody to evict either a tenant or a licensee from their home without a court order. This applies whether or not the tenancy is protected. The only exception to this provision is where the letting is an 'excluded letting' under the Housing Act 1988, in which case no court order is necessary to evict the occupant once their contractual right of occupation has been terminated. There is every chance, however, that in carrying out an eviction without a court order the landlord may commit an offence under s.6 of the Criminal Law Act which makes it an offence to use or threaten violence to enter any premises on which there is a person opposed to the entry. 'Excluded lettings' are as follows:

- Where the tenant/licensee shares accommodation with the landlord and it is the landlord's only or principal home. This exclusion does not apply if the shared accommodation consists only of storage areas or means of access such as staircases or corridors.
- Where the tenant/licensee lives in the same building as the landlord and shares accommodation with a member of the landlord's

family (which includes spouse, parents, grandparents, children, grandchildren, siblings, uncles and aunts). The same restricted definition applies to accommodation as for the previous exclusion. Neither of the above two exclusions apply where the building in question is a purpose-built block of flats.

- Where the tenancy/licence was granted as a temporary expedient to a person who was at that time a squatter.
- Where the tenancy/licence had been a genuine holiday let, which has now expired.
- Where the tenancy/licence was provided free of any charge.
- Where it is hostel accommodation provided by any of the list of organisations set out in s.31 of the Housing Act 1988 (includes local authorities, housing trusts, the Housing Corporation, housing action trusts and so on).

What is an illegal eviction?

Any act that prevents the tenant/licensee from entering their home, e.g. by changing the locks, removing their belongings, will amount to an illegal eviction. A landlord who has carried out an illegal eviction can be prosecuted in either the magistrates' or the crown court, and can be fined or imprisoned. In addition, the evicted person can apply immediately to the local county court to be reinstated, and can seek damages. In the past two years, damages awards in excess of £5000 have been recorded in a number of instances. In future, awards are likely to be much higher, as the 1988 Housing Act also allows victims of illegal eviction to sue the landlord for damages that reflect the difference in value to the landlord of the tenanted property and with vacant possession. This figure may well be very substantial. Such actions are likely to be in the High Court owing to the magnitude of the damages claims. Legal aid will be available to the tenant (see Chapter 1).

Harassment

If a landlord, or somebody acting on their behalf, does things likely to intimidate a tenant and encourage them to leave the premises (for example, by making threats, disconnecting services, sabotaging the property, or generally making life difficult or unpleasant) they may be guilty of the criminal offence of harassment. In these circumstances, the local Tenancy

Relations Officer should always be consulted. If they believe harassment is taking place they should take steps to prevent its continuance. If they are unsuccessful the tenant can apply to the county court as above under 'Illegal eviction' for similar remedies, and the Tenancy Relations Officer may prosecute the landlord. If the harassment amounts to racial harassment, consult CRE. Advisers should also obtain a copy of the CRE *Race Relations Code of Practice* (private renting) which should eventually become part of the housing legislation.

Assistance in harassment and illegal eviction cases

The Law Society and the Campaign for Bedsit Rights have published a directory of solicitors who have taken up cases for private tenants facing harassment and illegal eviction. It covers individual areas of the country (£3.50), and the whole of England and Wales (£10), and can be obtained from CBR, 7 Whitechapel Road, London E1 1DU.

Martin Wilcock, Environmental Health Officer, Rotherham MBC, Elmbank House, 73 Alma Road, Rotherham S60 2BU, can also provide copies of a *Harassment and Illegal Eviction Pack* used by local authorities (enclose sae).

Failure to provide name and address of landlord

Every tenant has the right to know the name and address of their landlord. If they do not have this information they should make a written request to the person who last collected any rent from them for it. If the rent collector fails to provide the information, the Tenancy Relations Officer has the power to prosecute them in the local magistrates' court, where they can be ordered to provide the information and can be fined.

Failure to provide a rent book

Every tenant with a weekly tenancy is entitled to a rent book, unless their tenancy includes substantial board (all or most meals). If a landlord refuses to provide a rent book, the Tenancy Relations Officer can prosecute them as above. The rent book must contain details of the name and address of the landlord and agent (if any), of the rent and council tax payable, and of the tenant's rights to have a fair rent fixed, to claim housing benefit, and of their protection from eviction without a court order. Newsagents frequently stock rent books.

FURTHER SOURCES OF REFERENCE

There are a number of useful guides and manuals on housing law that could be used by advisers to provide more detailed information. SHAC manages to include everything in outline in a single manual, the *Housing Rights Guide*, which is reissued annually. Together with CPAG they also produce a *Rights Guide for Home-owners*. Another straightforward guide for home-owners is Meadowcroft, C. (1987), *The Homeowner's Guide to the Law* (Fourmat Books). Specifically for flat-owners, SHAC have produced (1989) *Owning your own Flat: a Practical Guide to Problems with your Lease and Landlord*. Those living in bedsits should consult *Bedsit Rights* (1989), produced by the Campaign for Bedsit Rights, 7 Whitechapel Rd, London E1 1DU.

For more detailed information, advisers with some knowledge of the law should use the following (the title in each case indicates with precision the scope of the work):

Arden, A. (1993), *Manual of Housing Law* (5th edn, Sweet and Maxwell).

Barlow, A. (1992), *Living Together: a Guide to the Law* (Fourmat Publishing).

Campaign for Bedsit Rights (1993), *Living in Bed and Breakfast: An Advice Guide*.

Campbell, R., and Gallagher, J. (1992), *Security of Tenure in the Private Rented Sector* (looseleaf, SHAC Publications).

Hoath, D. (1989), *Public Housing Law* (Sweet and Maxwell).

Hughes, D. (1987), *Public Sector Housing Law* (2nd edn, Butterworths).

Hunter C., and McGrath, S. (1992), *Homeless Persons* (Legal Action Group).

Letall, M. (1988), *Mobile Homes: an Occupier's Guide* (Shelter).

Luba, I., Madge, N., and McConnell, D. (1993), *Defending Possession Proceedings* (3rd edn, Legal Action Group).

Martin, I. (1986), *Security of Tenure under the Rent Act* (Sweet and Maxwell).

Moroney, L., and Goodwin, J. (1992), *Homelessness: a Good Practice Guide* (Shelter).

Resource Information Service (1988), *Women's Housing Handbook.*
Sherriff, G. (1993), *Guide to Residential Tenancies* (Sweet and Maxwell).

The Housing Year Book 1992 (Longman) is a very useful directory that provides details on the entire range of housing-related organisations in the United Kingdom. The listings include all local authority housing and related departments, and a wide range of information on housing associations, specialist libraries and bookshops, professional bodies and associations, and special organisations dealing with single issues such as debt, homelessness, special housing and so forth.
Independent Funding for Tenants 1992, by Rosalind Dean of the Institute of Housing in Coventry, explains how independent resources can give tenants' groups the autonomy to be more equal partners with their landlords, and looks at schemes for giving such support and the legal, financial and practical issues involved.

For those interested in a broad overview of Britain's housing history, and some provocative solutions to some of the problems, the following two collections (both under £10) are well worth obtaining:

Grant, C., *Built to Last*, from Shelter, 88 Old Street, London EC1V 9HU
Darke, J., *The Roof over your Head*, from Spokesman, Bertrand Russell House, Gamble St, Nottingham, NG7 4ET.

The following organisations may also be of assistance:

The National Housing Law Service, Woolwich House, 43 George Street, Croydon CR9 1EY provides a comprehensive range of legal services in connection with housing law.

Federation of Black Housing Organisations, 374 Gray's Inn Road, London WC1X 8BB (tel: 071 837 8288). Voluntary organisation whose aim is to highlight the housing needs of black people and to campaign against racism in housing. Provides practical advice and information on setting up housing associations and co-ops (see p.342) and undertakes campaigns and lobbying. Publishes national directory of black housing and advice groups.

Federation of Private Residents' Associations Ltd, 11 Dartmouth Street, London SW1H 9BL (tel: 071 222 0037). Federation of voluntary groups representing the interests of private tenants. Provides free legal advice to its members.

SHAC, 189A Brompton Road, London SW5 0AR (tel: 071 373 7276) is a housing aid and advice centre for those living in Greater London which also provides a wide range of excellent and accurate guides.

Shelter is the leading organisation campaigning against homelessness. Produces numerous publications, videotapes, wallcharts, a bi-monthly magazine (*Roof*) and spearheads many campaigns. Provides independent housing advice, training courses and aid to individuals and communities on all aspects of homelessness.
Shelter (England): 88 Old Street, London EC1V 9HU (tel: 071 253 0202).
Shelter (Wales): 25 Walter Road, Swansea SA1 5NN (tel: 0792 469400).
Shelter (Scotland): 8 Hampton Terrace, Edinburgh EH12 5JD (tel: 031 3131550).

National Tenants Organisation, (England) HVA Centre, 12 School Road, Hounslow TW3 1QZ (tel: 0742 426177). Federation of tenants' organisations across the country with a number of regional branches. Provides lobbying, training, publication service covering all types of rented accommodation.

Tenants Participation Advisory Service (TPAS), 48 The Crescent, Salford, M5 4NY (tel: 061 745 7903). TPAS works with tenants, councils and housing associations to try to increase tenant involvement in housing management. Provides information, advice and training.

Private Tenants Rights Project (PTRP), 1 Nevern Place, Earl's Court, London SW5 9NR (tel: 071 370 7069) assists groups of private tenants in test case and development work to strengthen the position of private tenants in the housing market.

Chapter 11

Using legal rights to improve a home

Many hundreds of thousands of people, perhaps even millions, in the United Kingdom live in substandard accommodation. Social workers do not need to be told that poor accommodation is one of the major sources of family stress and breakdown. But the law is not entirely passive when it comes to improving housing conditions. It is the purpose of this chapter to outline in some detail the various ways in which people living in substandard accommodation, or accommodation that has not been kept in a proper state of repair, can use the law to improve their housing conditions. The chapter will also indicate the procedures whereby a tenant, living in accommodation where they consider the rent to be too high, can apply to have it reduced to a level that is fair, or if the rent is not reduced can seek financial assistance to meet the payment. Because the law provides little by way of extra assistance to owner-occupiers in substandard accommodation (with the exception of accommodation in which a disabled person is living: see Chapter 4), this chapter will focus primarily upon the rights of tenants. Some of the rights described in the chapter relate only to private tenants, others relate to all types of tenant regardless of the status of the landlord. A simple guide on disrepair and how to spot it is Morris, I. (1989), *Bazaar Property Doctor* (BBC).

GETTING THE LANDLORD TO DO REPAIRS: THE DIRECT APPROACH

What repairs is a landlord liable to carry out under contract law?

A landlord's liability to carry out the repairs set out below applies regardless of the type of tenancy. It therefore applies equally to private tenancies, council tenancies, and housing association tenancies. The liability does not apply if the letting is only a licence (see Chapter 10). Whenever there is a tenancy for which the initial term is less than seven years (it does not matter if the tenant in fact lives in the premises for more than seven years), and the tenancy commenced later than 24 October 1961, the landlord has a legal duty under s.11 Landlord and Tenant Act 1985 to keep in repair (which includes a duty to put in repair) the following parts of the dwelling:

1. The structure and exterior of the house, including drains, drainpipes and guttering. This will therefore include roofs, walls, floors, ceilings, doors, window frames, sills, sashes and glass (unless broken by the tenant). This duty will also extend to outside walls if they form an integral design feature and are actually fixed to the house, and will include the essential means of access to the property and common parts. It will not, however, extend to damage caused by design defects, e.g. condensation caused by a lack of proper insulation, unless the condensation actually caused damage to the structure or the exterior of the property (but see p.373), nor will it extend to damage caused by the tenant acting in an 'un-tenantlike' manner.
2. All installations for supplying or making use of water, gas and electricity, e.g. pipes, wiring, water tanks, toilets, basins. This does not extend to appliances which are not firmly fixed to the premises, and therefore excludes such things as cookers, plug-in electrical equipment and plumbed-in washing machines.
3. All installations for space or water heating, e.g. radiators, water heaters, and boilers. For tenancies which began on or after after 15 January 1989, installations include those directly serving the tenant's property, though not part of it, as long as they belong to the landlord.

The landlord's responsibility to keep all the above in repair is absolute, e.g. the landlord cannot contract out of the responsibility in the letting agreement. But this is also subject to the following conditions:

- Liability to repair (and also to provide compensation for the effects of living with disrepair) only begins at the moment that the landlord has, or is deemed to have (i.e. through an agent), notice of any disrepair. It is for this reason that it is essential for a tenant to ensure that their landlord (or the landlord's agent) is always informed of any defect or disrepair as soon as it is discovered, preferably in writing. If the landlord or agent ever visit the premises, the tenant should always record the details of the visit in writing.

- Liability to repair does not, however, extend to repairing property that has been destroyed or damaged by fire, storm, flood or other natural disaster or to keep in repair such of the tenant's belongings as he or she is entitled to remove from the premises at the end of the tenancy, e.g. fitted kitchens and heating systems installed by the tenant, unless the damage arises as a consequence of other disrepair for which the landlord is liable (e.g. the leaking roof that damages the heating system).
- The standard of repair that is expected by law is no higher than the general standard of repair in the area. Thus the standard of repair expected in a slum area is lower than that in a well-kept area.
- The landlord's liability is only to *repair* not to *improve* the property, unless the only way that the repair can be effected is by replacing an obsolete or out-of-date part with a more modern equivalent. The way in which the courts interpret this provision depends very much on the age of the property in question and the cost of the 'improvements' compared with the cost of the 'repair'. If the property in disrepair is relatively modern and the defect in question is caused by a design or construction defect, the courts can order repairing work that amounts to the use of a new and improved construction method, e.g. by using better methods of underpinning or by using expansion joints. This discretion is, however, used sparingly. If the property is older, the courts may authorise more extensive use of 'improvements' as the basis for repairing work, but in these circumstances they will always take account of the cost of the work, and will not order work that amounts to the virtual reconstruction of the property.

How can a tenant *make* a landlord do these repairs?

As soon as a tenant becomes aware of any disrepair in the above categories they should immediately inform their landlord. The landlord then acquires the right to enter the premises at a reasonable time to inspect the disrepair, subject to giving 24 hours' notice. With luck, the repairs will then be carried out by the landlord, and all will be well. If the landlord fails to do anything, the tenant has the right to issue proceedings in the local county court asking that the landlord be ordered to carry out the repairs, and also, if appropriate, for compensation for the inconvenience and discomfort caused to the tenant by the disrepair. Legal aid is available for such an action (see Chapter 1) and a solicitor should be consulted before any proceedings are initiated. It is essential to check the tenant's security of tenure (see Chapter 10) before taking action, for if a tenant has no security of tenure it will be open to the landlord to respond to the disrepair proceedings by eviction.

Can a court make a landlord do the repairs?

If the landlord does not agree to do the repairs, despite the tenant's summons, there will be a full hearing before the local county court. If the judge is satisfied that the disrepair exists, and that it is the landlord's responsibility to do the repairs, s/he will make an order setting out a schedule of work to be done by the landlord and a time scale. Compensation can also be ordered (see below).

Can the tenant do the repairs themselves and deduct the cost from future rent?

Yes, as long as the tenant first gives notice in writing to the landlord that this is their intention and gives the landlord one final opportunity to do the repairs. The cost of the repairs can only be deducted from that part of the rent that is actually 'rent', i.e. it cannot be deducted from any part of the rent that goes towards paying the council tax. Local authority tenants, and most housing association tenants, also have the right to receive grant aid to carry out these repairs (see Chapter 4 at p.101, and below at p.377).

How does the court work out the amount of compensation for disrepair?

Recent years have witnessed a considerable increase in the amount of money that courts are prepared to order landlords to pay in compensation to tenants who have been obliged to endure living in unrepaired premises. The first principle underlying the amount of compensation ordered is to return to the tenant a sum of money that represents the difference in value to the tenant between the premises in their repaired state and the premises in their disrepaired state. This sum should cover the entire period that the premises remain unrepaired from the moment that the landlord has notice of the disrepair. Thus, if half the premises are uninhabitable due to disrepair, the landlord should be ordered to pay back half the rent for the whole period they remain in disrepair.

The second principle is that there should be added to this figure a sum that reflects any general suffering, inconvenience or distress occasioned to the tenant by the disrepair (known as general damages). This figure is often a lump sum of several hundred pounds, depending upon the degree of distress.

The third principle is that the tenant should also be compensated for any specific damage to their property caused by disrepair (known as special damages). Thus the 'replacement cost' of furniture, clothes, bedding and other personal items damaged as a result of the disrepair (e.g. through water penetration) can also be claimed. 'Replacement cost' means the estimated cost of replacing the item in the state it was when damaged, not the cost of a brand new replacement. Since 1988, courts have been prepared to make awards well in excess of £4000 for serious disrepair. The leading case setting out the guidelines is *Chiodi* v. *De Marney* (1988), *Estates Gazette* 41 at 80.

How long does it take to process a claim against a landlord through the courts?

The least satisfactory aspect of this procedure is the time it takes to process the action. Proceedings should never be initiated until the landlord has been given written notice of each defect and a reasonable amount of time in which to carry out the necessary repairs, and has failed to do so. The preparatory work necessary to issue a summons, obtain reports and so on may take a further few weeks. If the landlord defends the action, it can take up to a year before a date is set for the court hearing. At the very least, a period of months is likely to pass before a date is set. Thus, a tenant should be under no illusion of the frustrations that lie ahead if they choose to take this type of action. It should, however, be made clear that the threat of such action is often sufficient to persuade a defaulting landlord to carry out the necessary repairs. For the truly resilient tenant, it is possible to conduct the action without using a lawyer. But take care! See *Taking your own Case to Court or Tribunal* (1985, Consumers' Association).

Can anybody other than a tenant exercise these repairing rights?

No. These rights arise exclusively by virtue of the status of a tenant, and are not available to licensees, squatters, subtenants, or family and friends of the tenant who are living with them.

What can somebody do who is not a tenant but who suffers injury or damage while on the disrepaired premises?

If a person is not a tenant they cannot use contract law. The law of tort states, however, that if a person is not the tenant of premises in disrepair, but they nevertheless suffer personal injury or damage to their property while on the disrepaired premises they may still, in certain circumstances, be able to sue the landlord for the damage or injury that they have suffered. The circumstances are as follows:

- They are a lawful visitor of the tenant (e.g. the tenant invited them to be there, either to live or as a visitor).
- The damage or personal injury was caused by a defect in the premises of which the landlord knew or ought to have known. In other words, if the damage or injury was caused by a defect (e.g. falling plaster) of which the landlord had no knowledge because of a failure to inspect the property at reasonable intervals, the visitor may still be able to sue the landlord.
- The defect that caused the damage or injury to the visitor must be a defect that the landlord has a legal obligation to put right (see above at p.372).

What happens if the damage or injury is the result of the defective work of a third party, e.g. a builder?

Anyone who carries out work of construction, repair, maintenance, enlargement, conversion, demolition or any other work in relation to premises owes a duty of care to all those who might reasonably be expected to be affected by resulting defects in that work. This means that they will be liable for any personal injury or damage suffered by anyone as long as the injury or damage was reasonably foreseeable. They will not, however, be liable for any reduction in the value of the property as a result of the defects, nor the cost of putting it right. The defect must cause actual injury. The injured person does not have to be on the premises in order to be able to sue for damages. They may, for example, be a neighbour or a passer-by, injured by falling debris. A landlord may also be liable for the negligent work of a contractor if reasonable care was not taken in the selection of a competent person for the particular job.

Most structural building work is now covered by the Building Regulations. If a person is injured or their property harmed as a result of a failure by a builder to comply with the Building Regulations, that person can take legal action against both the builder and the owner for compensation (unless the breach of the Building Regulations was actually condoned by the local authority, in which case they are the best party to sue). For further information on Building Regulations, contact the local authority Building Control Department. For further information, consult *Which? Getting Work Done on Your House* (Consumers' Association/ Hodder and Stoughton).

Special note on council housing repairs

As complaints about inadequate council housing repairs account for 8 per cent of the total complaints to the Local Ombudsman (see Chapter 3 at p.75) the office has now published *Guidance on Good Practice 3: Council Housing Repairs* (available from address on p.75). The guidance covers the 10 key areas in which it expects housing authorities to take special measures, including information to tenants, record-keeping, work organisation, compensation and complaints.

GETTING THE COUNCIL TO HELP: THE POSITION OF THE PRIVATE TENANT

There are a number of ways in which the local council can intervene in cases of serious disrepair to privately rented property. The extent to which a private tenant living in accommodation which is in a bad state of repair can enlist the assistance of their local council will depend upon three things:

1. Is the accommodation in a special category, i.e. a House in Multiple Occupation (HMO) or a Common Lodging House (CLH)?

2. How extensive is the disrepair?
3. What are the policies of the local authority concerning the exercise of its discretionary powers?

In addition, the general point should once again be made that before taking any action regarding disrepair a tenant should always begin by checking their security of tenure (see Chapter 10). There is little point in asserting legal rights to have repairs carried out, only to be subsequently evicted.

SPECIAL CATEGORIES OF ACCOMMODATION

There are certain types of private accommodation to which special laws apply, namely Houses in Multiple Occupation (HMOs) and Common Lodging Houses (CLHs). This section will look at the special provisions which apply to these two types of accommodation.

Houses in Multiple Occupation (HMOs)

If the building in which the tenant is housed is a House in Multiple Occupation (HMO) local authorities have available to them a whole range of special powers of intervention in the running of the house. Whether they exercise these powers is a political and a financial question: most of these powers need extra financial resources to back them up, otherwise they are of little value.

An HMO is 'a house or flat which is occupied by persons who do not form a single household'. This description covers accommodation where separate households are sharing bathrooms, toilets, cooking facilities, common living areas and the like, but does not extend to buildings in which there may be a number of self-contained flats, the only common parts being entrance halls and stairs. The description therefore covers such arrangements as houses divided into bedsits, hostels and hotels housing homeless families.

Some of the worst housing conditions in the country are to be found in HMOs. There is controversy surrounding the number of HMOs in the United Kingdom. There have been two surveys of HMOs, one carried out by the DOE to cover the whole of England and Wales (1986) and the other limited to the Greater London Area (1987). The official DOE estimate of the number of HMOs in England and Wales at that time of 334,000 was almost certainly an underestimate. (For further information contact Campaign for Bedsit Rights, see p.385.)

It has been estimated that 77 per cent of HMOs contain households who are living in substandard accommodation (and substandard means merely households who share or lack basic sanitary amenities such as baths or inside toilets). This figure of 77 per cent is a national average and rises to 90 per cent in parts of Greater Manchester, Sheffield, Bradford, Leeds and certain London boroughs. The government's own survey of conditions in hostels and lodging houses carried out in 1976 revealed that 85 per cent of hostels were built before 1914, and that 78 per cent of the hostels were in buildings that fell below the government's minimum standards for toilets, wash-basins and baths. By 1986 the Department of the Environment estimated that the 334,000 HMOs were housing in excess of 2 million people. Of these, 110,000 needed major repairs, 96,000 were lacking basic amenities, 53,000 were overcrowded, 77,000 were managed unsatisfactorily and 127,000 lacked legal fire hazard precautions. More recently, in 1991, the Audit Commission published *Healthy Housing: the Role of Environmental Health Services* (HMSO), which stated that about half the HMOs in England and Wales were damp, dangerous, overcrowded or unhygienic. And in 1993, the Campaign for Bedsit Rights published its own research report, *Houses in Multiple Occupation: Policy and Practice in the 1990s*. Among the alarming facts unearthed in this latest report were the following:

- Only 51 per cent of local authorities have any sort of written policy on HMOs.
- Only 15 per cent of authorities have a capital and revenue budget specifically for HMO work.
- More than three people die, and 68 people are injured, in fires in HMOs *every week* in England and Wales alone.

It is against these deeply depressing statistics that all that is written below on legal powers has to be read. It must, however, be accepted that enforcing these powers will be an uphill task for anybody. Despite numerous attempts at private member's legislation to improve the conditions in HMOs, only limited improvement has been seen in the past 20 years. The problem is compounded by the fact that inhabitants of HMOs may be highly vulnerable both legally (because they may not have the status of tenancy: see Chapter 10) and emotionally (because their occupation of an HMO has been forced upon them by a crisis such as divorce, homelessness, lack of money, eviction, or personal problems like drug or alcohol addiction). Despite these difficulties, there are nevertheless a number of powers available to councils to improve the conditions and safety of those living in HMOs. These powers relate to the following:

- execution of works to improve the conditions within the HMO;
- fire precautions;
- overcrowding.

Execution of works to improve the conditions within the HMO

The living conditions within an HMO are often of a very poor quality. The fact that complete strangers have to share many facilities often means that there is no clear agreement as to who is responsible for what duties, which means that little gets done by way of cleaning or repair. (This is notwithstanding the fact that each individual occupant of an HMO, provided they are a tenant and not a licensee (see Chapter 10), has the same repairing rights as tenants of other accommodation: see p.371). Many HMOs are large, impersonal edifices, crammed too full with lonely, isolated people with little money, and a limited sense of their rights to have improvements done to their home. The following description of a large hostel for single men in Tower Hamlets (an HMO) by an independent Environmental Health Inspector provides a chilling though accurate picture of much hostel accommodation:

> The room I was allocated was little larger than the bed it contained. Its thin wooden walls meant that I could hear everything in adjoining rooms. The bed linen was filthy and stained with excrement. The nearest toilets were damp and filthy and some were broken. The walls, floors and surfaces were dirty. The wiring to the electric light was perished, exposing live wires. Every fire door in the corridor was wedged open and the fire precautions were inadequate.

But local authorities do have legal powers to do something about such conditions if they can exercise the political will to produce the resources to use these powers. If an HMO is in a bad condition in respect of one or more of the list of matters set out below, a local authority has power to serve notices on the 'person in control' of the HMO requiring them to carry out specified works on the property to render it reasonably suitable for its existing inhabitants to continue living there. These works may relate to any of the following:

> satisfactory facilities for storage, preparation and cooking of food, including an adequate number of sinks with a satisfactory supply of hot and cold water; an adequate number of suitably located WCs, fixed baths or showers, and wash-hand basins for the exclusive use of the occupants, each with a satisfactory supply of hot and cold water; adequate means of escape from fire, and adequate other fire precautions.

It will be seen that the list is quite extensive, and the local authority has power to carry out the works in default if they are not done. In practice, however, local authorities do not make sufficient use of these powers. In any event, grant aid in the form of Common Parts Grants are available to the person in control, on whom the notice is served. There is also a further option of a Group Repairs Scheme, details of which can be obtained from the local authority.

Person in control of HMO

It will have been seen that many of the notices concerning HMOs have to be served on the 'person in control' of the premises. The law defines the 'person in control' as the person receiving the rent or other payments on the property from tenants or lodgers, whether as landlord or landlord's agent.

Fire precautions in HMOs

By their very nature, HMOs carry high fire risks (see above for government estimates). Between 1979 and 1981, 431 people died in fires in HMOs. The relative risk of death by fire for the occupant of an HMO is nine times greater than that for a person living elsewhere. Although many of these fires are simply the result of excessive strain being placed upon archaic electrical systems, there is clear evidence that many are also preventable by the installation of proper fire precautions within the HMO. Local authorities have strong legal powers relating to fire precautions in HMOs which they should be encouraged to utilise:

- Any HMO comprising three or more storeys (excluding a storey below the floor level of the principal entrance to the house), whose total floor space exceeds 500 square metres, must comply with fire precautions drawn up for that building by the local authority after consultation with the fire authority. These precautions will vary according to the conditions of the house and may include the addition of fire doors, smoke screens, fire detectors or proper means of escape. The local authority can serve notices on the person having control of the premises (see p.381) setting out the work that should be done, and can do the work in default if it is not done. It is clear from the evidence that there is widespread failure by local authorities to enforce these powers, which is a matter for deep regret. It would also appear that these provisions apply to less than 10 per cent of all HMOs.
- If the HMO is smaller than described above the local authority has powers to insist upon fire precautions but they are all discretionary. These powers relate principally to the installation of proper means of escape from fire. For details, consult the local Fire Authority or the local authority Environmental Health Department.

Overcrowding in HMOs

A local authority has the power to determine the maximum number of people who are allowed to live in a particular HMO, including the maximum number who are to sleep in each room in the house. These maximums can be age and sex related. This is a discretionary power, but local authorities should be encouraged to use the power in HMOs where overcrowding creates insanitary or dangerous conditions for the inhabitants. Once fixed, a 'maximum numbers order' is served on the 'person having control of the house' (see p.381) in the form of a notice. If there are more people in occupation than the maximum numbers, the notice does not require the reduction of the numbers by eviction, but merely forbids the replacement of departing occupants in excess of the maximum numbers contained in the notice. It is a criminal offence to fail to comply with an overcrowding notice, although in practice prosecutions under these provisions are very rare.

Can a local authority take over the running of an HMO if its owners or landlords persistently fail to manage it to a satisfactory standard?

The law provides local authorities with two special procedures to take over the running of HMOs when they consider they are being inadequately run. Both these procedures are discretionary and involve the local authority in extra management work that it may feel it has inadequate resources to provide. As the appalling conditions in many HMOs become more apparent, however, there has been a discernible increase in the use of these powers by local authorities. The two powers are *Management Orders* and *Control Orders.*

Management Order

If a local authority considers that an HMO is in an unsatisfactory state due to a failure to maintain adequate standards of management, they may serve a notice on the person who directly or indirectly receives the rent on the premises, ordering them to comply with the Management Regulations, a series of Regulations prescribed by the Secretary of State for the Environment. A copy of the notice must be posted in a prominent position in the house in order that all occupants are made aware of its existence. The Management Regulations cover a wide range of management functions, not all of which may be relevant to the particular property. They include:

> general repair, water supplies, cleaning of rooms and common parts, drainage, safety of the occupants, tidiness of any garden, fire escapes, good ventilation, proper space and water heating, refuse disposal, and proper electricity supplies.

A failure to comply with the Management Regulations, once served, amounts to a criminal offence and local authorities have wide powers to carry out any works in default. In 1987 there were approximately 4000 Management Orders in force, an entirely inadequate figure when set against the 77,000 households living in HMOs that were poorly managed (p.379).

CONTROL ORDER

The greatest power of all that a local authority possesses to intervene in the running of an HMO is the Control Order. If a local authority makes a Control Order over an HMO it may immediately enter into possession of the property and take such steps as it feels necessary to protect the safety, health or welfare of the inhabitants of the HMO. The local authority is entitled to collect and keep the rent payable on the property for the period of the Control Order, and must in return pay the owner an annual sum of money by way of 'compensation'. The local authority must also prepare within eight weeks a scheme of work designed to remedy the problems that brought about the Control Order. The Control Order can last up to five years, after which time it will automatically lapse. It can be seen that the dual effect of a Control Order is:

1. That the owner loses all control over their property for the period of the order;
2. That the local authority takes upon itself the full legal and financial burden of being a landlord of a property that by definition is likely to need a great deal of money spent on it.

It is therefore not surprising to learn that Control Orders are rare, running at present at around 40 per year across the entire country.

A Control Order can only be made on an HMO if there is already in existence on that HMO either a Management Order, or a notice concerning fire precautions, overcrowding, or the execution of works to improve conditions within the HMO, and that order or notice has not been effective.

Is there any appeal against the imposition of the above notices and orders?

Every one of the notices and orders that are outlined above concerning HMOs can be appealed against by the person on whom it is made, i.e. the person normally in 'control of the property' (see p.381). This creates yet more hurdles for the occupant of an HMO, as they will then have to await the outcome of the appeal, which may take several months, during which time both they and the local authority are powerless to do anything.

Further information

It is clear from the above that the conditions of those living in HMOs are a source for very serious concern. For those who wish to find out more about conditions in HMOs, the results of the two surveys mentioned above are essential reading. See Kirkby, K., and Sopp, L. (1986), *Houses in Multiple Occupation in England and Wales: Report of a Postal Survey of Local Authorities* (HMSO) and Thomas, A. (1987), *Greater London Houses in Multiple Occupation Survey* (Association of Metropolitan Authorities). The main organisation campaigning for an improvement in the prevailing conditions in HMOs and a strengthening of the legal rights of those who occupy HMOs is the Campaign for Bedsit Rights, which can be contacted at 7 Whitechapel Road, London E1 1DU (tel: 071 377 0027).

Common Lodging Houses (CLHs)

In some large cities in the United Kingdom there exist large HMOs, mostly of a dour Victorian red brick, that have the special function of providing basic accommodation to people who would otherwise be likely to find themselves on the streets. The law describes these premises as Common Lodging Houses (CLHs). They are defined as follows:

> A CLH is a house provided for the purpose of accommodating by night poor people who are not members of the same family and who are allowed to occupy one common room for the purpose of sleeping or eating.

If an HMO fits this description (and the 'common room' can be divided into cubicles) it has to be registered as a CLH with the local authority, which has the power to restrict the number of people who may sleep there on any one night. The local authority also has a number of powers relating to health controls within the CLH, and can close the CLH if it appears that the CLH is unfit because of inadequate sanitation, water supply, or means of escape from fire, or the keeper is unfit to be responsible for the CLH. It is clear from the evidence obtained by the DOE and GLC reports on HMOs, and the evidence obtained by the Campaign for Bedsit Rights, that very many CLHs fail to reach reasonable standards of care in respect of these duties, and yet their registration is not withdrawn.

Advisers who are concerned about the standards in a particular HMO should put pressure on their local authority to reconsider the registration (which in any event has to be reconsidered every 13 months) or should contact the Campaign for Bedsit Rights.

HOUSES THAT ARE GENERALLY UNFIT OR UNHEALTHY

The above section has detailed certain special categories of private sector rented accommodation which have special problems that local authorities have special powers to help resolve. This section will look at the general powers vested in local authorities to intervene in cases of serious disrepair in all privately rented accommodation. In each case the power to intervene is determined by:

- the extent of the disrepair;
- the attitudes and policies of the council.

Houses which are unfit for human habitation

The *1981 House Conditions Survey* found that of the 18.1 million dwellings in England and Wales approximately 1.1 million (6 per cent) were unfit to live in. A further 900,000 lacked basic amenities. The *1991 English House Conditions Survey* (HMSO) showed a continuing deterioration to 1.5 million, which amounts to a staggering 1 in 12 properties deemed unfit to live in. Of those 1.5 million properties, 20.5 per cent were in the private rented sector, 6.9 per cent were local authority owned, 6.7 per cent were with housing associations, and 5.5 per cent were owner-occupied (the remainder were generally unoccupied for dwelling purposes). Yet in 1990–1 only 7133 notices were served in respect of unfit dwellings (see below at p.388).

What does unfit for human habitation mean?

The law states that a home is unfit for human habitation (UHH) if it fails to meet accepted standards under one or more of the following heads, to the extent that it is not reasonably suitable for occupation:

> Free from serious disrepair; structurally stable; free from damp prejudicial to the health of the occupants; adequate provision for lighting, heating and ventilation; adequate piped supply of wholesome water; satisfactory facilities for the preparation and cooking of food, including a sink with a satisfactory supply of hot and cold water; effective system for the disposal of foul, waste and surface water; suitably located WC, fixed bath or shower, and wash-hand basin with appropriate hot and cold water, for exclusive use of the occupants.

The test is applied to the occupant's integral home whether it be a whole house, a flat or simply a room in a house (as in the case of the inhabitant of an HMO).

Special additional requirements apply to basements – consult the local Environmental Health Department for details.

Who decides if a home is UHH?

It is the duty of the local authority Environmental Health Department to inspect its area for homes that are UHH, and it is the local authority alone that has the power to determine the issue of unfitness (although the local authority EHOs will be using standard manuals and procedures in carrying out their inspections). A useful *Housing Standards Wallchart* can be obtained from PHAS Publications. If a local authority refuses to inspect a particular home for unfitness, despite a request by the occupant that it does so, it is open to the occupant to go to their local magistrates' court and ask a JP to order the local authority to carry out an inspection. The JP will only do this if the applicant can provide them with sufficient initial evidence that the home appears to be unfit. Even then it would appear that the local authority is under no obligation to find the house to be unfit following the inspection. In deciding whether a home is UHH, the Environmental Health Officer will follow guidelines contained in DOE circulars, the Institute of Environmental Health Officers' circulars and case law.

What happens if the local authority decides that the home in question is UHH?

If a local authority receives a report from its officer that a home is UHH the local authority *must* take one of two courses of action:

1. *Serve a Repairs Notice:* This notice will be served on the person in control of the premises enclosing a schedule of works, plus time scale, for rendering the house fit for human habitation. Failure to comply with the list entitles the local authority to do the work in default and charge it to the person in control, who can appeal against the order to the local county court. They are also eligible to apply to the local authority for a mandatory Renovation Grant to assist in the cost of the work.
2. *Serve a Control Order/Demolition Notice:* This order/notice will have the effect of closing down or ordering the demolition of all or part of the premises in response to the particular unfitness. The same appeal procedures apply. All occupants of the dwelling displaced by such an order will be rehoused by the local authority (see p.333).

In rare circumstances, where there are a number of properties in such condition in the area, the local authority can initiate an *area clearance procedure.*

Homes which are not UHH but are in a state of serious disrepair

What if the dwelling is in serious disrepair but not UHH?

There are two possible courses of action where homes in this category are concerned. (The contractual remedies between landlord and tenant outlined on pp. 371–78 are also available if the circumstances are appropriate. They can be used as an alternative remedy or in parallel.)

The local authority can serve a Section 190(1)(a) Notice (Housing Act 1985)

Under this procedure, if local authority Environmental Health Officers, having carried out an inspection of a home in disrepair, do not consider it to be UHH (see p.386), they can still serve a repairs notice on the person in control of the property, if they are satisfied that:

> the home is in disrepair having regard to its age, character and locality and substantial repairs are necessary to bring it up to a reasonable standard; or the disrepair of the property is such that the condition of

the home interferes with the material comfort of the occupying tenant, and the tenant has complained about its condition to them.

For further detailed information on all the above procedures, including information on grant aid, consult Edmunds, R. (1991), *Garner's Alteration or Conversion of Houses* (Longman).

THE STATUTORY NUISANCE PROCEDURE CAN BE INVOKED

Any premises in such a state as to be prejudicial to the health of the occupants (i.e. injurious, or likely to cause injury to health) or a source of something unhealthy that is interfering with a neighbour's enjoyment of their land (for example, by the escape of unsavoury smells from rotting wood or carpets) are described by law as a *statutory nuisance* (see below). This definition applies whether the premises are in the private or the public sector.

Local authorities have a duty to inspect their areas for statutory nuisances. Where a statutory nuisance is found to exist there is a set procedure that the Chief Environmental Health Officer is supposed to follow. If the local authority does not follow this procedure, and the statutory nuisance continues to exist, any person suffering as a result of its existence can take the landlord to court. It will be seen from the above definition that there are two distinct ways in which a statutory nuisance can arise. In practice it is the first type of statutory nuisance, where premises are prejudicial to the health of the occupants, that provides the most common course of action to a person who is living in premises that are in bad disrepair.

What does 'prejudicial to health' mean?

There are few helpful guidelines on what the law means by the phrase 'prejudicial to health'. It could be said that premises are 'prejudicial to the health of the occupants' if a qualified medical practitioner certifies this to be the case. Thus, if an already ill person is made worse by enduring the consequences of disrepair, e.g. damp, draughts, etc., those premises are 'prejudicial' to their health. Certainly, the evidence of a GP is of great importance in these circumstances. The word 'prejudicial' can incorporate not only actual but also potential damage to health, and thus it has been decided in one case that dangerous wiring can be 'prejudicial to the health' of the occupants. Similarly, if the occupant has a particular sensitivity, such as asthma, that is a relevant factor in determining whether the premises in which they live are 'prejudicial' to their health.

The statutory nuisance procedure

What should the occupant of premises that are a statutory nuisance do about it?

Anybody who is suffering from the presence of a statutory nuisance (i.e. they are a 'person aggrieved by it', whatever their legal status in the property) should report the existence of the statutory nuisance to the local authority Environmental Health Department. The Environmental Health Department will come and inspect the premises. If they are satisfied that the statutory nuisance exists, they must serve an *abatement notice* on the person responsible for it, telling that person to abate the statutory nuisance (i.e. to get rid of it). The only circumstances in which they are not obliged to serve such a notice are if they decide to use the Unfitness procedures described above (see pp. 386–8).

The 'person responsible' is the owner of the property if the statutory nuisance is caused by a structural defect (e.g. dampness caused by inadequate cavity wall insulation), otherwise it is the person who is responsible for causing the nuisance to exist or continue. This latter definition sometimes causes problems as it can be suggested that some statutory nuisances are caused by the occupants' own lifestyles, in which case the Environmental Health Officers will not agree to serve an abatement notice on anybody else. It is up to the occupants in these circumstances, perhaps with the help of a law centre or an expert voluntary surveyor who may be supplied by a local CAB scheme, to argue that the statutory nuisance emanates not from their lifestyle, but from the fact that they are alive!

Can the owner abate the statutory nuisance by evicting the occupants?

At first sight this would appear to be a risk to the occupier. In practice, however, the landlord can only take this course of action if an abatement notice has not yet been served at the time of the eviction, and nobody is moved into the premises after the eviction has taken place (in order to show that there is no 'person aggrieved' living in the premises). Chapter 10 has demonstrated that, in general terms, landlords have to follow fairly lengthy procedures before they can evict occupants, even licensees. Once an abatement notice has been served the landlord cannot seek to abate the nuisance by evicting the occupants, unless it can be shown beyond any doubt that the premises will not be re-let, e.g. a closing order has been served on the premises. In these circumstances the occupants will in any event have a statutory right to be rehoused (see Chapter 10 p.333) and also to receive compensation (see p.395).

What happens if the statutory nuisance is not abated?

If the statutory nuisance is not abated within a reasonable period it is the duty of the local authority to bring the matter before the local magistrates' court, where a magistrate will issue a summons against the person responsible. A date will be set for the hearing. The local authority as complainant will take responsibility for proving the matter at the hearing, and the occupant need not be involved, except as a witness. As the proceedings are criminal proceedings there is a heavy burden of proof on the local authority to prove their case, and in particular to show that the statutory nuisance is still in existence or likely to recur at the date of the hearing, which may be some months after the date that the summons was issued. This is of particular importance when the alleged statutory nuisance is weather-related, e.g. the disrepair causes rainwater to enter the premises, or there is seasonal damp. Advisers should be alert to the dangers of agreeing to hearing dates at which the statutory nuisance may well have temporarily disappeared and where likely recurrence will be hard to establish.

What happens if the local authority satisfies the magistrates that a statutory nuisance exists at the date of the hearing?

If the case is proved, the magistrates will impose an abatement order on the person responsible for the statutory nuisance and may also impose a fine. They also have powers to instruct the local authority to carry out the necessary remedial works in default and to compensate the occupants of the premises for any damage they may have suffered either to their health or to their property. The willingness of magistrates to make such compensation orders varies considerably from court to court.

Can the occupant of premises suffering from a statutory nuisance themselves apply to the court to issue a summons without using the local authority?

The law allows an individual to issue a summons against the person responsible for a statutory nuisance if they are a 'person aggrieved' by it. Legal aid is not, however, available to conduct such a case (see Chapter 1) and, unless they have the assistance of voluntary organisations such as a law centre, the applicant should be advised to leave the matter to the local authority to handle, however slow and frustrating this may be. It is better to put pressure on the local authority to speed up the proceedings than bear the cost of conducting the prosecution.

The one exception to the above advice is where it is the local authority who is the 'person responsible' for the statutory nuisance. In these circumstances, because most local authorities refuse to serve abatement notices on themselves, it will be necessary for the 'person aggrieved' to issue the summons themselves. This is a simple procedure, and advice can be sought from the *Shelter Public Health Practice Notes*: *Statutory Nuisances*. All the aggrieved person needs to do is to attend the local magistrates' court on a 'summons day', together with a doctor's letter confirming that their health is suffering from the state of the premises, and some evidence such as photographs, or a report, setting out the state of the premises. A useful guide, *How to Inspect a House or Flat*, can be obtained from TRIS, 1 Pink Lane, Newcastle upon Tyne, NE1 5DW. Most law centres and housing advice centres can assist in these cases (see Chapter 1).

ATTITUDES AND POLICIES OF THE COUNCIL

It cannot be stressed strongly enough that the majority of the rights to achieve better housing conditions that have been detailed above are heavily dependent upon the willingness of a local authority to enforce these rights. A few of the enforcement procedures set out above have been described as legal duties, which means that the local authority has no choice, they must take action. The majority of the enforcement procedures are not duties, they are merely powers, which means that the local authority will only use the procedure if it has both the political will and the finance to do so. Even where the enforcement procedure is a duty and not a power there will always remain the problem of what to do if the local authority does not carry out its duties. How can it be forced to do so? There are court procedures available in these circumstances (see Chapter 3, p.78) but they are costly and time-consuming. Advisers should therefore always be aware that persuasion based on knowledge of rights is their strongest weapon, and enforcement through legal process is an unlikely panacea for a large number of these rights.

OTHER SPECIAL POWERS OF LOCAL AUTHORITIES TO DEAL WITH SUBSTANDARD ACCOMMODATION

There are a number of further miscellaneous powers vested in local authorities to enable them to deal with specific housing problems as follows.

Emergency orders where there is a serious risk to health

In cases where there are serious health risks, e.g. blocked drains or toilets, badly leaking roofs, or flooding, the Environmental Health Department have emergency powers under the Building Act 1984 to serve a nine-day notice to abate the nuisance, which is a procedure it might use if sufficient pressure is placed upon it. For full details on this, see Webster, C. (1981), *Environmental Health Law* (Sweet and Maxwell); Hughes, D. (1987), *Environmental Law* (Butterworths), and Luba, J. (1986), *Repairs: Tenants' Rights* (Legal Action Group).

Orders in respect of dangerous buildings

If a local authority believes a building, or part of a building, to be dangerous it has the power to apply to the local magistrates' court to request that an order be served on the person having 'control of the house' (see p.381) requiring them to execute any works necessary to render the building safe. Any queries regarding this power should be addressed to the local Environmental Health Department.

Orders in respect of verminous or infested premises

The *Institution of EHO Statistics and Report 1990–1* revealed that in the previous year EHOs had dealt with 42,805 premises infested with cockroaches, 23,646 properties infested with Pharaoh's ants, and 250,000 premises had been treated for rats and other rodents! Where premises are verminous, or are in such filthy or unwholesome condition as to be prejudicial to health, the local authority has a duty to serve a notice on either the owner or the occupier of the premises ordering them to take steps to remedy their condition. It is an offence to fail to comply with such a notice, and the local authority may also do any necessary remedial work themselves and charge the defaulter should the notice be ignored. Where premises are infested with mice or rats the local authority must take steps to destroy them (if the land belongs to it) or to ensure that they are destroyed (if the land belongs to another).

Orders in respect of unsightly gardens, vacant sites or other open land

Where it appears to a local authority that the condition of any of the above three categories is so unsightly that it seriously offends the look of the immediate area, it has the power to serve a notice on the owner or occupier of the land ordering them to do something to improve the condition of the land. Enclosed sites, e.g. a breaker's yard, are not covered by this provision.

Further information

For further information on all the rights and powers set out in the above section, advisers should consult any of the following:

Burridge, R., and Ormandy D. (eds) (1993), *Unhealthy Housing: Research, Remedies and Reform* (E. and F. N. Spon). This is a collection of essays related to all of the above themes, written by 23 prominent specialists in the field.
Edmunds, R. (1991), *Garner's Alteration and Conversion of Houses* (Longman).
Luba, I. (1986), *Repairs: Tenant's Rights* (Legal Action Group).
Baublys, K. (1986), *Your Rights to Repair* (SHAC).

Public Health Practice Notes obtainable from Shelter Publications, 88 Old St, London EC1V 9HU (tel: 071 253 0202).
Webster, C. (1981), *Environmental Health Law* (Sweet and Maxwell).
Murdie, A. (1993), *Environmental Law and Citizen Action* (Earthscan).

Finally, it should be noted that the following organisation is willing, in cases of need, to provide free independent advice, house inspections, experts' reports and other environmental investigations from a team of independent and experienced advisers. It operates throughout the country: Health and Housing Group, 189 Old Brompton Road, London SW5 0AR (tel: 071 373 8028).

HOME LOSS AND DISTURBANCE PAYMENTS

Any person who is displaced from their home in any of the following circumstances may (in addition to being rehoused: see Chapter 10, p.333) be entitled to financial compensation in the form of a *home loss payment* and/or a *disturbance payment.* The circumstances are if displaced:

1. Following compulsory purchase.
2. By a local authority that has previously acquired the land and now wishes to redevelop or improve it.
3. By a local authority or housing association following the issue of a closing or demolition order under the unfitness provisions (see p.386).
4. By a local authority following the issue of an improvement notice under the Housing Act 1985.

All these circumstances will lead to compensation rights for private tenants and most housing association tenants, but only the first two will lead to compensation rights for local authority tenants.

Home loss payment

A home loss payment is paid by the local authority (or the Housing Association, if under the third head above) to any occupier of a home in the relevant premises who had a legal right to be there, and had lived there continuously as their main or only home for a period of at least five years at the date of the displacement. The claimant may be the tenant, or a person living with the tenant. The claimant cannot be a council tenant if the claim is under the second head. If the claim is by joint tenants the payment will be split equally between them. If the claimant has lived in a series of dwellings within the same building, for example in a succession of bedsits, during the five-year period, they will still be eligible. If the claim is under the first head the claimant does not have to remain in occupation until required by the local authority to leave, as long as they are in occupation on the date that the local authority are given permission to buy the property.

The amount of the home loss payment will vary according to the date of the displacement, and the figures should be carefully checked with an independent housing adviser. All claims must be made within six years of the displacement on a special form provided by a local authority. The form can also be obtained from a local Citizens' Advice Bureau, a Housing Aid or Action Centre, or a local law centre.

Disturbance payment

A person who is entitled to claim a home loss payment is also entitled to claim a disturbance payment. This is a sum of money to cover the reasonable expenses they have incurred as a result of their displacement and settlement in another home. It can thus cover not only removal expenses, but also the costs of setting up a new home, which may be substantial. Even if a person is not entitled to a home loss payment, e.g. because they have not lived in the premises for at least five years, the local authority still has a discretion to make them a disturbance payment.

Is there an appeal against a refusal to make either of the above two payments or the level of a disturbance payment?

Yes. An appeal lies to the Lands Tribunal, which is one of the few tribunals for which legal aid is available (see Chapter 1). The address of the Lands Tribunal is: 48–9 Chancery Lane, London WC2A 1JR (tel: 071 936 7200). See also 'How to Use the Lands Tribunal', 40 *Community Action* 33.

GETTING THE COUNCIL TO HELP: THE POSITION OF THE COUNCIL TENANT

The contractual obligations of a landlord to do repairs are the same in both the public and the private sector, and have been set out on p.371. In addition, it has been stated that where disrepair gives rise to a statutory nuisance it is open to the person aggrieved, in this case the council tenant, licensee or any person living with them, to issue a summons in the local magistrates' court requesting that the landlord council be ordered to abate the nuisance, hopefully by carrying out any necessary repairs or improvements in the process. It should, however, be stressed that, while this course of action provides a good way of taking direct action against the council landlord, the applicant cannot receive legal aid to help with their legal costs, and they should therefore be very careful to ensure that they make the best use of voluntary surveyor schemes at local CABs, or the special skills of law centres in this area.

Can a council tenant do their own repairs and send the bill to the council?

A council tenant (and any secure tenant: see Chapter 10, p.336) is in exactly the same position as a private tenant in this respect, i.e. they can do the repairs themselves and deduct the cost from future rent providing the repairs are the responsibility of the council and the council is given prior notice of this intention (see p.374). There is in addition a special scheme for secure tenants, including council tenants, called the Right to Repair Scheme, which is a formal procedure allowing tenants to carry out certain repairs to their own homes and claim the cost back from the council. Although the scheme has been criticised because it simply formalises existing rights of tenants and adds nothing new, it does nevertheless offer a proper claims procedure where previously nothing existed. The repair must be one for which the council is liable (see p.371) and which would cost the council between £20 and £200 if they did it. It must not be a repair to the structure or exterior of a flat.

A claim under this scheme is made on a special form, the Tenant's Repair Claim Form, on which the tenant will explain:

- what they intend to repair;

- why the repair is needed;
- what works they intend to do;
- what materials they intend to use.

The council should reply within 21 days, either accepting the claim or refusing it, in which case reasons must be given.

A detailed leaflet explaining more about the scheme, *Right to Repair: a Guide for Public Sector Tenants: Housing Booklet No. 2*, can be obtained from the Department of the Environment.

REDUCING THE RENT

Position for tenants with Rent Act protected tenancies still in existence on 15 January 1989

The rent officer service

If a tenant in this category finds it difficult to pay the rent, they should consider whether they can use the rent officer service (also known as the fair rent system). This service enables rent officers, who are under the general supervision and control of the Department of the Environment and work from regional offices spread throughout the country, to register a fixed rent on certain privately rented premises that will be the maximum sum that the landlord can charge for renting those premises for the next two years.

What premises does the rent officer service cover?

The service applies to any premises that are let to a tenant on a protected tenancy or statutory tenancy (see Chapter 10 at p.349) where the tenancy was in existence prior to 15 January 1989 and still subsists. It does not therefore apply to public sector lettings, unprotected lettings, licences or any lettings that commenced on or after that date.

Who can apply to register a fair rent?

Any tenant or landlord of premises in the above category may apply to register a fair rent. A local authority can also apply, even though they have no interest in the property. In practice, it is rare for a local authority to do so.

Are the means of the tenant or the landlord a relevant consideration?

No. The fair rent will be registered on the property, not on the tenant; consequently, the means of both the landlord and the tenant are irrelevant and are never taken into consideration. If the tenant's means are particularly low, they can always consider applying for housing benefit (see below at p.404) in addition to (or instead of) applying to register a fair rent, as housing benefit is means tested.

How does a rent officer set about fixing a fair rent?

In fixing a fair rent, the rent officer follows a formula set out in the Rent Act 1977 supplemented by internal codes of guidance and case law. The formula takes into account a number of factors, in particular the age, character, locality, state of repair and quality of the furniture provided in the letting. The rent officer is supposed to discount any scarcity of similar accommodation in the locality, in other words to ignore the fact that in the open market scarcity of that particular type of accommodation might be forcing its rental value higher.

Anybody thinking of applying to register a fair rent should also be aware that rent officers are very influenced by *comparables* when fixing the rent on a particular property, i.e. the rents that have already been fixed on similar properties in the area. As all information on fair rents is public information, it is thus advisable for anybody considering an application first to inspect the register at their local rent office in order to check the comparables currently operating in their area. Even this information should, however, be treated with caution because it may not include sufficient detail on such matters as the state of internal decoration and repair which could have influenced the decision. A figure for inflation should also be added if the registration date was some time in the past.

What is the procedure for applying to fix a fair rent?

The procedure is very straightforward. The applicant obtains a form from the local rent officer service (address in local telephone directory) and fills out a request for rent registration, providing basic details about the property. The rent officer then informs the other party (whether landlord or tenant) of the application, and arranges a date to visit the property. Both landlord and tenant are invited to attend the inspection, should they so wish, and to make any representation they wish. In cases of complexity or controversy, a further meeting at the rent officer's office can sometimes be arranged. Once the rent officer has obtained all the necessary information, a fair rent is fixed on the premises and this sum will be communicated to the parties as the maximum rent chargeable on the premises.

Is there an appeal against a rent officer's decision?

Yes. Either party may appeal against an unfavourable registration to the local Rent Assessment Committee (RAC), a specialist tribunal, normally with three members, set up to adjudicate on matters relating to housing cost. The RAC will consider the application afresh, will visit the premises and will make their own decision following a hearing which can be attended by all parties together with their representatives. As legal aid (see Chapter 1) is not available for RAC hearings, the cost of legal representation (at least for tenants) is normally prohibitive. There are, however, voluntary surveyor schemes operating in some parts of the country which can provide representation in such matters. For details, consult a local CAB. Tenants should be warned that RACs have a tendency to increase a rent officer's registration by an average of around 10 per cent, and it is less common for a tenant to achieve a reduction in the rent officer's fair rent registration.

From what date will a fair rent be effective?

The answer to this question will depend on a number of factors and in any event is not simple. As landlords often make mistakes on this particular matter, tenants in any doubt should consult a law centre, CAB or housing aid centre for advice. The answer in summary is as follows:

- The earliest date from which the registered rent is payable will be the date of registration, *not* the date that the application was filed (which may be several weeks earlier).

- During the *contractual period* of the tenancy, i.e. the period before either a fixed term tenancy or a Notice to Quit expires, the maximum rent chargeable is either the existing rent or the new registered rent, whichever is the lower. For further details on the contractual period, see Chapter 10, p.348.
- During the *statutory period* of the tenancy, i.e. the period after the contractual period has ended, but while the tenant remains in occupation under the protection of the Rent Act, the registered rent will be the new rent payable.
- If the new rent amounts to a rent increase it will not become operative on the premises until a Notice of Increase (a special formal document) has been served on the tenant. If the rent is decreased by the rent officer, a Notice of Increase will obviously be unnecessary and the decreased rent will be the effective rent from the date of registration.

How long will a fair rent remain effective on a property once registered?

Once registered, a fair rent will normally remain effective on that property indefinitely, or until one of two things happens (there are other special circumstances which are too rare to warrant special mention here):

1. The landlord applies successfully to remove the registration from the register. This is, however, only permissible once two years have passed since the registration date and then only if there is no protected statutory tenant living on the premises at the time of the application to remove. If a new tenancy with a new tenant begins, thereafter the relevant law will now be that contained in the Housing Act 1988 (see p.402).
2. The two years have expired, the tenancy is continuing, and either party applies for a re-registration (an application can in fact be made by a landlord after 21 months, to become effective as soon as the two years have expired). In exceptional circumstances, an application can be made before the two years have expired, as when there has been such a substantial change in the terms of the tenancy, e.g. as a result of improvements, refurnishing and so forth, that the existing fair rent is no longer 'fair'. Note, however, that while 'improvements' might

allow the landlord to reapply within the two-year period, 'repairs' will not. (On the distinction between 'improvements' and 'repairs', see p.373).

NB The rent is registered on the property, not the tenant, and therefore the fair rent will continue to operate regardless of any change of tenant. This important rule only applies, however, if the letting is of the same property, i.e. if, for example, the rent was registered on the premises as an unfurnished letting and the premises are now let furnished, the registered rent will not apply. If, however, the new letting is an assured or an assured shorthold tenancy (i.e. it commenced on or after 15 January 1989); the registered rent will no longer apply (see p.403).

It is worth noting that, since the introduction of the new assured and assured shorthold tenancies that are largely free of rent regulation, there is evidence that rent officers are being influenced by these far higher rents in setting their fair rents. The DOE in a consultation paper, *Rent Act Tenants: Rent Increases* (1992), reported that typical re-registration figures being reported to them were 20–30 per cent increases, with the figure rising in some cases to 50 per cent. This approach may have been influenced by a crop of cases in 1992 in which it was argued that where there was no evidence of any scarcity of comparable rented accommodation, the fair rent should be the market rent. For a useful summary of the best way to counter this argument and how to adopt a protective strategy in advising tenants on their fair rent application, see Roberts, D. (1992), 'Scarcity and fair rent registration', *Legal Action*, November, at 17–18.

What can a tenant do if they find out that the landlord has been charging in excess of an existing registered rent?

If a tenant finds, by searching the rent register, that they are being charged more than the fair rent registered on the premises, they can claim back from the landlord the excess paid, up to a maximum of two years' overpayment. This can be done either by deducting the money from future rent, or by an action for debt in the local county court. The letting must, however, be for an identical letting as that which was subject to the fair rent registration.

Can a tenant register a fair rent and claim housing benefit?

Yes. Although the government is theoretically committed to paying housing benefit on full market rents in all new types of tenancies under the Housing Act 1988 (see below at p.404), a local authority benefit office can insist that it will only pay housing benefit up to the level of a fair rent for tenancies that could be registered under the fair rent scheme. It is therefore likely that for those of small means the dual approach will be quite common.

Rent control for assured tenants

There is no restriction on the rent which landlords can initially charge assured tenants. Rent officers have no jurisdiction over the rents of assured tenants. At the end of the contractual period of the tenancy the landlord can increase the rent as long as the correct notices are served (advice should always be sought on this matter by the tenant, to check the validity of notices). In some circumstances, if the tenant wishes to object to the new rent, they can apply to the local rent assessment committee, which will then fix the rent following a number of set procedures. This rent will not, however, be a 'fair rent' along the lines of rents fixed by rent officers on Rent Act protected tenancies. It will be the rent at which the tenancy 'might reasonably be expected to be let in the open market by a willing landlord under an assured tenancy'. If the tenant cannot afford the rent they can apply for housing benefit, though this is subject to a means test (see p.404).

Rent control for assured shorthold tenants

Tenants in this category can apply to the rent assessment committee to determine what rent they should pay if they are dissatisfied with the amount. The rent assessment committee will not alter the rent, however, unless it considers that the rent is significantly higher than the amount which a landlord might reasonably be expected to obtain for similar tenancies in the locality. The committee can only do this if there are sufficient numbers of similar properties in the area on which to make a comparison. It seems unlikely, therefore, that there will be many applications to rent assessment committees under this category.

HOUSING BENEFIT: FINANCIAL ASSISTANCE IN PAYING THE RENT AND COUNCIL TAX

Rent

For those who have difficulty meeting their housing costs, it is always worth considering the possibility of applying for Housing Benefit (HB). The benefit is available both to council and to private tenants, to offset the cost of the rent. The benefit is means tested. What follows below is a summary of how to claim HB. For more detailed information, consult one of a number of guides as follows:

The National Welfare Benefits Handbook (CPAG).
Ward, M., and Zebedee, J., *The Guide to Housing Benefit* (Institute of Housing and SHAC).
Benefits Guide for Single People (CHAR).

For a detailed and more expensive annotated guide to all the relevant legislation, see Findlay, L. (1988), *CPAG's Annotated Housing Benefit Legislation* (CPAG).

The DSS also produce a Fact Sheet on HB: DSS leaflets, *Guide to Housing Benefit*, and *Help With Housing Costs*. Both leaflets are available from local councils, and RR1 can also be obtained from post offices. The detailed manual that DSS officers themselves use when assessing HB is *The Housing Benefits Guidance Manual* (DSS).

How is HB claimed?

HB is a government scheme that is administered by local councils. It is claimed by filling out a detailed form that is supplied by the local authority DSS (for all claimants in receipt of income support, see Chapter 8) or otherwise by the local authority HB section.

How is a claimant's entitlement to HB calculated?

Whatever a person's source of income, the same formula will be used for calculating whether or not they are entitled to receive any HB. The process appears complex, but if the stages set out below are followed the claimant or their adviser can quickly gain a clear idea of their level of entitlement.

Stage 1: is the claimant in receipt of income support? (see Chapter 8)

If the claimant is in receipt of income support, they will be entitled to receive the maximum level of HB, which will be 100 per cent eligible rent (see p.406 on what exactly is meant by eligible rent). They must, however, claim their HB separately from the IS (i.e. there is no automatic payment to an income support claimant). If the claimant is *not* in receipt of income support, proceed to Stage 2.

Stage 2: calculate the claimant's capital

Any capital below £3000 will be disregarded. If the claimant has between £3000 and £16,000, this capital will be deemed to generate £1 weekly income for every £250 (or part of £250) in excess of £3000. Thus a claimant with capital of £4400 will be deemed to generate income of £6 per week from their capital. (On the distinction between capital and income, see the *National Welfare Benefits Handbook*.) Capital includes money in bank and building society deposits, premium bonds, unit trusts, stocks and shares, lump-sum redundancy payments and cash savings. A child's capital is not treated as belonging to the claimant (but above a certain capital level the child cannot be included as a dependant). There are special rules on charitable payments (see *National Welfare Benefits Handbook*). Some items of capital are entirely disregarded. These are the same items that are disregarded for the purposes of a claim for income support (see Chapter 8). Any claimant with capital in excess of £16,000 will be ineligible for HB.

Stage 3: calculate the claimant's applicable amount

The formula for this calculation is exactly the same as for calculating eligibility for income support (see Chapter 8, p.265) but for the purposes of HB it is, of course, being applied to those who (for whatever reason) are not in receipt of income support. The amount will vary considerably according to the age and level of disability (if any) of the claimant and any dependants.

STAGE 4: CALCULATE THE CLAIMANT'S INCOME

The formula for this calculation is again the same as for calculating eligibility for income support (see Chapter 8, p.268).

STAGE 5: CALCULATE THE CLAIMANT'S ELIGIBLE RENT, I.E. AMOUNT OF RENT AGAINST WHICH THEY MAY CLAIM BENEFIT

Rent

Some parts of rent charges are not eligible for HB, i.e. they must be deducted by the claimant from their rent before filling out the form. The following charges are all ineligible: water and sewerage charges, charges for meals, laundry, leisure facilities, cleaning (except for common areas), transport, medical and nursing care, and alarm systems (except on accommodation for sick and elderly or disabled people). Service charges are eligible for HB, i.e. they can be included on the form, as long as they are reasonable and have to be paid as part of the tenancy. They would include such things as contributions towards the upkeep of lifts, common refuse chutes, and play areas. There are further complex rules regarding rent which include fuel charges, some of which will not be included in the eligible rent according to a scale that can be found in all the handbooks.

STAGE 6: IF THERE IS A NON-DEPENDANT LIVING IN THE CLAIMANT'S HOME, DEDUCT A FIXED SUM FROM THE ELIGIBLE RENT TO REFLECT THE AMOUNT THEY ARE DEEMED TO CONTRIBUTE

A non-dependant is someone who lives in the claimant's home and is not dependent on them, e.g. an adult relative (unless they are dependent), a child for whom the claimant does not receive child benefit, a friend or a lodger. Where there is a non-dependant living in the claimant's home there will be an automatic deduction from the HB otherwise payable, according to a set scale. This deduction is intended to reflect the amount of contribution that the non-dependant makes to the housing costs, regardless of whether they do make any such payment.

STAGE 7: COMPARE INCOME WITH APPLICABLE AMOUNT

- If income is less than applicable amount, maximum HB is payable, i.e. 100 per cent eligible rent.
- If income is higher than applicable amount, the following formula is applied:
  1. Work out excess of income over applicable amount = *X*
  2. Deduct 65 per cent of *X* from maximum eligible rent, and the resulting figures will be the HB payable. (No HB will be paid if the figure is less than 50p per week.)

What happens if the local authority considers that the rent is too high?

Regulation 11 of the Housing Benefit (General) Regulations 1981 sets out the grounds on which eligible rent can be restricted by the local authority for HB purposes. These Regulations have been further amended by the Rent Officers (Additional Functions) Order 1990, which effectively passes back to rent officers a significant role in determining rent levels, as it states that in certain defined situations a rent officer (see above at p.398) will be asked to determine whether a rent is reasonable for the purposes of housing benefit subsidy. Leaving aside this additional rent officer function, details of which can be obtained from the local housing benefit section, the law allows councils to restrict the 'eligible rent' on which they will pay housing benefit where they feel either that the dwelling is larger than reasonably required by the occupants or the rent is unreasonably high in comparison with similar accommodation elsewhere. They cannot, however, do this if the household includes any of the following:

- someone aged 60 or over;
- a sick or disabled person;
- a child or young person.

In extreme circumstances, as where the council believes that rents are being set deliberately high to take advantage of the housing benefit scheme, HB can be withdrawn completely, or until the rent is reduced to reasonable levels. For more detail on the complex developments in this area of law, read East, R. (1992), 'Housing Benefit and Unreasonable

Rent', *Legal Action*, October, 18–20, and for a first study of the impact of these changes on rent levels, see Sharp, C. (1991), *Problems Assured: Private Renting after the Housing Act 1988* (SHAC/Joseph Rowntree Foundation). As if all the above potential restrictions were not enough, it should also be noted that local authorities widely operate a policy of 'rent stop', whereby they will not pay HB on any sum in excess of the subsidy threshold laid down by the DSS for their area. Central government will pay 97 per cent of all HB paid out by local authorities, if it is below the threshold, but only 25 per cent of HB paid out above the threshold. As a result of this policy, many, if not most, local authorities, strapped for cash, are refusing to pay HB above the threshold except in very extreme cases.

Finally, a person may also be denied HB if their tenancy is too informal, i.e. they are renting on a non-commercial basis from a friend, or from a close relative or partner.

Special rules for students

There are special rules relating to the rights of students to claim HB, which are dealt with in detail in the *National Welfare Benefits Handbook* (CPAG) and Ward, M., and Zebedee, J., *Guide to Housing Benefit* (SHAC and Institute of Housing). Students living in halls of residence or similar college accommodation for which they pay rent to an educational establishment are not eligible at all for HB during the 'period of study', which amounts to term time and Easter and Christmas vacations (but not the summer vacation). All other students are eligible to claim HB, subject to special rules and restrictions.

What is the maximum period for which HB can paid?

The maximum benefit period is 60 weeks, though local authorities have a discretion to make the payments for a shorter period. Once the period has expired the claimant must resubmit their claim, which will be considered afresh.

Can HB be backdated and claimants be forced to repay overpayments?

Local authorities have the power to backdate HB for up to 52 weeks. They can also recover overpayments in certain circumstances. It is likely that they will have some incentive to claw back overpayments (unless they were themselves grossly negligent in the initial payment) and also not to backdate unless absolutely necessary, as they will get a lower subsidy on any such payments.

Can HB be paid direct to a landlord?

HB will normally be paid direct to the landlord in the following circumstances:

- where the claimant or their partner is receiving IS and the DSS decide to pay part of the benefit to the landlord to cover arrears;
- where the claimant has rent arrears of eight weeks or more.

In addition, the local authority may agree to pay the HB direct to the landlord if the claimant has so requested or if the local authority decides it is in the best interests of the claimant's family. In all these circumstances both the landlord and the tenant must be notified of the decision. The claimant can request a review of an unfavourable decision.

Can a dissatisfied claimant appeal against an adverse HB decision?

A procedure exists enabling a claimant to appeal (known as a review) against any decision regarding their claim. There is no independent tribunal appeal system, but there is a two-stage review procedure consisting of an internal review and an application to a review board (the latter can only be requested after an internal review has been carried out). The request for an internal review must be in writing (a letter will suffice) and it must arrive at the local authority no later than six weeks from the date that the letter of notification of the decision was posted. A request for a further hearing before a review board (which will consist of local councillors) must be made within four weeks of the posting of the notification of the decision of the internal review.

Council tax

Council tax came into effect on 1 April 1993 to replace the community charge. Each property has one council tax attached to it, regardless of how many people live there, and regardless of whether it is rented, owned, squatted or empty. The amount of the tax is linked to the estimated value of the property on 1 April 1991. Each property is placed in a band, from A (lowest) to H (highest). The tax is divided into two parts:

1. A 50 per cent property tax.
2. A 50 per cent personal tax.

The 50 per cent personal tax can be reduced to 25 per cent if there is only one person living in the property, and by 50 per cent if there are 'invisible' adults living there (some adults including those in hospital, carers, students, and several other categories are deemed 'invisible', i.e. they are not included as living in the house for the purpose of the personal tax). There are also a number of reductions available in the property tax, if one or more people with disabilities live in the home, the effect of which will be to place the property down a band. For a detailed stage-by-stage description of the tax and how it works, see a series of articles in *Legal Action*, 1992–3, by Alan Murdie, and also Zebedee (below at p.411).

What is Council Tax Benefit?

There are two types of council tax benefit available, *main council tax benefit* (CTB) and *alternative maximum council tax benefit* (AMTCB).

CTB

This can be claimed by anybody aged 18 or over who is liable to pay the council tax on their home, and who is resident in that home. The procedure for claiming CTB is exactly the same as for HB (see above at p.404), and it is normal to claim both benefits together. The only difference in the two procedures comes at Stage 5 (where the eligible council tax is the full council tax payable) and at Stage 7, where the percentage applied to *X* for purposes of the final calculation is 20 per cent and not 65 per cent (see p.407).

AMCTB

This benefit can be claimed even if the applicant's personal income and capital make them ineligible for CTB. It is commonly known as 'second adult rebate' and is designed to compensate council tax payers who share their homes with other adults who do not contribute anything towards the tax, and who cannot afford to do so. An applicant must be liable (or jointly liable) to pay council tax, and a person who would have had a 25 per cent status discount if they had been living alone, or with 'invisible' people (see p.410). Although AMCTB is claimed by the person liable to pay council tax, it is in fact calculated upon the income of a 'second adult' of 18 or over living on a non-commercial basis with the claimant, such as grown-up sons and daughters still living at home. The logic of the benefit is that the claimant would have expected the 'second adult' to contribute to the council tax, had they the money to do so. The rebate can apply even if there is more than one extra adult, in which case it is calculated on their combined incomes. Finally, note that there is no minimum amount of council tax benefit payable. For a more detailed explanation of how the system works, see Zebedee, J. (1993/4), *Guide to Council Tax* (SHAC).

Index